Ethno-Cultural Diversity and Human Rights

International Studies in Human Rights

VOLUME 122

The titles published in this series are listed at *brill.com/ishr*

Ethno-Cultural Diversity and Human Rights

Challenges and Critiques

Edited by

Gaetano Pentassuglia

BRILL
NIJHOFF

LEIDEN | BOSTON

Library of Congress Cataloging-in-Publication Data

Names: Pentassuglia, Gaetano, Editor.
Title: Ethno-cultural diversity and human rights / edited by Gaetano Pentassuglia.
Description: Boston : Brill, 2018. | Series: International studies in human rights ; Volume 122
Identifiers: LCCN 2017041380 | ISBN 9789004328778 (hardback : alk. paper)
Subjects: LCSH: Minorities–Legal status, laws, etc. | Minorities–Civil rights. | Human rights. | Discrimination–Law and legislation.
Classification: LCC K3242 .E84 2017 | DDC 342.08/7–dc23
LC record available at https://lccn.loc.gov/2017041380

Typeface for the Latin, Greek, and Cyrillic scripts: "Brill". See and download: brill.com/brill-typeface.

ISSN 0924-4751
ISBN 978-90-04-32877-8 (hardback)
ISBN 978-90-04-32878-5 (e-book)

This book is printed on acid-free paper and produced in a sustainable manner.

Printed by Printforce, the Netherlands

Contents

Preface

This collection of essays is the outcome of a collaborative project that brings together prominent scholars and experts from the United Kingdom, continental Europe and Canada to discuss some of the key challenges facing the international community and individual states in responding to increasing demands for ethno-cultural diversity in human rights law and policy, and human rights thinking more broadly.

An early articulation of this project was explored in the context of academic exchanges between the Liverpool Law School and European partners and culminated in a major international symposium held at the University of Liverpool in May 2016. In this sense, the volume is very much the result of a wider networking research process designed to assess and contrast several controversial aspects of the relationship between group diversity and human rights.

The resurgence of ethnic and regional conflicts in the 1990s in various regions of the world generated momentum for a large corpus of legal standards and measures relating to ethno-cultural minority groups, which added to ongoing institutional exercises and multiple domestic arrangements. As the body of practice continues to grow to the benefit of such groups worldwide, it also gives pause for thought about its normative underpinnings, the potential and limitations of human rights discourse, and the resonance of that discourse with security and other practical dimensions.

Against this backdrop, the main ambition of the present collection is, not to provide a comprehensive review of the field, but rather to offer a timely and selective engagement with its complexities and the different 'shades of grey' that tend to define discourses about the nature and reach of group claims, justifications, and policies relating to the group protection/human rights nexus.

The general approach of the volume is deliberately, and unsurprisingly, multidisciplinary, as we seek to advance our understanding of group issues through a mix of moral, political and legal perspectives that interface with international and domestic developments in human rights discourse and beyond. All essays are original and extensive, and they significantly contribute to a developing agenda of cross-cutting investigations into a range of old and new concerns in law and public policy – from the impact of collective interests on rights discourse and nation-building, to international law's responses to group claims to decision-making authority, to dilemmas over immigration, intersectionality, and peacebuilding.

As the scientific editor of this volume, I would like to extend my sincere gratitude to all contributors for their authoritative and thought-provoking analyses, and for the numerous and constructive conversations that I had the opportunity and privilege to have with them over a significant period of time around many of the arguments that these analyses espouse. I would also like to thank the University of Liverpool and the School of Law and Social Justice for generously funding the 2016 international symposium that shaped up the structure and content of the collection, and the European Society of International Law and the British Branch of the International Law Association for kindly supporting the dissemination process at various stages. In addition, my thanks go to the several colleagues from the Liverpool Law School and other institutions who provided valuable reactions to the symposium presentations on which this volume's chapters are based, and to those fewer colleagues who occasionally commented on earlier drafts of some of these chapters.

Finally, I remain grateful to Lindy Melman and Bea Timmer at Martinus Nijhoff Publishers for their characteristically helpful editorial suggestions and timely production.

G.P., Liverpool
May 2017

List of Contributors

Chris Chapman
is Adviser/Researcher on Indigenous Rights at Amnesty International, where he supports research and advocacy on land rights, free prior and informed consent, and violence against indigenous women, among other issues. From 2000 to 2013 he was at Minority Rights Group International, most recently as Head of Conflict Prevention. Chris has published a number of articles/reports on indigenous and minority rights, conflict prevention and transitional justice, including 'Resolving conflicts using traditional mechanisms in the Karamoja and Teso regions of Uganda' (Minority Rights Group, London, 2009) and "Leveraging the Rights of Minorities and Indigenous Peoples for Transitional Justice", in *Identities in Transition: Challenges for Transitional Justice in Divided Societies* (Cambridge University Press, Cambridge, 2010). From 1995-2000 Chris worked in conflict resolution, human rights monitoring and journalism in Haiti and Guatemala. He has a master's degree in Armed Conflict and Crisis Management from the Open University of Catalonia.

Malgosia Fitzmaurice
holds a Chair of Public International Law at Queen Mary University of London. She has published extensively on general aspects of international law (the law of treaties and sources of international law), indigenous peoples, and whaling. Her latest publication is a monograph entitled *Whaling and International Law* (Cambridge University Press, Cambrdige, 2015). She has taught as a Visiting Professor at many universities such as Paris I (Sorbonne-Panthenon), Berkeley Law School and the University of Kobe.

Felipe Gómez Isa
is Profesor Titular of Public International Law and Researcher at the Institute of Human Rights of the University of Deusto (Bilbao). He is National Director of the European Master in Human Rights and Democratisation (EIUC, Venice, Italy) and Director of the UN Fellowship Programme for Indigenous Leaders from Latin America. He is Visiting Professor at Washington College of Law of American University (Washington, D.C.), at Universidad Externado de Colombia (Bogotá), at Peoples' Friendship University of Russia (Moscow), and at the René Cassin Institute of Human Rights (Strasbourg). He has published extensively on international human rights law, transitional justice and indigenous peoples' rights.

Tom Hadden
is Emeritus Professor of Law at Queen's University Belfast and Honorary Professor at Kent Law School. He was a member of the Standing Advisory Commission on Human Rights in Northern Ireland from 1985 to 1990 and the Northern Ireland Human Rights Commission from 1999 to 2005. His major work in this area has been the production of a number of working papers for the United Nations Working Group on Minorities, leading to a series of related publications, notably 'The Pendulum Theory of Individual, Communal and Minority Rights' in S. Caney & P. Jones (eds.), *Human Rights and Global Diversity* (Frank Cass Publishers, Oxon, 2001), 'Integration and Separation: Legal and Political Choices in Implementing Minority Rights', in N. Ghanea and A. Xanthaki (eds.), *Minorities, Peoples and Self-Determination* (Martinus Nijhoff Publishers, Leiden, 2005), and 'Policing for Shared Societies', in Mari Fitzduff (ed.), *Public Policies for Shared Societies* (Routledge, London, 2013).

Peter Jones
is Emeritus Professor of Political Philosophy at Newcastle University. He is the author of *Rights* (Macmillan, London, 1994), the joint editor of *National Rights, International Obligations* (Westview Press, Boulder, 1996) and of *Human Rights and Global Diversity* (Frank Cass Publishers, Oxon, 2001) and the editor of *Group Rights* (Ashgate, Aldershot, 2009). Most of his published work has appeared as journal articles and contributions to edited collections. He has written on many different aspects of rights, including, human rights, group rights, democratic rights, welfare rights, and rights of free expression. He has also examined issues relating to cultural and religious diversity, toleration, identity, recognition, international justice, and discrimination law.

Padraig McAuliffe
is a Senior Lecturer in the School of Law and Social Justice at the University of Liverpool. He is the author of *Transitional Justice and Rule of Law Reconstruction: A Contentious Relationship* (Routledge, London, 2013) and *Transformative Transitional Justice and the Malleability of Post-Conflict States* (Edward Elgar, Cheltenham, 2017).

Dolores Morondo Taramundi
is currently Head of Research at the Human Rights Institute of the University of Deusto (Bilbao). She holds a PhD in Law from the European University Institute (Fiesole, 2003) and previously taught Legal Theory and Philosophy and Human Rights at the University of Urbino (Italy). She has acted as an independent expert for human rights projects of the European Commission. Her main

areas of research and publication are antidiscrimination law, human rights and diversity, feminist legal theory and legal methodology.

Dwight Newman

is Professor of Law & Canada Research Chair in Indigenous Rights in Constitutional and International Law, University of Saskatchewan; Visiting Fellow, James Madison Program, Princeton University (2015-16); Visiting Fellow, Université de Montréal, Faculté de Droit (2017). He has published widely on constitutional law and indigenous rights topics, as well as theoretical work on group rights generally. His books include *Community and Collective Rights: A Theoretical Framework for Rights Held by Groups* (Hart Publishing, Oxford, 2011). He is currently working on a project on political theory and indigenous rights and a project on collective aspects of religious freedom. He has served on a variety of boards or committees, including currently as a member of the International Law Association (ILA) Committee on the Implementation of the Rights of Indigenous Peoples.

Ephraim Nimni

is Senior Research Fellow, Centre for the Study of Ethnic Conflict, Queen's University Belfast, and Ikebasque Visiting Professor, University of the Basque Country, 2013-2014. He was previously a Reader on Nationalism and Ethnic Conflict Resolution at Queen's University Belfast. He has published widely in the areas of non-territorial autonomy, minority rights and national self-determination.

Lucía Payero López

is a Research Associate at the Department of Philosophy of Law, University of Oviedo, and a Research Associate in the ERC Project 'Federalism: Dividing Political Power among People(s)' at Durham Law School. Her research interests lie in the fields of Legal Philosophy, Political Theory and Constitutional Theory. She has published articles and presented papers at international conferences on issues relating to nationalism, self-determination of peoples, devolution in Spain and the United Kingdom, federal theory, constitutionalism, transitional justice in Spain and Latin America, citizenship and immigration.

Gaetano Pentassuglia

is a Reader in International Law and Human Rights at Liverpool University, and School-wide Director of Postgraduate Research within the Faculty of Humanities and Social Sciences. He has published widely in the field, especially on human rights issues relating to minority groups, including indigenous peoples, and broader aspects of public international law. He has taught as a visiting professor at several universities such as Munich, Lund, Toronto, Palermo, Milano-Bicocca, and the European University Institute in Florence, and was recently Visiting Professor at the University of Deusto (Bilbao). His latest books include *Minorities in International Law: An Introductory Study* (Council of Europe Publishing, Strasbourg, 2002) and *Minority Groups and Judicial Discourse in International Law: A Comparative Perspective* (Martinus Nijhoff Publishers, Leiden, 2009). He is Co-Editor of the *International Journal on Minority and Group Rights* (Martinus Nijhoff Publishers, Leiden) and member of the International Advisory Board of the *Yearbook of Human Rights and Identity* (Martinus Nijhoff Publishers, Leiden). He has acted as consultant to a number of international and non-governmental institutions and is a former member of the International Law Association Committee on the Rights of Indigenous Peoples. He is also a frequent online contributor to media outlets and think tanks.

Introduction: The Unpacking of Ethno-Cultural Diversity

Gaetano Pentassuglia

As I write this Introduction, Turkey's Kurdish conflict has surged again, various nationalist or autonomist disputes further engulf the political and diplomatic landscape – from Catalonia to Eastern Ukraine or Nagorno-Karabakh – while American Indian tribes from North Dakota and indigenous groups from Brazil claim their rights over traditional lands, sacred burial grounds, and clean water, and worries about migration and religious intolerance continue to rise. In these and many other cases (old and new), the direct or indirect salience of matters such as national and local identities, ethnicity, language, religion, or culture broadly defined, and how they play out in complex domestic circumstances, can hardly be disputed.

From a human rights perspective, however, there is no shortage of difficult questions for scholars and policy-makers: What is the actual role of ethno-cultural diversity in human rights discourse? Can the protagonist groups of our cases claim rights of their own as human rights? What are the collective interests they seek to protect and how such interests interact with those pursued by wider political communities, including interests in nation-building projects? Do ethno-cultural groups have a right to territorial or cultural autonomy or otherwise a measure of decision-making authority? How do we reconcile the state's legal obligation to respect cultural-religious diversity with its freedom to shape up immigration policies? Can we make sense of intersectional dimensions of inequality within and across ethno-cultural communities? Can we use ethno-cultural protections to prevent conflict or alleviate the fear of it, or simply to help restore a sense of stability and confidence in the aftermath of violent clashes? And if so, what does that tell us about the aims of human rights?

This volume begins to answer some of these difficult questions. It brings together international law scholars, legal and moral philosophers, political theorists, and human rights practitioners. The essential aim of the volume is to address contested dimensions of the field, and in so doing, to unpack the conceptual and practical relationship between ethno-cultural diversity and human rights.

Indeed, as ethno-cultural groups increasingly use international human rights law as the primary avenue for framing their claims vis-à-vis state

 | DOI 10.1163/9789004328785_002

authorities, the sphere of ethno-cultural diversity related to human rights standards exhibits a peculiar mix of promising legal developments, practical uncertainties, and conceptual instabilities. They mainly revolve around the actual and potential reach of human rights categories, the nature of the collective interests involved, and the very understanding of ethno-cultural claims in legal and policy discourse.

•••

The way in which human rights relate to the sort of collective interests addressed in this volume is largely a function of the context within which such interests, or some of them, need protecting. The substantive picture is one of undeniable gains and equally undeniable limitations.

For one thing, the recent renewal in equality-, culture-, and participation-based protections is clearly remarkable. A few brief examples can illustrate the point. Both the Inter-American human rights bodies (Court and Commission) and the African human rights structures under the African Charter on Human and Peoples' Rights (ACHPR) have increasingly worked on the premise that there is something inherently unfair or unjust in the way that the groups concerned have been treated in matters of land title and natural resources, cultural identity as well as wider participation in public life. The Inter-American Court, in particular, has used the standard of non-discrimination in this context as a fundamental basis for progressive readings of indigenous rights.[1]

Whether it is through the notions of 'equality in fact', 'indirect discrimination', 'full and effective equality', and/or 'positive action',[2] it now seems rather undisputed that the expansion of the scope of equality in recent human rights case law and legislation requires domestic authorities

1 *See e.g. Yakye Axa Indigenous Community v. Paraguay*, Judgment of 6 February 2006, Series C, No. 125 (2005), para. 51; *The Saramaka People v. Suriname*, Judgment of 28 November 2007, Series C, No. 172 (2007), para. 103.

2 *See e.g. Minority Schools in Albania* (Advisory Opinion) 6 April 1935, P.C.I.J. Series A./B., No. 64, p. 3; Framework Convention for the Protection of National Minorities (FCNM), 1 February 1995 CETS No. 157, Article 4 (2); Committee on the Elimination of Racial Discrimination, *The meaning and scope of special measures in the International Convention on the Elimination of Racial Discrimination*, General Recommendation No. 32 adopted by the Committee on the Elimination of Racial Discrimination at its 75th session, 24 September 2009, U.N. Doc. CERD/C/GC/32 (2009); Council Directive 2000/43/EC of 29 June 2000 implementing the principle of equal treatment between persons irrespective of racial or ethnic origin, OJ 2000 L180/22, Article 5.

to evaluate the real or potential impact of public policies on the position of particular groups (including, for example, in matters of language or education), and whether there is a need for corrections and improvements, or even (narrowly construed) forms of 'reasonable accommodation'. As implied by the 1992 United Nations Declaration on the Rights of National or Ethnic, Religious and Linguistic Minorities (Articles 4(2) and 8(3)), state-generated special arrangements for all or specific minority groups are presumed to be compatible with the principle of equality, subject to a challenge on proportionality grounds.

From a relatively more specific angle, Article 27 of the International Covenant on Civil and Political Rights (ICCPR) affirms rights of cultural integrity to the benefit of ethnic, religious and linguistic minority groups, which encompass but are not limited to, indigenous ways of life associated with the use of land and its resources. Together with other leading global and regional human rights instruments,[3] this body of practice has resulted in converting the cultural right-based argument upholding ethno-cultural diversity into a discussion about the extent to which particular state measures impact the level of cultural access and enjoyment for the group, and/or the rights and interests of non-members and dissenting members within the group.[4] Indeed, the open ended view of cultural rights in this area has led the Inter-American Court itself to clarify that the connection between traditional land and indigenous culture should be taken as a particular articulation of an underlying right to 'cultural identity' grounded in the "collective dimension of the cultural life of native, indigenous, tribal and minority peoples and communities".[5] It is in a sense unsurprising that the European Court on Human Rights, for instance, has recognised cultural pluralism as an important value to be protected

---

3 United Nations Declaration on the Rights of Persons Belonging to National or Ethnic, Religious and Linguistic Minorities, UN GA Res. 47/135 (1992); United Nations Declaration on the Rights of Indigenous Peoples (UDRIP), UN Doc A/61/L.67 (2007); FCNM (*supra* note 2); International Labour Organisation (ILO) Convention on Indigenous and Tribal Peoples in Independent Countries (No. 169).

4 For cases discussing the individual rights implications of Quebec's commercial sign policy and legislation and of a comprehensive agreement with the Maori in New Zealand, *see Ballantyne et al. v. Canada,* Comm. Nos. 359/1989, 385/1989, Views of 31 March, 1993, U.N. Doc. CCPR/C/47/D/385/1989 (1993); *Apirana Mahuika et al. v. New Zealand,* Comm. No. 547/1993, Views of 27 October 2000, U.N. Doc. CCPR/C/70/D/541/1993.

5 *The Kichwa Indigenous People of Sarayaku v. Ecuador,* Judgment of 27 June 2012, Series C, No. 245 (2012), para. 216.

under the European Convention on Human Rights (ECHR), in relation to narrower or broader aspects of minority and majority identity and their entitlement to recognition,[6] or that the Committee on Economic, Social and Cultural Rights, which is charged with overseeing compliance with the Covenant on Economic, Social and Cultural Rights (CESCR), has employed a dynamic (anthropological) concept of 'culture' in interpreting the right to take part in cultural life under Article 15(1)(a) to include, among others, "minorities", "migrants" and "indigenous peoples".[7]

On a more macro-level, the right to self-determination's entrenchment in common Article 1 of the United Nations Covenants on Human Rights, coupled with a string of developments in distinct areas of group protection (minority and indigenous rights featuring prominently among them), have gradually added to postcolonial extensions of the concept by viewing specific forms of 'effective' participation in, or control over, decision-making processes as the most significant ways of enriching the minimum legal standard of 'representative government' within the wider political community which was upheld by the 1970 United Nations Declaration on Friendly Relations.[8] This was implicitly confirmed by the Supreme Court of Canada in the 1998 *Reference* case.[9] By stating that "the right to self-determination of a people is normally fulfilled through internal self-determination", the Court ultimately spoke to a wider practice concerned with equal rights, rights of participation in decision-making, and a measure of territorial or cultural autonomy for

6 *See e.g. Chapman v. United Kingdom*, Application No. 27238/95, Judgment of 18 January 2001; *Muñoz Diaz v. Spain*, Application No. 49151/07, Judgment of 8 December 2009; *Lautsi v. Italy*, Application No. 30814/06, Judgment of 18 March 2011.

7 Committee on Economic, Social and Cultural Rights, *Right of everyone to take part in cultural life*, General Comment No. 21 adopted by the Committee on Economic, Social and Cultural Rights at its 43rd session, 21 December 2009, U.N. Doc. E/C.12/GC/21 (2009), paras. 12–13. All of them are regarded as being entitled to core rights of choice, non-discrimination and participation in relevant decision-making; *ibid.*, at Sections B-C.

8 Declaration on Principles of International Law Concerning Friendly Relations and Co-operation among States in accordance with the Charter of the United Nations, GA Res. 2625, UN GAOR, 25th Sess., Supp. No. 28, UN Doc. A/8028 (1970). *See e.g.* United Nations Declaration on the Rights of Persons Belonging to National or Ethnic, Religious and Linguistic Minorities, Article 2(2)-(4); UNDRIP, Articles 3, 4, 18, and 19; FCNM, Article 15; *see generally* G. Pentassuglia, 'Ethnocultural Diversity and Human Rights: Legal Categories, Claims, and the Hybridity of Group Protection', VI *The Yearbook of Polar Law* (2015) pp. 271–280; M. Weller (ed.), *Political Participation of Minorities: A Commentary on International Standards and Practice* (Oxford University Press, Oxford, 2010).

9 *Reference Re Secession of Quebec* [1998] 2 S.C.R. 217 (hereinafter: the *Reference* case).

distinctive ethno-cultural identities. The 2007 United Nations Declaration on the Rights of Indigenous Peoples (UNDRIP) importantly recognises the right of internal self-determination while still articulating the overall protective framework as an intertwined bundle of entitlements to cultural protection within the state that are rooted in patterns of historical and persistent injustice.

•••

As I mentioned, these are no doubt important developments. Yet, they can as much illuminate as obscure what is at stake when it comes to grappling with the role of ethno-cultural diversity in human rights discourse. For example, the anti-discrimination approach to indigenous property rights under the American Convention on Human Rights (ACHR) has raised the question of whether conditioning such (equality-based) rights on traditional social and economic activities may partly inhibit rather than empower indigenous communities' autonomy within their land.[10] Moreover, it is not clear that such an approach can consistently support group identities or even generate positive obligations to that effect. In *Chapman v. United Kingdom*, the European Court on Human Rights dismissed the notion that exemptions on cultural grounds from planning laws to the benefit of members of a minority group such as the Roma community could be treated as the subject of positive duties or indeed derived from the principle of equality itself. It is quite significant that Protocol 12 to the ECHR, which prohibits discrimination beyond the context of ECHR rights, does not resolve the matter, nor has it been widely ratified.[11] Indirect discrimination claims have remarkable potential but may be difficult to trigger unless state legislation is in place (as has been invariably the case before

10 *See e.g.* L. Rodríguez-Piñero Royo, 'El impacto international de la sentencia', in F. Gómez Isa (ed.), *El caso Awas Tingni: Derechos Humanos entre lo local y lo global* (Universidad de Deusto, Bilbao, 2013) pp. 178–181.

11 11 April, 2000 CETS No. 177; established Council of Europe states are conspicuosly absent from the list of those members who have ratified the protocol. In the context of European Union equality law, *see also* J. Marko, 'Five Years After: Continuing Reflections on the Thematic Commentary on Effective Participation: The Interplay between Equality and Participation', in T. Malloy and U. Caruso (eds.), *Minorities, their Rights, and the Monitoring of the European Framework Convention for the Protection of National Minorities – Essays in Honour of Rainer Hofmann* (Martinus Nijhoff Publishers, Leiden, 2013) p. 97, at p. 110 (noting that "[u]ntil today, neither primary nor secondary EU law prescribe a "positive duty" to take positive measures which must – by definition – be group-oriented").

the Strasbourg Court), and their individual, collective, contingent or structural consequences may or may not inform particular equality considerations, or may not derive from the equality argument alone.

While the articulation of ethno-cultural diversity as a quintessentially cultural matter partly removes that uncertainty, it still appears unable to make sense of a variety of individual and communal diversities that could qualify for protection. The Inter-American Court on Human Rights has extended the cultural justification for indigenous rights to non-indigenous groups such as Afro-descendants who are linked to patterns of abuse and exploitation dating back to European colonisation, but it is unclear the extent to which this cultural line can translate into an overarching 'cultural view' of the ACHR, one that benefits *every* conceivable ethno-cultural grouping within the state. Tellingly, broad interpretations of general terms, such as 'family' under the ICCPR and the ACHR, have been informed by cultural considerations, though in a context specific to indigenous identity.[12] The European Court on Human Rights, for its part, has acknowledged the cultural dimension of certain minority claims, and even of certain majority traditions, but has appeared less than forthcoming in using the cultural argument as a transversal category which is able to support reasonable accommodation in matters of religious or ethnic diversity in the public sphere in response to state defences based on respect for secularism, democracy or gender equality. This sceptical line seems to be echoed by the Luxembourg-based European Court of Justice in the recent case of *Achbita v G4S Secure Solutions NV*, ruling that a company's desire for neutrality in the workplace may justify restrictions on wearing religious clothing such as the headscarf as long as they only apply to public-facing staff.[13]

Similar ambiguities surround the capacity of Article 27 ICCPR to effectively address ethno-cultural claims. One of the early commentators of this provision went as far as to suggest that it was unclear what its specific contribution really was other than "avoiding the consequences of an unenlightened interpretation of other provisions".[14] While the prevailing reading of Article 27 has largely outweighed the provision's negative formulation, including positive

12 G. Pentassuglia, *supra* note 8, pp. 73–74.

13 *Achbita v. G4S Secure Solutions NV*, Case C-157/15, Judgment of 14 March 2017. *See* more broadly S. Borelli, 'Of Veils, Crosses and Turbans: The European Court of Human Rights and Religious Practices as Manifestations of Cultural Diversity', in S. Borelli and F. Lenzerini (eds.), *Cultural Heritage, Cultural Rights, Cultural Diversity: New Developments in International Law* (Martinus Nijhoff Publishers, Leiden, 2012) p. 55.

14 N. Rodley, 'Conceptual Problems in the Protection of Minorities: International Legal Developments', 17 *Human Rights Quarterly* (1995) p. 48, at p. 65.

duties in the private sphere or positive rights to effective participation, critical questions remain about the ability of this norm to operate meaningfully across the wide(r) spectrum of group diversity, including minority languages, minority education and/or minority religions.[15]

One typical critique of the cultural argument in this context is that it encourages the 'essentialisation' of group cultures at the expense of politically and legally more ambitious narratives including (where appropriate) autonomy or self-government. Nevertheless, it is difficult to argue that cultural groups, particularly those attached to a homeland, can ground a claim to self-determination (or autonomy) *solely* in their communal identity. As the post-1945 international law of self-determination gradually emerged out of United Nations practice, those groups claiming to have suffered discrimination at the hands of settler states or new sovereigns were in practice left with the option of aligning with the decolonisation paradigm or, later on, seeking redress for gross human rights violations committed against them by the state. Retrospectively, such groups, particularly indigenous communities, did not pursue the former argument with any degree of consistency. And as the recent case of Kosovo shows, international law has hardly endorsed separate statehood as a general international legal remedy for group-based human rights violations.[16] In the *Reference* case over Quebec, the Supreme Court of Canada noted that 'external' self-determination in the form of 'remedial secession' would be contingent upon the state failing to respect 'internal' self-determination, though it did question whether remedial secession could be considered an established international law standard.[17]

•••

15 *Leonid Raihman v. Latvia* Comm. No. 1621/2007, Views of 30 November 2010, U.N. Doc. CCPR/C/100/C/100/D/1621/2007 (2010), Appendix, Individual opinion of Committee members Mr. Rafael Rivas Posada and Mr. Krister Thelin (dissenting), para. 8.6; *Ballantyne et al. v. Canada, supra* note 4; *Waldman v. Canada,* Comm. No. 694/1996, Views of 5 November 1999, U.N. Doc. CCPR/C/67/D/694/1996 (1996); in *Rakhim Mavlonov and Shansiy Sa'di v. Uzbekistan* (Comm. No. 1334/2004, Views of 19 March 2009, U.N. Doc. CCPR/C/95/D/1334/2004 (2009)), the Committee conceded, without further elaboration, that "education in a minority language is a fundamental part of minority culture" in the context of Article 27 (para. 8.7).

16 *Accordance with International Law of the Unilateral Declaration of Independence in Respect of* Kosovo, Advisory Opinion, 22 July 2010, I.C.J. Reports 2010, p. 403, paras. 51, 56, 82.

17 *Supra* note 9, paras. 134–135.

This often-uneasy match of gains and limitations in human rights discourse speaks more broadly to the fluidity of collective interests in articulating the concept or boundaries of group protection. This is a multi-layered terrain which has unsurprisingly drawn the attention of a variety of legal scholars and political and moral theorists.

By generally accepting Joseph Raz's interest-based conception of rights,[18] several scholars have grounded both individual and collective human rights in the interest of individuals in the quality of their own lives, including lives in communities. Variations on this theme are largely a function of the extent to which groups, including ethno-cultural groups, are thought to be reducible to a set of individuals enjoying rights of their own or entities that can themselves be the bearers of rights (moral and/or legal). In both cases the rights of group members are regarded as instrumental in protecting and largely defining the group's collective interests, though scholarly positions vary on the permissibility of restrictions on the rights of members and non-members. In this regard, lines of argument range from narrow views of 'internal protections' to broader views allowing for restrictions on the individual rights of insiders (and possibly outsiders) as long as such restrictions (such as taxation by religious schools, language requirements by autonomous provinces, or powers embedded in self-government agreements), are meant to protect a right-supporting community, that is, a viable group that is necessary to protect the autonomous choices of their members or otherwise serve members' interest in general and respect the equivalently weighty interest of non-members as well.[19] From this broader perspective, some authors have argued that there exist good reasons for intervention or deference, or for modulating the type of intervention, by the state and/or human rights adjudicators, in cases other than those where dramatic violations – such as 'honour killings' or female genital mutilation – have occurred. On a more general level, there is the recognition, as in Peter Jones' chapter in this volume, that the relationship between collective and individual interests within groups can be a multifaceted one, cutting across legal and extra-legal accounts of the field, possible asymmetries between broad moral premises and specific legal rights, and complex articulations of ethno-cultural claims themselves.

---

18 *See* especially Raz, Joseph. *The Morality of Freedom* (Clarendon Press, Oxford, 1986).

19 For range of views, *see e.g.* W. Kymlicka, *Multicultural Citizenship: A Liberal Theory of Minority Rights* (Oxford University Press, Oxford, 1995); M. Freeman, 'Are there Collective Human Rights?', in D. Beetham (ed.), *Politics and Human Rights* (Blackwell Publishers, Oxford, 1995) p. 25; D. Newman, *Community and Collective Rights: A Theoretical Framework for Rights Held by Groups* (Hart Publishing, Oxford, 2011); M. Jovanović, *Collective Rights: A Legal Theory* (Cambridge University Press, Cambridge, 2012).

Matters become even more complicated as we step outside the strict minority prism through which all of these discussions are conducted and look at collective interests through a wider set of communities, be they majorities within distinct political units, similarly situated individuals within and across groups, or extended communities such as the international community or the human rights movement itself. For example, authors of the likes of Dwight Newman (in this volume), Alan Patten, and more recently, Liav Orgad, have noted that the collective interests of national and certain local majorities in a culturally agile integration of immigrants, or in regional autonomy, respectively, are just as important as the collective interests pursued by other groups, including cultural minorities or other types of groups within the relevant unit.[20] On the hotly contested immigration issue, in particular, Alan Patten has argued that, while immigrants should never be deemed to have waived non-discrimination rights, or basic dimensions of religious freedom and possible accommodation, receiving states (and their majorities) can legitimately take reasonable steps to make their own cultural and linguistic rights explicit to potential immigrants. He seeks to expose the limitations of the cultural argument in the immigration debate by drawing an important distinction between securing access to a public culture that is tolerant and respectful of diversity within, and guaranteeing open-ended access to one's own societal culture through specific cultural rights.

Equally, complications arise in the context of intersectional aspects of discrimination that may occur within and across groups. Focusing on minority religious women, Ayelet Shachar has proposed a model of regulated and shared jurisdiction between the state and the group in matters that intersect with the cultural-religious (*de jure* or *de facto*) autonomy of the group, including issues pertaining to family law such as marriages and their dissolution, property and inheritance.[21] However, as the case of Muslim women brought to the fore by the famous 1985 *Sha Bano* case before the Supreme Court of India and its subsequent developments illustrate, gender-based intersectionality may be as much a matter of securing the rights of individuals as a valid indicator of the state's underlying deficiencies in engaging with particular identities and diversities in order to foster

20 A. Patten, *Equal Recognition: The Moral Foundations of Minority Rights* (Princeton University Press, Princeton and Oxford, 2014), ch. 8; L. Orgav, *The Cultural Defense of Nations: A Liberal Theory of Majority Rights* (Oxford University Press, Oxford, 2016).

21 A. Shachar, *Multicultural Jurisdictions: Cultural Differences and Women's Rights* (Cambridge University Press, Cambridge, 2001).

'negotiated' social and political orders that can accompany and sustain the language of rights.[22]

On a more systemic level, the complexities of ethno-cultural diversity in legal and policy discourse partly replicate broader tensions between traditional universalist accounts of the field, with their typical call for some form of uniform and unlimited application of human rights, and more particularist views keen to prioritise the national or local level as a basis for moral and legal action. Many of the chapters in this volume attest – explicitly or implicitly – to the simplistic nature of this divide and the need to dig deeper into the proper functions and ramifications of human rights within the international system as they deal with the different historical circumstances of groups, overlapping dimensions, issues of mobility, or security threats. If anything, the challenge of ethno-cultural diversity is above all one of identifying the nature and scope of the collective interests involved, as well as reasonable criteria to constructively manage the relationship between domestic law and policy and international norms in the field.

More specifically, as Neil Walker has insightfully argued from a general perspective and is broadly echoed in some of this volume's contributions, it may well be that human rights cannot cover all conceivable spaces of policy action or political morality or that, conversely, there is something inevitably open-ended about human rights as they strive to achieve some form of cross-cultural convergence across a plurality of conceptions of 'just' social and political orders, or a plural configuration of institutions and political communities below and above the surface of the state.[23] In this context, interlocking collective interests can sit alongside competing collective and individual claims. Malgosia Fitzmaurice's chapter on indigenous rights and intergenerational equity offers one example of how the collective interests pursued by ethno-cultural groups can provide opportunities for a partial legal and policy realignment with equally cherished global values endorsed by international law itself.

•••

22 M. Walzer, *The Paradox of Liberation: Secular Revolutions and Religious Counterrevolutions* (Yale University Press, New Haven and London, 2015) pp. 114–121; from a broader anti-discrimination perspective, *see* the chapter by Dolores Morondo Taramundi in this volume.

23 N. Walker, 'Universalism and particularism in human rights', in C. Holder and D. Reidy (eds.), *Human Rights: The Hard Questions* (Cambridge University Press, Cambridge, 2013) p. 39, at pp. 49–50; from the specific angle of immigration, *see also* the chapter by Tom Hadden in this volume.

Against such a backdrop of normative and policy complexity, the relatively narrower level of international human rights law relating to ethno-cultural claims seems increasingly to be less a function of the straightforward application of discrete and self-standing rights (as important as they certainly are), and more of a by-product of cumulative and 'systemic' readings of standards, complex balancing acts in particular instances, 'frontier management' exercises between the international and domestic legal orders, or otherwise wider processes of accommodation of individual and collective interests within the political community.

Article 27 ICCPR, for example, has mirrored to some extent the porous boundaries of this discourse, especially in the context of competing claims made by the group and its members relating to membership issues or internal dissent. The Human Rights Committee has ruled, depending on the case, in favour of the group member based on a sensitive account of internal community debate, in favour of the group as protected by national legislation, and in favour of both the majority of the group and the dissenting minority within.[24] While the Committee is generally keen to interpret Article 27 rights in ways which are as consistent as possible with their individual dimension, the contingency of the assessments reflects not only their contextual nature, but more generally, the sort of discourses that these types of assessment may entail in rather difficult scenarios. It is quite telling that human rights practice has focused less on exit strategies (à la Shachar) in the event of internal restrictions and more on reconciling community practices and interests with the rights of individuals from within the group.[25]

More broadly, the interplay of legal developments and conceptual fluidity in the field paradoxically results, not in inhibiting further progress, but in the proliferation of hybrid sites of protection for ethno-cultural diversity. Rigid dichotomies between the individual and the group in human rights law are giving way to complex, yet practical, articulations of what is loosely perceived as a bundle of claims pervasively linked to one another, the hybrid outlook of which opens up possibilities for various degrees of protection. Practice around Article 27 rights as collective rights and certain collective dimensions of freedom of religion and family life – such as the viability of religious communities

---

24 *Sandra Lovelace v. Canada*, Comm. No. 24/1977, July 30 1981, U.N. Doc. Supp. No. 40, Annex 18, U.N. Doc. A/36/40 166 (1981); *Ivan Kitok v. Sweden*, Comm. No. 197/1985, July 27 1988, U.N. Doc. Supp. No. 40, Annex 7, U.N. Doc. A/43/40 229 (1988); *Apirana Mahuika v. New Zealand*, *supra* note 4.

25 G. Pentassuglia, *Minority Groups and Judicial Discourse in International Law: A Comparative Perspective* (Martinus Nijhoff Publishers, Leiden, 2009) pp. 136–141.

or the protection of religious sites or burial grounds[26] – tends to hybridise distinctions between rights in the name of comparable collective interests. Similarly, the Committee on Economic, Social and Cultural Rights has sought to bridge the gap between individual and group protection by acknowledging individual and collective dimensions of cultural rights under the CESCR. The right to take part in cultural life has been very loosely framed as *both* a right of individuals and a right of groups built around a bundle of entitlements to freely choose a specific set or multiple sets of cultural goods, to be able to access such goods and to participate in the design and implementation of laws affecting them. The Committee has indicated that such a participation should involve "their free and informed prior consent" when their "cultural resources ... are at risk".[27]

This heightened level of hybridity is anything but unique to these more general human rights instruments. It has effectively become something of a hallmark of much of human rights practice, including more complex cases. For all of its significance and transformative potential, the recognition of indigenous autonomy in the UNDRIP, for example, still requires the group to engage in negotiations with the state (and vice versa) over the exact terms of its political status, its cultural autonomy and/or legal systems where they exist, as well as to work out regimes that are consistent with the rights of individual members and non-members. Other global and regional practice has developed a discourse whereby formally individual and group rights not only meet, but are explained in light of each other's cross-cutting and intertwined dimensions, be they religion, culture, property, self-determination, participation, or a combination of these. Certain individual rights have been re-read to incorporate group rights at sub-state level, and group rights (e.g. rights to natural resources) have been re-read to partly endorse the logic of the individual rights (e.g. property rights) to which they are said to be intimately related as a matter of substance and process.[28] Ambitious peace settlements in conflict and non-conflict scenarios have equally appealed to cumulative hybrid views of standards, including hybrid self-determination arrangements,

26 *See e.g.* the European Court on Human Rights' decision in *Metropolitan Church of Bessarabia and Others v. Moldova*, Application No. 45701/99, Judgment of 13 December 2001; P. Jones, 'Groups and Human Rights', in C. Holder and D. Reidy (eds.), *supra* note 23, p. 107; *Hopu and Bessert v. France*, Comm. No. 549/1993, July 29, 1997, U.N. Doc. CCPR/C/60/D/549/1993/Rev.1. (1997).

27 *See supra* note 7, para. 15(a); *see also* para. 55(e).

28 G. Pentassuglia, 'Toward a Jurisprudential Articulation of Indigenous Land Rights', 22 *European Journal of International Law* (2011) p. 165, at pp. 187–190, 198.

in an attempt to govern competing individual and group claims across the political community.[29] In a non-conflict scenario, the Draft Nordic Saami Convention, produced in 2005 by Norway, Finland and Sweden together with the respective Nordic Saami parliaments, exemplifies a major attempt at institutionalising aspects of the Saami legal order as a central component of Saami self-determination within wider state systems, including conflicts of law norms, forms of territorial and cultural autonomy, and weaker translations of Saami legal practices into state law.[30]

In sum, the role of ethno-cultural diversity in human rights discourse is increasingly multi-layered, and increasingly hybrid at that. In some cases, human rights practice will enable vitally important group activity. In other cases, it will protect the distinctive collective interest in group flourishing through measures that target specific rights. In still other cases, it will create a framework for institutional and policy action to be worked out at the local level.

For all the progress that has been undisputedly made on several fronts of human rights law, and for all the hybridity and innovation that have come with recent attempts to navigate the complexities of ethno-cultural diversity, there is a sense, though, that the international human rights regime still leaves significant space for conceptual ambiguity as to the paths on which it needs to be set for ethno-cultural groups to be taken seriously. In this sense, hybrid solutions are not only valuable legal (doctrinal) tools in the wake of ever more dynamic readings of human rights norms; they also mirror – to greater or lesser extent – genuine normative or conceptual dilemmas as to the significance of ethno-cultural diversity, the status of groups, and the ways in which the law can or should respond to ethno-cultural claims.

•••

29 For excellent discussion in conflict contexts, *see* C. Bell, *On the Law of Peace: Peace Agreements and the Lex Pacificatoria* (Oxford University Press, Oxford, 2008) chs. 5,11 (arguing that hybrid self-determination, including autonomy arrangements, from the Bougainville to the Belfast agreements, can be pursued as "the best application of the law in situations of intrastate ethnic conflict", p. 225).

30 For this gamut of models, *see* J. W. Hamilton, 'Acknowledging and Accommodating Legal Pluralism: An Application to the Draft Nordic Saami Convention', in N. Bankes and T. Koivurova (eds.), *The Proposed Nordic Saami Convention: National and International Dimensions of Indigenous Property Rights* (Hart Publishing, Oxford, 2013) pp. 45–77.

Certain ambivalences in the field are in part the upshot of narratives that question the very validity of claims relating to ethno-cultural identity. Much of this thinking essentially seeks to deconstruct the meaning(s) of such claims from a critical, 'post-cultural' (post-modern), or cosmopolitan angle. Martti Koskenniemi, for example, has argued that, since there is no natural standard to assess the existence of 'national' (ethno-cultural) communities, 'national' self-determination claims (and by analogy, ethno-cultural claims more broadly) should be understood essentially as ways "to enlist popular support for the struggle against political oppression", be they in the form of anti-colonialism as we have known it, or some other form of resistance or reaction as a legitimate process of political contestation.[31] Others have gone as far as to question the plausibility of coherent cultural, national, or identity claims as significant drivers of human identity in an era of globalisation and mobility. For them, if there is any culture or identity at all, it is a global one that dissolves, not affirms, differences built around "natural languages" and "natural cultures"; it is one that operates in circumstances of "radical heterogeneity and fragmentation" which are no longer capable of sustaining any serious concept of group identity within or across state boundaries.[32]

Needless to say, several of these perspectives also reiterate concerns about essentialism and varying degrees of hostility or suspicion towards right claims attached to a community defined in (broadly understood) ethno-cultural terms (be it a minority or majority group).[33] A strand of practice has gone on to draw the conclusion that community identity is, at best, little more than shorthand for the individual's subjective choice. In *Ciubotaru v. Moldova* before the European Court of Human Rights,[34] Judge Mijović went as far as to contend that self-identification was primarily "a matter of personal perception rather than a matter based on objective grounds"; he concurred with the majority's finding of a breach of Article 8 (private and family life), not on the basis (upheld by the Court) that Moldova had failed to provide the applicant with an

---

31 M. Koskenniemi, 'National Self-Determination Today: Problems of Legal Theory and Practice', 43 *International and Comparative Law Quarterly* (1994) p. 241, at p. 262.

32 For discussion and critique of this line, *see e.g.* J. Tully, *Strange Multiplicity: Constitutionalism in an Age of Diversity* (Cambridge University Press, Cambridge, 1995) pp. 45–47 (citing the work of James Clifford and Peter Emberley).

33 F. Tesón, 'Ethnicity, Human Rights, and Self-Determination', in D. Wippman (ed.) *International Law and Ethnic Conflict* (Cornell University Press, Ithaca and London, 1998) p. 86; *id.*, 'Introduction: The Conundrum of Self-Determination', in F. Tesón (ed.), *The Theory of Self-Determination* (Cambridge University Press, Cambridge, 2016) p. 1.

34 Application No. 27138/04, Judgment of 27 April 2010.

opportunity to adduce evidence in support of his identity claim, but rather on the basis that the applicant's self-identification choice should have been respected *regardless* of any objective parameters to establish affiliation with a particular group. These lines of thinking hardly fit in with established international law and human rights practice,[35] though they most certainly offer a critique of such practice. Under international human rights law, compulsory individual identifications with (or membership in) the group are not permitted, be they enacted through legislation or other domestic practices. However, it is one thing to mark out the limits of state action in recording and classifying ethno-cultural groups, and to expose challenges that arise in the context of particular group arrangements like certain power-sharing agreements,[36] and it is quite another to reconceptualise ethno-cultural claims in ways that break them down into a highly contingent set of separate and self-contained views of individual identity, one that fails to engage with the legitimacy of core interests that attach to individuals *and* groups alike.[37]

In fact, while it may be historically accurate to link several group claims to positive emancipatory projects, and others to more destructive projects of political manipulation, aggressive chauvinism, and/or cultural essentialism, it would be wrong to assume either that group identities can be reduced to

---

35 *See generally* G. Pentassuglia, *Minorities in International Law: An Introductory Study* (Council of Europe Publishing, Strasbourg, 2002) pp. 72–74; it can also be argued that the European Court of Human Rights does not regard self-identification as an exclusive criterion: *see* the Chamber's ruling in *Ciobutaru* (*supra* note 34, paras. 57–58) and *Gorzelik and Others v Poland*, Application No. 44158/98, Judgment of 17 February 2004 (for commentary, *see* G. Pentassuglia, 'Protecting Minority Groups Through Human Rights Courts: The Interpretive Role of European and Inter-American Jurisprudence', in A. F. Vrdoljak (ed.), *The Cultural Dimension of Human Rights* (Oxford University Press, Oxford, 2013) pp. 104–106).

36 In terms of European practice, the focus has often been on the effects of precluding free self-identification or making it subject to certain legal consequences linked, for example, to political offices or types of employment. *See e.g.* FCNM Advisory Committee, Third Opinion on the United Kingdom, 30 June 2011, paras. 44–47; Third Opinion on Cyprus, 19 March 2010, para. 39; Fourth Opinion on Cyprus, 18 March 2015, paras. 11–12; Third Opinion on Italy, 15 October 2010, para. 53.

37 *See e.g.* Thematic Commentary No. 4, *The Scope of Application of the Framework Convention for the Protection of National Minorities*, 27 May 2016, ACFC/56DOC(2016)001, para. 10. Indeed, the logical implication of the subjective approach is that individual choice would be (ontologically and legally) *constitutive* of the identity phenomenon itself, not (or not only) an ex post facto safeguard against certain pre-existing socio-cultural communities that people are born into (whatever their legal characterisation) and that they can perceive as a significant part of their core identity.

patterns of discourse, or that all identity claims involve a fundamental reengineering of the state as opposed to more limited forms of recognition. For one thing, social science research has convincingly shown that, whatever their origins and form, and whatever their openness and potential for negotiation and revision, group identities must be taken seriously as they are no less real underlying social determinants than the political projects or priorities that help mediate them (or some of them).[38] On the other hand, virtually no states are home to homogenous socio-cultural 'nations', yet most states seek to secure one version or another of a uniform public culture, of a uniform cultural paradigm, that poses a threat (in principle or in practice) to inter-group diversity. In other words, the reality of states as legal entities is almost invariably the reality of a public culture coalescing around a dominant group. The very emergence of new states in the name of 'national' independence, or the continuing running of states as nation states – from Europe, to the Americas, to Africa and Asia – have consistently raised very real questions about the rearrangement of authority within the newly constituted or established entity in order to meet certain group demands. Although, as explained by Michael Walzer, not all nation-building projects have proved wholly incapable of recognising the need for some form of group diversity within (at least in some of their founding documents),[39] they certainly indicate the salience of community identity of one form or another *across* the fabric of emerging or established states. The chapters of this volume by Chris Chapman, Dwight Newman, Tom Hadden, and Ephraim Nimni and Lucia Payero tell us in different ways of the genuine complexities associated with the constant interplay of homogenising tendencies and group representation, on the one hand, and cultural claims and the state's own pursuits of social and cultural protection or integration, on the other.

•••

38 *See e.g.* the insightful analyses of I. Berlin, 'Nationalism: Past Neglect and Present Power', in H. Hardy (ed.), *Against The Current: Essays in the History of Ideas* (The Hogarth Press, London, 1979) p. 333; C. Geertz, *The Interpretation of Cultures* (Fontana Press, London, 1973); *id., Mondo globale, mondi locali: cultura e politica alla fine del ventesimo secolo* (il Mulino, Bologna, 1995) chs. II and IV; J. Tully, *supra* note 32; M. Walzer, *supra* note 22.

39 M. Walzer, *supra* note 22. For a review of similar debates in South East Asia, *see e.g.* J. Castellino, 'Autonomy in South Asia: Evidence for the Emergence of a Regional Custom', in T. Malloy and F. Palermo (eds.), *Minority Accommodation through Territorial and Non-Territorial Autonomy* (Oxford University Press, Oxford, 2015) p. 217.

These discussions are of course amplified by long-standing debates over the legal status of ethno-cultural groups in international human rights law, and the competing ideas underlying those debates. A prime example of this is the rather complex discussion over so-called 'new' minorities as distinct from 'old' or traditional (national) minorities. The argument in favour of extending the concept to include immigrants and similar groupings rests essentially on the notion that cultural identities or cultural differences inhere in all individuals regardless of communal or situational circumstances; as long as access to a cultural 'context of choice'[40] affects virtually everyone, there would be no reason, so the argument goes, for denying minority status to immigrants while granting it to other groups within the state. In terms of the legal categories mentioned earlier in this Introduction, the point appeals to the necessarily universal scope of rights to culture in (explicit or implicit) conjunction with the principle of equality.

While the argument has become increasingly popular in some expert circles, it still faces a range of rather formidable legal and policy challenges. For one thing, there is virtually no empirical evidence that indicates an emerging international consensus on the above extension as a matter of law. Take, again, the FCNM. Although the Advisory Committee has consistently supported the idea of a broader application of this treaty, a large number of the current states parties that have taken a stance on this matter (*at least* more than half of the current treaty membership) has equally consistently held on to a more restrictive understanding of the concept of 'national minority'. As I suggested in my earlier work,[41] it is entirely possible (in some cases, perhaps even advisable) for individual states to provide extended protection on a *de facto* (discretionary) rather than *de jure* (obligatory) basis, as evidenced by a limited number of later cases. Equally, it is *not* permissible for states to make group status dependent upon exceedingly restrictive (discrimination-inducing) criteria, such as state recognition, territorial concentration, or state kinship, which lie beyond minimum parameters supplied by international human rights law. In conceptual terms, though, the key point is that, while the cultural argument can (indeed, must) support essential elements of protection under general human rights norms (e.g. access to non-discrimination tout court, or to basic religious rights), it struggles to make sense of those largely contextual considerations that underpin the *prioritisation* of certain group interests over others within state

40 W. Kymlicka, *supra* note 19.

41 G. Pentassuglia, *supra* note 35, pp. 65–66.

jurisdictions, including specific levels of decision-making authority involving minority and majority communities.[42]

An adapted cultural argument that has proved relatively more successful so far has emerged in the context of debates over indigeneity. As I mentioned, the Inter-American Court of Human Rights has broadly interpreted that concept to include certain non-native and land-dependent traditional communities. Similarly, the African Commission on Human and Peoples' Rights has linked selective 'peoples' rights' under the ACHPR – mainly the right to existence and self-determination, Article 20; the right to natural resources, Article 21; and the right to development, Article 22 – to an expansive concept of indigeneity that is not dependent upon 'prior occupancy' of traditional communal lands and resources.[43] In the ground-breaking *Endorois* case against Kenya, for example, the Commission recognised the pastoralist community in question as an indigenous community on account of the group's long-established cultural and land tenure practices, "beyond the "narrow/aboriginal/pre-Colombian" understanding of indigenous peoples".[44] In addition to criteria of self-identification, territorial connection, and cultural distinctiveness, notions of social marginalisation, discrimination and non-dominance have informed such a re-thinking to a significant degree.

Despite a measure of relative jurisprudential success, questions have nonetheless been raised about the longer term sustainability of this particular way of (re-)conceptualising certain ethno-cultural groups. For example, legal theorists of the likes of Patrick Macklem and Dwight Newman have warned against the danger of over-emphasising generic non-dominance at the expense of a more coherent account of the normative purposes of the field,[45] while

---

42 The FCNM Advisory Committee, for example, has encouraged the enjoyment of specific language and education rights under the FCNM irrespective of traditional residency or numerical requirements, in the name of promoting multilingualism and diversity as well as equality (*see supra* note 37, paras. 31, 42, and 79).

43 Report of the African Commission's Working Group of Experts on Indigenous Populations/Communities, submitted in accordance with the Resolution on the Rights of Indigenous Populations/Communities in Africa, IWAGIA (Copenhagen) and ACHPR (Banjul) (2005), Section 4.2.

44 *Centre for Minority Rights Development (Kenya) and Minority Rights Group International on behalf of Endorois Welfare Council v. Kenya*, Comm. No. 276/2003, 4 February 2010, para. 159.

45 P. Macklem, *The Sovereignty of Human Rights* (Oxford University Press, Oxford, 2015) ch. 6; D. Newman's chapter in this volume; *see also* F.M. Ndahinda, *Indigenousness in Africa: A Contested Legal Framework for Empowerment of 'Marginalized' Communities* (T.M.C. Press, The Hague, 2011).

other prominent voices such as Will Kymlicka and Benedict Kingsbury have, in different ways, exposed critical dimensions of the ambivalent relationship between 'indigenous peoples' and 'national minorities' or otherwise traditional ethno-cultural communities.[46] In fact, the flexible view reflected in the Inter-American and African case law seeks to render international human rights law more responsive to the position of the groups concerned. However, in ways that are highly reminiscent of the old/new minorities debate in Europe, the deployment of the cultural argument in connection with broader social equality concerns does not *ipso facto* settle group status issues, nor does it invite to address the underlying reasons why certain ethno-cultural groups merit protection in the way they do.

Probably the holy grail of legal discussions about group status is tied to popular claims to 'national' self-determination made by groups that perceive themselves as fairly coherent cultural communities linked to a traditional homeland. Neither the United Nations decolonisation paradigm nor the later shift towards issues of governance within the framework of the state makes it obvious that such claims can be accommodated by appealing to 'peoplehood' (or 'nationhood') in international law. The problem is unlikely to be resolved through precise definitions or judicial or quasi-judicial pronouncements over the status of a claimant as a 'people' or a 'nation' within an emerging or established state. For example, the-then European Community Arbitration Commission on Yugoslavia located the position of the Bosnian Serbs around hybrid notions of 'population', 'minority' and 'ethnic group' for purposes of self-determination within Bosnia.[47] The International Court of Justice, for its part, held that Kosovo's Declaration of Independence was not, in and of itself, at odds with international law, but still refrained from recognising the population of Kosovo, let alone the Kosovar Albanians, as a people in a legal sense.[48] Critics have suggested that the awkwardness surrounding these rulings reflect a failure to recognise sub-unit claims from within the internal federal boundaries of collapsing Yugoslavia or a failure to genuinely engage with self-determination issues from within Serbia as

46 B. Kingsbury, 'Reconciling Five Competing Conceptual Structures of Indigenous Peoples' Claims in International and Comparative Law', 34 *New York University Journal of International Law and Politics* (2001) p. 189, at pp. 233, 244; W. Kymlicka, *Multicultural Odysseys: Navigating the New International Politics of Diversity* (Oxford University Press, Oxford, 2007) pp. 273–91.

47 European Community Arbitration Commission, Opinion No. 2, 11 January 1992, 31 *International Legal Materials* (1992) p. 1497.

48 *Supra* note 16, paras. 51, 56, 82, 89, 105, 109.

an established state.[49] Yet, it can be argued that these pronouncements underscore a deeper tension between human rights law and claims to self-determination made by 'national' groups, one that can be resolved neither through carving out entire states out of a 'national' *droit acquis* in 'abnormal' circumstances of territorial and political transition,[50] nor through outright rejection of such claims or some alternative version of them.[51] As I discuss in my essay, the 1998 *Reference* case before the Supreme Court of Canada was not premised on any assumption about the status of the French-speaking community of Quebec, or indeed of any other group within Quebec, as a 'people'. The focus was on the acknowledgment of inter-group diversity within the state and the requirement of constitutional conversations to address that diversity.

The central point here is not that sub-national groups can never be viewed as 'peoples' for legal purposes, however hybrid and highly contingent such a recognition may be,[52] but rather that the matter is only part (most likely a minimal part) of a much more complex story about the co-existence of groups and the reasons why some of them and not others require the protection that they do. In this sense, legal arguments squarely built around 'peoplehood' (or 'nationhood') are either implausible or incomplete.

•••

The various attempts at (re-)conceptualising ethno-cultural identity ultimately account for the role of law, not only in addressing a variable range of collective

49 *See e.g.* R. Falk, *Human Rights Horizons: The Pursuit of Justice in a Globalizing World* (Routledge, New York and London, 2000) pp. 115–116 (commenting on H. Hannum's 'Self-Determination, Yugoslavia, and Europe: Old Wine in New Bottles?', 3 *Transnational Law and Contemporary Problems* (1993) p. 59).

50 *The Aaland Islands Question (On Jurisdiction)*, Report of the International Committee of Jurists, League of Nations Official Journal, Special Supplement No. 3 (1920); *The Aaland Islands Question (On the Merits)*, Report by the Commission of Rapporteurs, League of Nations Council Document B7 21/68/106 (1921). Just as the international community's intervention in the transitional circumstances of the case did not use the 'nation' as the ultimate controlling legal principle, so too the European Community's heightened competence in Yugoslavia did not buttress the equation between 'natural' (national) communities and nation states.

51 For commentary, *see* my chapter in this volume, and more broadly, G. Pentassuglia, 'Self-Determination, Human Rights, and the Nation-State: Revisiting Group Claims through a Complex Nexus in International Law', 19 *International Community Law Review* (2017), forthcoming.

52 *Ibid.*

and individual interests as previously discussed, but also in calibrating responses at a more systemic level. From a human rights perspective, the tension between uniformity and differentiation in tackling ethno-cultural claims broadly mirrors the oscillation between decostructivist approaches to ethno-cultural identity and comprehensive views of the field that ultimately lump the diverse body of groups together through single and self-sustaining human rights categories such as equality or culture. The blend of human rights protections and security arrangements in complex group accommodation models adds to the dilemmatic aspects of these debates, as illustrated by the *Sejdić and Finci v. Bosnia and Herzegovina*, where the European Court of Human Rights concluded that Bosnia's power-sharing agreement signed at Dayton in 1995 was incompatible with Article 14 ECHR insofar as it excluded members of communities other than the Bosniak, Croat and Serbian ones (who had freely so self-identified) from certain political offices.[53]

Much of this discourse – wittingly or unwittingly – fails to unpack the ethno-cultural phenomenon; it misses the contingent legitimacy of community arrangements, or the differential impact of international law-making on groups and the limits of cultural claims, or the varying degrees to which human rights-based group safeguards can prevent conflict in particular instances or help contain belligerent groups' more mundane priorities in post-conflict scenarios. Several chapters of this volume can be taken to cumulatively begin to fill that gap by exploring the bases, developments, potentials, and/or limitations of human rights law and policy in relation to a whole host of different claims and contexts involving ethno-cultural diversity.

•••

This interdisciplinary collection is divided into four parts, each of which seeks to deepen our understanding of commonly and less commonly examined aspects of ethno-cultural diversity. Part I offers moral, legal and political theory perspectives on the complex relationship between ethno-cultural groups and collective interests and their implications for human rights discourse. Part II looks at this nexus from the perspective of the international legal system, specifically human rights-based arrangements for particular groups and the impact of such arrangements on other interests protected by international law. Part III explores policy dilemmas generated by ethno-cultural concerns in the context of immigration and intersectional discrimination. Part IV discusses the role of ethno-cultural diversity, or lack of it, in preventing or fomenting

53 Applications Nos. 27996/06 and 34836/06, Judgment of 22 December 2009.

conflict, and the asymmetries between human rights and security concerns in post-conflict peacebuilding.

The division is not meant to suggest sharp distinctions in content or approach, but rather an indication of the prevailing focus of each cluster of essays across a range of cross-cutting dimensions. Indeed, many of them variably address foundational or conceptual questions from their specific angle, and all of them anchor their analyses in various areas of group diversity practice.

Peter Jones (Chapter 1) argues that the rights of ethno-cultural minorities, including indigenous peoples, can be both collective and group-specific and still be human rights. He contends that this is so because what undergirds people's human rights is the universality of human status, not the universality of right; human rights can deal with the different circumstances of groups on a moral and legal levels while still taking the 'human' in human rights seriously. Dwight Newman (Chapter 2) acknowledges the significance of such rights in human rights discourse but suggests that the framework of relevant collective (community) interests should include the rights of majorities within state-wide and sub-state units alongside minority and indigenous rights. He contends that, the moral considerations that militate in favour of such a view are just as important as the human rights that are already legally ascribed to minority groups, even though they may or may not be enumerated in legal form. From a more traditional minority angle, Ephraim Nimni and Lucia Payero-López (Chapter 3) seek to expose the human rights relevance of group representation deficits that stem from monolithic views of the nation state in liberal democracies anchored in notions of undivided sovereignty. They argue that the proclivity to secessionism by the affected national minorities can be avoided by converting nation states into plurinational states, and discuss how this could help resolve Spain's recently rekindled constitutional dilemmas.

In different ways, my chapter (Chapter 4), and the following two by Felipe Gómez Isa (Chapter 5) and Malgosia Fitzmaurice (Chapter 6), exemplify ethno-cultural conundrums in international law. I look at autonomy claimed by ethno-cultural minority groups as a bundle of contingent legal, conceptual and policy issues rather than a problem to be solved through ready-made and generally applicable or 'inherent' rights. I seek to move away from traditional concerns with group status and right-holding matters to investigate the legitimacy of autonomy arrangements in international human rights law. Felipe Gómez Isa traces the history of international law's legacy of conquest and exclusion of indigenous peoples and argues that such a legacy still defines the position of these communities within societies. Against this backdrop, he discusses the potential of contemporary international human rights instruments, including the UNDRIP, to become transformative tools in law and policy. Malgosia Fitzmaurice, for her part, values such developments while still situating the issue of ethno-cultural diversity within a broader context of collective interests, including international environmental law's endorsement of intergenerational equity and what this tells us about the content and methods of indigenous whaling. She suggests that enhanced participation of indigenous peoples in inter-state relations and within indigenous groups themselves may help address these questions.

The remaining four chapters weave conceptual dimensions into particular issues that lie at the intersection of human rights and practical domestic policies, particularly migration, intersectionality and security. Tom Hadden (Chapter 7) addresses the vexing question of immigration and migrant rights and draws a distinction between basic human rights for all and more flexible standards in such areas as education, housing, employment, or culture. He argues that in the latter areas the state can make legitimate choices, including encouraging greater ethnic, linguistic and cultural integration and/or modulating protection depending on the generation, size and/or concentration of the migrant group involved. He offers a word of caution against overloading human rights discourse with rigid requirements that may sidestep practical state choices at national and local levels. Dolores Morondo Taramundi (Chapter 8) takes on the question of internal minorities by combining minority rights accounts of the issue with insights from anti-discrimination law and policy, specifically in the context of intersectionality. She argues that framing the debate in terms of a binary choice between the cultural autonomy of the group and the rights of individuals within the group tends to downplay the underlying collective and cross-cutting dimensions of inequality claims, especially in the case of sex equality.

Looking at security, Chris Chapman (Chapter 9) examines the link between ethno-cultural diversity and conflict prevention and management by discussing approaches that incorporate assimilationist and integrationist methods. He notes that the suppression of diversity facilitates rather than contains conflict and looks at a range of violent conflicts where group rights issues have proved one of their main drivers. From the perspective of post-conflict peacebuilding, Padraig McAuliffe (Chapter 10) argues that ethno-cultural protections in peace agreements tend to be under-used or under-enforced. For McAuliffe, the security priorities pursued by the belligerent majority and minority groups in the aftermath of a civil war typically outweigh human rights concerns; they tend to inform most trusted forms of power-sharing or autonomy solutions and put pressure on desirable longer term approaches that blend holistic rights-based frameworks with security-based conflict management strategies.

Few, if any, would dispute the ever expanding use of human rights to frame a variety of ethno-cultural claims in several legal and policy settings. Yet, under international human rights law, standards are unclear and ambivalent, while traditional analyses have often failed to elucidate and dissect the complexities involved. This edited volume does not cover the full spectrum of ethno-cultural issues but I hope it can at least begin the process of unpacking what is actually at stake and encourage more nuanced and cross-cutting responses to a field all too often infused with minimalist, absolutist, or overly sectorial understandings of rights.

PART I

Ethno-Cultural Diversity and Collective Interests

CHAPTER 1

Collective and Group-Specific: Can the Rights of Ethno-Cultural Minorities be Human Rights?

Peter Jones[1]

1 Introduction

The human rights tradition has viewed the idea of minority rights with ambivalence. On the one hand, the tradition has been protective of minorities simply by virtue of according them the same fundamental rights as majorities. If human rights are universal, minority individuals necessarily have those rights on the same terms as everyone else. Moreover, the protection afforded by universal rights is often of greater significance for minorities, simply because, as minorities, they are more vulnerable than majorities to mistreatment or to less than equal treatment.

On the other hand, the kinds of claim associated with minority rights, especially the rights of ethno-cultural minorities, have not always sat comfortably within the human rights tradition. One reason is that minority claims are sometimes collective in nature. Culture, language, nationality, religious affiliation, and the like are collective phenomena and the rights minorities seek in relation to them often make sense only as collective rights – as rights possessed by the minority as a group rather than by its members severally. Those rights are at odds with the tradition that conceives human rights as rights possessed only by human individuals. While some have dissented from that tradition, the idea that human rights can be held by groups has generally been resisted, either because it has been deemed incoherent or because it has been thought to endanger individual human rights.

Minority rights have also proved difficult for human rights thinking insofar as they are rights that are in some way special to minorities. That specialness is at odds with the belief that human rights are necessarily universal.

1 Earlier drafts of this chapter benefited from discussions at the Symposium on Ethno-Cultural Diversity and Human Rights held at the School of Law and Social Justice, University of Liverpool; the inaugural meeting of the Globalising Minority Rights Project held at the Department of Philosophy, University of Tromsø; and a meeting of the Durham and Newcastle Political Theory Group. Special thanks to Gaetano Pentassuglia, Kaspar Lippert-Rasmussen and Annamari Vitikainen.

 | DOI 10.1163/9789004328785_003

Consider language rights. If human rights are universal rights, majorities and minorities can have human rights in respect of their language only insofar as they are precisely the same rights. If there is good reason why the language rights of majorities and minorities, or of different minorities, should differ, those different rights cannot be human rights. That simple all-or-nothing dichotomy, forced on us by the demands of universality, seems too stark. There is often good reason why language rights should differ. For example, the cost and inconvenience a society would incur if it were to make a minority's language an official public language on terms precisely equal with the majority language could be prohibitive, especially if the society contained more than one linguistic minority. On the other hand, it might be equally inappropriate that a minority should possess no rights in respect of its language beyond those possessed indiscriminately by all, including a single individual who was the only individual in the society to speak his or her language. If human rights are always and only universal rights, those sorts of consideration would seem to be, of necessity, excluded from the purview of human rights thinking.

In this chapter, I shall challenge the orthodoxies that human rights must be individually-held and universally-held. I shall argue that human rights can remain authentically 'human' and yet be collective in form and 'group-specific', that is, different for different groups. Human rights thinking need not therefore be embarrassed by the rights of ethno-cultural minorities.

Making an argument of that sort has been complicated by the emergence in recent years of different conceptions of what we should understand a human right to be. The traditional moral conception of human rights takes seriously the 'human' in 'human right', so that a human right is a right we hold in virtue of being human. People may have rights as citizens and other rights as members of non-state associations, but they possess some rights just as human beings. Those are human rights. That has been the dominant conception amongst those who have conceived human rights as moral rights, at least in the first instance, including those who have undertaken philosophical analyses of human rights. I shall follow Pablo Gilabert in describing that traditional conception as 'humanist'.[2] Some contemporary philosophers who keep faith with it are James Griffin,[3] John Tasioulas,[4] and Carl Wellman.[5]

---

2 P. Gilabert, 'Humanist and Political Perspectives on Human Rights', 39 *Political Theory* (2011) p. 439.

3 J. Griffin, *On Human Rights* (Oxford University Press, Oxford, 2008).

4 J. Tasioulas, 'The Moral Reality of Human Rights', in T. Pogge (ed.), *Freedom from Poverty as a Human Right* (Oxford University Press, Oxford, 2007).

5 C. Wellman, *The Moral Dimensions of Human Rights* (Oxford University Press, Oxford, 2011).

Human-rights thinking has always been highly political in inspiration. It has been strongly motivated by what follows politically if people possess human rights; but for humanists those political implications are just that, 'implications'. They are not part of the very idea of human rights. In that respect, the humanist conception contrasts with the 'political' conception espoused by John Rawls,[6] Charles Beitz,[7] and Joseph Raz.[8] On their view, we should understand what a human right is with reference to the meaning the term has, and the role human rights perform, in contemporary political practice. A human right is a right that is legitimately of concern to the international political community and a right whose violation may justify (albeit defeasibly) some form of international intervention – military, economic or diplomatic. Exponents of the political conception differ in their accounts of quite how human rights figure in international political practice, but they agree in conceiving them in terms of their international political role rather than with reference to a supposed link to our humanity.

'Political' theorists do not deny that determining which rights should fall into the category of human rights is properly a matter for moral argument. What makes their view 'political' is their conception of what it is that we justify when we justify a human right. Their thinking can be distinguished from a third school of thought whose conception of human rights I shall describe simply as 'legal'. Legal human rights have existed ever since they were incorporated in international law many decades ago and the legal conception is not distinguished by mere recognition of that fact. Rather, it is distinguished by the sharp separation it makes between moral human rights and legal human rights. Moral thinking on human rights has often assumed that legal human rights are, or should be, merely moral human rights translated into international law. Allen Buchanan describes that as the 'mirroring' view.[9] He believes it to be profoundly mistaken, since all sorts of consideration other than moral human rights actually feed into, and rightly feed into, the make-up of legal human rights. Moreover, many legal human rights have no moral equivalents. While he does not reject the very idea of moral human rights or deny that moral human rights can sometimes be relevant to the justification of legal human rights, he believes it quite wrong to suppose that a system of international human rights law either can be, or should be, merely the legal instantiation of a philosophical

---

6 J. Rawls, *The Law of Peoples* (Harvard University Press, Cambridge, MA, 1999).

7 C. R. Beitz, *The Idea of Human Rights* (Oxford University Press, Oxford, 2009).

8 J. Raz, 'Human Rights without Foundations', in S. Besson and J. Tasioulas (eds.), *The Philosophy of International Law* (Oxford University Press, Oxford, 2010) p. 321.

9 A. Buchanan, *The Heart of Human Rights* (Oxford University Press, Oxford, 2013).

theory of moral human rights.[10] Patrick Macklem separates legal human rights from moral thinking even more radically.[11] He conceives both the substance of, and the case for, legal human rights as entirely internal to international law. Legal human rights are rights through which international law has sought to correct pathologies of its own making. In investing sovereign power in states, international law has distributed political power in a way that makes possible seriously adverse consequences; human rights law is the device international law has used to curb the power that it has itself conferred upon states.

In considering whether rights that are collective to and specific to ethno-cultural minorities can also be human rights, I shall take seriously the 'human' in human rights. I shall assume, along with the humanist conception, that human rights are rights people hold in virtue of being human. If we do not make that assumption, the issue of whether human rights can be collective or group-specific can easily become a non-issue. If legal human rights are whatever international law declares them to be and if international law declares collective rights or group-specific rights to be human rights, that declaration settles the matter. Similarly, on the political conception, if collective rights or group-specific rights figure amongst the rights that are of legitimate international concern and whose violation can justify international political action, that suffices to make them human rights. So the question of whether there can be collective human rights or group-specific human rights remains a significant question only if the 'human' in human rights continues to have something like its traditional meaning.

In following the humanist tradition in that respect, I do not mean wholly to reject the claims of either the political or the legal theorists. The political theorists are right to challenge the assumption that we can leap straight from human rights traditionally understood to rights that are serious candidates for international political action. If we take a hard-headed look at the political structures and the political realities of our world, and give due weight to the limits, costs and dangers of international action, there may well be moral rights that people possess as human beings which are insufficiently important to warrant international political action. Not all of the humanist's human rights need therefore rank as the political theorist's 'international human rights'. Similarly, the legal theorists make a convincing case against supposing that legal human rights can be, or should be, merely legalised moral human rights, which take no account of the consequences of making rights part of international law or of the larger purposes of an international legal human

10 Although Carl Wellman, *supra* note 5, aligns himself with the humanist conception of moral human rights, he, like, Buchanan, argues that other sorts of consideration bear on the appropriate content of legal human rights.

11 P. Macklem, *The Sovereignty of Human Rights* (Oxford University Press, Oxford, 2015).

rights system. There is also no reason to jettison legal positivism's insistence on separating what law is from what it ought to be, just because the subject of law happens to be human rights.

On the other hand, the political and legal conceptions can take forms that render the 'human' in human rights of little or no consequence. If human rights are no more than rights that the international political community recognises as sovereignty-limiting, why should we persist in describing them as 'human' rights? We might ask the same of legal conceptions, if the 'human' in human rights law turns out to be no more than a conventional but misleading tag. We have reason to pause before tossing aside the very idea of human rights along with humanist thinking in general.

In making my arguments, I shall mix modes. I shall use a conception of human rights largely associated with humanist thinking but I shall make extensive use of UN and regional human rights declarations and conventions; I shall draw, in other words, on soft and hard forms of international human rights law. I do so partly because examples and instances that are already recognised formally as human rights are likely to carry greater weight than rights of my own devising. I also have an eye to extending the relevance of my arguments beyond humanist approaches to human rights. However, I do not aim to give a comprehensive account of the human rights currently ascribed to ethno-cultural minorities. I mean only to point out instances in which those rights are already collective or group-specific in nature, or cases in which rights could be collective or group-specific consistently with their remaining human rights.

The term 'ethno-cultural minority' sometimes includes, and sometimes excludes, indigenous peoples. I shall include indigenous peoples in the groups I consider but, since they are now treated as a separate category for human rights purposes, I shall consider them alongside, but separately from, other sorts of ethno-cultural group.

2 Collective Human Rights

2.1 *Indigenous Peoples and Collective Rights*

The human rights instrument that attributes rights to groups most expressly and most abundantly is the United Nations Declaration on the Rights of Indigenous Peoples (UNDRIP), 2007. Here are some examples:

> Article 4
> Indigenous peoples, in exercising their right to self-determination, have the right to autonomy or self-government in matters relating to their internal and local affairs ...

> Article 5
> Indigenous peoples have the right to maintain and strengthen their distinct political, legal, economic, social and cultural institutions, while retaining their right to participate fully, if they so choose, in the political, economic, social and cultural life of the State.
>
> Article 10
> Indigenous peoples shall not be forcibly removed from their lands and territories.

These rights are self-evidently group rights. They ascribe rights to indigenous people as peoples rather than to indigenous people as discrete individuals. Of the thirty-seven articles of UNDRIP that expressly declare rights, twenty-six declare group rights in the form of rights ascribed to indigenous peoples. Of the remaining eleven, nine articles ascribe rights to both indigenous peoples and indigenous individuals; two ascribe rights to indigenous individuals only.

There may be reason to doubt whether the group rights that UNDRIP ascribes to indigenous peoples should really be understood as human rights. The Declaration's Preamble includes the following clause:

> *Recognizing and reaffirming* that indigenous individuals are entitled without discrimination to all human rights recognized in international law, and that indigenous peoples possess collective rights which are indispensable for their existence, well-being and integral development as peoples.

That clause may suggest that, while the individual rights of indigenous people are human rights, the collective rights of indigenous peoples belong to a separate category of peoples' rights. Yet the first article of UNDRIP contradicts that interpretation:

> Article 1
> Indigenous peoples have the right to the full enjoyment, *as a collective or as individuals*, of all human rights and fundamental freedoms as recognized in the Charter of the United Nations, the Universal Declaration of Human Rights and international human rights law. (My emphasis)

That article indicates that UNDRIP intends its collective rights to be human rights, so that the rights it ascribes to indigenous people as peoples are also rights that those peoples hold as human beings.[12] Why should there be any objection to that? Why should not indigenous people hold human rights both as individuals and as groups?

2.2 *Both Human and Collective*

For some objectors the answer lies in the very idea of group rights, particularly the idea of group moral rights. Groups, as distinct from their members taken severally, are not, they would protest, the types of entity that are capable of bearing moral rights.[13] Other objectors are willing to accept that groups can hold rights; they deny only that group rights can be human rights. The most common objection to ascribing human rights to groups is succinctly stated by Jack Donnelly:

> If human rights are the rights that one has simply as a human being, then only human beings have human rights. Because only individual persons are human beings, it would seem that only individuals can have human rights. Collectivities of all sorts have many and varied rights, but these are not human rights.[14]

Before we can assess Donnelly's claim, we need to look more closely at what a group right is. A group right is generally understood as a right that a group holds as a group and only as a group. It is not a right that each of the group's members holds individually, such as the right of a university student to use the university's library or the right of an adult citizen to vote in her country's

---

12 On this issue, see S. J. Anaya, 'The right of indigenous peoples to self-determination in the post-Declaration era', in C. Charters and R. Stavenhagen (eds.), *Making the Declaration Work: The United Nations Declaration on the Rights of Indigenous Peoples* (International Work Group for Indigenous Affairs, Copenhagen, 2009) p. 184.

13 E.g. M. Hartney, 'Some Confusions Concerning Collective Rights', 4 *Canadian Journal of Law and Jurisprudence* (1991) p. 292; J. Narveson, 'Collective Rights?', 4 *Canadian Journal of Law and Jurisprudence* (1991) p. 329.

14 J. Donnelly, *Universal Human Rights in Theory and Practice*, third edition (Cornell University Press, Ithaca, 2013) p. 30. See also, J.A. Graff, 'Human Rights, Peoples, and the Right to Self-Determination', in J. Baker (ed.), *Group Rights* (Toronto University Press, Toronto, 1994) p. 186; J. Griffin, *supra* note 3, pp. 256–276; M. A. Jovanović, *Collective Rights* (Cambridge University Press, Cambridge, 2012) pp. 166–195; J. W. Nickel, *Making Sense of Human Rights*, second edition (Blackwell, Oxford, 2007) pp. 163–166; J. Waldron, *Liberal Rights* (Cambridge University Press, Cambridge, 1993) pp. 339–369; C. Wellman, *supra* note 4, pp. 66–69.

elections. A right is a group right only if it is possessed by the group as a group rather than by its members taken severally.

When we move beyond that basic idea, we encounter widespread disagreement on how we should conceive a group right. We can, however, distinguish two fundamentally different conceptions, which I shall describe as 'corporate' and 'collective'.

The corporate conception of group rights might also be described as the traditional conception in that it is the way in which group rights have been most commonly understood until recently. On this conception, we should conceive a right-holding group on analogy with a right-holding individual person. A person holds his rights as a single integral entity and so too must a group (which is why I describe this conception as 'corporate'). We might think of the right-holding group as a group-individual or a group-person. In law this can be achieved by the ascription of legal personality to a group; having recognised the group as legal person, law can then assign that artificial person legal rights and legal responsibilities. The attribution of the properties of a natural person to a group is more problematic but proponents of the corporate conception need attribute to a group only those natural properties that they reckon are essential for right-holding.[15] For the groups it conceives as moral right-holders, the most fundamental distinguishing feature of the corporate conception is its ascription of moral standing to the group as a group. Moral standing is a precondition of moral right-holding, just as legal standing is a precondition of legal right-holding, and that leads easily to the thought that, if groups can possess moral rights, they must possess moral standing as groups – a standing that is separate from, and independent of, the moral standing of the individuals who make up the group's members.

It is this conception of group rights that most frequently attracts scepticism. The sceptics are unwilling to accept that we should conceive groups as person-like entities or as possessing moral standing in their own right. I shall pass over those issues. Here the relevant question is whether group rights corporately conceived might be human rights. The answer is fairly obviously 'no'. On the corporate conception, the entity that holds a group right is quite different from a natural human being so that, if we take seriously the 'human' in human right, group rights corporately conceived cannot be human rights.

We can, however, conceive group rights in a quite different fashion. We can conceive them as rights that the members of a group hold collectively rather

15 E.g. P. A. French, *Collective and Corporate Responsibility* (Columbia University Press, New York, 1984).

than separately, jointly rather than severally. I describe this conception of a group right as 'collective'. I do so because something that is held 'collectively' is, by implication, something that has more than one holder and, as I use the term, a collective right does indeed have a plurality of holders. By contrast, a group right corporately conceived has a single holder, the group conceived as a unitary entity.[16]

On the collective conception, there is no right-holding group that has a being and moral standing separate from the people who make it up. The right-holding group is simply the set of individuals who constitute the group and the moral standing that underwrites their collective right is that of the several individuals who make up the group. But the collective right they hold is an authentic group right since it is a right that they hold only together and not separately. The conception here is not therefore one in which individuals hold rights as separate individuals and in which they, or we, somehow aggregate their individual rights into a collective right. On the contrary, a collective right is a right that the group's members hold jointly and *only* jointly. If, for example, we conceive the right of a people to collective self-determination as a collective right, it will be a right possessed by the flesh-and-blood individuals who make up the relevant people and who hold their right only collectively. If a linguistic minority which is concentrated in a particular region of a society has a collective right that public signage in that region should be in the minority's language as well as in the society's official public language, that right will be a right that the individual members of the minority hold jointly but not separately. In both cases, the group's members will hold a right together that none of them holds individually.

Provided a group right takes that form, there is no obvious barrier to its being a human right. Donnelly's objection to the possibility of collective human rights is that, since human rights are held by human beings and since human beings are individual persons, only individual persons can hold human rights. But collective rights *are* held by individual persons; they are distinguished only by being rights that individual persons hold collectively rather than separately.

Of course, whether we should deem a particular collective right a human right will need to be argued. Not all collective rights will be human rights, just

16 Even so, proponents of the corporate conception most commonly use the adjective 'collective' to describe group rights; e.g. P. A. French, *supra* note 15; M. A. Jovanović, supra note 14; D. Newman, *Community and Collective Rights: A Theoretical Framework for Rights held by Groups* (Hart, Oxford, 2011). There is no commonly accepted vocabulary that marks the distinction I make between the two conceptions. I use the terms 'corporate' and 'collective' only because each seems aptly to describe its conception of a right-holding group.

as not all individual rights are human rights. But the mere fact that a right is a collective right should not, of itself, stand in the way of its being a human right. We might argue over whether all or any of the collective rights in UNDRIP should figure in a human rights declaration, but that argument should not be foreclosed merely because many of those rights are collective rights.

2.3 *Ethno-Cultural Minorities and Collective Rights*

If we turn from UNDRIP to human rights instruments that are intended to provide for the ethno-cultural groups usually described as 'minorities', we have to search much harder for any hint of group rights. That is because the drafters of those instruments made studied efforts to avoid ascribing rights to groups, perhaps in the belief that, if the rights were to remain human rights, they could not be held by groups.[17]

That is true of the Declaration on the Rights of Persons Belonging to National or Ethnic, Religious, and Linguistic Minorities, 1992 (hereinafter the 'Declaration on Minorities'), and the European Framework Convention for the Protection of National Minorities, 1995 (hereinafter the 'European Framework Convention'). Both ascribe rights not to minorities as groups but to 'persons belonging to minorities'.

In fact that form of words lends itself easily to collective right-holding. 'Persons belonging to minorities' might hold rights collectively just as they might hold rights individually. However, neither the Declaration on Minorities nor the European Framework Convention means to concede that possibility. Both impose upon states obligations that are directed at the collective interests of minorities and, had those interests been made the objects of rights, those would have been rights that minorities possessed collectively. Thus, the first article of the Declaration on Minorities reads:

> States shall protect the existence and the national or ethnic, cultural, religious and linguistic identity of minorities within their respective territories and shall encourage conditions for the promotion of that identity.

---

17 The Human Rights Committee, in adjudicating cases relating to article 27 and other articles of the ICCPR that bear on the rights of ethno-cultural minorities, has been willing to take account of the collective dimensions of minority claims. See P. Macklem, *supra* note 10, pp. 112–114, and Y. M. Donders, *Towards a Right to Cultural Identity?* (Intersentia, Antwerp, 2002) pp. 176–191. For a comprehensive analysis of judicial discourse on international law relating to minority rights, see G. Pentassuglia, *Minority Groups and Judicial Discourse in International Law: A Comparative Perspective* (Martinus Nijhoff, Leiden, 2009).

The Declaration's fourth article requires states to take several measures that will establish background conditions favourable to the maintenance and promotion of minority identities. The European Framework Convention imposes on Parties to the Convention an even wider range of obligations in respect of minorities and, if those obligations were tied to rights, many of those rights would be collective rights. But neither the Declaration nor the Convention takes that extra step.[18]

Even so, neither document wholly ignores the collective character of much that matters to ethno-cultural minorities. Both allow that, while the rights they recognise are always and only rights possessed by persons individually, those persons may nevertheless join with others in exercising their individual rights; so, while the *possession* of rights may be individual, their *exercise* can be collective. Article 3.1 of the Declaration on Minorities provides:

> Persons belonging to minorities may *exercise* their rights, including those set forth in the present Declaration, *individually as well as in community with other members of their group*, without any discrimination. (My emphases)

Similarly, Article 3.2 of the European Framework Convention provides:

> Persons belonging to national minorities may *exercise* the rights and enjoy the freedoms flowing from the principles enshrined in the present framework Convention *individually as well as in community with others.* (My emphases)[19]

---

18 I do not mean to suggest that either document refrains from recognising a greater range of rights only because those would have been collective rights. The primary purpose of a convention is to set out the obligations of those who are party to it and it makes sense therefore that its articles should give primacy to those obligations. In addition, both the Declaration and the Convention sometimes require states to take measures of a very general background nature and recognise that the appropriate measures can vary legitimately according to local circumstances; that too may have encouraged sparing use of the language of rights.

19 Article 27 of the ICCPR implies that individuals will exercise the rights it recognises only along with others: "In those States in which ethnic, religious or linguistic minorities exist, persons belonging to such minorities shall not be denied the right, *in community with the other members of their group*, to enjoy their own culture, to profess and practise their own religion, or to use their own language" (my emphasis).

If members of minorities have the option of exercising their individual rights in community with others, do they need collective rights? Can they, through collectively exercising their individual rights, be entitled to all to which they would be entitled were they to possess collective rights?

That is a possibility that must tempt those who want human rights to provide for the needs, vulnerabilities and identities of ethno-cultural minorities but who shun the idea of collective human rights. The proposition we need to examine then is that, through exercising their individual rights together, individuals can gain access to the collective goods that are possible objects of collective rights. To test that proposition, consider rights to the two goods that I previously instanced: a linguistic minority's right to public signage in its own language and the right of a people, including an indigenous people, to collective self-determination. Could a group of individuals secure a right to those goods through the simultaneous exercise of their individually-held rights?

Individuals can exercise only rights they possess. Might an individual member of a linguistic minority possess, as an individual, a right that the public signage in his region should be in his language? That is highly improbable. The right we are considering is a claim-right and therefore a right that would impose a duty on the rest of the society to provide public signage in the individual's language. Given the cost of making that provision, it is most unlikely that a single person's interest in having public signage in his language would suffice to justify that duty and, if it does not suffice, the individual will possess no corresponding claim-right. If individuals, qua individuals, start out with no right to public signage in their language, it is hard to see how they could arrive at a shared right to that signage merely by exercising their individual rights. If, on the other hand, we consider the interest of the entire linguistic minority in having public signage in their language, their combined interest may well suffice to justify the duty.[20] In that case, they will possess a right to public signage collectively that none of them possesses individually.

The case of public signage is an example of a good that is only contingently collective.[21] Having public signage in one's language is a good (let's suppose) but its goodness is not dependent on its being shared with others. Even if a person were the only person in a society to speak his language, he could still have an interest in there being public signage in his language. Some goods are,

20 I follow here the reasoning of J. Raz, *The Morality of Freedom* (Oxford University Press, Oxford, 1986) pp. 207–209.

21 On the relationship between collective rights and collective goods, see further P. Jones, 'Collective rights, public goods, and participatory goods', in G. Calder, M. Bessone and F. Zuolo (eds.), *How Groups Matter* (Routledge, London, 2014) p. 52.

however, necessarily collective. They can be the goods they are only if they are shared with others. An example is the good for a society of being collectively self-determining. Could a single individual have a right to that good? Logically, that is possible. I could be the only individual in my society who is entitled to its being collectively self-determining, perhaps because my interest in its being self-determining is the only interest that counts; my fellow citizens may possess interests identical with my own but, for some reason, their interests do not count.[22] While that is a logical possibility, it is not a moral possibility that need detain us, since we are operating on human rights assumptions. If I were to have an individual right that my society should be collectively self-determining, I would have a right not only over the organisation of my own life but also over the organisation of the lives of all of my fellow citizens, and that right would be inconsistent with each of my fellow citizens' having a status equal to my own – an equality that is fundamental to human rights thinking. Unsurprisingly therefore, no individual can possess, qua individual, a human right to a society's collective self-determination.[23]

Suppose we attribute to each individual a right to that individual's self-determination. Could individuals then exercise their individual rights of self-determination to achieve the collective self-determination of themselves as a group? There is no immediate route from one right to the other. An act of collective self-determination is not the same as a multitude of simultaneous acts of individual self-determination and individuals cannot, merely through exercising rights over their own lives, turn those rights into collective rights over the lives of one another.

If, however, individual rights of self-determination are alienable, individuals might trade in their rights, partially if not wholly, in order to form themselves into an association. They might, that is, follow the path of John Locke's social contractors and agree to become members of a common association and to subordinate themselves to the authority of that association. They might also each agree that their association should be collectively self-determining. In that case, they will have exercised their individual rights to create a self-determining

22 Note that the individual right here is not a right that only the individual right-holder shall determine the course of the society's life since that would not be a right to collective self-determination. Rather the right-holder possesses a right that the society shall be determined by himself along with his fellow-citizens. The right-holder might declare to his fellow citizens, "I have the right that we shall be self-determining".

23 See further, P. Jones, 'Human Rights and Collective Self-Determination', in A. Etinson (ed.), *Human Rights: Moral or Political?* (Oxford University Press, Oxford, 2017) forthcoming.

association which, as an association, can have collective rights to goods that are collective to the association.

The context in which that move from the individual to the collective is most plausible is religious practice. Article 18 of the UDHR gives people the freedom to manifest their religion "either alone or in community with others", as do the International Covenant on Civil and Political Rights (ICCPR) (Art. 18) and the European Convention on Human Rights (ECHR) (Art. 9).[24] Much of religious practice takes a collective form. People practise their religion through becoming members of religious organisations, such as churches and mosques. They also engage in collective religious practices, such as a nagar kirtan (a public religious procession) staged by a Sikh community, or an integrated act of Christian worship in which the participants assume different roles and play different parts. If there is a right to stage a nagar kirtan, or a right to a collective act of worship as a collective act, it must be a collective right. Individual participants may have individual rights to participate in the collective act but those individual rights should not be confused with a right to the collective act as a collective act. That collective right will be held collectively by the participants in the act. Similarly, if we think of the rights of a religious organisation as rights possessed by the organisation's members, those will be rights held collectively by the members. But we can then ask how there came to be those collective rights. If membership of a religious organisation is voluntary and if participation in a collective religious act is also voluntary, the answer will be through individuals' exercising their individual rights of religious freedom. It is through their exercise of those rights that they have become members of religious organisations or participants in collective religious acts.[25] In that way, collective religious rights can be grounded in the exercise of individual religious rights and the violation of a collective religious right can be, at a deeper level, the violation of several individuals' individual religious rights.

We can, then, tell something like the social contract story to explain how people can, by exercising their individual rights together, gain access to collective religious goods which, if they are objects of rights, will be objects of collective rights. That story depends crucially on people's religious membership and participation being matters of choice which is not always the sociological reality, especially when religion forms part of an ethno-cultural identity; but, according to the human rights canon, it ought to be the reality. To what extent can we apply

24 The ECHR uses the same words. The ICCPR's phrasing is, "either individually or in community with others".

25 Cf. the European Framework Convention, Art. 8: "The Parties undertake to recognize that every person belonging to a national minority has the right to manifest his or her religion or belief and to establish religious institutions, organisations and associations".

that model more generally to the collective aspects of the lives of ethno-cultural minorities? It certainly applies to some. Members of minorities might, for example, exercise their individual rights of freedom of association to establish or join associations devoted to their shared culture, language or history. But it does not apply to all. Consider the two examples I gave previously. People do not join their native language group; they simply find themselves to be members of it. Similarly, they cannot join an indigenous people; they just are, or are not, members of that people. If they are members of an indigenous people, they might opt to abandon that people, either territorially or culturally, just as individuals might choose to give up their native tongue for another language. But they cannot wilfully become members of an indigenous people or wilfully turn a non-native language into their native language. Nor can they wilfully adopt a nationality that is not already their nationality (in the sense of 'nationality' relevant here) or lay claim to a culture of the kind we associate with ethnicity if it is not already their culture. Hence, the contractual route from individual rights to collective goods and collective rights will be more often than not unavailable. We cannot plausibly use the idea of social contract to ground the collective right to self-determination of indigenous peoples in the joint exercise of their members' individual rights. Nor can we use that idea to explain how it is that a linguistic minority might have a right to public signage in its own language.

In large measure therefore, people will not be able to secure rights to the collective goods associated with their ethno-cultural identities merely by exercising human rights that they possess as discrete individuals. In general, if there are, or ought to be, human rights to those collective goods, they must be collective human rights and, what is more, rights that are fundamentally collective rather than collective rights brought into existence by the simultaneous exercise of individual rights.

2.4 *Collective Human Rights – A Threat to Individual Human Rights?*

Even if the notion of collective human rights is both coherent and plausible in the form I have proposed, that notion is likely to attract another sort of doubt. People often shun group rights because they fear those rights will be used to the detriment of individuals, particularly the individuals who constitute the group's members. That fear is likely to be exacerbated if we assert group rights in the context of human rights and if the right-holding groups have, like ethno-cultural minorities, involuntary memberships. Should that fear make us reluctant to concede that groups might hold human rights?

The principal source of that fear is the possibility that a group may wield its rights over its own members and do so in a way that significantly impairs their freedom or harms them in some other way. If we accord human rights to groups, we may simultaneously imperil the human rights of those who fall under the authority of those groups. Group human rights may therefore exist to the detriment of individual human rights.

In considering that possibility, the distinction between the corporate and collective conceptions of group rights is once again crucial. A group right corporately conceived creates the possibility that a group will hold rights against its own members. It does so because, on the corporate conception, a right-holding group is an entity that is distinct from its members and that possesses moral standing independently of that of its members. If we separate the group from its members in that fashion, we make it possible for the group as one party to hold rights against its individual members as other parties. On the collective conception, however, there is no group that exists independently of its members; the group is simply the individual members who jointly hold the right. It makes no more sense to hold that the rights jointly held by those individuals might be rights that they hold against themselves than it does to hold that a right held by a single individual might be a right he holds against himself. So, if we operate with the collective conception, a collective right can be directed only outwardly as a claim upon parties external to the right-holding group. It cannot be directed inwardly towards the collectivity's own members.

If that simple logic is less than fully reassuring, the obvious course is to provide that collective human rights must always be consistent with individual human rights. The individuals who hold human rights collectively will be the same individuals who hold human rights individually, so that collective and individual human rights must together form a coherent set. Safeguards for individual human rights of the relevant sort are already written into UNDRIP (Arts 1, 46), the Declaration on Minorities (Arts 3.2, 8.2), and the European Framework Convention (Arts 3.1, 22).[26]

3 Group-Specific Human Rights

By a group-specific right I mean a right that is specific to a particular group rather than universal to mankind. Group-specific rights can also be group rights, but they do not have to be. I borrow the term 'group-specific' from Will

26 I consider the issues raised in this section more fully in P. Jones, 'Cultures, Group Rights, and Group-Differentiated Rights', in M. Dimova-Cookson and P. M. R. Stirk (eds.), *Multiculturalism and Moral Conflict* (Routledge, London, 2010) p. 38, at pp. 46–53; and 'Groups and Human Rights', in C. Holder and D. Reidy (eds.), *Human Rights: the Hard Questions* (Cambridge University Press, Cambridge, 2013) p. 100, at pp. 109–112.

Kymlicka.[27] Most of the group-specific rights that Kymlicka identified and defended in his *Liberalism, Community and Culture* were also collective rights[28] but, as he has been subsequently at pains to point out, the group-specific nature of those rights was logically independent of their being collective rights, and the issue of whether those rights were rightfully group-specific was quite separate from controversy over whether they could or should be collective rights.[29] A right specific to an ethno-cultural group can be a right held by the group's members severally rather than collectively. For example, Sikhs in Britain have legal rights specific to themselves to ride a motorcycle, or to work on a construction site, without wearing a safety helmet provided they wear a turban. They also have the right to carry a knife (the kirpan) in public while most other British citizens do not. Those rights are entirely intelligible as rights possessed and exercised by individual Sikhs.[30]

The general run of rights, other than human rights, are group specific; e.g. rights that people possess as citizens of particular countries or rights they have as members of particular associations. Rights may also be specific to different categories of individual; e.g. rights specific to children or the elderly, such as rights to special care and protection. Thus, the 'group' in 'group-specific' can signify a group that takes the form of a community or an association but it does not have to. A right can also be group-specific in being specific to a particular type of group rather than to each token of that type.

The challenge facing the idea of group-specific human rights is readily evident. I have defined group-specific rights in opposition to rights that are universal to human beings, yet human rights are commonly thought to be universal rights. That universality is generally reckoned a defining feature of human rights.[31] How then can a right be both group-specific and human? Before turning to that question, I want to comment briefly on how far the rights currently ascribed to indigenous peoples and ethno-cultural minorities are group-specific.

---

27 W. Kymlicka, *Multicultural Citizenship* (Clarendon Press, Oxford, 1995).

28 W. Kymlicka, *Liberalism, Community and Culture* (Clarendon Press, Oxford, 1989). *E.g.* the rights of aboriginal groups to self-government, their rights over their territories, and their right to restrict the mobility, property and voting rights of non-aboriginal people with respect to aboriginal communities and their lands.

29 W. Kymlicka, *supra* note 27, pp. 45–47.

30 For a different view, see M. A. Jovanović, *supra* note 14, p. 123.

31 'Generally' here includes my former self; for example, P. Jones, *Rights* (Macmillan, Basingstoke, 1994), pp. 81–82.

3.1 *Indigenous Peoples and Group-Specific Rights*

Some of the rights found in UNDRIP are rights ascribed to indigenous peoples or indigenous individuals in common with other peoples or other individuals. Article 3, for example, ascribes to indigenous peoples the same right of self-determination as the first articles of the International Covenant on Economic, Social and Cultural Rights (ICESCR) and the ICCPR ascribe to all peoples.[32] Other articles ascribe rights to indigenous individuals that the UDHR and the International Covenants ascribe to everyone. Article 7.1, for instance, states that indigenous individuals "have the rights to life, physical and mental integrity, liberty and security of person".[33] Article 2 ascribes to both indigenous peoples and indigenous individuals "the right to be free from any kind of discrimination, in the exercise of their rights".[34]

For the most part, however, the rights that appear in UNDRIP are clearly tailored to indigenous peoples – to their specific character, circumstances and historical treatment. Here are three examples:

> Article 25
> Indigenous peoples have the right to maintain and strengthen their distinctive spiritual relationship with their traditionally owned or otherwise occupied and used lands, territories, waters and coastal seas and other resources and to uphold their responsibilities to future generations in this regard.
>
> Article 28.1
> Indigenous peoples have the right to redress, by means that can include restitution or, when this is not possible, just, fair and equitable compensation, for the lands, territories and resources which they have traditionally owned or otherwise occupied or used, and which have been confiscated, taken, occupied, used or damaged without their free, prior and informed consent.
>
> Article 31
> Indigenous peoples have the right to maintain, control, protect and develop their cultural heritage, traditional knowledge and traditional cultural expressions, as well as the manifestations of their sciences, technologies and cultures, including human and genetic resources, seeds, medicines,

---

32 "All peoples have the right of self-determination. By virtue of that right they freely determine their political status and freely pursue their economic, social and cultural development."

33 Cf. UDHR Art. 3; ICCPR Arts 6.1, 7, 9.1.

34 Cf. UDHR Art. 2; ICESCR Art. 2.2; ICCPR Art. 2.1.

> knowledge of the properties of fauna and flora, oral traditions, literatures, designs, sports and traditional games and visual and performing arts. They also have the right to maintain, control, protect and develop their intellectual property over such cultural heritage, traditional knowledge, and traditional cultural expressions.

It is hardly surprising that a declaration devoted to the rights of indigenous peoples should address the specific character, circumstances and experience of indigenous peoples. But, insofar as those rights are specific to indigenous peoples, they confront us with the question of how they can also be human rights.

Earlier I raised and dismissed the suggestion that the collective rights that UNDRIP ascribes to indigenous peoples could belong to a special class of peoples' rights that is separate from human rights. But suppose that suggestion were correct. The issue of universality would still arise. If the rights of peoples are supposed to be universal to all peoples, just as human rights are commonly supposed to be universal to all human beings, how can rights be both rights of peoples and rights specific to indigenous peoples?

3.2 *Ethno-Cultural Minorities and Group-Specific Rights*

If we turn to UN and regional instruments designed to provide for ethno-cultural minorities, we find a mixed picture. We can take as our starting point rights that minorities possess along with everyone else. Some of the rights ascribed to minorities in the Declaration on Minorities and the European Framework Convention are not group-specific at all. Both the Declaration on Minorities (Art. 4.1) and the European Framework Convention (Art. 4.1), for example, assert the right of persons belonging to minorities to equality before the law, a right already ascribed to all in the UDHR (Art. 7) and the ICCPR (Art. 14). The European Framework Convention (Art. 7) replicates the UDHR (Arts 18–20) and the ECHR (Arts 9–11) in asserting the rights of minority individuals to freedom of peaceful assembly, association and expression and to freedom of thought, conscience and religion. Emphasising that minorities possess those rights equally with everyone else is not without practical point since, *ceteris paribus*, minorities are more vulnerable to their denial or infringement, but reasserting those rights does no more than confirm their universality.

The term 'minority rights' is normally reserved for rights that are specific to minorities – rights that are "special rights recognised to the exclusive benefit of minority groups".[35] An example is article 27 of the ICCPR.

---

35 G. Pentassuglia, *Minorities in International Law* (Council of Europe, Strasbourg, 2002) p. 48.

> In those States in which ethnic, religious or linguistic minorities exist, persons belonging to such minorities shall not be denied the right, in community with the other members of their group, to enjoy their own culture, to profess and practise their own religion, or to use their own language.[36]

No similar article caters for majorities. The Declaration on Minorities and the European Framework Convention similarly ascribe a number of rights specifically to minorities. The Declaration (Art. 2.3) attributes to persons belonging to minorities the right to participate in national and, where appropriate, regional decision-making. The Convention, while allowing policies of integration, requires its Parties to refrain from policies or practices aimed at assimilation (Art. 5.2), and it attributes to persons belonging to minorities rights to use their language in private and public (Art. 10.1), to be addressed in a language they understand should they be accused or arrested (Art. 10.3), to use their name and have it recognised in their own language (Art. 11.1), to display signs in their language (Art. 11.2), to manage and maintain their own private educational and training establishments (Art. 13), and so on.

Both documents also oblige states to take measures designed to protect the rights and identities of minorities. The Declaration on Minorities requires states to create favourable conditions enabling persons belonging to minorities to "express their characteristics and to develop their culture, language, religion, traditions and customs" (Art. 4.2); to secure adequate opportunities for minority persons "to learn their mother tongue or to have instruction in their mother tongue" (Art. 4.3); and "to encourage knowledge of the history, traditions, language and culture of minorities existing within their territory" (Art. 4.4). The European Framework Convention includes similar provisions (Arts 5.1, 6.1, 12, 14).

These rights, and the state-obligations with which they are associated, are clearly group-specific, but they do not privilege minorities. Rather, they address and aim to provide for the disadvantaged position in which ethnocultural minorities are liable to find themselves relative to majorities. There is no article providing for majorities, equivalent to Article 27 of the ICCPR, not because majorities matter less than minorities but because the working assumption is that majorities, since they are majorities, will experience no obstacle to enjoying their culture, professing and practising their religion, or using their language. If that assumption proved misplaced because a minority dominated a society and used its dominance to prevent the majority

36 The text of the article reappears in modified form in article 2.1 of the Declaration on Minorities. The Declaration substitutes "have the right" for "shall not be denied the right".

from enjoying its culture, professing and practising its religion, or using its language, persons belonging to that majority would suffer a violation of their rights (morally if not legally) no less than had they been a minority. Similarly the special rights and measures set out in the Declaration on Minorities and the European Framework Convention are not replicated for majorities simply because, it is assumed, majorities have no need of them. Thus, while the rights and measures instanced above are clearly group-specific, they aim only to narrow the gap between minorities and majorities by securing states of affairs for minorities that majorities can take for granted. That is why they do not privilege minorities even though they are special to minorities. We might describe them as group-specific devices that are ultimately universal in aspiration.

That description would, however, be less than accurate since there are differences in the end-states that current provision for minorities aims to achieve. According to Article 4.2 of the European Framework Convention:

> The Parties undertake to adopt, where necessary, adequate measures in order to promote, in all areas of economic, social, political and cultural life, *full and effective equality* between persons belonging to a national minority and those belonging to the majority. (My emphasis)

On inspection, however, the rights the Convention assigns to minorities fall short of the "full and effective equality" it ostensibly requires. The Convention does not require, for example, that a minority's language must be an official language of its society.[37] Nor does it require that a minority's culture must figure equally with the majority's in the society's public culture, or that its religion must figure equally with all other religions in the society's public ceremonies, or that a society should not have an officially established religion. There is nothing necessarily untoward in those states of affairs but they do indicate a significant way in which the rights of ethno-cultural majorities and minorities can be group-differentiated and so group-specific.

Still more striking is the way in which rights of different minorities can differ. The European Framework Convention provides differently for differently situated minorities. It requires Parties to the Convention to endeavour, as far as possible, that "in areas inhabited by persons belonging to national minorities traditionally or in substantial numbers", those persons should be

---

37 "The Parties' obligations regarding the use of minority languages do not in any way affect the status of the official language or languages of the country concerned." Council of Europe, *Explanatory Report on the European Framework Convention for the Protection of National Minorities* (Strasbourg, 1995), para. 66.

able to use their language in their relations with the administrative authorities (Art. 10.2).[38] In the case of such minorities, the Parties should also endeavour to ensure that persons belonging to those minorities "have adequate opportunities for being taught the minority language or for receiving instruction in this language" (Art. 14.2). It also requires Parties to endeavour "in areas traditionally inhabited by substantial numbers of persons belonging to a national minority" that "traditional local names, street names and other topographical indications intended for the public" shall be displayed in the minority's language as well as the majority's (Art. 11.3). None of these articles is formulated in the language of rights, but the implication of each is that minorities that meet the qualifying conditions (those that have been "traditionally" present in an area and/or that exist "in substantial numbers") have claims that minorities who fail to meet them do not.

The European Framework Convention is more explicit than the Declaration on Minorities on the different provision that should be made for differently situated minorities, but the Working Group on Minorities of the Sub-Commission on the Promotion and Protection of Human Rights, in commenting on the Declaration, is still more forthright.[39] It expressly recognises "factors that can be relevant in distinguishing between the rights that can be demanded by different minorities":

> Those who live compactly together in a part of the State territory may be entitled to rights regarding the use of language, and street and place names which are different from those who are dispersed, and may in some circumstances be entitled to some kind of autonomy. Those who have been established for a long time on the territory may have stronger rights than those who have recently arrived.[40]

Again, there is nothing necessarily untoward in these differences in minorities' rights and I do not cite them in a spirit of criticism. They have eminently reasonable justifications.[41] I cite them only to highlight how the rights that figure

---

38 "This provision does not cover all relations between individuals belonging to national minorities and public authorities. It only extends to administrative authorities." Ibid., para. 64.

39 *Commentary of the Working Group on Minorities to the United Nations Declaration on the Rights of Persons Belonging to National or Ethnic, Religious and Linguistic Minorities*, E/CN.4/Sub.2/AC.5/2005/2.

40 Ibid., para. 10; see also paras 60–64.

41 The most contentious form of differentiation is the privileging of 'old' over 'new' (i.e. migrant) minorities. For a recent examination of that issue and a qualified defence of the

in human rights instruments can differ between different minorities as well as between majority and minority. The overall picture is one of rights that differ between groups according to relevant differences in their circumstances.

3.3 *Making Sense of Group-Specific Human Rights*

How then can rights be both human and group-specific? The apparent conflict between those two adjectives arises from the widely-shared assumption that human rights must be universal rights. Must they?

3.3.1 The Primacy of Human Status

Take the phrase commonly affirmed by adherents of the humanist conception of human rights: a human right is a right we possess 'in virtue of being human'. What does that phrase mean? It does not present us with a mere biological description; more importantly, it affirms a status, either moral or legal. A human right is a right that we hold in virtue of possessing the status of being human. It is a right that we hold because we are human. In like fashion, a right we hold in virtue of being citizens is a right we hold because we are citizens and a right we one hold in virtue of being a member of an association, such as a natural history society, or a member of an institution, such as a legislature, is a right we hold as a member. That is what a right's being a citizen's right or a member's right connotes. In like manner, a 'human right' connotes a right we possess as human beings.

In the first instance, therefore, the 'human' in 'human right' signals the status in virtue of which the bearer holds the right, rather than the scope of those who hold the right. It will, in the second instance, imply a description of scope if we can infer, as people commonly do, that a right that someone holds in virtue of his or her human status must be a right that every other human person holds too – if, that is, we can infer universality of right from universality of status. Before proposing that we should not draw that inference, I say a little more about the primacy of human status in the idea of human rights.

The words most commonly used in UN documentation to refer to the moral status that people possess as human beings are 'dignity' and 'worth'. The opening lines of the UN Charter affirm the UN's "faith in the fundamental human

---

old/new distinction, see A. Patten, *Equal Recognition: The Moral Foundations of Minority Rights* (Princeton University Press, Princeton, NJ, 2014) pp. 269–297. The European Charter for Regional or Minority Languages, 1992, Art. 1(a), excludes altogether the languages of migrants from its remit; however, the Charter is less concerned to provide for the rights of language-speakers than to preserve, protect and promote European regional and minority languages as goods in their own right.

rights" and "in the dignity and worth of the human person". That faith is restated in the preamble to the UDHR, which also recognizes "the inherent dignity" and "the equal and inalienable rights of all members of the human family". According to the preambles to the ICESCR and ICCPR, "the equal and inalienable rights of all members of the human family" are rights that "derive from the inherent dignity of the human person". Similarly the Preamble to the Vienna Declaration and Programme of Action, 1993, recognizes and affirms "that all human rights derive from the dignity and worth inherent in the human person, and that the human person is the central subject of human rights and fundamental freedoms". The word 'derive', rather than indicating only a status that undergirds human rights, may imply that the entire catalogue of human rights can be inferred from human dignity and human worth. That is hard to find plausible and it is perhaps idle to look for analytic precision in these preambles. Certainly, the term dignity occurs in them with more than one meaning.[42] Nevertheless, amongst those various usages, 'dignity', along with 'worth', is used to indicate that people possess moral status as human beings and that, as bearers of that status, they bear human rights.

Something else affirmed in human rights declarations and conventions, not only in their preambles but also in the rights and standards they set out, is the equal status that people possess as human beings and as the bearers of human rights.[43] We therefore have a double-barrelled claim: human beings have both *status* and *equal* status; they *matter* and they matter *equally*. Thus, whatever rights people hold in virtue of possessing human status must be rights that are consistent with their equal status. If human rights can differ for different people, as I shall suggest, those differences must be compatible with the equal status of their holders. They must be 'horizontal' rather than 'vertical' differences of right; they cannot imply that some matter more than others and are, for that reason, entitled to more and better than others.

The status in virtue of which we hold human rights is also crucial to the political role we look to those rights to perform. In the humanist conception, unlike the political conception, that role does not figure in the very idea of

42 C. Beitz, 'Human Dignity in the Theory of Human Rights: Nothing But a Phrase?', 41 *Philosophy and Public Affairs* (2013) p. 259; J. Habermas, 'The Concept of Human Dignity and the Realistic Utopia of Human Rights', 41 *Metaphilosophy* (2010) p. 464. On the idea of dignity more generally, see G. Kateb, *Human Dignity* (Harvard University Press, Cambridge, MA, 2012); M. Rosen, *Dignity: Its History and Meaning* (Harvard University Press, Cambridge, MA, 2012); J. Waldron, *Dignity, Rank, and Rights* (Oxford University Press, Oxford, 2012).

43 On which see Buchanan, *supra* note 9, pp. 28–31, 68–72, 88–92, 134–145.

human rights; rather, it is an implication that follows from the possession of human rights. The status in virtue of which we hold those rights is critical to that implication. If we conceive a right as a right we hold as human beings, we do not conceive it as a gift of the state. It is not granted by the state, nor is the state at liberty to remove it. Even if a human right imposes positive rather than merely negative obligations on the state, it is still not a right we possess by the grace of the state. Thus, if we look to human rights to play their familiar role of limiting the sovereignty of states – limiting what states may do but also what they may not do – the status in virtue of which we hold human rights is crucial to their performing that role.

3.3.2 Both Group-Specific and Human

Why do commentators so frequently suppose that human rights must be universal? The answer may be simply that they treat universality as an axiomatic feature of human rights: human rights, they may suppose, simply *are* rights possessed by all humans. But, amongst humanist theorists, there may be another answer: rights that we possess in virtue of being human must be rights that derive from, and only from, our common human nature, and rights so derived will be rights common to all human beings. However, if human rights are to reach beyond the natural rights of the seventeenth century and to bear any resemblance to the rights incorporated in the UDHR, that view is unsustainable. Certainly human rights need to take account of our natures as human beings, but they must also take account of the conditions and circumstances in which we live. The extent to which the rights in the UDHR are geared to particular socio-political conditions is frequently noticed. Rights relating to judicial processes and to legal punishment, to personal security, to nationality and asylum, to education and to other welfare goods and services, provide examples.

The account of human rights given by James Griffin comes close to a 'human nature only' account. For Griffin, the foundation of human rights lies in the human capacity for normative agency; human rights properly conceived are rights that protect the development and exercise of that agency. The most basic of those rights are rights to autonomy, liberty and minimum material provision. But even Griffin accepts that, in order to give determinate shape to those very general rights, we must take account of 'practicalities', including the nature of human societies.[44]

Of course, once we have taken account of those practicalities, the rights that emerge may still be universal rights. Griffin ensures that outcome by allowing

44 J. Griffin, *supra* note 3, pp. 37–39.

practicalities to figure in his argument only insofar as they are practicalities common to the human condition across time as well as space. Why impose such an extraordinarily exacting constraint? The answer seems to lie in Griffin's determination to ensure that human rights will remain universal across both time and space. Others, such as John Tasioulas, suggest that we should impose a time-constraint upon the universality of human rights, so that we can claim human rights in the contemporary world without their having to make sense for people living in the mediaeval era or the Stone Age.[45] But, if temporal differences can compromise the universality of human rights, why should not other sorts of difference?

In fact, amongst the rights already recognised as human rights by the UN, some do. Consider the rights of children recognised in the Convention on the Rights of the Child, 1989, and its two Optional Protocols.[46] Some of those are also held by adults; e.g. the right to life (Art. 6) and the right not to be tortured (Art. 37). Some are formulated in the same language as the rights of adults but, assuming the Convention does not mean to challenge traditional parental authority (cf Art. 5), cannot be precisely the same rights; e.g. rights to freedom of association and religion (Arts 14, 15). Still others are rights special to children; e.g. rights to care and protection (Arts 3, 20), the right not to be separated from their parents (Art. 9), rights relating to their development (Art. 27), the right to be protected from any form of exploitation (Arts 32–36), and special rights relating to armed conflict (Art. 38 and Optional Protocol I). All adults will have had a childhood and most children will go on to have an adulthood so that, in the course of a normal human life, a person will have held rights both as a child and as an adult. But that does not remove the puzzle of how human rights can be universal and yet different for children and adults. However, there is no puzzle if what makes them human rights is the common status in virtue of which the rights are held. Human rights so understood can be rights that provide differently for the conditions of childhood and adulthood, and it would be decidedly odd if they did not.

For the most part, the human rights of women and men are the same, even though women are often more vulnerable than men to violations of some of those rights. But some rights differ because women, unlike men, are capable of pregnancy and child-bearing. Two striking examples are the rights of women not to be subjected to forced pregnancy and to forced abortion.[47] Here too it

45 J. Tasioulas, 'Taking rights out of human rights', 120 *Ethics* (2010) p. 647, at pp. 666–672.

46 The UDHR (Art. 25.2), the ICESCR (Art. 10), and the ICCPR (Art. 24), also include children within their purview.

47 Beijing Declaration and Platform for Action, Fourth World Conference on Women: Action for Equality, Development and Peace (1995), Annex II, para. 11.

would be perverse to insist that rights providing against such grotesque wrongs cannot be human rights, simply because they are possessed only by women. Their being less than universal is no bar to their being human rights if what makes them 'human' is the status in virtue of which they are held.

Human rights theorists sometimes wring their hands over the case of people who are comatose or who have lost command of their faculties through illnesses such as dementia. Clearly, these conditions will affect the rights of those who suffer them. We do people no favours if we continue to ascribe them freedoms that presuppose a self-direction of which they are no longer capable. But we also have reason to ascribe them rights to special care and protection that non-sufferers do not possess. The non-universality of these rights is entirely consistent with their being human rights – rights that people hold in virtue of their equal status as human beings.

Consider now differences that we might describe as differences of circumstance rather than condition. One such is the different circumstances in which human beings have lived in different centuries. Those differences are inescapably relevant to the content of some rights, such as welfare rights, which in turn creates difficulty for those, like Griffin and Wellman, who insist that human rights must be universal through time as well as space.[48] That difficulty disappears if rights are 'human' in virtue of the status of the holder rather than the universality of the right. The rights that people can possess in virtue of their human status will vary, intelligibly and reasonably, according to the different historical circumstances in which they live.

Now let's return to the human rights of ethno-cultural minorities and consider those that depart from universal rights in the most radical way: the different language rights of differently situated linguistic minorities. We have seen how the language rights of a society's majority may differ from those of its minorities and how the rights of its different minorities may differ according to circumstances, such as their relative size and geographical concentration. Those differences in right can be entirely consistent with the equal human status of all whose rights are at stake. They hold different rights neither because they are differently valued as persons nor because their languages are differently valued, but because they are differently circumstanced in relation to the make-up of the society to which they belong. The differences in right are neutral with respect to both the identity of particular persons and the identity of their language in that *any* person speaking *any* language in the same circumstances would possess the same rights. Different language speakers can

48 J. Griffin, *supra* note 3, pp. 48–51; C. Wellman, *supra* note 5, pp. 27–28.

therefore possess different rights in respect of the public use of their language, even though the rights at stake are rights they possess as human beings and therefore human rights.

The case of linguistic minorities is noteworthy because the language rights of different minorities can differ in extent. In that respect, their rights can be correctly described as unequal but, so long as that inequality is justified, they are unequal in a way that is consistent with the equal human status of those who make up the relevant minorities. The more common case will be rights that differ according to the different conditions and circumstances of groups, but which we have no reason to describe as unequal. The human rights of indigenous peoples exemplify that more common case. In many respects those rights are more complex than the rights of linguistic minorities, since they range over multiple aspects of people's lives and have to provide for people whose specific circumstances and ways of life differ and whose members may adhere in different degrees to the ways of life traditionally associated with their group. Here I shall not enter into any of those complexities. I draw attention only to the way in which rights that indigenous people hold in virtue of their human status can still be rights that are sensitive to their special features and circumstances as indigenous people. Just as Kymlicka has argued that rights can be justifiably group-differentiated even though they are rights that people hold as citizens of the same society,[49] so rights can be justifiably group-differentiated even though they are rights that people hold in virtue of their common status as human beings.[50]

3.3.3 Group-Specific Human Rights – Apparent Rather Than Real?

Those who cling to the belief that human rights must be universal can deal in one of three ways with the rights I have suggested are both human and group-specific. They might accept that the rights are indeed human rights but deny that they are (fundamentally) group-specific; or they might accept that the rights are group-specific but deny they are human rights; or they might deny that they are rights of any kind.[51] How might the first sort of denial be

49 W. Kymlicka, *supra* notes 27 and 28. See also W. Kymlicka and W. Norman, 'Citizenship in Diverse Societies: Issues, Contexts, Concepts', in W. Kymlicka and W. Norman (eds.), *Citizenship in Diverse Societies* (Oxford University Press, Oxford, 2000) p. 1.

50 For another argument that arrives at the conclusion that human rights need not be universal, though in a different way and in a more radical form, see R. Cruft, 'Human rights, individualism and cultural diversity', 8 *Critical Review of International Social and Political Philosophy* (2005) p. 265.

51 Griffin and Wellman, whose thinking on this issue I consider *infra*, deny that some of the rights I have identified as group-specific human rights are moral human rights or

made? How might apparently group-specific rights be reconfigured as universal rights? Two sorts of strategy are available: we might show that an apparently group-specific right is either (a) merely a variant of a universal right, or that it is (b) a universal but conditional right – a right that is possessed universally but that applies conditionally. My principal objection to both strategies is that they are wrongly motivated; they are driven by the mistaken belief that rights have to be universal to be human. That said, I comment briefly on each.

Proponents of the first strategy usually characterise a non-universal human right as a right that 'derives' from a higher-level universal right. The derived right is then accounted a human right because of its derivation. Wellman, for example, accepts that both children and pregnant women possess human rights to special care which other people do not.[52] What makes those non-universal rights human rights is their deriving from a basal human right that *is* universal: the right to be rescued from potential harm.[53]

If a human right must be universal, it is unclear how a non-universal right can satisfy that criterion merely by being linked to a right that is universal. That objection might be met by reconceptualising what a derived right is. Rather than being separate from the right from which it derives, as a child is separate from its parent, it may be no more than an aspect or application of a universal right. That is implicit in Griffin's notion that all other human rights cascade from the three basic human rights to autonomy, liberty and minimum provision.[54] But we then need to be convinced that all non-universal rights can be accounted for fully as mere realisations of abstract higher-level rights. The rights in UNDRIP do not lend themselves easily to that task, nor do language rights. James Nickel suggests that the right of minority individuals to use their native language can be derived from the universal right to freedom

moral rights of any kind. Both deny that young children and severely mentally incapacitated adults possess moral human rights, while allowing that they can be the objects of moral duties. For Griffin, the foundation of all human rights lies in the capacity for normative agency so that those who lack that capacity have no human rights. For Wellman, the capacity for moral agency is a precondition for holding moral rights, so that those who lack that capacity cannot bear moral rights of any sort. (Both allow that children can bear moral human rights once they have acquired a capacity for agency.) Both also deny that groups can bear moral human rights and are sceptical about moral group rights more generally. J. Griffin, *supra* note 3, pp. 83–95, 256–276; C.Wellman, *supra* note 5, pp. 21–22, 27–28, 66–69; C. Wellman, *Real Rights* (Oxford University Press, Oxford, 1995) pp. 113–132, 157–177.

52 His words echo those of the UDHR Art. 25.2.

53 C. Wellman, *supra* note 5, p. 29.

54 J. Griffin, *supra* note 3.

of expression or communication.[55] That proposal is unconvincing on three counts: the considerations that motivate language rights are quite different from those that motivate the right to free expression; free expression provides no rationale for prioritising native language-use over other language-use; and it does not explain how different linguistic groups can legitimately have different language rights.

The other possible strategy – the 'conditional' strategy – works by characterising an apparently non-universal right as a right which is held universally but applies only in specific conditions. Wellman presents the right to social security as a right of that sort.[56] The right itself is possessed irrespective of time and place but its 'application' depends on conditions that make its realisation possible. Thus, while people in the ancient world possessed the same right to social security as people living now, the right did not 'apply' in the ancient world because the circumstances necessary for its enjoyment were absent. That seems little more than a makeshift designed to maintain an appearance of universality. While human status is universal across time, the rights which that status grounds are not. If people in the ancient world were living now, they would have the same right to social security as we have now, and, if we had been living in the ancient world, our right to social security would have amounted only to what was possible then. It is not merely the application of the right that is conditional but the content of the right itself.

Even rights that are more straightforwardly conditional, such as rights to assistance if we are disabled or involuntarily unemployed, are arguably non-universal. If these are human rights, all human beings will be eligible for them, but only those who meet the qualifying condition will actually have the right to assistance. Here again, it is the status that is universal and the eligibility that follows from it, rather than the right. That may seem unnecessarily precise given that unemployment and disability are misfortunes that may befall any of us. But it would not be overly precise if we were to use Wellman's conditional strategy to transform all group-specific into universal rights – if, for example, we were to say that all human beings possess rights relating to pregnancy conditional on their being women, or that all possess the rights in UNDRIP conditional on their being indigenous, or that all possess certain sorts of language right conditional on their belonging to a linguistic minority of a particular type.

55 J. W. Nickel, *supra* note14, p. 161.

56 C. Wellman, *supra* note 5, pp. 28–29.

4 Conclusion

My main purpose has been to argue that there is scope for the rights of indigenous peoples and those of ethno-cultural minorities to be both collective and group-specific and still be human rights. That argument does not require us either to abandon or to trivialise the 'human' in human rights. On the contrary, we can conceive human rights as rights that we possess in virtue of being human whilst allowing that some of those rights can be collective or group-specific or both. Collective human rights are rights that are held jointly by individuals in virtue of their status as human beings. Typically, they will be rights to collective goods, such as collective self-determination. Group-specific human rights are rights that are specific to a group rather than rights held by all, but are still rights which the group's members hold, either individually or collectively, in virtue of their status as human beings. The universality of the status upon which human rights are founded, and in virtue of which they are 'human', does not entail that rights themselves can be human rights only if they are universal across space or time or both.

In making that argument, I have drawn on UNDRIP and declarations and conventions relating to the rights of ethno-cultural minorities. In doing so, I have not attempted to argue that the rights announced in those documents can be claimed, with full justification, as human rights. My claim has been more limited; I have argued only that their authenticity as human rights need not be in doubt merely because they are either collectively-held or less than universal in scope.

In a similar fashion, my conception of what makes a right a 'human right' has been modest and minimal: it is a right that people possess in virtue of their human status. My argument is not therefore tied to any particular justificatory theory of human rights or to any substantive account of the content of human rights. It is a conceptual rather than a normative argument. It therefore stands free of any particular normative theory of human rights, although it may be more congenial to some normative theories than to others.

The idea that rights are 'human' in virtue of the status in which they are held is one that is most associated with the traditional moral thinking about human rights that I have described as 'humanist'. Little distinguishes my argument in this chapter as 'humanist' beyond my use of the idea that human rights are rights we hold in virtue of our human status. Is it the case, even so, that my argument remains trapped within the confines of humanism and has no significance beyond humanist thinking about human rights?

While proponents of the political conception continue to use the language of human rights, their understanding of what a human right is renders the adjective 'human' of little or no significance, although that is more clearly true of Beitz's and Raz's versions of the political conception than of Rawls's. Political theorists are therefore likely to remain unmoved by an argument that rights grounded in human status can be collectively-held or group-specific, even though the individualism and universalism commonly associated with the idea of rights held 'in virtue of being human' contribute to Beitz's and Raz's reasons for dismissing that idea.[57]

My argument is more significant for legal conceptions of human rights. Here, of course, the status relevant to the bearing of human rights will be legal rather than moral, even though, if we sought a moral justification for that legal status, we might find it, with Allen Buchanan, in an equivalent moral status.[58] If we conceive legal human rights as rights that are so-called because their legally recognised bearers are human beings, legal human rights can still take the form of collective rights or group-specific rights. The legal ascription of human rights to indigenous peoples and ethno-cultural minorities in those forms need not betoken either adhockery or incoherence at the heart of human rights law. Rather, those rights can be part of a logically coherent scheme of legal human rights.

---

57 Rawls, by contrast, shows no inclination to deviate from a conception of human rights as rights held by human beings individually and universally. For critical discussions of the political conception, see P. Gilabert, *supra* note 2; S. M. Liao and A. Etinson, 'Political and naturalistic conceptions of human rights: a false polemic?', 9 *Journal of Moral Philosophy* (2012) p. 327; D. Miller, 'Joseph Raz on human rights: a critical appraisal', in R. Cruft, S. M. Liao and M. Renzo (eds.), *Philosophical Foundations of Human Rights* (Oxford University Press, Oxford, 2015) p. 232; J. Tasioulas, 'Are human rights essentially triggers for intervention?', 4 *Philosophy Compass* (2006) p. 938.

58 A. Buchanan, *supra* note 9, p. 89.

CHAPTER 2

Why Majority Rights Matter in the Context of Ethno-Cultural Diversity: The Interlinkage of Minority Rights, Indigenous Rights, and Majority Rights

Dwight Newman[1]

1 Introduction: The Interlinkage of Minority and Majority Rights

Discussions of minority rights and indigenous rights often proceed as if all pertinent rights were determined on the basis of ethno-cultural minority status or indigenous status, rather than based on a broader theory of collective interests. A focus on marginalized identities is particularly apparent in the discourses of recognition and of multiculturalism[2]—even where these discourses sometimes contain competing elements.[3] A focus on rights arising from a marginalized minority status is even more particularly apparent in theories of so-called liberal multiculturalism—those theories, offered by the likes of Will Kymlicka, of multiculturalism grounded in liberal egalitarian values.[4] And a

1 I am grateful for having had the chance to present a draft version of this paper at the University of Liverpool International Symposium on Ethno-Cultural Diversity and Human Rights in May 2016 and for comments there from Peter Jones, Gaetano Pantassuglia, and Alexandra Tomaselli. I am also grateful for conversations related to the paper with Jean Leclair, Michael Plaxton, Luc B. Tremblay, and Han-Ru Zhou and to Gaetano Pentassuglia for his rich comments on an earlier draft of the chapter.

2 On the politics of recognition, *see e.g.* C. Taylor, 'The Politics of Recognition', in A. Guttman (ed.), *Re-Examining the Politics of Recognition* (Princeton University Press, Princeton, 1994) p. 25; J. Tully, *Strange Multiplicity: Constitutionalism in the Age of Diversity* (Cambridge University Press, New York, 1995). On multiculturalism, *see* W. Kymlicka, *Multicultural Citizenship: A Liberal Theory of Minority Rights* (Oxford University Press, Oxford, 1995); N. Glazer, *We Are All Multiculturalists Now* (Harvard University Press, Cambridge, 1998).

3 Charles Taylor, for example, would subscribe simultaneously to aspects of multicultural recognition and aspects of tradition that could be in competition with multiculturalist claims.

4 W. Kymlicka, *supra* note 1. *See also* W. Kymlicka, *Liberalism, Community, and Culture* (Clarendon Press, Oxford, 1989). On the inability of Kymlicka to provide for majority rights,

 | DOI 10.1163/9789004328785_004

focus on rights arising from a marginalized indigenous status is apparent in practical political instruments, such as constitutional provisions on indigenous rights or as the internationally adopted United Nations Declaration on the Rights of Indigenous Peoples (UNDRIP),[5] and in much of the theorizing about these instruments.[6]

To the extent that discussions proceed in this way, they are arguably unnecessarily polarizing. Within these discourses, no language acknowledges that majority communities could also hold rights.[7] The assumptions are all that minorities need protections from majorities,[8] that indigenous communities need protections from so-called "settler colonialists",[9] and that historic or contemporary victimhood is the grounding of significant rights.[10]

At the same time, the political arena sees increasing assertiveness by historical majorities in the face of pressures on their own cultures. Throughout Europe, worries about influxes of immigrants have led to a variety of policy responses

---

see M. Seymour, 'Collective Rights in Multi-nation States', in M. Seymour, ed., *The Fate of the Nation-State* (McGill-Queen's University Press, Montreal, 2004) pp. 105, 112.

5 Declaration on the Rights of Indigenous Peoples, GA Res. 61/295, UN Doc. A/RES/47/1 (2007) ("UNDRIP"). On the development of the UNDRIP, *see generally* M. Barelli, *Seeking Justice in International Law: The Significance and Implications of the UN Declaration on the Rights of Indigenous Peoples* (Routledge, London, 2016).

6 *See e.g.* the discussion of UNDRIP at various points in P. Macklem, *The Sovereignty of Human Rights* (Oxford University Press, Oxford, 2016). Some conceptions of the purposes of UNDRIP are significantly different from the mainstream liberal egalitarian analysis and treat it, for instance, as an instrument of legal pluralism that is recognizing indigenous traditions. These conceptions are not subject to all of my critiques but also have not become as prominent as the liberal egalitarian account. For an example of such a conception, *see* F. Gómez Isa, 'Cultural Diversity, Legal Pluralism, and Human Rights from an Indigenous Perspective: The Approach by the Colombian Constitutional Court and the Inter-American Court of Human Rights', 36 *Human Rights Quarterly* (2014) p. 722. On the transformative nature of the UNDRIP generally, *see* M. Barelli, *supra* note 5.

7 *See* the discussion concerning the absence of such discourse in L. Orgod, *The Cultural Defense of Nations: A Liberal Theory of Majority Rights* (Oxford University Press, Oxford, 2015).

8 *See generally* L.-A. Thio, *Managing Babel: The International Legal Protection of Minorities in the Twentieth Century* (Martinus Nijhoff, Leiden, 2005).

9 *See e.g.* P. Wolfe, 'Settler Colonialism and the Elimination of the Native', 8 *Journal of Genocide Research* (2006) p. 387; P. Wolfe, *Settler Colonialism and the Transformation of Anthropology: The Politics and Poetics of an Ethnographic Event* (Cassel, London, 1999).

10 *See* R. Meister, 'Human Rights and the Politics of Victimhood', 16 *Ethics & International Affairs* (2002) p. 91; J. Manning and B. Campbell, 'Microaggression and Moral Cultures', 13 *Comparative Sociology* (2014) p. 692.

involving reassertions of historical European values,[11] also now finding gradual expression by individuals ranging from scholars to essayists to novelists.[12]

In the Canadian province of Quebec, various iterations of policy debate have seen rounds of debate on the limits of reasonable accommodation of minority practices, on the possibility of a more deliberately established shared set of values or traditions, and on the possibility of a new model going beyond multiculturalism.[13] The latter has seen the vibrant cultivation of models of so-called 'interculturalism' in various forms, providing accounts of cultural interaction that preserve a place for the historic identity and traditions of an existing national community.[14]

These specific examples of increasing policy debates could be multiplied. In any event, one response of political theorists is to condemn what they term the backward responses of majority populations to modernity, seeing minority rights as ongoing essential protections against oppressive majorities.[15] Many political theorists see no basis, for instance, for immigration policies that pursue any place for the historic identity of a state and call instead for effectively open borders based on abstracted, generalized liberal egalitarian concerns.[16]

---

11 *See e.g.* P. Jenkins, *God's Continent: Christianity, Islam, and Europe's Religious Crisis* (Oxford University Press, Oxford, 2007); M. Emerson, 'Interculturalism: Europe and Its Muslims in Search of Sound Societal Models', in P. Justino, T. Brückand and P. Verwimp (eds.), *A Micro-Level Perspective on the Dynamics of Conflict, Violence, and Development* (Oxford University Press, Oxford, 2014).

12 *See e.g.* J. Finnis, 'On the Nature of a Free Society', *Notre Dame Law School Legal Studies Research Paper No. 1709* (2017); P. Manent, *Situation de la France* (Groupe Artège, Paris, 2015), translated as P. Manent, *Beyond Radical Secularism: How France and the Christian West Should Respond to the Islamic Challenge,* trans. R. Hancock (St. Augustine's Press, South Bend, 2016); M. Houllebecq, *Soumission* (Flammarion, Paris, 2015), translated as M. Houllebecq, *Submission,* trans. L. Stein (Farrar, Struass & Giroux, Paris, 2015).

13 A major report on these debates was issued as G. Bouchard and C. Taylor, *Building the Future: A Time for Reconciliation* (Québec Commission de consultation sur les pratiques d'accomodement reliées aux différences culturelles, Québec, 2008).

14 *See* G. Bouchard, 'What is Interculturalism?', 56 *McGill Law Journal* (2011) p. 435; G. Bouchard, *Interculturalism: A View from Quebec,* trans. H. Scott (University of Toronto Press, Toronto, 2015).

15 N. Lerner, *Religion, Secular Beliefs and Human Rights* (Martinus Nijhoff, Leiden, 2nd edn., 2012) pp. 99–116.

16 *See* especially J. Carens, *The Ethics of Immigration* (Oxford University Press, Oxford, 2013). A recent take that considers a wider range of interests, but is still not highly attentive to the identity of the existing state, is J. J. Mendoza, *The Moral and Political Philosophy of Immigration* (Lexington Books, Lanham/Maryland, 2017).

Somewhat prominently amongst these arguments, one could arguably even characterise a whole 'Toronto school' of scholars arguing for unrestricted migration,[17] with the internal debates at Toronto seemingly being just about whether it is legitimate for the state to consider any economic factors in choosing how much immigration to allow[18]—without anyone being ready to consider potential cultural arguments.[19]

Many liberal theorists, then, effectively recharacterise every act of what historic communities might consider self-preservation into an act of aggression against minorities and indigenous communities, often without any distinction whatsoever based on circumstances. That said, the idea that there could be particular circumstances in which majority rights warrant more respect has received some important recent attention. This attention is not simply to procedural majority rights, such as rights in relation to the implementation of a democratic majority vote in certain circumstances,[20] but is attention to the idea that in at least some circumstances it is analytically helpful to think of a majority as holding substantive rights to act in certain ways.

17 The full-fledged call for open borders is perhaps most clear in Joseph Carens' work: *see e.g.* J. Carens, 'Aliens and Citizens: The Case for Open Borders', 49 *Review of Politics* (1987) p. 251; *Id.*, *The Ethics of Immigration* (Oxford University Press, Oxford, 2013). However, others at Toronto also suggest profound unfairness in immigration restrictions. For example, Ayelet Schachar writes of the violations of egalitarian principles arising from immigration restrictions (A. Schachar, *The Birthright Lottery: Citizenship and Global Inequality* (Harvard University Press, Cambridge, 2009)). Michael Trebilcock approaches matters from a law and economics perspective but nonetheless comes to a very optimistic account of benefits from immigration: N. Kelley and M. Trebilcock, *The Making of the Mosaic: A History of Canadian Immigration Policy* (University of Toronto Press, Toronto, 1998). And others spend significant effort on arguing against particular immigration-related rules, such as the removal of citizenship from terrorists: A. Macklin, 'Citizenship Revocation, the Privilege to Have Rights, and the Production of the Alien', 40 *Queen's Law Journal* (2014) p. 1; K. Roach and C. Forcese, *False Security: The Radicalization of Canadian Anti-Terrorism* (Irwin Law, Toronto, 2015).

18 *See e.g.* A. Macklin, 'Freeing Migration from the State: Michael Trebilcock on Immigration Policy', 60 *University of Toronto Law Journal* (2010) p. 315.

19 There are of course some prominent political theorists elsewhere who permit some degree of restriction on immigration on some grounds. *See e.g.* M. Walzer, *Spheres of Justice* (Basic Books, Boston, 1983); D. Miller, 'Immigration: The Case for Limits', in Andrew Cohen and Christopher Wellman (eds.), *Contemporary Debates in Applied Ethics* (Blackwell, Oxford, 2005) p. 193; D. Galloway, 'Liberalism, Globalism and Immigration', 18 *Queen's Law Journal* (1993) p. 266.

20 On such procedural majority rights, *see e.g.* W. Kendall, *John Locke and the Doctrine of Majority-Rule* (University of Illinois Press, Urbana, 1941).

The important new work of Liav Orgod, *The Cultural Defense of Nations: A Liberal Theory of Majority Rights,*[21] argues that there are specific, definable circumstances in which majority rights warrant respect. I put the claim in this somewhat vague manner of 'warranting respect' so as to avoid dwelling too long on matters of whether what is at stake are legal rights (justified claims within a legal system that are valid on a correct interpretation of the legal system) or simply moral rights (justified claims that are valid independently of any legal system).[22] As with human rights more generally, the claims at issue here concern rights that ought to be respected, with perhaps a prima facie case for legal recognition, but whether they assume precisely parallel legal form is in some respects a detail of means of implementation.[23]

In his important new work on majority rights, Orgod focuses on four principal circumstances, in all of which he suggests that majorities take on some of the characteristics usually applicable to minorities, referring particularly to situations in which majorities are diminishing, majorities are actually regional minorities, majorities are victimized, or majorities have become trapped into the mindset of minorities.[24] In justifying the claim that majority rights deserve respect in such circumstances, Orgod largely argues that the same bases that justify minority rights in a variety of circumstances would justify majority rights in the delineated circumstances. He puts the fundamental point as follows:

> Cultural minority rights have paved the way for cultural majority rights. The moral interests of the majority in adhering to its culture and preserving fundamental elements of that culture are based on rationales which are similar to those that first justify the cultural rights of minority groups.[25]

In arguing in such a manner, Orgod both offers a grounding for majority rights that would potentially be accepted by many of those who argue for minority rights and situates that grounding within relatively unaltered dominant discourses of minority rights.

---

21 L. Orgod, *supra* note 7.

22 D. Newman, *Community and Collective Rights: A Theoretical Framework for Rights Held by Groups* (Hart Publishing, Oxford, 2011) p. 11.

23 *Ibid.,* p. 11; P. Jones, 'Group Rights and Group Oppression', 7 *Journal of Political Philosophy* (1999) pp. 353, 355.

24 L. Orgod, *supra* note 7, pp. 9, 189–95.

25 *Ibid.,* p. 196.

In a sense, Orgod argues that some majority identities can become marginalized in certain circumstances and thus worthy of protection.[26] That approach effectively locks in a focus on marginalization as a grounding for rights. In pursuing such an argument, I will argue, Orgod both accomplishes much and stops short of the sort of altered basis for group rights analysis that would ground a better account of both minority and majority rights and an appropriate reconciliation of these different categories of rights.

One might draw a more specific distinction here. Orgod develops a liberal account of what we might term *weak majority rights*, with these rights being claimed only on the basis of a majority group taking on characteristics of a minority group; the account I will offer is of *strong majority rights*, with these rights arising based on characteristics of groups themselves. Though my argument for majority rights will build from majority rights being based on some of the same foundations as minority rights, I will argue that those foundations are not solely those of minority disempowerment so much as collective interests of groups. To be clear, however, I certainly do not accept all claims that are floated under the name of 'majority rights', and indeed I consider some of its usages quite unfortunate, and I also would not personally support some of the policy choices I think majorities are entitled to make. Nonetheless, I will offer an account of *strong majority rights*.

In this chapter, I argue that approaches to the discussion of group rights need to shift to some degree to a focus on collective interests, rather than simply minority and/or indigenous identity. I will make three main arguments grounded in the circumstances of minority and indigenous communities themselves: (1) that a focus on minority and/or indigenous identity actually has tendencies to lock minority and indigenous groups into disadvantage; (2) that situations where ethno-cultural or cultural-linguistic minority groups have a majority status within some level of political unit are not uncommon and that such situations need the new analysis prescribed; and (3) that situations where an indigenous community takes on a majority status in a political unit also call for this new analysis.

However, I will also be arguing more broadly that a conceptual shift away from responses to marginalized identities toward responses to collective interests is appropriate and necessary to a full response to the set of minority and majority rights questions at stake. In putting that argument, I will offer a broader account grounded in my past work on collective interests and collective rights,[27] and I will argue that such an account can provide a nuanced set

26 *Ibid.*, pp. 189–95.

27 *See* especially D. Newman, *supra* note 22.

of tools for recognizing generally reconcilable majority and minority rights. Such a conceptual shift, I note, is not mere verbal jockeying. I will show that it has significant conceptual implications for the potential acceptability of some policies, including for the acceptability of versions of 'interculturalism' in place of 'multiculturalism'. I make my three main arguments, then, based on the situation of minority and indigenous groups, but my claim is ultimately broader and actually envisions the need also to find appropriate reconciliations between minority and majority rights.

2 Locking Groups into Disadvantage and Victimhood

Turning to the first argument, my claim is that a focus on minority and/or indigenous rights can have tendencies to lock minority and indigenous groups into disadvantage. That claim stands, I will suggest, despite some initial complications, and it offers some telling considerations against dominant approaches to relying on non-dominance in grounding minority rights.

This claim is somewhat complicated by the determination not to offer legal definitions of "minorities" or of "indigenous peoples" in central instruments that bear on their rights.[28] Neither the 1992 UN Declaration on the Rights of Minorities nor the 2007 UNDRIP defines its respective rights-holders.[29] Yet, these definitions are important to who holds what legal rights. Interestingly, the two definitions are actually interconnected to some degree. In the cynical realpolitik of negotiation processes, Will Kymlicka describes how some states agreed to support the UNDRIP only on the basis that the rights at issue were being extended to a limited set of indigenous groups, with a so-called 'firewall' between them and other minority groups.[30] In light of that negotiating history, the definition of indigenous communities is implicitly narrowed compared to what it might have been, such that there must be a separate definition of minorities.

---

28 *See also* B. Saul, *Indigenous Peoples and Human Rights: International and Regional Jurisprudence* (Hart Publishing, Oxford, 2016) p. 25 (noting the lack of international law development of such a definition).

29 Declaration on the Rights of Persons Belonging to National or Ethnic, Religious and Linguistic Minorities, UN GA Res 47/135, UN Doc A/RES/47/135 (1992) ('UN Declaration on the Rights of Minorities'); UNDRIP, *supra* note 5.

30 W. Kymlicka, 'Beyond the Indigenous/Minority Dichotomy?', in S. Allen and A. Xanthaki (eds.), *Reflections on the UN Declaration on the Rights of Indigenous Peoples* (Hart Publishing, Oxford, 2011) p. 187. *See also* H. Quane, 'The UN Declaration on the Rights of Indigenous Peoples: New Directions for Self-Determination and Participatory Rights?', *Ibid.*, p. 267.

Nonetheless, there have been since the adoption of the UNDRIP ongoing efforts by various groups to characterise themselves as indigenous communities.[31]

The 1995 Council of Europe Framework Convention on the Protection of National Minorities goes further than the 1992 UN Declaration on the Rights of Minorities in the minority rights it identifies, albeit in the context of a different international organization.[32] These more extensive rights are also not simply based on "national or ethnic, cultural, religious and linguistic identity" as in the 1992 instrument.[33] Rather, they apply to "national minorities".[34] Effectively, there are at least two different definitions of minorities in international law, one of them narrower than the other.

The 2007 UNDRIP ascribes a much more extended set of rights to indigenous peoples than apply in respect of minorities, without a definition of the indigenous peoples holding those rights in the instrument itself.[35] Although aspects of the UNDRIP recognize the preferred position of indigenous communities themselves that indigenous identity is based largely on self-identification—Article 33 states that "[i]ndigenous peoples have the right to determine their own identity or membership in accordance with their customs and traditions"[36]—that concept is not all-encompassing as to definition given the legal consequences of indigenous identity. International law has gone on to develop some degree of definition of the concept.[37]

In ongoing attempts to define these concepts, non-dominance ends up playing a significant role.[38] For example, on the influential definition of minorities developed by Francesco Capotorti, a minority is a:

> [G]roup numerically inferior to the rest of the population of a State, in a non-dominant position, whose members – being nationals of the

31 W. Kymlicka, *ibid.*; D. Hodgson, *Being Maasai, Becoming Indigenous: Postcolonial Politics in a Neocolonial World* (Indiana University Press, Bloomington, 2011). *See also* S. Balaton-Chrimes, 'Indigeneity and Kenya's Nubians: Seeking Equality in Difference or Sameness?', 51 *Journal of Modern African Studies* (2013) p. 331 (discussing claims to indigeneity as an equality-seeking strategy).

32 Framework Convention for the Protection of National Minorities, Council of Europe, ETS No. 157 (1 February 1995, entered into force 1 February 1998).

33 UN Declaration on the Rights of Minorities, *supra* note 29, Arts. 1(1), 2(1).

34 Framework Convention for the Protection of National Minorities, *supra* note 32, Art. 1.

35 UNDRIP, *supra* note 5.

36 *Ibid.* The article would seem to be primarily about membership, but the reference to identity itself is consistent with the broader notion of self-identification of indigenous peoples.

37 B. Saul, *supra* note 28, pp. 22–53

38 *Ibid.*, pp. 32–33.

> State – possess ethnic, religious or linguistic characteristics differing from those of the rest of the population and show, if only implicitly, a sense of solidarity, directed towards preserving their culture, traditions, religion or language.[39]

Others have raised issues about the nationality requirement and even the numerical inferiority as inapplicable to the circumstances of some groups that clearly count as minorities, but the idea of non-dominance has been seen as vital. What that means in legal terms, though, is not straightforward and has actually occasioned ongoing debates.[40] Some see the concept as just restating that of numerical inferiority, but that would imply an implausible redundance.[41] But if the requirement is of "economic, social, and cultural domination", as on one description,[42] or even "a state of dependence and subordination", as on another,[43] various groups that would be popularly regarded as minorities might well not qualify, such as in the case of various minorities that are not totally dominated but are still distinctive communities warranting some protections. In any event, non-dominance has taken on a role in the legal definition.

Non-dominance is similarly a central part of the working definition of indigenous peoples developed in Martinéz Cobo's 1986 Report to the UN Sub Commission on the Prevention of Discrimination of Minorities.[44] In this definition:

> Indigenous communities, peoples and nations are those which, having a historical continuity with pre-invasion and pre-colonial societies that developed on their territories, consider themselves distinct from other sectors of the societies now prevailing in those territories, or parts of

---

39 United Nations Sub-Commission on Prevention of Discrimination and Protection of Minorities, *Study on the Rights of Persons belonging to Ethnic, Religious and Linguistic Minorities*, UN Doc. No. E/CN.4/Sub.2/384/Rev.1.1979 (United Nations, New York, 1979), para. 568 ('Capotorti Report').

40 *See e.g.* Steven Wheatley, *Democracies, Minorities, and International Law* (Cambridge University Press, Cambridge, 2005), p. 20.

41 *Ibid.*

42 *Ibid.*

43 José Pergoa, 'The Existence and Recognition of Minorities', UN Doc. E/CN.4/Sub .2/AC.5/2000/WP.d (3 April 2000), para. 17.

44 J. Martínez Cobo, *Study of the Problem of Discrimination Against Indigenous Populations*, UN Doc. E/CN.4/Sub.2/1986/7 (1986/87).

> them. They form at present non-dominant sectors of society and are determined to preserve, develop and transmit to future generations their ancestral territories, and their ethnic identity, as the basis of their continued existence as peoples, in accordance with their own cultural patterns, social institutions and legal systems.[45]

The element of non-dominance has similarly played a central role in other more recent attempts to engage with the legal definition of indigeneity in complex circumstances like those in Africa and Asia.[46] In the 2005 report of the African Commission's Working Group on Indigenous Populations/ Communities, the emphasis on non-dominance is clear:

> The overall characteristics of groups identifying themselves as indigenous peoples are that their cultures and ways of life differ considerably from the dominant society, and that their cultures are under threat, in some cases to the point of extinction.[47]

The subsequent discussion goes on to describe various related characteristics, with the concept of non-dominance being pervasive throughout the various characteristics.[48]

Within liberal accounts, of course, it makes sense that non-dominant groups might receive some particular protections. Scholars like Will Kymlicka and Patrick Macklem have developed liberal egalitarian accounts of indigenous rights and minority rights that fit such protections neatly within liberal theory. Kymlicka's 1989 book *Liberalism, Community, and Culture* made the fundamental point that indigenous groups would face inequalities in preserving their cultures within the state and therefore would warrant special protections.[49]

---

45 *Ibid.*

46 These contexts have always presented greater complexities. *See e.g.* B. Kingsbury, '"Indigenous Peoples" in International Law: A Constructivist Approach to the Asian Controversy', 92 *American Journal of International Law* (1998) p. 414; D. Newman, 'The Law and Politics of Indigenous Rights in the Postcolonial African State', 102 *Proceedings of the Annual Meeting (American Society of International Law)* (2008) p. 98; D. Newman, 'Africa and the United Nations Declaration on the Rights of Indigenous Peoples', in S. Dersso (ed.), *Perspectives on the Rights of Minorities and Indigenous Peoples in Africa* (Pretoria University Law Press, Pretoria, 2010) p. 141.

47 African Commission on Human and Peoples' Rights, *Indigenous Peoples in Africa: The Forgotten Peoples?* (International Work Group for Indigenous Affairs, Copenhagen, 2006) p. 10.

48 *Ibid.*, pp. 10–11.

49 W. Kymlicka, *Liberalism, Community, Culture*, *supra* note 4.

Macklem's 2001 *Indigenous Difference and the Constitution of Canada* drew meaningfully upon this idea in explaining Canada's constitutional provisions on aboriginal rights,[50] so Macklem's structure of argumentation once appeared relatively closely aligned with Kymlicka's, notably in so far as he drew directly upon Kymlicka in framing his argument.[51] Macklem's 2016 *The Sovereignty of Human Rights* resituates his argument into the international arena in some new ways.[52] In this arena, Macklem sees norms of international human rights as effectively responses to the international legal order's distribution of power and thus sees indigenous rights as a primary human right that responds to the circumstances of marginalized communities within a legal order that otherwise results in injustices due to its state-based organization.[53]

The idea could be seen as extending to minority rights as well in both of these scholars, with Macklem then capturing it perhaps most neatly in his statement that minority rights arise for distributional reasons because "[m]inorities exist in relation to majorities, and majorities exist because international law distributes sovereign power over territory and people to certain collectivities and not to others."[54] Macklem's later work in the *Sovereignty of Human Rights* does question the justice of a state-based organization of the international system in a way that neither Kymlicka nor Macklem's *Indigenous Difference and the Constitution of Canada* did. Thus, for instance, his larger argument also addresses the need for self-government for certain groups in order to try to face legitimacy challenges to the state to the extent possible.[55] Nonetheless, to the extent that significant norms of international human rights, including minority rights and indigenous rights, still function as responses to a distribution of power, they have a redistributive character analogous to that they held in his earlier work which was more closely connected to a Rawlsian liberal egalitarian framework. It may be that Macklem has now partly transcended such a framework, but to the extent he has, he is an exception within a group of scholars who have continued to use it. Scholars like Kymlicka, with his absolutely enormous influence on scholarship and policy-makers, have certainly continued to see minority and

50 P. Macklem, *Indigenous Difference and the Constitution of Canada* (University of Toronto Press, Toronto, 2001).

51 *Ibid.*, pp. 71–74, 77.

52 P. Macklem, *The Sovereignty of Human Rights* (Oxford University Press, Oxford, 2016).

53 *Ibid.*

54 P. Macklem, 'Minority rights in international law', 6 *International Journal of Constitutional Law* (2008) p. 531.

55 P. Macklem, *supra* note 52.

indigenous rights as a sort of redistribution to non-dominant communities, flowing from a Rawlsian liberal egalitarian framework.

The unfortunate effect of this legal definition and this scholarly account comes from its very normative basis. The definition implies that indigenous peoples and minority groups must be 'non-dominant' to receive rights and thus in some respects locks them into a position of non-dominance if they are to retain their rights. In so far as the idea is to remedy an ongoing disadvantage, the disadvantage seemingly must be ongoing for these communities to benefit from the rights at issue. There is thus the potential either for these rights to be only temporarily justified or for their ongoing justification to be dependent upon ongoing marginalization.

In his discussion of the legal definition of indigenous peoples, Ben Saul notes briefly this point in the legal context. He states that a:

> [P]aradox in the strict application of this [non-dominance] criterion is that the attainment of equal rights could render a population no longer indigenous (as no longer being disadvantaged). However, UN practice suggests that the historical experience of marginalisation is also critical, not whether it always persists (if it does, it affects the measures that may be necessary to improve the situation rather than the existence of the group as such).[56]

Saul is at least sensitive to the potential paradox that arises. However, his one-line dismissal of it based on alleged practices of the United Nations (UN) is too quick. First, nobody would say that a group ceases to exist when it does well, as Saul's last sentence peculiarly seems to suggest. Rather, the effect of basing indigenous rights on non-dominance by defining indigenous groups as being those that are non-dominant is that an indigenous community that does well might cease to qualify for indigenous rights. It would cease to be 'indigenous' in the legal sense, but it would not necessarily cease to 'exist' as a group. Second, despite Saul's quick claim, it is far from obvious that the UN carries out any extensive work on behalf of highly advantaged indigenous groups because of historical experiences of past marginalization. His point comes across as pure assertion, and a somewhat implausible one at that. Third, even were the UN to act in some such ways, that point would still say nothing about what states do or are obligated to do under pertinent rights instruments or international law norms or what normative theory on the point would commend. If the definition

56 B. Saul, *supra* note 28, pp. 32–33.

of indigenous rights requires non-dominance or marginalization, whatever some UN body might be doing would not alter the negative effects in the circumstances arising from cessation of state respect for indigenous rights and removal of the existing normative arguments for the group to hold indigenous rights. Saul might have further argument on the point, but for present purposes, although he is seemingly attentive to a potential paradox at issue, his consideration of it is ultimately underdeveloped.

The effects of non-dominance or disadvantage playing a central role in the normative argumentation on minority and indigenous rights actually cut rather deeply. Indeed, were indigenous or minority communities simply to be better off in economic terms, arguably that fact alone would have the potential to undermine their claims within liberal egalitarian arguments oriented to non-dominance or relative disadvantage. Someone might properly say that economic status does not imply that a community is not politically dominated, but the point would be that different aspects of non-dominance could presumably set one another off within a purely equalization-based model. Communities becoming sufficiently better off in one aspect would see their overall position potentially become one of relative advantage, undermining claims to equalization.[57] Someone might try to respond by focusing on just some aspect of non-dominance, perhaps most plausibly political non-dominance, and then presuming that other aspects of a community's status cannot offset this aspect, on which there must be equalization. But that approach arguably weakens the plausibility of a claim to equalization—while overall equality might seem like a plausible aim, precise political equality does not seem so compelling an aim if it is known that the communities in question could differ dramatically inversely on other dimensions. I ultimately find no particular model of non-dominance currently compelling, but the approach for which I will ultimately argue also does not rest on any definition of non-dominance.

If communities' rights flow only from equalization, their rights are vulnerable to these communities' own successes. So, there are reasons to be profoundly concerned with resting on the argumentation of the liberal egalitarian frameworks of the likes of Kymlicka. As I have argued previously against Kymlicka, a significantly problematic effect of his argument is to make indigenous rights temporary rights and rights that exist only in the context of indigenous communities that are disadvantaged and poor.[58] Legal frameworks based on a definition involving non-dominance partly replicate this dimension and

57 D. Newman, *supra* note 22, pp. 74–75.

58 *Ibid.*

implicitly threaten the withdrawal of rights from minority or indigenous communities that do too well.

This sort of threat, of course, is not discontinuous with the types of threats routinely posed by liberal egalitarian policies, at least as coming from the dominant Rawlsian stream of liberal egalitarianism. One of the major critiques of such strands of egalitarianism has been their difficulty in avoiding the so-called 'levelling down objection', an objection that their preferred outcomes might be achieved as much by simply taking away from those who have more as by actually raising up those with less.[59] Liberal egalitarian accounts may thus struggle more generally with appropriate responses to success. That they do so in respect of indigenous communities and minorities, though, is the concerning point in the present context.

3 Geographically Concentrated Minorities

Turning to the second part of the argument, I want to emphasize that the issue of minority and indigenous communities being required to be non-dominant in order to retain their rights relates to a very real concern raised by current conditions and is not just something raised by hypothetical future circumstances of prosperity. In particular, where certain minorities or indigenous communities have geographical concentrations, approaches focused on minority or indigenous identity actually risk undermining the claims of minority and indigenous communities.

In respect of minorities, some minorities are geographically concentrated within a state and may then take on majority status within, for instance, a federal subunit. Although the Capotorti definition refers only to a minority within a state, the challenge is that there will often be a Russian doll phenomenon in which different minorities take on majority status within some power-holding unit but then have different minorities within that unit.[60] In one sense, this is the flip side of what Orgod directly recognizes as one of the situations in which majorities become minorities,[61] and it is one that makes clear that minorities sometimes require protection directly via a mechanism of majority rights.

To take the example of the Canadian province of Quebec, francophones are in a significant minority position in North America and in the Canadian state

59 D. Parfit, 'Equality and Priority', 10 *Ratio* (1997) p. 202.

60 *See generally* A. Eisenberg and J. Spinner-Halev (eds.), *Minorities Within Minorities* (Cambridge University Press, Cambridge, 2005).

61 L. Orgod, *supra* note 7, pp. 189–95.

in particular, but within the province of Quebec they are a majority, and it is anglophone residents of Quebec who face some of the circumstances of a minority, at least in certain types of power, despite their strong economic position and their connections to a larger anglophone majority outside Quebec. Referring simply to the francophone and anglophone communities understates of course the complexities of the actual situation. The 'allophone' community, made up of immigrant communities with other languages who have historically tended to assimilate linguistically to the anglophone community, is seen by some within the francophone community as posing an additional sort of demographic threat. They face their own circumstances of intersecting minority status, as do Quebec's indigenous communities.

This situation is by no means an isolated example. Many minority communities are majorities in some political subunit (whether numerically or in terms of some form of power), and often in complex ways with intersecting communities. Such situations will arise especially where a state's constitutional design has sought to be responsive to the existence of geographically concentrated minorities within the state, such as in many federal states where the structure of federalism acts as a means of protecting diversity.[62]

Only an analysis that furthers the possibility of recognizing rights held by a majority actually offers full protection to those minorities that constitute majorities within some political subunit. That claim may or may not correspond to the legal structures for minority rights, as the main minority rights instruments are effectively silent as to the possibility at hand. However, normative claims concerning minority rights frequently pertain to restraints on the exercise of state power and would typically be thought to entail constraints on whatever level of the state holds particular powers.

The effect of such constraints on state power, paradoxically, may be to constrain the level of government developed precisely in order to safeguard a minority within the state from taking steps to protect that minority. And some liberal nation-building efforts have actually developed in precisely that way. Taking up again the example of the Canadian province of Quebec, the development of language rights policies as part of Canada's 1982 constitutional amendments was significantly part of a Canadian nation-building project as envisioned by then-Prime Minister Pierre Trudeau.[63]

---

62 On federalism, *see generally* A. Lev (ed.), *The Federal Idea* (Hart Publishing, London, 2017).

63 P. Russell, 'The Political Purposes of the Canadian Charter of Rights and Freedoms', 61 *Canadian Bar Review* (1983) p. 30.

Within this nation-building project, the idea of minority language rights for the two official language communities was partly to assure francophone Canadians as to their recognition throughout Canada, but that assurance does not necessarily serve the interests of the geographically concentrated francophone community of Quebec, which has a distinctive Québécois identity. The idea of constitutionalized minority language rights was also partly to alter the dynamics of language policy in the province of Quebec by restricting the development of any effort to use the educational system to try to make the use of the French language the default language within the public arena.[64] That statement, notably, is distinct from litigation around commercial sign laws and concerns simply a description of one of the purposes of constitutionalized minority language rights. Protecting anglophones in Quebec was partly a means of limiting Québécois nation-building—what purported to be a minority rights protection regime was actually quite deliberately a means of limiting the nation-building efforts of a particular minority group.[65]

More recently, the Canadian federal government has at times tended to emphasize indigenous rights issues in Quebec as one means of posing an additional obstacle to any choice by Quebec for self-determination in the form of secession.[66] The prospect of indigenous communities within Quebec holding equivalent rights of self-determination as those held by Quebec itself effects a significant constraint on Quebec secession.[67] Though some Québécois political theorists have tried to put arguments that self-determination rights are properly held only by the people of the full unit of potential statehood and not by groups within,[68] that argument struggles in the context of the Canadian normative debate. Notably, even though international law has focused on self-determination within whole territorial entities and secession

64 *See generally* D. Salée, 'Quebec Sovereignty and the Challenge of Linguistic and Ethnocultural Minorities: Identity, Difference, and the Politics of Ressentiment', in M.D. Behiels and M. Hayday (eds.), *Contemporary Quebec: Selected Readings and Commentaries* (McGill-Queen's University Press, Montreal, 2011) p. 472.

65 *Ibid.*

66 *See generally* J.F. Lisée, *Octobre 1995: Tous les espoirs, tous les chagrins* (Québec Amérique, Montréal, 2015) pp. 191–98.

67 Lisée notes that the Supreme Court of Canada actually makes effects on Aboriginal rights part of what needs to be negotiated in the course of any secession negotiations: *ibid.* pp. 192–93. *See also Reference re Secession of Quebec,* [1998] 2 S.C.R. 217 (Supreme Court of Canada) para. 139.

68 *See e.g.* M. Seymour, *De la tolérance à la reconnaissance* (Éditions du Boréal, Montréal, 2008).

applying only to whole territorial units under the doctrine of *uti possidetis*,[69] the Supreme Court of Canada was ready in its *Secession Reference* to allude implicitly to the possibility of something different in its indications that effects on Aboriginal rights would need to be one of the objects of negotiation in the event of secession. Within the Canadian normative environment, the more promising response from a Québécois secessionist perspective is the development of strategic approaches to align indigenous interests with Québécois interests.[70] Having to do as much, though, adds a complex strategic dimension to Québécois politics and illustrates again that indigenous or minority rights claims within the territory of a geographically concentrated minority may actually serve as a means of limiting the rights of that minority which has geographical majority status.

Saying as much arguably speaks to some eccentricities of the Canadian context, in which minority nationalism and a secessionist movement are strongly linked. The national government's affirmations related to indigenous rights effectively help to contain Québécois nationalism, even at the same time that one might raise even more complicated claims as to how attitudes to Québec nationalism or secessionism probably also shape aspects of the Canadian state's complex relationship to the scope of indigenous rights it is willing to accept.

Some theoretical accounts do permit some steps by geographically concentrated minorities, although the inconsistences in which they end up show the policy fruit of accounts that are not geared to the problems at hand. For example, Will Kymlicka is ready to defend temporary constraints on voting by new residents of areas with large indigenous populations, but he is generally skeptical of language policies that would allow concentrated minorities to preserve their cultures.[71] Arguing for temporary protections while denying more permanent protections seems like something of a classic band-aid approach that does not address underlying issues. To take another example, although he is by no means a simple liberal egalitarian, Joseph Carens has somewhat

69 For an extended discussion, see S. Lalonde, *Determining Boundaries in a Conflicted World: The Role of Uti Possidetis* (Montréal: McGill-Queen's University Press, 2000).

70 J.F. Lisée, *supra* note 66, pp. 193–96.

71 Such skepticism follows logically from his rejection of so-called 'internal restrictions': *see generally* D. Newman, 'Putting Kymlicka in Perspective: Canadian Diversity and Collective Rights', in S. Tierney (ed.), *Accommodating Cultural Diversity* (Routledge, London, 2007) p. 59. But *see* his seemingly nuanced view on Quebec's language law in W. Kymlicka, *Politics in the Vernacular: Nationalism,Multiculturalism, and Citizenship* (Oxford University Press, Oxford, 2001) pp. 286–88.

paradoxically argued both for open borders and in favour of language policies that may help to preserve an existing cultural community in the context of a geographically concentrated minority holding political power.[72] Arguing for defences of cultural communities through language policy while subjecting them to the vagaries of open borders shows a peculiar inconsistency in whether they are to be able to defend themselves or not.

Liberal egalitarian accounts of reasons for minority rights effectively skirt the issues of geographically concentrated minorities that become majorities. In effect, they either insist on denying the power of the minority and thereby maintain its rights, or they begin to treat it as a majority and insist that all of its decisions are heavily constrained by its responsibilities to minorities within. Saying as much is of course potentially overgeneralized. But any solutions within liberal egalitarian approaches are, in general terms, heavily undertheorized, simply nonexistent, or enmeshed in contradictions or at least significant tensions.

4 Indigenous Governments and the Challenges of Theoretical Approaches Based on Lack of Power

Indigenous groups may not be in a majority position in a political subunit as commonly as minorities are. However, it is very possible that they will be if they are within a state that is trying to respond to their rights. In such circumstances, theoretical accounts oriented toward non-dominance and lack of power face difficulties in grappling with the claims of these indigenous communities.

The basic point is that states that have recognized self-governing powers for indigenous communities or that have territorial subunits with majority indigenous populations create settings in which indigenous communities may hold power to some degree. In the negotiation of modern treaties with indigenous communities, for example, Canada has been ready to negotiate the recognition of power within certain spheres of jurisdiction in which the indigenous government becomes the constitutionally recognized governmental authority.[73] And, in the creation of the Nunavut Territory in the Eastern Arctic, Canada

---

72 On open borders, *see* J. Carens, *supra* note 16; *Id.*, 'Aliens and Citizens: The Case for Open Borders', *supra* note 17. On language policies, *see* various parts of J. Carens, *Culture, Citizenship, and Community: A Contextual Exploration of Justice as Evenhandedness* (Oxford University Press, Oxford, 2000).

73 On these negotiations, *see e.g.* C. Alcantara, *Negotiating the Deal: Comprehensive Land Claims Agreements in Canada* (University of Toronto Press, Toronto, 2013).

deliberately created a federal subunit in which there would be a majority Inuit population, meaning that indigenous communities would exercise majority control of a public government and thus hold power.[74]

When indigenous communities take on governmental power in such ways, they could begin losing the characteristics of non-dominance and vulnerability that are said to make up part of their definition. Paradoxically, in such circumstances, recognizing the rights of indigenous communities may actually have tendencies toward eliminating them. A related paradox, of course, arises more broadly given the actual rights of indigenous communities to autonomy: fulfilling that right may actually, over time, diminish other rights claims or, in some contexts, even undermine the claim to indigenous status in a way that nobody could intend.

That point, of course, needs further unpacking. Nobody would suppose that the granting of governmental powers to indigenous communities in Canada immediately causes them to cease to be indigenous or to hold indigenous rights. On the contrary, the Canadian constitutional text would actually seem to result in such powers, along with any other aspects of the treaty relationships in which they are embedded, becoming constitutionally entrenched. After all, the constitutional text entrenches "Aboriginal and treaty rights", and the definition of treaty rights specifically includes rights held under modern treaties.[75] At a normative level, too, nobody would suppose that an indigenous community attaining recognition of self-governmental jurisdictional authority is instantaneously transformed into a dominant community such that it loses all its rights.

The point is subtler than that. Once indigenous communities accede to governmental authority, they obviously do not instantly become dominant. But one of the bases of their prior non-dominance has shifted, and that may be accompanied by shifts in other bases at the same time if the governmental authority is accompanied by control over resources or altered economic arrangements around resources. There may be no particular move to declare a particular indigenous group no longer to meet the definition of an indigenous community, but the urgency with which liberal egalitarian theories might have emphasized its circumstances may well fade.

Indeed, there are actually tendencies by liberal egalitarian theorists of multiculturalism to focus rapidly on potential problems with self-governing indigenous communities as soon as those communities act in respect of their

---

74 *See generally* J. Hicks and G. White, *Made in Nunavut: An Experiment in Decentralized Government* (UBC Press, Vancouver, 2016).

75 *See Constitution Act, 1982*, s. 35 (Canada).

indigenous identity. The argument for any sort of self-determination is all well and good so long as the assumption is that indigenous communities will act as liberals might prefer. However, where they act in ways considered 'illiberal', especially if they can be accused of theocratic tendencies, critiques rapidly emerge.[76] Within Kymlicka's account, for instance, Kymlicka's long-standing distinction between internal restrictions and external protections enacts a presumption that indigenous and minority communities with power cannot act in ways diverging from liberalism in respect of their members, having to prioritize individual autonomy as their key value whether or not this would have actually been the key value of these communities.[77] There is a problem, then, that the actual exercise of self-governmental authority becomes rapidly questioned—indigenous communities receive a defence from liberal theorists only so long as they are non-dominant.

Consider the further example of the (admittedly tenuous and uncertain) moves toward statehood for Greenland.[78] If Greenland did move forward to statehood, it would become a majority-indigenous state. Would it be right for that state to be immediately one in which the indigenous majority holds no special rights and must defer in some ways to minority rights of the non-indigenous residents? Putting the point in this manner must surely identify a peculiarity in the arguments made for indigenous and minority rights that are grounded in a lack of power. As soon as these communities attain power, are they then to have lesser rights?

The current language of minority rights and indigenous rights has an inherent weakness. It is inherently remedial rather than fully responsive to these communities and their flourishing. In the process, it actually offers less possibility to these communities than an approach that would ground itself in the interests of these communities, regardless of their position in terms of dominance or non-dominance. Different minority communities and indigenous communities have collective interests that properly ground opportunities for them to flourish as communities, and focusing on these interests avoids the necessity for a particular disadvantaged circumstance before they can be

---

76 For a discussion of liberal theorists' rush to attack illiberal practices of indigenous communities, especially if associated with religion, *see* A. Riley, 'Sovereignty and Illiberalism', 95 *California Law Review* (2007) p. 1. *See also* D. Newman, 'Liberal Multicuturalism and Will Kymlicka's Uneasy Relation with Religious Pluralism', 64 *Bijdragen International Journal of Philosophy & Theology* (2003) p. 265.

77 *See* D. Newman, *supra* note 22, ch. 1. *See also* A. Riley, *supra* note 76.

78 *See e.g.* U.P.G. Gad, 'Greeland: A Post-Danish Sovereign Nation State in the Making', 49 *Cooperation and Conflict* (2014) p. 98.

respected, thus allowing for ongoing respect for these communities in the context of their future flourishing.

5 Analysis of Group Rights Claims in Terms of Collective Interests

In my broader theoretical account of collective rights, developed mainly in *Community and Collective Rights: A Theoretical Framework for Rights Held by Groups*,[79] I have argued previously that ethno-cultural groups meeting the requirements for being a collectivity (as opposed to simply a set, or large number of people) can, in principle, hold moral rights at a group level. However, I also argue that the legitimacy of group rights claims depends on their appropriate reconciliation with individual rights of members and reciprocity with claims of those outside the group, including other groups.[80] This sort of approach, I would argue, more appropriately respects the existence of rights held by majority groups as well as minority groups. Though I can develop it in only a limited way in the current paper, and must thus refer readers to my longer work on the topic, it is important to set out some of the basic structure of the argument so as to press to some present implications.

The concept of a collective interest parallels that of an individual interest and refers to something that makes a community's life go better. In other words, it is something that makes a community flourish, that makes the bases of shared life within that community most meaningful.[81] Without diverging from the assumption of a thin version of moral individualism as expressed in Joseph Raz's 'humanistic principle'—that individual well-being is of 'ultimate concern'[82]—it is possible to identify some collective interests as sufficiently morally valuable as to ground duties owed by others. The simplest examples will arise in those situations in which the fulfillment of a collective interest is actually necessary to the fulfillment of individual interests that are themselves

79 D. Newman, *supra* note 22; *Id.*, 'Theorizing Collective Indigenous Rights', 31 *American Indian Law Review* (2006/07) p. 273; *Id.*, 'Value Collectivism, Collective Rights, and Self-Threatening Theory', 33 *Oxford Journal of Legal Studies* (2012) p. 197.

80 D. Newman, *supra* note 22, pp. 107–52.

81 *Ibid.,* pp. 59 *et seq*. This approach also appears in D. Newman, 'Collective Interests and Collective Rights', 49 *American Journal of Jurisprudence* (2004) p. 127, and it builds upon the approach to the common good found in J. Finnis, *Natural Law and Natural Rights* (Clarendon Press, Oxford, 1980).

82 D. Newman, *supra* note 22, p. 12, citing J. Raz, *The Morality of Freedom* (Clarendon Press, Oxford, 1985) p. 194.

significant enough to be rights,[83] although such situations need not be the limit of those in which collective interests warrant respect or even rights protection.

Where individuals' flourishing actually depends significantly upon the fulfillment of an interest that can be described properly only in terms of the claims of a group or community, then individual interests drive the identification of a collective interest as worthy of rights protection. For example, where individuals flourish in the context of a particular religious community, their flourishing depends upon that community having certain basic interests respected, including non-interference with its basic liturgy or respect for the property of that religious community. Where such conditions obtain, then respect for individuals drives respect for the community as a necessary means of respecting the individuals who associate in that community.

Operating within such an understanding, it makes no immediate difference whether the community at issue is a minority community or a majority community. The adherents of a minority faith or those of a majority faith both need respect for their faith community and its institutions as a precursor to their full flourishing. Thus, this sort of approach rooting itself in collective interests rather than in some form of minority status—or some particular aspect of minority status, such as disempowerment—is ready to respect minority rights but is also ready to respect majority rights. Here, though, someone might quibble and ask about the nature of the majority community at issue in this claim to 'majority rights', suggesting that the rights adhere to it not because it is a community that is a majority but because it is a particular type of community that happens to be in the position of a majority. And that claim would be quite correct. A purely statistical majority would not typically be identifiable as a community or group, as opposed to a set of individuals. On the conception indicated earlier,[84] not only the character but potentially even the whole identity of any such majority group would shift significantly as one substituted members, unless it actually has its own character and values. However, having character and values would typically be enough to set off a group, whether a statistical minority or statistical majority, as a community that could then provide meaning within the lives of members and thus potentially warrant respect. The point is not to support majorities for the sake of supporting majorities but to respect communities in light of their contribution to the lives of individual members associating within them.

To put the point bluntly, though, not every community warrants such respect. A community that is actually entirely negative for its own members—say,

83 *See e.g.* D. Newman, *supra* note 22, pp. 76–82.

84 On sets versus collectivities, *ibid.*, p. 4.

a destructive cult—can still be said to flourish or not flourish, but its flourishing is of no value in light of the humanistic principle that it is ultimately the interests of individual human beings that matter. Thus, its interests do not deserve respect. And, with somewhat more complexity, we can also say that a community that fails to maintain appropriate reciprocity with other communities or non-members of that community more generally is similarly subject to not warranting respect.[85]

This latter claim is slightly more complex in so far as the flourishing of the community in question may still appear to be such as to contribute to the lives of its own members, thus making it of some value. However, it enters into a self-performative contradiction in its claims to respect, grounded in its contribution to the interests of its members, when it does not show reciprocal respect for other communities or non-members of the community.[86] This point may, of course, be a matter of degree. But at an abstract level of the legitimacy of claims, it is an important point. And it is one that potentially enables the finding of a reconciliation between majority and minority rights.

6 Reconciling Majority and Minority Rights

The principal objection some will have to the concept of majority rights, of course, is the old trope that majorities are already powerful and that the point of rights is actually to provide protections against majorities rather than to further empower them. Indeed, we could rummage through our old Ronald Dworkin texts for quotations about why rights must inherently be anti-majoritarian. For example, in *Taking Rights Seriously*, he puts the point as follows:

> The existence of rights against the Government would be jeopardized if the Government were able to defeat such a right by appealing to the right of a democratic majority to work its will. A right against the Government must be a right to do something even when the majority thinks it would be wrong to do it, and even when the majority would be worse off for having it done.[87]

85 *Ibid.*, p. 139.

86 *Ibid.*, p. 140.

87 R. Dworkin, *Taking Rights Seriously* (Belknap Press, London, 1978) p. 194.

This passage is, of course, pregnant with many of the aspects of rights culture that have been socially destructive, ranging from its assumptions of rights as inherently oppositional to its sheer libertinism. For present purposes, though, it is the fearsome, alliterative warning about the majority that would "work its will" that is at issue. The old tropes would claim that respecting majority rights means an end to other rights. However, if majority rights are grounded on the same considerations as minority rights and subject to expectations of reciprocity, as discussed above, then majority rights are inherently limited to those that do not inappropriately harm other communities—just as other communities' rights are similarly limited. The ultimate outcome is actually a set of reciprocally reconciled rights, with the possibility that each community can flourish without dragging down other communities.

That said, some might argue that this possibility is overly saccharine and that conflicts between different rights claims will inevitably emerge. This possibility cannot be entirely avoided. However, there is also a tendency on the part of many to overstate the extent to which different rights are in conflict. There are three principal reasons for this. First, many rights have been assumed to have overextended forms such that they have the potential to run up against many other rights, when they should actually be understood in more specified ways. Second, even when rights are considered more specifically, there are assumptions that their implications are broader than they are. Specific rights give rise to specific duties, some of which are of relatively limited extent or implications, and only when different duties emanating from rights are actually impossible to fulfill simultaneously is it actually proper to speak of conflicting rights.[88] Third, there is quite possibly simply some hyperbole at play, perhaps even as a rhetorical strategy to discourage the recognition of majority rights.

Where, though, there are genuine conflicts between majority rights and minority rights, there may be some moral issues as to the priority between these rights. These issues must be considered in a nuanced way, with attention to the variety of moral considerations at play. In facing them, though, the fact that majority rights have often been under-recognized ought not to imply any automatic preference for the claims of minorities, as has perhaps often become the default in latter-day liberal egalitarianism.

Indeed, plausible means of choosing between conflicting rights when it is necessary to do so may actually prefer the claim of the group that happens to be in a majority much more often than many would assume. Any reference to choosing as between the 'weight' of the claims, of course, might well do

---

88 J. Waldron, 'Rights in Conflict', 99 *Ethics* (1989) p. 503.

so based on the number of people affected, but those consequentialist-style considerations might not seem in a good fit with rights issues anyway. However, deeper methodologies, such as considering the impact of particular rights on the integrity of different groups and the integrity of the individuals within them, may well also favour groups that happen to be in majorities more commonly than assumed. That they will have that tendency arguably arises from considerations like rootedness in place. Some examples might make the point clearer.

Consider, first, a potentially claimed conflict between a nation-state's control over its immigration policy in light of its desire to protect its dominant existing culture (which provides meaning to its members lives) versus the claims of foreign nationals to immigrate into that state in an effort to improve their lives. As noted earlier, in the absence of recognition of majority rights, many left liberal theorists have leaned toward arguing that the state must admit immigrants, perhaps even without restriction.

My claim would be that the state may permissibly make a variety of choices on that question, generally with priority over the claims of potential migrants, and might wish to make a variety of choices in light of the nature of its current common culture. A state that has an existing ethno-national identity, such as Japan, might even restrict immigration in light of that ethno-national identity, as Japan does. A state grounded around a set of national ideals might make choices concerning admission of immigrants who will subscribe to those national ideals or, at least, can be assimilated to them. And, of course, some states might have a fully multicultural identity with a thinner set of values and might make the decision to have relatively open borders, albeit perhaps considering whether potential immigrants will themselves ascribe to that ideal.

Those who argue that migrants' choices should take priority over the state's choices on maintaining its own identity and character would, of course, focus on the potential significance of the effects on migrants' lives from immigration to another state and the injustice of the so-called "birthplace lottery".[89] However, by definition, the potential migrants have assumed mobility, whereas the existing nation-state is rooted in place. So long as potential migrants have opportunities to better their lives somewhere, the existing nation-state's rights, which must be exercised where it is, would generally have priority over their claims in the place where the state is. That said, there could of course be exceptions to this priority if either there are insufficient places for the rights claims of potential migrants to be realized and/or if there were an emergency

89 A. Schachar, *supra* note 17.

situation in which many refugees were fleeing a well-founded fear of persecution. And our legal frameworks recognize such notions, with international refugee conventions taking priority over state interests on certain specific legal grounds,[90] albeit often narrower ones than are often portrayed.

There are, of course, situations where minority groups have a strong rootedness in place. Where that is the case, my initial indication that majority rights will often have priority based on this consideration may well not apply in the same way. For example, where a long-standing historic minority within a state seeks to maintain its culture through maintaining minority-language schooling even while the state has embarked on majoritarian nation-building policies, there is a challenging rights conflict at issue. The majoritarian nation-building policy will relate to certain majority rights in relation to cultural identity and certain shared rights in terms of security, but the minority community, unlike potential migrants, can realistically pursue its cultural flourishing only in the same place. Its rights claims in relation to the preservation of its cultural identity and character have essentially the same rootedness in place as those of the state's majority. Accordingly, so long as the minority's claimed rights operate in a way that shows reciprocal respect for majority rights, they may well take some degree of priority, depending on a larger set of factual considerations.

Some of what I have said here might strike some as having a resemblance to some of Kymlicka's distinctions between different types of groups, such as between indigenous groups, national minorities, and immigrant groups.[91] Indeed, here, there is an aspect of Kymlicka's approach that has some significant value. Indigenous groups or historic national minorities do have a different rootedness in place as compared to recent immigrant groups. And they have this rootedness regardless of whether they are more concentrated or more dispersed, although that latter factor may play into what the effects of their claims are on specific issues in specific factual contexts. Indeed, I would push matters further than Kymlicka does and would argue that concentrated minority groups, which thus potentially become regional majorities, with rootedness in place may sometimes appropriately hold majority rights that may include what he would call impermissible internal restrictions, being policies that limit some aspects of the autonomy of their own members. As I have argued elsewhere, Kymlicka's refusal to recognize such rights in some circumstances is inconsistent

90 W.T. Worster, 'The Evolving Definition of the Refugee in Contemporary International Law', 30 *Berkeley Journal of International Law* (2012) p. 94.

91 This distinction is prominent throughout W. Kymlicka, *Multicultural Citizenship* (Oxford University Press, Oxford, 1995).

with policies he purports to uphold in general terms and is inconsistent with the potentially necessary rights for some communities to flourish.[92]

At the same time, nation-building policies of a historic majority may actually warrant significant respect in some contexts, perhaps even at the expense of certain minority claims. Assuming the national majority also has long-standing rootedness in place, and thus legitimately claims to be able realistically to flourish in the place where it now is, the reciprocal relations between it and minority communities would suggest that each should potentially sometimes yield to the other. There are no simple solutions, but broad questions of statecraft. But it makes a difference that within that statecraft, it is sometimes entirely proper to make choices that favour the majority. Majority rights help to shape appropriate paths forward, and their recognition corrects an imbalance that has been all too present in many recent discussions. Majority rights are not in contradiction to minority rights and indigenous rights but are part of an interlinked reciprocally respecting set of majority rights, minority rights, and indigenous rights.

7 Policy Implications

It has probably become implicitly apparent by now that the policy implications of the present claims could actually be far-reaching. In his seminal work on majority rights, Liav Orgod tended to argue for a limited range of implications from the recognition of majority rights. In particular, he argued for a major distinction between immigration contexts and non-immigration contexts, suggesting that there might be more majority rights than traditionally recognized in relation to immigration but that in relation to non-immigration matters, "the majority does not usually need a 'right' to protect its culture because it can utilize its numerical superiority to perpetuate its culture."[93]

However, majority rights have implications beyond the immigration context, and appropriately so. Although, in theory, a majority could use its numerical superiority within democratic processes to enact culturally sustaining policies within a state, the same could actually be said in respect of immigration so long as the majority actually existed. If Orgod argues for rights of majorities to make choices concerning immigration, there is arguably no inherent reason why this point should not extend to rights concerning choices on other

92 D. Newman, *supra* note 71.

93 L. Orgod, *supra* note 7, p. 197.

policies. His caveat has a puzzling aspect. Orgod's reluctance to go further in terms of the scope of majority rights might conceivably have been a rhetorical/ strategic choice in some measure, so as to avoid showing the full scope of implications from majority rights. Or, it might have reflected a reasonable worry about rights inflation, with Orgod considering it unnecessary to use the term 'majority rights' to refer to policy implementation that he genuinely saw as already available to majorities through democratic processes.

Concern that talk of majority rights amounts to a further rights inflation relates to a real worry about rights culture. This worry is that more policy considerations than warrant it are translated into a language of rights and thus rendered into more antagonistic considerations that have further negative effects such as enhancement of judicial power. However, failing to recognize majority rights when minority rights and indigenous rights are recognized in ways that might otherwise unduly constrain majority communities has a distorting effect. Moreover, majorities may be less able to achieve policy implementation through democratic processes than often assumed, with various institutional factors complicating that otherwise simple assumption. For example, complex normative forces on behalf of historically marginalized communities circle round in ways that make it seem inappropriate for majority communities to pursue their legitimate aspirations.[94] Similarly, entrenched interests within bureaucracies and governmental institutions that have been responsive to other communities make it surprisingly challenging for majority communities to exercise the levers of power.[95] If any such considerations apply, Orgod's assumptions that majority rights are not needed actually significantly falter—there could be not just symbolic but actual practical reasons why majority rights are needed in a range of policy areas.

In terms of the account developed here, it is clear that the focus of majority rights is not specifically on immigration but on a range of policies whereby a community might pursue its collective interests, including in its own survival as a community offering meaning within its members' lives. In one sense, immigration issues might actually appear to be some of the more challenging issues to analyze, because they concern issues on the boundaries of membership in the community when collective interests may presuppose something concerning the scope of the community, although it is possible to offer responses to

---

94 See D. Salée, *supra* note 64.

95 A more elaborate claim would be that the 'deep state'—a set of organs not responsive to the democratically elected government—significantly impedes alteration of policy by the majority community: see e.g. M. Lofgren, *The Deep State: The Fall of the Constitution and the Rise of a Shadow Government* (Penguin Books, New York, 2016).

this seeming paradox in much more extended forms.[96] Collective interests may ground a range of policies to sustain the identity and character of an existing community and may well ground majority rights to maintain those policies.

I have argued for a conceptual shift based on the circumstances of minorities and indigenous communities themselves, and the ways in which these communities would tangibly benefit from majority rights in certain circumstances, but there are obviously broader policy implications to a principled acceptance of majority rights. Several examples are illustrative.

First, the conceptual shift at issue has significant background implications for the potential acceptability of some policies, including for the acceptability of versions of 'interculturalism' in place of the 'multiculturalism' policies that many have tended to treat as morally mandatory in discussions of ethno-cultural diversity. Interculturalism has been under much discussion in the Canadian province of Quebec as a different response to circumstances of diversity that does not involve the majority population surrendering its own culture. There, the concept received some degree of expression in the Bouchard-Taylor Commission.[97] More recently, Gérard Bouchard has written a book-length work on the topic, first in French and more recently released in English-language translation.[98]

In this model, the orientation of policies of management of ethno-cultural diversity is neither multiculturalism nor assimilation but an integrative pluralism seeking the integration of all members of society, integration into a historic shared language, reciprocity in cultural differences, promotion of exchange, and development of a shared culture. Such a model, more so than multiculturalism, sees some specific place for the historic majority in, for instance, its language policy. At the same time, it seeks to reconcile the interests of majorities and minorities in a manner not dictating special rights for ethno-cultural groups based on their present status but based upon arrangements that can enable all to flourish together.[99] Such a model shows respect for majority rights along with minority rights and is thus a tangible policy expression of an approach that recognizes majority rights.

Second, the conceptual shift may not only make certain policies acceptable, but it might actually support arguments that certain policies should be pursued. If majority communities matter, and if majorities hold rights such as

96 I provide that at various points in D. Newman, *supra* note 22.

97 G. Bouchard and C. Taylor, *supra* note 13.

98 G. Bouchard, *L'Interculturalisme: Un point de vue québécois* (Éditions du Boréal, Montréal, 2012); G. Bouchard, *supra* note 14; G. Bouchard, 'What is Interculturalism', *ibid.*

99 *See generally* G. Bouchard, *Interculturalism, ibid.*

cultural survival, it actually becomes not only permissible but actually appropriate, desirable, or mandatory to pursue policies that support such cultural survival. The moral call of majority rights might include a call for such policies as regulation to maintain a particular linguistic context (what Quebec has often called a 'visage linguistique', which there supports survival of the majority francophone community as a cultural community). It might also encompass efforts to support families, policies to support historic faiths, policies to maintain cultural ideals, and various sorts of policies to sustain local communities. Variations of these different policies are being pursued at present in different locales across the Western world, often to the chagrin of liberal theorists and denunciations from liberal political actors. To mention just one simple albeit symbolically significant example, when the European Court of Human Rights in *Lautsi* permitted Italy to continue to have crucifixes in school classrooms and it did continue to do so,[100] thus continuing representation of the country's majority religion in a non-accommodationist way, that decision has continued to be critiqued by many liberal theorists and political actors. Policies that defend majority rights have stronger justifications in political and legal theory than they are often recognized as having.

8 Conclusions

If we break away from the liberal egalitarian model that offers temporary and highly contingent defences for minority and indigenous rights, claims to respect for minority groups and indigenous groups actually depend on the placement of value on groups. It would be highly ironic to suppose that only minority groups could be valuable. In reality, the arguments underlying the sounder justifications for minority and indigenous rights call for a conceptual framework that shows respect to collective interests writ large, and thus even to the collective interests of majority groups.

In supporting majority rights, though, there is no argument here against minority rights or indigenous rights. On the contrary, these different categories of rights of particular communities are actually interlinking and self-reinforcing. Along with minority communities and indigenous communities, majority communities matter. But minority and indigenous communities benefit from this recognition as well, as it liberates them from the need to remain marginalized to retain their rights. An approach based on collective

100 *Lautsi v. Italy*, Application No. 30814/06, Judgment of 18 March 2011.

interests rather than response to marginalization has the potential to uplift all communities—majority communities, minority communities, and indigenous communities—while offering a principled defence of the rights of each community.

Of course, one issue that could be raised is what this conclusion means for the ongoing role of human rights doctrine in regulating ethno-cultural diversity. If some minority rights are actually properly subsumed into majority rights and additional communities hold rights in so far as certain communities hold majority rights, does this scenario complicate the role that human rights even play in managing ethno-cultural diversity? On the one hand, one might first resist the query in that I would say that the implementation of this model will not necessarily be in the form of translating each moral right into a precisely parallel legal right. But that statement actually says that there are considerations beyond the present set of legally recognized human rights, or any set of legally recognized human rights, that may be as significant as those rights in determining the appropriate management of ethno-cultural diversity. Legally recognized minority rights and indigenous rights may have a role to play because of the institutions that enforce them, but the overall balance of considerations legitimately at play ought simply to be recognized as involving moral considerations that may be as strong as human rights but not necessarily enumerated in the form of human rights. In that sense, human rights are a particular part of the picture in managing ethno-cultural diversity, but they are a limited part. We need properly to think of a variety of moral considerations that include but are not limited to rights.

CHAPTER 3

The Liberal Democratic Deficit in Minority Representation: The Case of Spain

Lucía Payero-López and *Ephraim Nimni*

1 Introduction

The unforeseen Western key political events of 2016, the success of the Brexit referendum and the election of Donald Trump in the US, are interpreted as resulting from the alienation from dominant elites of large sections of the traditional working class and other unskilled labourers.[1] Here workers and labourers were alienated because their historical representatives pursue the politics of globalisation without adequate redistribution or compensatory mechanisms.[2] This situation touched upon a recurrent democratic deficit in liberal democracies. Dominant elites or establishment politicians fail to be in tune with constituents when representation takes the form of an excessive delegation.[3] In abstract terms, delegation is the transfer of responsibility or authority. Self-delegated legislators shield themselves from the need to account to their constituents for a course of action, and attempt to silent the degree to which the public holds them accountable for policy outcomes.[4] There are many different variations to this general idea, but the common denominator is that a democratic deficit occurs when supposedly democratic organisations or institutions fall short of representing constituents by concealing to them policies and objectives that are incompatible with the interests of

1 S. Gietel-Basten, 'Why Brexit? The Toxic Mix of Immigration and Austerity', 42 *Population and Development Review* (2016) pp. 673–680.

2 "The reason of their angst is not immigration but a form of globalization that, in absence of adequate redistributive policies, creates winners and losers". *See* I. Colantone and P. Stanig, 'Global competition and Brexit', 2016–44 *BAFFI CAREFIN Centre Research Paper* (2016); and https://www.knowledge.unibocconi.eu/notizia.php?idArt=17195.

3 J. Goldsmith, 'Should International Human Rights Law Trump US Domestic Law?', 1 *Chicago Journal of International Law* (2000) p. 33.

4 J. Fox and S.V. Jordan, 'Delegation and Accountability', 73 *The Journal of Politics* (2011) pp. 831–832.

 | DOI 10.1163/9789004328785_005

these constituents. Thus, delegation ceases to be a form of representation by hiding the incompatibility of government policies with the interests of the represented.[5]

It will be argued here that this form of deficit of representation is not the result of circumstantial factors, such as the interests of dominant elites, manipulative politicians, or the triumph of specific economic interests. The deficit of representation is a by-product of a democratic deficiency in the process of liberal representation itself, which has the tendency to transform political representation into delegation.[6]

It will be impossible to focus on the multiple aspects of this phenomenon in this chapter. Instead, we will concentrate on what is not only a historically recurrent expression of this form of representative deficit, but also one that has disrupted the life and times of liberal nation states since their inception: the serious deficit of representation of national and ethnic minorities in liberal democracies. We shall first set out the conceptual and analytical problem and then exemplify the argument in the case of the Spanish state.

2 Minority Representation as an Issue for Human Rights

In a recent important book on Parliaments and Human Rights, the speaker of the British House of Commons, John Bercow MP, argues in the preface that in many liberal democracies there is a growing and genuinely-held concern that the institutional arrangements for the protection of human rights suffer from a "democratic deficit".[7] Yet, surprisingly, the volume does not systematically consider the most conspicuous case of such a deficit in liberal democracies, the predicament of national and ethnic minorities. In the research grant report that preceded the book to the British Art and Humanities Council,[8] the authors cite the liberal theorist Ronald Dworkin, who argues that "legislatures are

5 'Representation', in *Concept and Form: The Cahiers pour l'Analyse and Contemporary French Thought*, at http://cahiers.kingston.ac.uk/concepts/representation.html.

6 *See* S. Piattoni, 'Representation as delegation: a basis for EU democracy?', 20 *Journal of European Public Policy* (2013) pp. 224–242.

7 J. Bercow, 'Preface', in M. Hunt, H. Hooper and P. Yowell (eds.), *Parliaments and Human Rights: Redressing the Democratic Deficit* (Hart Publishing, Oxford, 2015).

8 M. Hunt, H. Hooper and P. Yowell, 'Parliaments and Human Rights. Redressing the Democratic Deficit', *Research Report to the Art and Humanities Research Council* (2012), at http://www.ahrc.ac.uk/documents/project-reports-and-reviews/ahrc-public-policy-series/parliaments-and-human-rights-redressing-the-democratic-deficit/.

systematically biased against minority interests because representatives must, to be re-elected, side with the majority"[9] and calls instead upon the judiciary to protect the interests of minorities. But in the book, unfortunately, no systematic analysis takes place to evaluate the causes of this repetitive event, which needs to be squarely located as a systemic democratic deficit at the heart of the one person one vote system of governance.[10]

A democratic deficit occurs when ostensibly democratic governments, organisations or institutions fall short of fulfilling the principles of democracy in their practices or operation.[11] This is particularly the case in two contrasting situations: when there is a disparity in the mechanisms for the representation and evaluation of different kinds of equal citizens (the case of women's and men's pay for the same job, for example), and paradoxically, in the contrasting case, when institutions of plural societies, composed by different ethno-national communities, are 'colour blind'.[12] This is to say, when the institutions of the state perceive citizens as individual and equal homologous quantities, effectively not recognising their cultural specificity. When this cultural specificity is the cause of segregation and alienation from the majority society, the lack of recognition of the specific cultural and representational needs of minority citizens becomes a serious democratic deficit.[13]

Here the principle of mechanical equality between citizens, understood as sameness, clashes with social plurality and the democratic need

9 R. Dworkin, *Law's Empire* (Harvard University Press, Cambridge, Mass., 1988) p. 375.

10 G.M. Hayden, 'The False Promise of One Person, One Vote', 10 *Michigan Law Review* (2003), pp. 213–214.

11 S. Levinson, 'How the United States Constitution Contributes to the Democratic Deficit in America', 55 *Drake Law Review* (2007) pp. 859–860.

12 'Colour Blind racism' is a term that emerged in the US to define those liberals that ignore the phenotypical or cultural differences between individuals that are determining factors in the behaviour of the individual. Liberal principles, such as 'equal opportunity', 'meritocracy', and 'individual effort', are used in an abstract and decontextualised way, creating misrecognition of difference by dumping all individuals into the individual characteristics of the dominant group. *See* E. Bonilla-Silva, *Racism Without Racists and the Persistence of Racial Inequality in America* (Rowman & Littlefield Publishers, Lanham, 2009) pp. 28–30.

13 M. Threlfall *et al.*, 'Remaking Political Citizenship in Multicultural Europe: Addressing Citizenship Deficits in the Formal Political Representation System', in B. Halsaa, S. Roseneil and S. Sümer (eds.), *Remaking Citizenship in Multicultural Europe* (Palgrave Macmillan, Basingstoke, 2012) pp. 141–165.

of minorities to be recognised in their specific difference to the majority community. As these groups are not only cultural but often are also numerical minorities, these minority communities are prevented from exercising their right to democratic representation. Of course, in liberal democracies they have the right to free speech and to stand for office, but their numerical status fatally curtails their ability to be elected in majoritarian electoral systems.

An important question needs to be asked: Is this impediment to minority representation a violation of human rights? In an important work Will Kymlicka and Christine Straehle argue that even where boundaries coincide with the territories of national minorities, meaningful autonomy could be undermined if the central government usurps most of the subunit powers. They further argue that this usurpation is a clear injustice that can occur without violating individual civil and political rights. So long as individual members maintain the right to vote and run for office, human rights principles pose no obstacle to the majority's efforts to disempower the minority community.[14]

But is this correct? Are human rights individual or collective and how this equation can be balanced? Perhaps the view of Kymlicka and Straehle is somewhat narrow, constrained by a dogmatic liberal interpretation of human rights as individual rights in which individuals are the privileged transcendental actors. But human rights cannot be an abstract universal category because this defies the foundational plural characteristic of human beings. Our common human characteristics are precisely constituted through our insertion in time and space into a community. *We are human not despite diversity, but because of diversity*. To deny the importance and value of cultural diversity, and of our cultural insertion, denies a key component of the notion of human rights, as this means denying an important constitutive element of our humanity. Yvonne Donders makes a significant point in that the rigid division between individual rights and collective rights can be disputed. Many individual rights are historically given to individuals, but are to be enjoyed or exercised as members of a collective entity, or at least jointly with others.[15] So, the behaviour described by Kymlicka and Straehle above is a violation of human rights, even if individual members of these communities are conferred all individual

---

14 W. Kymlicka and C. Straehle, 'Cosmopolitanism, nation-states and minority nationalism: a critical review of recent literature', 7 *European Journal of Philosophy* (1999) pp. 75–76.

15 Y. Donders, 'Foundations of Collective Cultural Rights in International Human Rights Law', in A. Jakubowski (ed.), *Cultural Rights as Collective Rights: an International Law Perspective* (Brill, Leiden, 2016) pp. 87–112.

democratic rights. Human rights are violated if the right to collective group representation is violated.

Further to this, the recent movements for the emancipation of indigenous peoples show that there are cultural dimensions to the exercise of human rights, and that these can only be exercised collectively.[16] A view of human rights that is only oriented towards individual rights, risks undermining the cultural identity and way of life of minorities. This is because it does not include the important dimension of the right to culture and self-determination that can only be exercised collectively. Culture gives individuals and communities a sense of belonging and an insertion in time and space. As such, culture concerns their human dignity, which is a crucial ingredient of the project of human rights.[17] In this regard, human rights for minorities will not be complete without incorporating the collective right of national minorities to the recognition of their culture in the public domain.[18] For this reason, minority representation must transcend the numerical constraint. As Charles Taylor famously argues:

> [M]isrecognition shows not just a lack of due respect. It can inflict a grievous wound. Due recognition is not just a courtesy we owe people. It is a vital human need.[19]

This is therefore an inextricable part of any conception of human rights.[20] The question of the recognition of the collective dimensions of human rights directly leads to two important issues: Why are liberal democratic nation states averse to recognising stateless nations? And, could self-determination be understood in other ways than nation state independence?

---

16 On indigenous peoples and human rights, *see* the influential monograph by P. Thornberry, *Indigenous Peoples and Human Rights* (Manchester University Press, Manchester, 2002).

17 Y. Donders, Y. 'Do cultural diversity and human rights make a good match?', 61 *International Social Science Journal* (2010) pp. 15–35.

18 *See* Miodrag A. Jovanovic, "Recognizing Minority Identities Through Collective Rights", 27 *Human Rights Quarterly* (2005) pp. 625–651.

19 C. Taylor, 'The Politics of Recognition', in A. Gutmann (ed.) *Multiculturalism: Examining the Politics of Recognition* (Princeton University Press, Princeton, 1994) p. 26.

20 For a recent comprehensive discussion of the politics of recognition and its implications for a theory of human rights, *see* C.T. Arruda, 'What We Can Intend: Recognition and Collective Intentionality', 54 *The Southern Journal of Philosophy* (2016) p. 5.

3 Why Liberal Democracies are Averse to Recognising Stateless Nations in their Midst?

First, a platitude that is often forgotten. The prevalent form of political organisation across the world is the nation state, yet a nation is not a state.[21] A state is a governmental and administrative apparatus and the nation is a kind of a cultural community – self-defined or otherwise –, similar but not identical to an ethnic group. There is a continuous and protracted confusion between these terms, both in academic writing and in political parlance. This leads to serious misunderstandings in the relation between nation and state, one that is detrimental to the many nations that are stateless. This is particularly so when the nation is conflated with the body of citizens. When this happens, members of minority nations are misrecognised, and subject to something akin to the 'colour blind racism' discussed above. This alienates and antagonises minority nations as evidenced by the case of the Spanish state, a de facto multination state, which will be discussed below.

To be sure, there are many differing definitions of a nation. There is no consensus, but there might be a common denominator, thus we shall use the general term 'cultural community'. Few will dispute that nations are in the abstract a certain kind of cultural community (real or imagined, historical or constructed, invented or actual, created by states or perennial, etc.).[22] The European absolutist state was not necessarily a nation state, for there was no conception of a 'juridical citizen' and even less so a sense of a common nation, for 'divinely ordained' monarchs would have found it objectionable to say that they belonged to the same nation as their peasant subjects.[23] The term 'nation state' emerged eventually to foster the unification of Germany and Italy. It signified the formation of large states with an ambition of cultural homogenisation, a monocultural form of state liberal democratic nationalism, which followed the model first developed by the French Revolution.[24] The Spanish

21 M. Caminal, 'Democracy, federalism and plurinational states', in M. Caminal and F. Requejo (eds.), *Political Liberalism and Plurinational Democracies* (Routledge, London, 2011) p. 226.

22 There is in the literature a confusing proliferation of definitions. A very helpful article on this protracted confusion is L.W. Barrington, '"Nation" and "Nationalism": The Misuse of Key Concepts in Political Science', 30 *Political Science and Politics* (1997) pp. 712–716.

23 P. Anderson, *Lineages of the Absolutist State* (Verso Books, New York, 2013, 3rd ed.) p. 35.

24 I. Hont, 'The Permanent Crisis of a Divided Mankind: "Contemporary Crisis of the Nation State" in Historical Perspective', 42 *Political Studies* (1994) p. 229.

case developed much later, but it was above all the French Revolution the great unifier of nation states as we shall see in a moment.

Second, the problem is the term 'nationalism'. Definitions are even more confusing. There does not seem to be any common denominator. Most scholars agree that it is an important political phenomenon, but explanations of what it is are obfuscated and confusing.[25] Unfortunately, there is in the study of nations and nationalism a 'chicken and egg syndrome'. For some writers, nations are ancient communities that create a modern ideology called nationalism.[26] For others, nationalism is a phenomenon related to the advent of modernity, and it is nationalism that creates nations, not the other way around.[27] Anthony Smith argues for the chicken first, and Ernest Gellner for the egg first. As this cannot be mediated or resolved, we shall skip definitions. Nationalism is a floating signifier,[28] or if you prefer the terminology of the late Anthony Smith, it has a chameleon-like quality.[29] It is almost always part of different, contrasting and competing ideologies.

Nationalism is neither 'left' nor 'right' nor 'green' or whatever political project you wish to name. In an abstract sense, *it is an arena for struggle for competing ideologies that wish to become hegemonic in a nation*. This is why the definition is so slippery. Nationalism does not exist in a 'pure' form, but it operates intermingled with political ideologies of different kinds. It is a struggle for the appropriation of the hegemonic representation of a cultural community. Nationalism is often considered Conservative, or 'Right-Wing'. But, successful leftist nationalisms are not a rarity. Consider among many others, Cuban,

25 *See*, for example, E.B. Haas, 'What is nationalism and why should we study it?', 40 *International Organization* (1986) pp. 707–744. Haas parades you through a myriad of definitions and at the end we are more confused than when we started.

26 A.D. Smith, *National Identity* (Penguin Books, London, 1991) and *Nationalism and Modernism: A Critical Survey of Recent Theories of Nations and Nationalism* (Routledge, London, 1998).

27 E. Gellner, *Nations and Nationalism* (Blackwell, Oxford, 2nd ed., 1983).

28 'Floating signifiers' is a term used in semiotics to denote signifiers without referents, such as a word that does not point to any actual object or agreed upon meaning. This is precisely what nationalism is. Ernesto Laclau sets the floating signifier in a milieu of social interactions. The floating signifier is the hegemonic representative of a gathering of different demands, as elements that exist only in their differences to one another. They, nevertheless, combine through a system of equivalences. This chain of unsatisfied demands creates an empty totality, inside of which one signifier subordinates the rest and assumes their representation via a hegemonic process. This is a very good description of the role of nationalism in contemporary societies. *See* E. Laclau, *Emancipation(s)* (Verso, London, 1986).

29 A.D. Smith, *Nationalism and Modernism* (Routledge, London, 1998) p. 44.

Chinese, Basque, Kurdish, Scottish, and even Turkish leftist nationalisms. The Cuban revolution is a pertinent example. The discourse of Fidel Castro refers to the 'Cuban people' and makes many references to ikons or nationalist symbols, all incorporated into the revolutionary vision: the poet and hero of Cuban independence, José Martí,[30] for example. Likewise, the Cuban exiles in 'Little Havana' Florida, arch enemies of the Cuban revolution, refer to the same symbols, but incorporated into a drastically opposed ideology, and both claim to be the 'real' Cuban nationalists.[31]

To complete the picture, we need to discuss the relation between nation and nation state. Political theorists and political practitioners tend to assume that a world of nation states is a fact.[32] However, this is a seriously mistaken assumption. Nation states in the strict sense of the term, states whose entire or nearly entire population belongs to one nation are a very rare occurrence.[33] With some small exceptions, these homogeneous states represented in the UN are small isolated islands, or small states with a very small population. Furthermore, the alleged homogeneity of states was never correct, and is even less correct nowadays, with the considerable movement of peoples through migration.[34]

With the recent admission of South Sudan to the United Nations, there are precisely 193 states represented in the UN, of which less than 15 per cent are completely homogeneous. James Minahan in a monumental study of stateless nations puts the number of nations in this world to near 9,000 and the number of ethnic groups even higher.[35] Minahan further argues that only 3 per cent of all nations have achieved statehood. Whether these numbers are correct or not, it is abundantly clear that not all nations in this world can aspire to have

30 Fidel Castro, the leader of the Cuban Revolution, is buried next to the grave of José Martí, at http://www.miamiherald.com/news/nation-world/world/americas/fidel-castro-en/article117762148.html.

31 *See*, for example, "Radio y Televisión Jose Martí", a US radio and television international broadcaster based in Miami, financed by the US government, managed by counterrevolutionary exiles, which transmits political propaganda to Cuba, at http://www.martinoticias.com/.

32 W. Kymlicka and C. Straehle, *supra* note 14, p. 68.

33 S. Walby, 'The Myth of the Nation-State: Theorizing Society and Polities in a Global Era', 37 *Sociology* (2003) p. 529.

34 On the impact of immigration on the nation state, *see* I. Bloemraad, A. Korteweg and G. Yurdakul, 'Citizenship and Immigration: Multiculturalism, Assimilation, and Challenges to the Nation-State', 34 *Annual Review of Sociology* (2008) p. 524.

35 J. Minahan, 'Preface', in *Encyclopaedia of the Stateless Nations: Ethnic and National Groups Around the World* (*vol. 1*) (Greenwood Press, Westport, 2002) p. XIII.

a state of their own. There is a considerable disparity between the number of nations that have a state and those that do not. The number of nations is not very precise, but even in a very restrained and conservative calculation, there are more than ten times more nations than nation states, and often, nations inhabit overlapping territories, and their desire to build homogeneous nation states leads to intractable conflicts and genocides.[36] Ernest Gellner explains it clearly:

> [To] put it in the simplest possible terms: there is a very large number of potential nations on earth. Our planet also contains room for a certain number of independent or autonomous political units. On any reasonable calculation, the former number (of potential nations) is probably much, much larger than that of possible viable states.
>
> If this argument or calculation is correct, not all nationalisms can be satisfied, at any rate at the same time. The satisfaction of some spells the frustration of others. This argument is further and immeasurably strengthened by the fact that very many of the potential nations of this world live, or until recently have lived, not in compact territorial units but intermixed with each other in complex patterns. It follows that a territorial political unit can only become ethnically homogeneous, in such cases, if it either kills, or expels, or assimilates all non-nationals.[37]

Of course, Gellner is also a prisoner of his own conceptual framework, which leads him to argue that the function of nationalism is to build nation states and he cannot conceive of other forms of self-determination for minority nationalisms.[38]

Here we begin to detect a partial answer to our question. Liberal democratic nation states are averse to recognising stateless nations in their midst because of the fear of secession and disintegration of the existing state. There is here

36 On this point, *see* the seminal monograph by M. Mann, *The Dark Side of Democracy: Explaining Ethnic Cleansing* (Cambridge University Press, Cambridge, 2005). Itamar Magid explains in a review that Mann sheds light on democracy's more nefarious aspects by exemplifying the horrific consequences of an ethnic majority tyrannising ethnic minorities by majoritarian means. *See* 'Review', 2 *Amsterdam Law Forum* (2010), at http://amsterdamlawforum.org/article/view/150/296.

37 E. Gellner, *supra* note 26, p. 2.

38 E. Gellner defines nationalism as "primarily a political principle that holds that the political and the national unit should be congruent". *Ibid.*, p. 1. There is no space for nationalisms not wishing to construct a political unit.

a process of securitisation taking place.[39] As it is not possible for all nations to have their own state without infringing the territorial space of others, to put it colloquially, in this world of ours, there are insufficient pieces of real estate to satisfy demands from every nation to have their own territorial nation state. Established nation states fear that any concession to stateless nations is opening a Pandora's box that leads to disintegration and secession, and tend to see minority nations demands as infringing state security. We shall see below how this syndrome plays out in the Spanish state.

But there is a second significant dimension to the liberal democratic nation state aversion of stateless minority nationalisms which is important when discussing the Spanish state. As mentioned earlier, the principle of mechanical equality between citizens, understood as sameness, clashes with social plurality and the democratic need of minorities to be recognised in their specific difference to the majority community. This conflation of equality with sameness leads to the development of egalitarian citizenship laws in which citizens enjoy equal rights through a common culture, usually the culture of the dominant nation. The institutions of the state declare that the state should be 'of and for' the nation. In law and state administration, the dominant nation's language becomes the official language. The religion of the nation is privileged even in secular societies – consider Christmas – and the culture of the dominant nation is privileged in state symbols such as the flag and national anthem. Furthermore, broadcasting and educational outlets emphasise the culture of the dominant nation. Yet this is done while democratic policies in the state-making process highlight a broad and inclusive citizenship that provide equal individual rights to all.[40] All individuals are equal under the culture of the dominant nation, but minority nations tend not to have collective representation. Here the minorities' accusations of hypocrisy are difficult to refute.

The motivation for the liberal democratic nation state structured above comes from the two most important sources of contemporary liberal democracy. The French Revolution, Abbé Sieyès and the Jacobins, on the one hand, and John Stuart Mill, the founding father of Anglo-liberalism, on the other.

---

39 Securitisation is the process of states transforming certain types of subjects (usually members of a minority) into matters 'endangering state security' (minority nationalisms for example). This results in exceptional means to be used in dealing with them in the name of security. *See* B. Buzan, O. Wæver and J. de Wilde, *Security: A New Framework for Analysis* (Lynne Rienner Publishers, Boulder, 1998).

40 J.J. Linz and A. Stepan, 'Toward Consolidated Democracies', 7 *Journal of Democracy* (1996) pp. 22–23.

In *What Is the Third Estate?* (*Qu'est-ce que le Tiers-État?*), a political pamphlet written shortly before the French Revolution, Abbé Emmanuel Sieyès, a clergyman that was on the side of the revolution, argues vehemently for the elimination of the nobility and the church from the body of the French nation. The Third Estate, he says, the common people of France, are the complete nation. This political pamphlet had an immense impact on the revolution, and shaped the attitude of the radical section of the revolutionaries, the Jacobins, towards the non-French-speaking population in France. The goal of the revolutionaries was to transfer the sovereignty of the French State from the Monarch flesh and bones, to the collective French nation, and Sieyès responded to the question what is the Third Estate?, by saying that the Third Estate was the nation, and the nation was the new sovereign. Crucially here Sieyès conflates the principle of democratic representation in the state, with the body corporate it represents, the nation. But the nation is simultaneously a cultural community. And this cultural community replaces the sovereign flesh and bones with a cultural collective.[41]

To put the argument in contemporary terms, Sieyès was the first to conflate ethnos with demos. The *demoi* is the sovereign and *ethnie* is the nation, the cultural community that sustains the unity of the demos. The aim is to invoke the power of the nation to build a democratic society based on a common culture. It is at this point that the principle of conflating equality with sameness emerges, and the invitation to minority cultures to assimilate 'with democracy as compensation'. Also, it is here that the origin of the democratic deficit of liberal democracy can be found: the reduction of participation and belonging to the body politic to belonging to a given egalitarian political culture. The Jacobins implemented this policy with enthusiasm, and ruthlessly campaigned to assimilate all cultural minorities to the nation of the citizens.[42]

---

41 G. Noiriel, 'Socio-histoire d'un concept. Les usages du mot "nationalité" au XIXe siècle', 20 *Genèses* (1995) pp. 4–23.

42 Henri Grégoire was the author of the famous report to the French National Assembly 'On the necessity and the means of annihilating the patois and of universalising the use of the French language' (*Rapport sur la nécessité et les moyens d'anéantir les patois et d'universaliser l'usage de la langue française*) which asserted, inter alia, "it is possible to unify the language of a great nation. This undertaking, which has not been fully executed by any people, is worthy of the French people, who centralize all branches of social organization and who must be jealous of consecrating, as soon as possible, a single and indivisible Republic with the unique and invariable use of the language of liberty" (*On peut uniformer le langage d'une grande nation ... Cette entreprise qui ne fut*

A surprisingly similar argument came from the English-speaking world. John Stuart Mill was an English political philosopher, and perhaps the most influential thinker in the history of liberalism. His work exerted a long lasting influence on the development of liberalism in the English language. In one of his most important and influential works, *Considerations on Representative Government*, first published in 1861, on the section "On Representative Government", he writes:

> Free institutions are next to impossible in a country made up of different nationalities. Among a people without fellow-feeling, especially if they read and speak different languages, the united public opinion, necessary to the working of representative government, cannot exist.[43]

The democratic deficit in the representation of national and ethnic minorities has been present, as indicated above, since the creation of the liberal democratic nation state. It results in part from the conflation of ethnos with demos and in part from the mechanical equality of citizens in liberal democratic nation states whose cultural and ethnic plurality stands at odds with the institutional symbiotic relation between nation and state. As liberal democracies have few if any mechanisms available to ameliorate this situation, national minorities become alienated from the central state, and appeal to the only remedy on hand: secession and the creation of a new nation state, one that is likely to reproduce the same situation with regards to other minorities. In the contemporary world, national and ethnic communities live in an unavoidable plural embrace and the search for a culturally homogeneous territory is futile. The problem will be now exemplified in the case of the Spanish State.

However, the problem is not beyond resolution. It could be resolved if liberal democratic nation states become plurinational states that allow for the representation of their citizens and constituent communities.

---

pleinement exécutée chez aucun peuple, est digne du peuple français, qui centralise toutes les branches de l'organisation sociale et qui doit être jaloux de consacrer au plus tôt, dans une République une et indivisible, l'usage unique et invariable de la langue de la liberté). https://fr.wikisource.org/wiki/Rapport_sur_la_n%C3%A9cessit%C3%A9_et_les_moyens_d%E2%80%99an%C3%A9antir_les_patois_et_d%E2%80%99universaliser_l%E2%80%99usage_de_la_langue_fran%C3%A7aise

43 J.S. Mill, *Considerations on Representative Government* (Cosimo Classics, New York, 1861/2008) p. 230. There are many other versions and editions.

4 From Nation States to Plurinational States

The liberal democratic nation state is ceasing to exist in empirical terms, while the officialdom of most liberal democracies continues to hang on to the theory of this unviable idea. It is also likely that the idea of one nation in one state was an illusion since its inception. As liberal democracy was forged in the furnace of the nation state, it remains in a symbiotic relation to it without realising that the value of the nation state is seriously challenged by the real plurality of nations that demand self-determination. To some extent, the problem is not with liberal democracy itself, but with the original individualist dimension of nineteen century liberalism, and, the anomaly of plurinational states that call themselves nation states. If this is the case, it might be possible to adapt liberal democracy together with collective rights, to a liberal democratic model in a plurinational state. For this to happen, liberal democracy must thus accept the collective representation of national minorities.

The limitations of the nation state and the impossibility of creating states for every nation is finally giving way towards a change of thinking in the direction of a more pluralist and multidimensional understanding of the relationship between nationalism and democratic governance. This occurs in settings that encourage multiple jurisdictions. This leads to a shift from nation states to plurinational states. These are states with several nations: nationalist movements no longer need to aim to the creation of separate states.

These new theoretical insights advocate, in a vast display of empirical and comparative cases, a system of governance based on the participation of several democratically organised, ethno-national communities with multiple jurisdictions. Here the governmental process is not of discrete, centralised, homogenous units, as in the old nation state model, but one in which governance is understood as a multilayered and multicultural mechanism. The shift responds to the need to break with the oppressive governance of cultural minorities and the need to find ways to provide national minorities with equal rights, governance, and political participation – without dismembering existing states, but transforming them from nation states into plurinational states.

What follows will schematically show a few of these models.

4.1 *Demoicracy*

This is a promising new development in Political Theory and European Studies. Demoicracy (plural of democracy) is a polity of multiple distinct peoples (*demoi*), a polity of polities. It was designed to become an alternative to democracy, understood as power of a single *demos*. While liberal democracy always understands democracy as a mechanism tailored to a single demos, demoicracy refers to a plurality of demos (demoi) and therefore incorporates mechanisms for collective representation. If applied to a multination state, it creates the conditions for the representation of different national minorities without dismembering an existing state. The theoretical discussion of demoicracy and its application to the international arena is advanced in the important work of James Bohman,[44] and its application to Europe is developed by Francis Cheneval and Kalypso Nicolaïdis.

Francis Cheneval argues that the EU is a commonwealth of demoi and not a single democracy. For this reason, he argues that it is a mistake to analyse the European Union and its democratic deficit from a nation state perspective. From here, any normative assessment of democracy in the European Union should start from the premise that it is an organisation with multiple demoi and not a nation state. For Cheneval, the EU is a demoicracy, not a democracy.[45]

Kalypso Nicolaïdis follows a similar line of reasoning. She defines 'demoicracy' as a union of peoples, understood as a plurality of states and citizens, which govern together, but not as one; and like Cheneval, she argues that the concept of a multinational demoi encapsulates better the specificity of the EU. She further suggests that the concept of 'demoicracy' can serve both as an analytical lens for the European Union and as its normative benchmark. Consequently, she argues, the normative discussion should follow different lines of argumentation to those used to evaluate democracy in nation states.[46]

4.2 *National Cultural Autonomy*

The principle of National Cultural Autonomy (NCA) was developed by Otto Bauer and Karl Renner, twice president of Austria. The idea was to organise the geographically divided members of the same nation on a non-territorial

44 J. Bohman, *Democracy Across Borders: From Demos to Demoi* (MIT Press, Cambridge, Mass., 2007), and 'From Demos to Demoi: Democracy Across Borders', 18 *Ratio Juris* (2005) pp. 293–314.

45 F. Cheneval and F. Schimmelfenning, 'The Case for Demoicracy in the EU', *Paper prepared for EUSA Conference Boston, March 2011* at https://www1.ethz.ch/eup/people/schimmelfennig/publications/Demoicracy_Cheneval_Schimmelfennig_Boston_2011.pdf; F. Cheneval, S. Lavenex and F. Schimmelfennig, *European Democracy as Demoicracy* (Routledge, London, 2015).

46 K. Nicolaïdis, (2012) 'The Idea of European Demoicracy', in J. Dickson and P. Eleftheriadis (eds.), *Philosophical Foundations of European Union Law* (Oxford University Press, Oxford, 2012), at http://kalypsonicolaidis.com/wp-content/uploads/2015/02/2013_TheIdeaofDemoicracy.pdf.

basis, that is "to organize nations not as territorial bodies but as association of persons", thus separating nation from territory and making the nation a non-territorial association.[47]

This principle was later adopted by various socialist organisations, the Jewish Socialist Party from its foundation in 1906, the Jewish Labour Bund, the Armenian social democrats, the Russian Constitutional Democratic Party (Kadets) and the Salonica Greek Socialist Workers' Federation. The left-wing Zionists that favoured a binational solution in Palestine, the founding father of the academic study of nationalism, Hans Kohn, argued in the late 1920's for a binational state in Palestine based on a national cultural autonomy model, the Jewish Folkspartei, and the Democratic Union of Hungarians in Romania (DAHR) after 1989. It was also adopted as an official policy in the short-lived Ukrainian People's Republic (1917–1920), in the interwar Estonian Republic, and more recently by the Russian Duma in 1988. These are just a few examples; there are many others, such as legislation in Estonia and Hungary.

5 The Case of Spain

The Spanish case illustrates two different things. Firstly, it shows that the nation state gives rise to a democratic deficit which results in the misrepresentation of national minorities. The democratic deficit is caused by the 'colour-blind' character of the institutions of plural societies with a variety of ethno-national communities in their midst. Secondly, the Spanish case also highlights that misrepresented minorities tend to opt for secession when the central authorities do not offer them any other option. This course of action may end up in the disintegration of the state.

The analysis is divided into three parts. In the first section, the democratic deficit of the model of territorial organisation in Spain will be explained. The second section will be focused on the way in which the Spanish authorities are tackling Catalan demands of self-determination and how their centralist policy

47 For a discussion of the National Cultural Autonomy model, *see* E. Nimni, 'The Conceptual Challenge of Non-Territorial Autonomy' (2013), in E. Nimni, A. Osipov and D.J. Smith (eds.), *The Challenge of Non-Territorial Autonomy Theory and Practice* (Peter Lang, Bern, 2013) p. 1; 'National Cultural Autonomy as an Alternative to Minority Nationalism', 3 *Ethnopolitics* (2007), p. 354; also published in D. Smith and K. Cordell (eds.), *Cultural Autonomy in Contemporary Europe* (Routledge, London, 2008) p. 9; and 'Nationalist Multiculturalism in Late Imperial Austria as a Critique of Contemporary Liberalism: The Case of Bauer and Renner', 4 *Journal of Political Ideologies* (1999) p. 289.

fuels independence support. In the third section, a model of plurinational democracy will be proposed as an alternative to secession.

5.1 *Territorial Organisation in Spain*

Any observer wanting to know how Spain is nationally organised should read the Constitution and the interpretation given by the Constitutional Court to its provisions. Regarding the Constitution,[48] Articles 2 and 1.2 are of crucial importance to understand the territorial structure of Spain. Article 2 establishes:

> The Constitution is based on the indissoluble unity of the Spanish Nation,[49] the common and indivisible homeland of all Spaniards; it recognises and guarantees the right to self-government of the nationalities and regions of which it is composed and the solidarity among them all.

Article 2 must be read together with Article 1.2, which states: "National sovereignty belongs to the Spanish people, from whom all state powers emanate".

In accordance with the 1978 Constitution, Spain is a nation state. Constitutionally, there is only one official nation, the Spanish nation, and such nation cannot be divided. Even more, the indissoluble unity of this nation is the basis of the Constitution. The Spanish nation is sovereign, and therefore, entitled to a right of self-determination.

Alongside the Spanish nation, there are also nationalities and regions. Although the Constitution does not explain what territorial entities are included in each of these two categories, the use of the term 'nationality' to refer to Catalonia and the Basque Country is widely accepted. For the Constitution, nationalities are not nations;[50] thus, they lack sovereignty

48 Spanish Constitution, passed by the Cortes Generales in Plenary sittings of the Congress and the Senate held on 31 October 1978; ratified by referendum of the Spanish people on 6 December 1978; and sanctioned by His Majesty the King before the Cortes Generales on 27 December 1978. English version available at https://www.constituteproject.org/constitution/Spain_2011.pdf.

49 It is interesting to note that in the Constitution the term 'Spanish Nation' is written in capitals. This wording aims to stress that this nation enjoys supremacy over peripheral nations, which the Constitution calls 'nationalities.'

50 During the constitutional debates, two visions were confronted regarding the national question. On the one hand, some Parliamentarians held that the terms 'nation' and 'nationality' were synonymous. Two different strategies were used to defend this position. First, members of Alianza Popular (a political party later renamed Partido Popular), argued for the deletion of the term 'nationality' as a form of preserving national unity. Second, Catalan and Basque nationalist parties suggested avoiding any reference to the

and, instead of a right to self-determination, a right to autonomy is conferred on them.[51]

The Constitutional Court, the supreme interpreter of the Constitution, offers a particularly strict exegesis on national matters which narrows even more the range of options nationalities have. According to its case law, nationalities are not entitled to call a referendum[52] since this is a reserved matter included in Article 149.1, 32nd of the Constitution.[53] Even a non-binding referendum needs to be authorised by the Congress of Deputies, as established in Article 92:

1. Political decisions of special importance may be submitted to all citizens in a consultative referendum.
2. The referendum shall be called by the King on the President of the Government's proposal after previous authorisation by the Congress.

Spanish nation in order to leave room for the self-determination of peripheral nations. On the other hand, the majority of the House (The Union of the Democratic Centre –UCD–, The Spanish Socialist Workers' Party –PSOE–, the Spanish Communist Party –PCE– and the Catalan Minority –right-wing nationalists–) wanted to make the unity of the Spanish nation and the existence of peripheral nations within the same territory compatible. For doing this, it was necessary to confer a divergent essence on both political communities (the Spanish and peripheral nations), and employing different names for referring to each of them (nation *vs.* nationalities) could help. If nations are sovereign by definition, there cannot be more than one within the same territory. The solution was found in Hegelian distinction between 'nation' and 'people.' According to Hegel, a nation possesses a political essence and is sovereign, whereas a people has a cultural nature and, consequently, is deprived of sovereignty. When this theory was applied to Spain, it was said that the Spanish nation was a political entity with sovereign features, while nationalities were cultural entities (peoples, in the Hegelian sense) and, as such, they lacked sovereign attributes. For a detailed explanation of the influence of Hegel on the Spanish Constitution, *see* X. Bastida, *La nación española y el nacionalismo constitucional* (Ariel, Barcelona, 1998); *Miseria de la autonomía. Una filosofía del Estado autonómico* (Universidad de Oviedo, Oviedo, 1999).

51 The right to 'self-government' that Article 2 confers on nationalities and regions means autonomy. The right to autonomy implies that Autonomous Communities can exercise legislative and executive powers within the framework of the Constitution. However, autonomy does not entail sovereignty; thus, the unity of the Spanish Nation is not call into question.

52 Constitutional Court Judgment (CCJ) 103/2008, 11 September 2008, Legal Basis 2. In this judgment, the Act 9/2008, 27 June 2008, of the Basque Parliament convening and regulating a popular consultation for the purpose of ascertaining public opinion in the Autonomous Community of the Basque Country on commencing negotiations for achieving peace and political normalisation was repealed.

53 Article 149.1, 32nd reads: "The state shall have exclusive competence over (...) [the] authorisation of popular consultations through the holding of referendums."

3. An organic act[54] shall lay down the terms and procedures for the different kinds of referendum provided for in this Constitution.

The state could transfer the power to call a referendum to the Parliament of an Autonomous Community under the terms of Article 150.2 of the Constitution:

> The state may transfer or delegate to the Self-governing Communities, through an organic act, some of its powers which by their very nature can be transferred or delegated.

However, the Constitutional Court has clarified that the decision on whether or not an Autonomous Community wants to be integrated within the state directly affects the basis of the constitutional order as contained in Article 2. Since the relationship between the state and the Autonomous Communities is unilaterally established by the will of the state, the only referendum which can be held on this issue is the one established in Article 168. Article 168 contains one of the procedures for constitutional amendment, the more rigid one.[55] Among all the requirements which should be met to carry out the reform, is that a referendum must approve the proposed constitutional amendment. In this consultation the whole of the Spanish people is entitled to vote:[56]

1. If a total revision of the Constitution is proposed, or a partial revision affecting the Preliminary Part, Chapter II, Division 1 of Part I; or Part II, the proposed reform shall be approved by a two-thirds majority of

---

54 According to Article 81 of the Constitution, "1. Organic acts are those relating to the implementation of fundamental rights and public liberties, those approving the Statutes of Autonomy and the general electoral system and other laws provided for in the Constitution. 2. The approval, amendment or repeal of organic acts shall require the overall majority of the Members of Congress in a final vote on the bill as a whole."
Therefore, differences between organic and ordinary acts lie in their content (some matters are reserved for an organic act), but also in their formal procedure of approval.

55 The Spanish Constitution contains two different mechanisms of reform, namely those included in Articles 167 and 168. The use of each one depends on the issue subject to amendment. Any reform affecting the territorial organisation of the state must comply with the requirements established in Article 168. The procedure is so strict that has never been used, and will predictably remain untouched. As its proponents meant, far from being a mechanism of reform, Article 168 actually prevents constitutional amendment. *See* P. de Vega, *La reforma constitucionaly la problemática del poder constituyente* (Tecnos, Madrid, 1985).

56 CCJ 103/2008, 11 September 2008, Legal Basis 4.

the members of each House, and the Cortes Generales [the Spanish Parliament] shall be immediately dissolved.

2. The Houses elected thereupon must ratify the decision and proceed to examine the new constitutional text, which must be passed by a two-thirds majority of the members of each House.
3. Once the amendment has been passed by the Cortes Generales, it shall be submitted to ratification by referendum.

Even a non-binding referendum in which the citizens of a particular territory were called upon to vote only over the relationship between their Autonomous Community and the state is forbidden.[57]

At this point it is interesting to note that there was a slight (and brief) change in the case law of the Constitutional Court in 2014. The judgment 42/2014 that declared the Resolution 5/X adopting the Declaration of sovereignty and of the right to decide of the people of Catalonia[58] partially unconstitutional acknowledged the possibility of understanding the right to decide as something different from the right to self-determination. Construed in this sense:

> 'The right to decide held by the citizens of Catalonia' is not proclaimed as a manifestation of a right of self-determination not recognised in the Constitution, or as an unrecognised attribution of sovereignty, but as a political aspiration that may only be achieved through a process that conforms to constitutional legality and follows the principles of 'democratic legitimacy,' 'pluralism' and 'legality,' expressly proclaimed in the Declaration in close connection to the 'right to decide.'[59]

The exercise of such a right to decide would be two-fold:[60] in a first phase, the proposal of reforming the territorial order would be formulated, whereas at a later stage, the reform would be implemented. In order for this to occur, constitutional amendment would be required.[61] Therefore, in its judgment 42/2014,

57 *Ibid.*

58 Resolution 5/X adopting the Declaration of sovereignty and of the right to decide of the people of Catalonia, issued by the Catalan Parliament on 23 January 2013.

59 CCJ 42/2014, 25 March 2014, Legal Basis 3. In this judgment the Court declared the Declaration of sovereignty and of the right to decide of the people of Catalonia partially unconstitutional.

60 M. Barceló, 'Reconocimiento y construcción del derecho a decidir en el sistema constitucional español,' in M. Barceló *et al.*, *El derecho a decidir. Teoría y práctica de un nuevo derecho* (Atelier, Barcelona, 2015) p. 104.

61 CCJ 42/2014, *supra* note 59, Legal Basis 4c.

the Constitutional Court recognised that the capacity to call an independence referendum falls within the state's remit,[62] and also that before starting the process of constitutional amendment, a referendum or other kind of non-binding consultation in which only the citizens of a particular Autonomous Community would vote can be held.[63]

Nonetheless, in its subsequent case law the Constitutional Court modified this line of argument, coming back to the criterion stated in 2008.[64] This course of action has a far-reaching impact, the consequences of which, largely unforeseen, may end up being detrimental to the purpose of keeping Spain together. Two main reasons can explain this position. First, the Constitutional Court states that the only referendum which can be held to change the territorial order is the referendum established in Article 168 for constitutional amendment. This means that, according to the Court, not even the Spanish government is authorised to call an independence referendum unless constitutional reform is initiated. The result of maintaining this argument is quite serious, since the Constitutional Court is deactivating the institution of consultative referendum established by the Constitution (Article 92) and the power to call referenda (Article 149.1, 32nd).

---

62 *Ibid.*, Legal Basis 3.

63 J. Ridao, 'La juridificación del derecho a decidir en España. La STC 42/2014 y el derecho a aspirar a un proceso de cambio político del orden constitucional', 91 *UNED. Revista de Derecho Político* (2014) p. 96; J.M. Castellà, 'Derecho a decidir, secesión y formas de democracia. Un diálogo constitucional entre Italia y España', in L. Cappuccio and M. Corretja (eds.), *El derecho a decidir. Un diálogo ítalo-catalán* (Institut d'Estudis Autonòmics, Barcelona, 2014) p. 48; M. Corretja, 'El derecho a decidir en clave económica', in L. Cappuccio and M. Corretja (eds.), *El derecho a decidir. Un diálogo ítalo-catalán* (Institut d'Estudis Autonòmics, Barcelona, 2014) p. 191.

64 CCJ 31/2015, 25 February 2015, Legal Basis 6b; CCJ 138/2015, 11 June 2015, Legal Basis 3a.
The first judgment declared unconstitutional most provisions of the Act of the Parliament of Catalonia 10/2014, 26 September 2014, on non-referendum popular consultations and other forms of citizen participation. This Act was passed with the aim of legally support the call of an independence referendum on 9 November 2014 (9N). The central government brought the norm before the Constitutional Court and the challenge suspended its operation. Finally, Catalans voted on 9N, but the initially planned referendum was changed for a 'citizen participation process,' which lacked the legal guarantees of a plebiscite. For an analysis of 9N, *see* L. Payero, 'The "citizen participation process" in Catalonia: past, present and future,' 36(3) *Liverpool Law Review* (2015) pp. 237–242.
The second judgment declared unconstitutional the actions carried out by the Catalan government to call the 'citizen participation process' on 9N.

Second, by adopting this position the Constitutional Court has reduced the possibilities of nationalities to legally change the territorial organisation of the state to just one: constitutional reform through the mechanism established in Article 168. This basically means that nationalities will be able to decide on national matters only if they use factual channels, since Autonomous Communities do not take part in the process of constitutional amendment. Existing constitutional procedures then render any exercise of self-determination impossible. The path currently followed by Catalonia in order to implement the right to decide seems to inexorably lead to the disobedience of the Spanish law and, consequently, to an abrupt break-up of the relationship with Spain: the central government flatly refused to negotiate with the Catalan authorities, the Congress of Deputies did not allow the Catalan Parliament to call a non-binding independence referendum, and the Constitutional Court systematically rules against any legal initiative adopted by Catalonia.

5.2 *Dealing with Catalan Demands of Self-determination*

From a legal point of view, it could be said that the Constitution favours Spanish nationalism over any other, leaving a narrow scope for the self-determination of nationalities. In addition to this, the Constitutional Court interprets the territorial Constitution in a very restrictive sense. Indeed, the Court is playing a strong activist role in defending national unity.[65] Its recent case law represents a powerful tool in the development of the current centripetal policy carried

65 This poses a major problem, since the Constitutional Court is competent to solve "conflicts of jurisdiction between the state and the Autonomous Communities" (Article 161.1c of the Constitution). However, as many scholars have pointed out, the Court is a non-neutral referee when it comes to deciding on national matters. Among others, *see* J. Bengoetxea, 'Seven theses on Spanish justice to understand the prosecution of judge Garzón,' 1 *Oñati Socio-Legal Series* (2011) pp. 3–4; J. Pérez-Royo, 'Avería grave,' *El País*, 13 November 2012, at http://politica.elpais.com/politica/2012/11/13/actualidad/1352832544_039639.html; A. Buchanan, 'Prólogo a la edición española. ¿ Tiene Cataluña derecho a la secesión?,' in *Secesión. Causas y consecuencias del divorcio político* (Ariel, Barcelona, 2013) p. 20; J. Cagiao, 'El federalismo ante la consulta catalana. Una lectura federal del derecho a decidir,' in J. Cagiao and V. Martin (dirs.), *Federalismo, autonomía y secesión en el debate territorial español. El caso catalán* (Le Manuscrit, Paris, 2015) p. 90. The bias of the Court is even more salient due to the fact that its composition does not reflect territorial plurality: four of the twelve members of the Constitutional Court are nominated by the Congress, another four by the Senate, two by the Government and the remaining two by the Council of the Judicial Power (Article 159.1 of the Constitution). Whereas the first three are state organs, the last one is as much politicised as the Constitutional Court itself.

out by central Spain against peripheral nations.[66] Aware of this fact, the Spanish government employs the legal argument to reject nationalities' demands of wider self-government.[67] Catalonia, the Basque Country and any other Autonomous Community are not entitled to decide on national matters because the Constitution does not permit it in accordance with the interpretation provided by the Constitutional Court. There is no need of reaching a compromise, since the government cannot dispose of issues which fall within the remit of the Spanish people as a whole.[68]

Nonetheless, "the (...) law often has limited purchase, particularly when dealing with broader political upheaval".[69] That is why "where there is a political will, there is a legal way".[70] The main problem in Spain is that political will to solve the national question is lacking. It is not only the People's Party (PP) that rejects the right to decide of Catalonia with the weak argument that the Constitution bans it; the Spanish Socialist Workers' Party (PSOE) and Citizens Party (C's) are also against it. Let us illustrate this assertion with two instances.

---

66 The term 'peripheral' refers to the geographical location of these nations: the Basque Country and Catalonia lay, respectively, to the north and east north of Spain, whereas Madrid, the capital, is situated in the centre of Spain.

67 The use of the legal argument by the Spanish government has been criticised in L. Payero, '¿ Por qué Cataluña no puede autodeterminarse? Las razones del Estado español,' in J. Cagiao and G. Ferraiuolo (coords.), *El encaje constitucional del derecho a decidir. Un enfoque polémico* (Los Libros de la Catarata, Madrid, 2016) pp. 193–208.

68 The central government sometimes combines legal reasoning with an appeal to some pre-positivists foundations of the Constitution. A good example of this strategy is illustrated by the statement of the previous Home Secretary, Jorge Fernández-Díaz (PP), who after saying that "no legal referendum will be agreed with the government of Mariano Rajoy or any other because the Constitution forbids it," added that the reform of the Constitution would not be enough to hold the consultation; rather a new Constitution with an alternative foundation would need to be elaborated, as the current one is based on the "indissoluble unity of the Spanish Nation." *See* 'Fernández Díaz dice al Círculo de Economía que "no habrá referéndum pactado" porque la Constitución lo impide,' *Europa Press*, 17 September 2015, at http://www.europapress.es/sociedad/sucesos-00649/noticia-fernandez-diaz-dice-circulo-economia-no-habra-referendum-pactado-porque-constitucion-impide-20150917111727.html.

69 N. Torbisco and N. Krisch, 'Using Spanish law to block Catalonia's independence consultation may simply encourage Catalans to construct their own "alternative legality,"' *Blog LSE*, 4 November 2014, at http://blogs.lse.ac.uk/europpblog/2014/11/04/using-spanish-law-to-block-catalonias-independence-consultation-may-simply-encourage-catalans-to-construct-their-own-alternative-legality/.

70 K. Nicolaïdis, 'Scotland and the EU: Comment,' *Verfassungsblog*, 9 September 2014, at http://www.verfassungsblog.de/en/scotland-eu-comment-kalypso-nicolaidis/.

The first example revolves around the recognition of the right to decide, included in the political programme of Podemos for the 2015 general election.[71] One of the thorniest issues during the negotiations among the PSOE, C's and Podemos to form the government in early 2016 was the acceptance of the right to decide by the first two political formations. In April 2016, Podemos penned a document with twenty points containing the basic issues on which agreement was necessary to create an alternative government to Mariano Rajoy's. Point 19 included the right to decide.[72] Aware of the difficulty of making a compromise on the reformulation of the territorial structure, and taking into consideration that the voice of the territories was essential, Podemos accepted to change the composition of the negotiation table: instead of being made up of PSOE, Podemos and C's, this table would be comprised of representatives from En Comú Podem and the Socialists' Party of Catalonia (PSC), the brands of PSOE and Podemos in Catalonia.[73] In the end, no agreement was signed and a new general election was held on 26 June 2016.

The second example relates to the holding of an independence referendum in Catalonia, similar to those held in Quebec and Scotland. In the previous term of office (2011–2015), with a conservative majority in Madrid, the Catalan Parliament requested of the Congress of Deputies that the power to call a referendum be transferred to it. Although the Constitution allows it,[74] most deputies in the Congress rejected the proposal. Members of the PP,

71 Podemos proposed the constitutional recognition of the plurinational nature of Spain, the opening of a citizen debate on the recognition and forms of exercising the right to decide, and guaranteed that Autonomous government would be allowed to call popular consultations on the territorial organisation of the state. More specifically, Podemos undertook the organisation of a referendum in Catalonia. *See* 'Queremos, sabemos, podemos. Un programa para cambiar nuestro país,' *Political programme of Podemos for the general election held on 20 December 2015*, pp. 188–189, at https://lasonrisadeunpais.es/wp-content/plugins/programa/data/programa-es.pdf.

72 '20 propuestas para desbloquear la situación política y posibilitar un Gobierno del cambio,' at http://estaticos.elmundo.es/documentos/2016/04/07/20_propuestas_desbloquear_Podemos.pdf.

73 'Podemos plantea el derecho a decidir como condición para un pacto de investidura,' *Expansión*, 7 April 2016, at http://www.expansion.com/economia/politica/2016/04/07/57064b2d46163f0b248b4610.html.

74 Article 150 (2) reads: "The state may transfer of delegate to the Self-governing Communities, through an organic act, some of its powers which by their very nature can be transferred or delegated."

PSOE and Union Progress and Democracy (UPyD)[75] can be counted among the parliamentarians who voted against the motion.[76]

A side effect of this centralist policy is, paradoxically, a growing support for independence in Catalonia. Because of the flat refusal of the Spanish government to negotiate with the authorities of Catalonia, or even to hold a referendum on self-determination, and due to the case law of the Constitutional Court, one that interprets the Constitution very restrictively, an increasing number of Catalans are in favour of secession. The conclusion which can be drawn from this course of action is that maintaining a unitary conception of Spain proves unable to solve the national problem and can end up prompting the disintegration of the state. In fact, the reluctance showed by nation states to recognise national minorities in their midst due to the fear of disintegration produces exactly the effect they would try to avert. Lack of recognition fosters secessionism.

5.3 *A Plurinational Model of Democracy for Spain*

From a sociological point of view, Spain is a plural state where several nations coexist. This is something that even the Constitutional Court recognises.

> In view of the categorical meaning of Article 2 of the Constitution, the reference to the national reality of Catalonia (…) has no legal interpretive scope, even though out of the legal-constitutional context, there is room in a democratic order for the self-representation of a group as a national reality in an ideological, historical or cultural sense. It expresses a perfectly legitimate idea.[77]

---

75 UPyD was a political party with a history and programme quite similar to that of C's. Both parties were created with the aim of combatting peripheral nationalism and representing non-nationalists (that is, supporters of the Spanish nation) living in the Basque Country and Catalonia, respectively. However, they both obtained seats in the Spanish Parliament, although in different moments. In fact, the electoral success of C's coincided with the defeat (and practical disappearance) of UPyD.

76 *See* Journal of Debates of the Congress of Deputies, no 192, 8 April 2014.

77 CCJ 31/2010, 28 June 2010, Legal Basis 12. This judgment ruled out several articles of the Catalan Statute of Autonomy, passed by the Organic Act 6/2006, 19 July 2006, and became highly controversial in Catalonia. In fact, the ruling was interpreted as an attack on regional autonomy, since not only had it been passed by the Catalan and the Spanish Parliaments, but the people of Catalonia had endorsed the final text in a referendum. Four years after coming into force, the Constitutional Court overturned a number of articles of the Statute and stated the correct reading of many others. *See* L. Moreno's opinion, 'La independencia catalana en un Estado federal,' *La Voz de Galicia*, 5 January 2017 at http://www.lavozdegalicia.es/noticia/opinion/2017/01/05/independencia-catalana-espana-federal/0003_201701G5P15994

It seems logic that when reality is sociologically plural the legal-political answer given to it is equally plural. However, the Constitution is rigidly unitary. This causes a serious democratic deficit in the representation of minority nations at the central level. Indeed, both the Constitution (Article 2) and its official interpreter (CCJ 31/2010) conflate the notion of nation and that of state, in line with the Jacobin conception of the nation state: each state is only composed of a single nation, so the nation becomes indistinguishable from its state, and vice versa.

So what can be done to ameliorate this situation? At least three options are available for those policy-makers interested in soothing national tensions and enhancing the democratic quality of the Spanish State. Let us examine them.

1) In the short term, and without any legal reform, it would be possible to interpret the Constitution differently. For the particular case of the Catalan referendum, the Constitution does not forbid it:[78] the Catalan Parliament would have been able to call the consultation in 2014 providing the Congress of Deputies had transferred the power to do so. It is one thing for Catalans to be able to vote in a non-binding referendum on the inclusion of Catalonia within the rest of Spain, and quite another thing to argue that, according to the Constitution, the unity of Spain can only be called into question by means of a referendum where all Spaniards, not only Catalans, vote.[79] Both issues are not necessarily connected, despite the case law of the Constitutional Court and the mainstream academic literature on this topic. In the event that the referendum results favour secession, negotiations should start between Spanish and Catalan representatives, which may probably lead to constitutional reform. But a majority vote against independence

---

.htm. According to this author, the judgment broke with the territorial compact contained in the 1978 Constitution.

78 E. Vírgala, 'Algunas reflexiones jurídicas sobre la Ley de Consultas catalana,' *El Diario*, 19 September 2014, at http://www.eldiario.es/agendapublica/reforma-constitucional/reflexiones-juridicas-despues-septiembre_0_304820367.html; J. Cagiao, '¿ Es posible un referéndum de independencia en el actual ordenamiento jurídico español? El Derecho explicado en la prensa,' in J. Cagiao and G. Ferraiuolo (coords.), *El encaje constitucional del derecho a decidir. Un enfoque polémico* (Los Libros de la Catarata, Madrid, 2016) pp. 161–169.

79 The reason is that the deletion of the unity of Spain would entail the reform of Article 2 of the Constitution, so the use of the rigid mechanism of amendment is required. As has been explained (*supra* section 5.1), Article 168 establishes that the new constitutional text shall be ratified by referendum.

appears to be fairly likely, given the difficulty supporters of secession find to win a referendum in democratic contexts: uncertainty and fear help to keep the status quo.[80] Therefore, even under the assumption that the unity of the nation should be respected, an open-minded government, Parliament and Constitutional Court would arrive to an alternative solution which may satisfy Catalans.

2) In the medium term, an *ad hoc* solution that forces changes to the constitutional framework may be found. We use the term 'forces' because even in an ideal situation in which all political parties and the majority of the Spanish citizens agree on the amendment of the Constitution, the implementation of that reform would be too complex. Article 168 contains such stringent requirements that constitutional reform – although legally possible – becomes materially impossible. Far from being a mechanism of reform, Article 168 may be said to introduce a procedure to prevent any amendment.[81] Thus, a good deal of flexibility on the part of the political actors involved is required in order to circumvent the legal obstacle that Article 168 poses. Indeed, in case two-thirds of the members of each House decided to amend the Constitution, they would firstly agree on avoiding the use of Article 168. The *ad hoc* solution that we propose would entail the adoption of factual channels[82] so that the territorial organisation would be materially changed obviating both the constitutional ban on peripheral self-determination and the indivisible unity of the Spanish nation. It would be an illegal course of action, but in all likelihood, legitimate and sensible.

---

80 J. Cagiao, 'Tres reflexiones rápidas tras el No en el referéndum escocés,' *Publius & Brutus. Un blog para hablar de federalismo ... y otros temas*, 19 September 2014, at http://cartasfederalistas.blogspot.com.es/2014/09/tres-reflexiones-rapidas-tras-el-no-en.html.

81 In this sense, it is interesting to know the factual origin of the more rigid mechanism of constitutional reform. Article 168 was designed with the goal of preserving the monarchic regime, which had been de facto re-established by Franco. Instead of introducing explicit limits to the reform of certain constitutional matters, just like the Fundamental Laws of the Realm (constitutional norms which organised Spanish political powers during the dictatorship) did, a stringent procedure of amendment was passed. Intangibility clauses were excluded from the Constitution because constituents aimed to evade francoist references.

82 The term 'factual channels' refers to the exercise of self-determination on the fringes of legal proceedings. Given that constitutional reform by means of Article 168 is not viable, the use of factual channels may represent a suitable alternative to circumvent that legal obstacle.

Some scholars have suggested another option which, though not strictly illegal, can be included in this strategy.[83] On the basis of the literal wording of Article 168, which does not include itself among the protected provisions,[84] these academics propose a double constitutional reform by using the more lenient Article 167.[85] Firstly, Article 168 would be amended in order to exclude Article 2 from its scope; then, Article 2 would also be reformed in a self-determining sense.[86] This option does not meet serious objections, and in the case constitutional reform was undertaken political reasons would strongly justify recourse to this method. However, even if Article 167 was used, the final decision falls on the political and judicial institutions of Spain, such as the Cortes Generales, the Spanish people or the Constitutional Court. Thus the proposal of a

83 *See* J.L. Requejo-Pagés, *Las normas preconstitucionales y el mito del poder constituyente* (Centro de Estudios Políticos y Constitucionales, Madrid, 1998) pp. 107–108; F. Laporta, 'Las dos vías para la reforma de la Constitución,' 145 *Claves de Razón Práctica*, pp. 23; R. Punset, *La reforma de la Constitución. Aporías del cambio constitucional en el derecho español* (Universidad de Oviedo, Oviedo, 2012) p. 12; B. Clavero, 'La buena mala conciencia de la Constitución,' *El Diario*, 2 December 2015, at http://www.eldiario.es/contrapoder/buena_mala_conciencia_constitucional_6_458514167.html.

84 Matters subject to reform by means of Article 168 are fundamental rights and public liberties, the monarchy, the Preliminary Title, where both Article 1.2 and Article 2 are included, and a total revision of the Constitution.

85 Article 167 of the Constitution reads: "1. Bills on constitutional amendments must be approved by a majority of three-fifths of members of each House. If there is no agreement between the Houses, an effort to reach it shall be made by setting up a Joint Committee of an equal number of Deputies and Senators which shall submit a text to be voted on by the Congress and the Senate.
2. If approval is not obtained by means of the procedure outlined in the foregoing subsection, and provided that the text has been passed by the overall majority of the members of the Senate, the Congress may pass the amendment by a two-thirds vote in favour.
3. Once the amendment has been passed by the Cortes Generales, it shall be submitted to ratification by referendum, if so requested by one tenth of the members of either House within fifteen days after its passage".

86 'Self-determination' is a polysemic word which can adopt different meanings depending on the normative intention of the speaker. In some cases, self-determination is interpreted as synonymous of a certain type of autonomy, either territorial or non-territorial; in other cases, liberal democracy is understood as a sufficient condition for presupposing that the constituent parts of a plural state enjoy self-determination; in other contexts, self-determination comprises a variety of results freely decided by the members of the political entity to which this right is recognised, including the ability to secede. In the Spanish context, peripheral nations' demands fit better the latter concept of self-determination, *i.e.* secession should be an option to be discussed and voted on, but the people may decide differently (*e.g.* a federal arrangement could be agreed).

peripheral nation seeking to exercise a right to self-determination by means of Article 167 will be predictably voted down. Norman regards this situation as unjust, so he suggests the following:

> If a subunit wanted to secede because it found itself exploited or systematically outvoted in majoritarian decision-making – a condition that most theorists believe justifies secession – it would have to rely on the support of the very groups and institutions that had flouted its interests up to that point. A just secession clause would, presumably, make the will of the people in the subunit (...) a decisive condition for secession, or at least for the legitimacy of negotiations leading to secession.[87]

3) In the long term, the best option – at least from a scholarly point of view – would be the modification of the territorial Constitution on the basis that Spain is a plurinational state. The final aim would be to work out an agreement between socio-political and constitutional realities in order to reduce the democratic deficit. Some necessary changes would entail the suppression of any reference to the unity of the Spanish nation in Article 2 ("the Constitution is based on the indissoluble unity of the Spanish Nation, the common and indivisible homeland of all Spaniards"), which should be rewritten in a multinational sense. Possibilities range from the swap of the term 'nationality' for 'nation' to the use of the word 'nationality' exclusively.[88] Stress should be put on giving all the political communities in the midst of the state the same status and legal treatment. Modifications should also affect Article 1.2, which instead of "national sovereignty," should read "*popular* sovereignty belongs to the Spanish people." Here the expression

---

87 W. Norman, 'Secession and (Constitutional) Democracy,' in F. Requejo (ed.), *Democracy and National Pluralism* (Routledge, London, 2001) pp. 89–90.

88 The first draft of the Constitution, which was leaked to the press in November 1977, did not contain any reference to the Spanish nation. The original text read as follows: "The Constitution recognises and the Monarchy guarantees the right to self-government of the different nationalities and regions of which Spain is composed, the unity of the state and the solidarity among its peoples." It is important to remark upon the big difference that exists between the unity of the state, mentioned in the preliminary version of Article 2, and the unity of the nation, consecrated in the current Article 2. Whereas the recognition of the unity of the state is compatible with a plurality of nations, the unity of a unique nation prevents any competing nation from existing within the same state. For an explanation of how the modification of Article 2 took place, *see* J. Solé-Tura, *Nacionalidades y nacionalismos en España. Autonomías, federalismo y autodeterminación* (Alianza, Madrid, 1985).

> 'Spanish people' would mean 'the whole of the citizens of the Spanish State' rather than 'the Spanish nation.' Alternatively, and following the theory of demoicracy explained above, sovereignty could rest on a plurality of *demoi*, rather than on a single political body.

Once the previous changes have been carried out, two alternative strategies to deal with peripheral nations' demands of wider self-government can be adopted, depending on whether or not the right to self-determination is recognised.

In line with the first strategy, Spain is composed of several nations, but those nations are not entitled to self-determination. Sovereignty is vested in the citizens of the state as a whole. Nonetheless, if a clear majority of the inhabitants who are concentrated in a specific portion of the state territory (Catalonia, for instance) claims self-determination, the government should enter into negotiations with the representatives of the region. This duty derives, not from the minority nation's entitlement to a right to self-determination, but from the democratic principle, which requires that the government is consented by the governed. This is the opinion set by the Supreme Court of Canada in 1998.[89]

According to the second strategy, all the nations within the state are entitled to self-determination, not only the Spanish nation. Consequently, it would be necessary to establish a procedure to exercise that right, even before a concrete claim arises. The amendment to Article 2 proposed by Euskadiko Ezkerra during the constitutional debates represents a good example. The alternative text read as follows:

> The Constitution is based on the plurinationality of the Spanish State, the solidarity among its peoples, the right to autonomy of the regions of which it is composed, and the right to self-determination of those regions.[90]

A concordant Title VIII A was drafted, which developed the procedure to exercise the right to self-determination. However, the amendment was outvoted by the Parliament.

The solution of the national problem in Spain requires a change to the territorial Constitution and the adoption of a multinational conception of the state. If Spain is conceived of as a plural state, constitutional correctness could

---

89 *Reference re Secession of Quebec* [1998] 2 S.C.R. 217, at https://scc-csc.lexum.com/scc-csc/scc-csc/en/item/1643/index.do.

90 F. Letamendía, Journal of Debates of the Congress of Deputies, no 66, 12 May 1978, p. 2263.

not be used as a basis for failing to recognise citizens' will. As the Canadian Supreme Court stated, "the Constitution is not a straitjacket" that consecrates its content once and forever:

> Democratic institutions necessarily accommodate a continuous process of discussion and evolution which is reflected in the constitutional right of each participant in the federation to initiate constitutional change.[91]

That is how constitutions adapt to the historical evolution of society. Nevertheless, in Spain constitutional interpretation has turned the text into a legend, a curious phenomenon which has been called "constitutional fundamentalism".[92] Such strategy creates more problems than it is able to solve: in fact, extremely rigid constitutions render the institution of reform ineffective.

It is arguable which one of these two plural strategies (to pay attention to the democratic voice of the citizens, or to confer a right to self-determination on nationalities) is preferable. On the one hand, it may be argued that both political representatives and members of the Spanish nation, which are the majority of the Spanish population, will be more prone to accept the first option: *i.e.*, when a clear majority of the population living in a certain region expresses dissatisfaction with the existing territorial organisation, there is an obligation to enter into negotiations with the 'renegade' community, so that a new political arrangement is made. On the other hand, there is a solid theoretical basis for the second version of the plural argument:[93] the recognition of a right to self-determination for peripheral nations. This option is particularly attractive for minorities, since the emotive and positive connotations attached to the term 'right' would contribute to the general acceptance of self-determination, understood as a people's ability to decide the type of political relationship which should be maintained with the rest of the state. Should self-determination be introduced into the Constitution, citizens would get used to it and centralism would gradually lose supporters. This change in mind-set could be explained by the sanctifying power of law: Hegelian assertion that reality

91 *Reference re Secession of Quebec*, *supra* note 89, para. 150.

92 J.C. Velasco, 'Patriotismo constitucional y republicanismo,' 125 *Claves de Razón Práctica* (2002) p. 38.

93 L. Payero, 'El derecho de autodeterminación en España: breve explicación para extranjeros estupefactos y nacionales incautos,' 23 *Revista d'Estudis Autonòmics i Federals* (2016) pp. 46–79.

is rational could be paraphrased in the following sense: in Spain, legality – and, more specifically, the Constitution – is believed to be moral.[94]

Nevertheless, the constitutional recognition of the plural nature of Spain is an absolute necessity, and will serve as a starting point to solve the national question, reducing the democratic deficit of the state. Central authorities should become aware of the urgency of this issue, adopting political measures aimed to the implementation of a basic principle of democracy – that the government rests on the consent of the governed. Otherwise, the spectre of nationalism will continue to haunt Spain.

6 Conclusions

Liberal democratic states present a democratic deficit, the most significant manifestation of which concerns national and ethnic minorities. The misrepresentation of minorities occurs because liberal institutions are not sensitive to cultural plurality; rather, they are modelled on the pattern set by the national majority of the state. Yet, the liberal state declares itself to be neutral on cultural matters, and by means of the recognition of equal individual rights to all citizens, including members of minority groups, seeks to circumvent any democratic objection.

This is the case of Spain. In accordance with the Constitution, Spain is a nation state, whereas from a sociological perspective several nations coexist within its boundaries. Some of these national communities, especially Catalonia, claim a right to decide on their territorial integration with the rest of the state. However, the central authorities – the government, most members of Parliament, and the Constitutional Court – reject this vehemently. Arguments against Catalan demands range from legality (the Constitution prevents one peripheral nation from deciding on the territorial structure of the state) to pre-positivist impediments to constitutional reform. Negotiation and political flexibility are excluded from this reasoning in which democracy is conceived of as synonymous of honouring the Constitution adopted in 1978, regardless of its factual origin, its rigidity, or the evolution of the Spanish society after forty years. Any modification of the territorial

94 X. Bastida, 'La Constitución vertical. El constitucionalismo y la cuestión nacional,' in F. Quesada (ed.), *Pluralismo y ciudadanía* (Biblioteca Nueva, Madrid, 2003) pp. 257–283; L. Payero, 'El esencialismo constitucional: la Constitución española al servicio de la unidad nacional,' 6 *Oñati Socio-Legal Series* (2016) pp. 733–741.

Constitution should necessarily involve a state-wide referendum in which the national interests of the Spanish nation would be favoured.

As argued above, the solution to this problem requires the adoption of a plural conception of the state so that all the nations in its midst are constitutionally recognised and equally represented in the state institutions. In plural societies, the best antidote to disintegration is the recognition of minorities. The Spanish experience shows how the misrepresentation of national communities, far from averting the threat of secession, exponentially increases the risk of state fragmentation and support for independence among citizens.

PART II

Ethno-Cultural Diversity and the International Legal System

CHAPTER 4

Do Human Rights Have Anything to Say about Group Autonomy?

Gaetano Pentassuglia

1 Introduction: Bridging Self-Determination, Autonomy, and Human Rights

As recent secessionist crises rekindle international lawyers' traditional focus on external group disputes,[1] self-determination as an international human rights category arguably continues its transition from a mechanism used primarily to redistribute sovereign power amongst states to an entitlement driven by concerns for the adequacy of states' own legal orders.[2] The Supreme Court of Canada has gone as far as to argue that "[t]he recognized sources of international law establish that the right to self-determination of a people is normally fulfilled through internal self-determination – a people's pursuit of its political, economic, social and cultural development within the framework of an existing state".[3]

A typical way in which expert discourse addresses the issue of group autonomy in the context of 'internal' self-determination (as opposed to state-building claims) is through an investigation into whether a right to territorial autonomy

1 *See e.g.* Y. Shany, 'Does International Law Grant the People of Crimea and Donetsk a Right to Secede?' 21 *Brown Journal of World Affairs* (2014) p. 233; J. Vidmar, 'Crimea's Referendum and Secession: Why it Resembles Northern Cyprus More than Kosovo', at www.ejiltalk.org/crimeas-referendum-and-secession-why-it-resembles-northern-cyprus-more-than-kosovo.

2 The scholarly literature on the subject is immense. For a recent insightful account of the right to self-determination in international law, *see* P. Macklem, *The Sovereignty of Human Rights* (Oxford University Press, Oxford, 2015) pp. 163–184. For a classic treatment, *see* A. Cassese, *Self-Determination of Peoples: A Legal Reappraisal* (Cambridge University Press, Cambridge, 1995).

3 *Reference Re Secession of Quebec* [1998] 2 S.C.R. 217 (hereinafter: the *Reference* case). Tellingly, 'external' self-determination in the form of 'remedial secession' would be contingent upon the state failing to respect 'internal' self-determination; *ibid.*, paras. 134–135. For a similar thesis, *see* D. Raič, *Statehood and the Law of Self-Determination* (Kluwer Law International, Dordrecht, 2002) ch. 7.

 | DOI 10.1163/9789004328785_006

for a 'people' is (or ought to be) available under international law.[4] More broadly, attempts have been made at various junctures to characterise the right to self-determination as a right which accrues to a 'nation', whatever its internal or external implications.[5]

Aside from the pre- and post-World War I political notion of 'national' self-determination and its hybrid – largely implicit – legal articulations,[6] this line is not an entirely new one in modern international legal discourse. Writing in the late 1980s, Ian Brownlie, for instance, argued for a comprehensive approach to "the issue of self-determination, the treatment of minorities, and the status of indigenous populations" by noting that there existed a core set of rights and claims in this context that were "in principle the same", except that in his view, they required different ways of implementing them due the varied nature of the "facts" involved. Sub-state ethno-cultural groups such as national minorities and indigenous communities could thus be seen as 'peoples' entitled to some form of autonomy within the boundaries of the state.[7]

4 The focus here is exclusively on ethno-cultural groups, most notably national minorities and indigenous peoples. For recent illustrations from a range of narrower or broader perspectives, *see* T. Koivurova, 'Can Saami Transnational Indigenous Peoples Exercise Their Self-Determination in a World of Sovereign States?', in N. Bankes and T. Koivurova (eds.), *The Proposed Nordic Saami Convention: National and International Dimensions of Indigenous Property Rights* (Hart Publishing, Oxford, 2013) p. 105; E. Ruiz Vieytez, 'Réflexions sur la nature de l'autodétermination de la perspective des droits de l'homme', 3 *Les Cahiers du Centre de Recherche Interdisciplinaire sur la Diversité* (2012) p. 7.

5 *See e.g.* H. Moodrick-Even Khen, *National Identities and the Right to Self-Determination of Peoples* (Martinus Nijhoff Publishers, Leiden, 2016).

6 H. Hannum, *Autonomy, Sovereignty, and Self-Determination: The Accommodation of Conflicting Rights* (University of Pennsylvania Press, rev. edition, Philadelphia, 1996) pp. 35–36. For earlier articulations of the concept within Marxist socialist thought, *see* H. Davis (ed.), *The National Question: Selected Writings by Rosa Luxemburg* (Monthly Review Press, New York and London, 1976).

7 I. Brownlie, 'The Rights of Peoples in Modern International Law', in J. Crawford (ed.), *The Rights of Peoples* (Oxford University Press, Oxford, 1988) p. 1, at pp. 5–6, 16 (noting that the core meaning of self-determination lies in the "right of a community which has a distinct character to have this character reflected in the institutions of government under which it lives"). *See also* J. Crawford, 'The Right of Self-Determination in International Law: Its Development and Future', in P. Alston, *Peoples' Rights* (Oxford University Press, Oxford, 2001) p. 6, at pp. 64–65 (arguing that distinctions based on classes or of categories of groups such as minorities and indigenous groups "are imprecise at best", and that all these groups "can, depending on the circumstances, properly claim to be 'peoples'" for purposes of internal self-determination, though the effects of the recognition of that claim also depend on the circumstances).

This approach is seemingly consistent with the idea, first implicitly articulated in relation to dependent territories under the 1970 United Nations General Assembly Resolution 2625 (XXV), that autonomy could represent an alternative constitutional arrangement to be "freely determined" by the "people" concerned.[8] It also broadly chimes with various parallel standard-setting processes that have been promoted over the years in order to put a 'right to autonomy' on firmer legal grounds, whether or not in direct or explicit connection with self-determination.[9] However, experience shows that autonomy arguments based on 'peoplehood' or direct rights, while not entirely unsuccessful, are characteristically elusive, and at times plainly incorrect.[10] Crucially, they tend to obscure the complexities surrounding the question of autonomy from a legal and policy perspective.

There are at least three factors that complicate the autonomy debate. First, the relationship between self-determination and human rights – indeed, the role of self-determination as itself a human right – suggests that 'autonomy' is less a matter of unilateral, let alone 'inherent', right and more of an element of a wider puzzle involving the accommodation of individual and collective interests within the political community.[11] Secondly, research from the past several years convincingly shows that autonomy regimes can usefully take a variety of forms. Territorial autonomy in the sense of a grant of decision-making authority in a number of areas intended to benefit a sector of the population which is located within a geographically defined unit, may not be the only – or even the most desirable – solution in all

8 Declaration on Principles of International Law Concerning Friendly Relations and Co-operation among States in accordance with the Charter of the United Nations, GA Res. 2625, UN GAOR, 25th Sess., Supp. No. 28, UN Doc. A/8028 (1970). According to Hannum, mentioning "the emergence into any other political status" recognises "the potential for new inter- and intra-state relations", *supra* note 6, p. 41.

9 *See e.g.* Liechtenstein's UN proposal in the early 1990s for a 'post-colonial' view of self-determination based on a right to autonomy within the state (UN Doc. A/48/147 (1993)); or the Council of Europe Parliamentary Assembly's proposal for a right to autonomy for national minorities under a protocol to the European Convention on Human Rights through Recommendation 1201 (1993), Article 11. More recently, the United Nations General Assembly adopted the United Nations Declaration on the Rights of Indigenous Peoples which does articulate autonomy as a form of internal self-determination (Article 4).

10 As noted by Koskenniemi, 'national' self-determination has essentially buttressed the consolidation of the state system in international law rather than specific communal affiliations. M. Koskenniemi, 'National Self-Determination Today: Problems of Legal Theory and Practice', 43 *International and Comparative Law Quarterly* (1994) p. 241, at pp. 251–257.

11 *See e.g.* H. Hannum, *supra* note 6.

circumstances requiring group accommodation.[12] Territorial autonomy, just as non-territorial one (or a combination of both), is a means to an end, not an end in itself. Thirdly, and relatedly, such regimes require a proper understanding of the interests or purposes they are meant to protect or serve, and why the law – international human rights law, in our case – is or ought to become actively involved in it. Arguing that the claimant qualifies as a 'people' for purposes of internal self-determination or that territorially concentrated groups benefit (or ought to benefit) from a specific right to autonomy in international law do not advance our thinking very far. We need to understand "the interests behind demands based on supposedly timeless or historical or primordial rights" [13] in order to develop an approach that focuses on the legitimacy of claims and the reasons why the law should respond to those claims.

Against this backdrop, I intend to pursue a more complex line of reasoning by contending that autonomy may or may not be a matter of right; it may or may not involve territorial control; it may or may not benefit an entity recognised as a 'people' (let alone a 'nation'); and it may or may not be based on international law. I argue that, while there is a clear need for international human rights law to engage constructively with group claims to autonomy, there is much more to the story than free-standing rights, territorial exclusivity or distinct peoplehood (or nationhood, for that matter). For one thing, human rights discourse, particularly human rights instruments and adjudication, has increasingly challenged a strict distinction between the individual and the group in addressing ethno-cultural claims, to a point where legal protection has taken on multiple hybrid forms and opened up several lines of interpretation.[14] This, in turn,

12 Territorial autonomy has of course proved vitally important in several cases. The point here is that this chapter does not assume or endorse a particular definition of autonomy but works loosely within the wider spectrum of institutional possibilities identified in scholarly and public policy discourse, including hybrid forms of cultural autonomy and/or legal pluralism. For discussion, *see e.g.* T. Malloy and F. Palermo (eds.), *Minority Accommodation through Territorial and Non-Territorial Autonomy* (Oxford University Press, Oxford, 2015); M. Suksi, 'Functional Autonomy: The Case of Finland with Some Notes on the Basis of International Human Rights Law and Comparisons with Other Cases', 15 *International Journal on Minority and Group Rights* (2008) pp. 195–199; H. Quane, 'Legal Pluralism and International Human Rights Law: Inherently Incompatible, Mutually Reinforcing or Something in Between?', 33 *Oxford Journal of Legal Studies* (2013) p. 675.

13 H. Hannum, *supra* note 6, p. 503.

14 G. Pentassuglia, 'Ethnocultural Diversity and Human Rights: Legal Categories, Claims, and the Hybridity of Group Protection', VI *The Yearbook of Polar Law* (2015) p. 250.

suggests that the question of autonomy should not be seen in isolation from the general human rights framework but it can and should be broken down into a number of human rights elements or dimensions that appear relevant to this debate instead. More broadly, autonomy issues in the context of human rights call for an assessment of the pathologies or anomalies that need to be addressed within the framework of the state. What is at stake when it comes to autonomy? Do autonomy claims seek to achieve basic spaces of political and/or economic freedom, more robust identity-based protections, and/or certain degrees of decision-making authority? When stepping back from legal detail, such claims typically come into view as part of a larger pattern of allocations and reallocations of sovereign power that have been buttressed by international law, of which human rights law is very much an integral part.

This chapter thus addresses the subject of autonomy at two levels. At the level of rights and obligations – legal standards and practice – it aims to engage with international human rights dimensions that are frequently overshadowed by group status and right-holding concerns and yet play (or ought to play) an increasingly vital role in capturing the various functions of international human rights norms in handling autonomy matters within domestic legal orders (Section 2). Following on from this, and at a more 'systemic' level, the chapter discusses general approaches and ambivalences towards autonomy in rights and public discourse, and why autonomy has more to do with the contingent legitimacy of claims than with 'universal' or 'inherent' legal rights under international human rights law (Section 3). I ultimately look at autonomy as a bundle of legal, conceptual and policy issues rather than a problem to be solved through ready-made and generally applicable rights. In so doing I seek to provide a constructive view that shifts the focus towards the possibilities offered by the human rights framework in tackling ethno-cultural claims and the process needed to strike a balance between seemingly unconditional rights and the legally crude role of effectiveness or political realities.

2 Disaggregating the Debate: A Closer Look at the Faces of Group Autonomy in International Law

2.1 *Autonomy as a Platform for Articulating Claims*

In its most obvious and most basic sense, autonomy for minority groups implies the need for some distance, a distinct space within which the group and its members can articulate, debate and protect their identity and self-governing capacities. As Hurst Hannum puts it, "[p]ersonal and political autonomy is in some real sense the right to be different and to be left alone".[15] Indeed, a variable measure of autonomy from the central government or otherwise the broader society is arguably the hallmark of minority claims throughout history.

Seen through the lens of human rights law, autonomy can and should be articulated, first of all, as a matter of enabling actions and a wider political discourse. The right to form and participate in associations recognised under international human rights law provides an indispensable context within which minority groups are allowed to claim and assert their identities, and partly project their communal interaction – their horizontal relationships – onto the public sphere. Markku Suksi, for example, refers to "personal autonomy" to imply "the use of the freedom of association as a general civil right in the horizontal dimension between persons belonging to a minority group for carrying out different cultural and other activities that the minority might feel are important".[16] More generally, private/civil law institutions such as associations, foundations, or political parties, generate legally protected platforms for a range of activities specific to the group concerned to be conducted without interference from state authorities. There is a strong case for this dimension to be encompassed by a variety of general and special human rights instruments, including Article 27 of the International Covenant on Civil and Political Rights (ICCPR) and the Council of Europe Framework Convention for the Protection of National Minorities (FCNM).[17]

Though intended to have an impact on civil society and the larger political community, this minimum approach to autonomy is predicated on a formal distinction between the 'private' nature of the activities in question and the 'public' functions of the state. In other words, the outer limit of 'personal autonomy' so understood is defined by the inability of the group to claim regulatory and/or decision-making powers that are typically the preserve of public authorities. However, there are two aspects to this that should be kept in mind from an autonomy point of view.

First, group autonomy through private law institutions (or otherwise structures that are not allowed to perform actions on behalf of the state) represents a

15 H. Hannum, *supra* note 6, p. 4.

16 M. Suksi, 'Personal Autonomy as Institutional Form – Focus on Europe Against the Background to Article 27 of the ICCPR', 15 *International Journal on Minority and Group Rights* (2008) pp. 160–161.

17 P. Vermeersch, 'Minority Associations: Issues of representation, internal democracy, and legitimacy', in M. Weller (ed.), *Political Participation of Minorities: A Commentary on International Standards and Practice* (Oxford University Press, Oxford, 2010) p. 682, at pp. 686–687.

fundamental baseline the absence of which would be in breach of human rights standards. This has been made clear by the European Court of Human Rights under the European Convention on Human Rights (ECHR). Not only has the Court openly acknowledged the link amongst associative freedoms (including freedom of religion), the articulation of group identities under conditions of political and cultural pluralism, and the autonomous existence of minority communities,[18] but it has also firmly dismissed approaches aimed to curtail such space on security or other public grounds. A stream of cases decided against Greece, Turkey and a few other states in the context of pro-group activities (e.g. pro-Kurdish demands for constitutional changes and language rights) is a case in point. These cases variably involved the refusal by state authorities to register associations claiming to represent a national minority group or to be pursuing a pro-minority agenda, the dissolution of political parties having similar objectives, or bans on public meetings. The Court's response has been unequivocal:

> [T]here can be no justification for hindering a political group solely because it seeks to debate in public the situation of part of the State's population and to take part in the nation's political life in order to find, according to democratic rules, solutions capable of satisfying everyone concerned.[19]

The case of Turkey is particularly telling as matters of personal autonomy for Kurdish or pro-Kurdish structures strongly resonate with more general attempts to redefine 'national' identity and the approach to the treatment of minority groups within the state through new constitutional arrangements, regardless of the 1923 Treaty of Lausanne which delineated a space for the protection of non-Muslim minorities upon the establishment of the Republic of Turkey.[20] This sort of organisational freedom thus operates in two overlapping

---

18 *See generally* G. Pentassuglia, 'The Strasbourg Court and Minority Groups: Shooting in the Dark or a New Interpretive Ethos?', 19 *International Journal on Minority and Group Rights* (2012) p. 1; *id.*, *supra* note 14, p. 300.

19 *United Communist Party of Turkey and others v. Turkey*, Judgment of 30 January 1998, Reports 1998-I, para. 57. *See also Stankov and the United Macedonian Association Ilinden v. Bulgaria*, Applications Nos. 29221/95 and 292225/95, Judgment of 2 October 2001, para. 97 ("[i]n a democratic society based on the rule of law, political ideas which challenge the existing order and whose realisation is advocated by peaceful means must be afforded a proper opportunity of expression through the exercise of the right of assembly as well as by other lawful means").

20 For a critical assessment of the scope of this treaty and national legislation, *see* D. Bayir, *Minorities and Nationalism in Turkish Law* (Ashgate, Aldershot, 2013).

directions. It is suitable for enabling degrees of pluralism in the relationship between the state and the group, and it can be instrumental in pursuing new institutional or constitutional arrangements through democratic means. It can also work within the group itself to the extent that sectors of it have a different understanding of the group's identity and/or intend to pursue particular activities as part of that broader identity.

Secondly, one can argue that there is nothing in international human rights law that precludes the delegation of public functions to this sort of group (non-governmental) entities. While there is no automatic right to public status as a result of the setting up of such entities,[21] the latter are arguably entitled to seek a measure of decision-making (public) authority in pre-defined areas. For instance, the right of minority groups to establish their own private schools was one of the very first rights to attract international legal protection in the history of the field.[22] In principle, the setting up of such schools does not involve the allocation or exercise of public powers or indeed the discharge of public tasks – only compliance with certain requirements set out by international conventions.[23] Nevertheless, it is far from uncommon for such private schools to be granted certain 'functional' public powers, such as the power to award degrees, or otherwise the capacity to operate under a common legislative framework that recognises their special status.[24] While it would be difficult to establish a specific international legal obligation upon the state to grant such powers and/or public tasks, it is reasonable to argue that such prerogatives are fully compatible with minimum forms of group autonomy under international human rights law, and may even be required in circumstances where those prerogatives would be essential to the effective exercise of certain associative rights.[25]

---

21 *Gorzelik v. Poland*, Application No. 44158/9820, Judgment of 17 February 2004, Eur. Ct.H.R.

22 *Minority Schools in Albania* (Advisory Opinion) 6 April 1935, P.C.I.J. Series A./B., No. 64.

23 *See e.g.* UNESCO Convention Against Discrimination in Education, 14 December 1960, Article 5(1)(c).

24 M. Suksi, 'Non-Territorial Autonomy: The Meaning of '(Non-)Territoriality'', in T. Malloy and F. Palermo (eds.), *supra* note 12, p. 82, at p. 88.

25 For example, it can be argued that the right to set up a private minority school under Article 27 ICCPR may indeed require the recognition of certain legal 'public' capacities to enable the school to operate as an effective educational structure in circumstances in which private minority schools are the only institutional option available to the group for a measure of mother tongue education. *See* by implication the Permanent Court of International Justice's Advisory Opinion from 1935, *supra* note 22.

2.2 *A Story within a Story: Autonomy as a Narrow Legal Entitlement*

If autonomy as a minimal space for articulating human rights-based claims within society lies at one end of the spectrum, the specific recognition of rights or otherwise international legal mechanisms to support particular forms of autonomy lies at the opposite end of it.

In fact, far from being a concept or category alien to international legal practice, autonomy has been employed time and again throughout history as a tool for accommodating the position of certain ethno-cultural groups. "[F]ullest degree of self-government compatible with the unity of Czecho-Slovak State" was granted to the Ruthene territory under the 1919 Treaty of Saint-Germain-en-Laye. The Aaland Islands received autonomy within newly established Finland with full backing from the League of Nations, which called for its further strengthening by way of internal legislation. The League Council upheld the 1920 Report of the International Commission of Jurists – one of the bodies appointed by the Council to consider the status of the Aaland Islands – despite the fact that, at least initially, territorial autonomy as opposed to reunification with Sweden had not been supported by the local population. Similar legal iterations can be found in other settings, including the 'autonomous territory of Eastern Carelia' under the 1920 Peace Treaty between Finland and Russia; the 'local autonomy' for the Kurds provided under the 1920 Treaty of Sèvres, in line with US President Woodrow Wilson's Fourteen Points' commitment to, *inter alia*, the 'autonomous development' of non-Turkish minorities within the Ottoman empire; or the autonomy enjoyed by the Memel Territory under Lithuanian sovereignty which was designed to preserve "the traditional rights and culture of its inhabitants" under the 1924 Convention and Transitory Provision concerning Memel. In all of these cases, autonomy meant the actual or proposed transfer of a considerable set of legislative and administrative powers, generally in predefined areas, to the unit concerned. More limited forms of autonomy were also part of the Versailles settlement, normally involving a degree of self-rule in education and religious matters.[26]

For a variety of reasons, some of these arrangements were short-lived (e.g. Memel Territory); others remained unimplemented (e.g. Ruthenia or Kurdish autonomy); yet others survived legal and political developments (e.g. Aaland Islands). On the whole, they did nevertheless provide a fertile ground for the legal and policy conceptualisation of autonomy in later cases. Indeed, similar approaches re-emerged, in whole or in part, in post-World War II and

26 For reviews of some of these arrangements, *see* H. Hannum, *supra* note 6, chs. 9, 17; P. Thornberry, *International Law and The Rights of Minorities* (Oxford University Press, Oxford, 1991) ch. 3; *Status of Eastern Carelia* (Advisory Opinion), 1923 P.C.I.J. Series B, No. 5, p. 7.

post-Cold War scenarios. Italy and Austria, for example, entered into an agreement in 1946 to grant a special statute of autonomy for the German-speaking population of South Tyrol/Alto Adige. The United Nations fostered consensus on autonomy for Eritrea within Ethiopia in the 1950s. Some form of autonomy was attempted in 1996 under the basic treaties between Hungary and Slovakia, and Hungary and Romania. Both Slovakia and Romania clarified that they had not endorsed ethnically-based territorial autonomy, though a convincing argument has since been made that non-ethnically-based territorial autonomy or cultural autonomy are compatible with those treaties.[27]

These cases undoubtedly reflect selective experiments or techniques (others would parallel or follow them at different junctures). Despite the obvious human rights undertones or dimensions of these approaches (all such regimes flexibly framed the question in the context of individual and communal rights, or specifically, as a 'modern' human rights matter), autonomy never turned itself into a general entitlement capable of cutting across the canon of international human rights law. True, autonomy was (and still is) a legitimate option – indeed a legal right – during the process of decolonisation or freeing populations equally entitled to self-determination in circumstances of occupation or foreign domination. Puerto Rico agreed to 'free association' with the United States under the terms of the 1960 United Nations Declaration on the Granting of Independence to Colonial Peoples and Countries.[28] This has in practice given Puerto Rico a significant amount of autonomy within the United States, and the people of Puerto Rico crucially retain the right to modify such an arrangement unilaterally. Substantial autonomy was endorsed, at least as an interim solution, for entities endowed with a similar legal status, such as East Timor or Palestine.[29]

However, these autonomy regimes were never meant to signal a broader right for distinct ethno-cultural groups under the legal register of external self-determination, let alone a more general right to autonomy for ethno-cultural groups under human rights law. A different view would effectively derive from

---

27 *See generally* P. Kovács, *Le droit international pour les minorités face a l'état-nation* (Miskolci Egyetemi Kiadó, Miskolc, 2000).

28 GA Res. 1541, UN GAOR 15th session, Supp. No. 15, UN Doc. A/4654, Principle VII.

29 *See e.g.* L. Hannikainen, 'Self-Determination and Autonomy in International Law', in M. Suksi (ed.), *Autonomy: Applications and Implications* (Kluwer Law International, Dordrecht, 1988) pp. 89–90. It is a different matter whether a move from interim autonomy to independence can be given effect through a wholly unilateral process. For the case of Palestine, *see e.g. Legal Consequences of the Construction of a Wall in the Occupied Palestinian Territory* (Advisory Opinion), 9 July 2004, I.C.J. Reports 131, Separate Opinions of Judge Higgins, Judge Kooijmans, and Judge Elarby.

a broader argument about the nature of colonial self-determination. The argument suggests that mention of a "territory which is geographically separate and is distinct ethnically and/or culturally" in United Nations General Assembly Resolution 1541 as a basis for identifying the colonial units which qualified for self-determination under the terms of the 1960 Declaration amounted to acknowledging 'national' self-determination in its multiple variants. It represented, in other words, some kind of iteration of the concept that was deemed acceptable (at least politically) at Versailles. While this argument is used, rather curiously, to both support and challenge an ethno-nationalist view of self-determination (particularly through the overwhelmingly chosen pattern of liberation: independence),[30] it does not stand the test of a rigorous scrutiny of practice. If it ever meant anything specific, the ethno-cultural reference in Resolution 1541 applied to the relationship between the coloniser and the colonised rather than the ethno-cultural features of any particular community – the myriad of them encompassed by the administrative boundaries of the crumbling empires. It contributed at best to marking off a space separate from the metropolitan state where sovereign power exercised by a distant ruler was no longer legitimate. The decolonisation that became acceptable as an international law standard was unsurprisingly built around geography, not demography, territory, not nationhood or ethno-cultural identity. In fact, the national liberation movements that eventually achieved independence on behalf of the colonies were amongst the most determined supporters of this line, pre- and post-independence.[31]

That being said, the United Nations Declaration on the Rights of Indigenous Peoples (UNDRIP) adopted by the General Assembly in 2007 has arguably propelled the question of autonomy for particular ethno-cultural groups back into the human rights agenda. Article 4 affirms the right of indigenous peoples "to autonomy or self-government in matters relating to their internal and local affairs" as a way of exercising their right to self-determination. The UNDRIP

30 *Compare e.g.* A. Patten, 'Self-Determination for National Minorities', in F. Tesón (ed.), *The Theory of Self-Determination* (Cambridge University Press, Cambridge, 2016) pp. 126–129; E. Rodríguez-Santiago, *The Evolution of Self-Determination of Peoples in International* Law, *ibid.*, p. 238.

31 M. Koskenniemi, *supra* note 10, pp. 254–255 ("[w]hat was important for the liberators was to seize the particular forms of State power ... that had been introduced by colonial rule, not to re-establish whatever tribal or statal entities preceded colonialism"); in his 1990 book, Hurst Hannum went as far as to note that, because of the extreme ethnic heterogeneity of most African states post-independence "Africa may simply be more honest than the rest of the world in admitting that self-determination *of the state* has replaced the theoretical self-determination of peoples", *supra* note 6, p. 47.

specifically recognises the right of indigenous peoples to their own "institutions" while at the same time acknowledging their right to participate (in a non-coercive manner) in the political, economic, social and cultural life of the state (Articles 5, 18, and 19). The mainstream argument about indigenous autonomy in international human rights law goes broadly as follows: 1) there exists a clear 'right' to autonomy; 2) such a right accrues to indigenous groups as 'peoples' (unlike 'national minorities' or other ethno-cultural groups); 3) indigenous autonomy thus responds to wholly unique circumstances, which are then reflected in equally unique legal arrangements.[32]

Reasonably convincing on its face, I would submit that this argument suffers from an excessive focus on right-holding/group status matters and tends to obscure a more legally fluid and conceptually open-ended picture. It is certainly the case that international human rights law does not recognise autonomy as a matter of general right. However, this is by no means the whole story. For one thing, when we zoom in on the international legal approach to indigenous rights, including the crucial issue of autonomy, human rights responses appear far more nuanced and hybrid than a straightforward 'right to autonomy' might seem to suggest. Regardless of whether there is a genuine international consensus that the UNDRIP's 'soft' right to autonomy arises as a matter of 'hard' international customary law,[33] the human rights practice of indigenous rights shows that elements that are essential to autonomy regimes (such as land tenure systems) are largely considered and defined in international legal contexts in which no right to autonomy exists as a direct entitlement.[34] More importantly, looking at autonomy only or primarily through the prism of a specific right for tightly construed categories of 'peoples' ends up downplaying – unintentionally perhaps – the plurality of ways in which autonomy is susceptible to broader application both in relation to the implementation of existing human rights obligations, and in the context of those cross-cutting dimensions that defy strict group classifications in human rights practice. I will next take a closer look at each of these dimensions in turn.[35]

---

32 Indigenous communities have consistently claimed to be 'more than' minorities.

33 *See generally* M. Barelli, *Seeking Justice in International Law: The Significance and Implications of the UN Declaration on the Rights of Indigenous Peoples* (Routledge, London, 2016). *See also* the chapter by Felipe Gómez Isa in the present volume.

34 G. Pentassuglia, 'Towards a Jurisprudential Articulation of Indigenous Land Rights', 22 *European Journal of International Law* (2011) p. 165.

35 It should be noted that a specific discussion of how group categories such as indigenous peoples and national minorities relate to one another is beyond the scope of this chapter. The conceptual implications of the cross-cutting dimensions of autonomy will be discussed in Sections 2.4 and 3.

2.3 *Autonomy as a 'Living' Human Rights Practice*

While the UNDRIP's articulation of indigenous self-determination as autonomy has been presented as a remarkable innovation in international law theory and practice (which partly is), the underlying link between self-determination and autonomy, consistent with demands for appropriate levels of control over decision-making, is as old as the idea of self-determination itself.

In the Aaland Islands case, both commissions appointed by the Council of the League clearly implied that granting (or reinforcing) autonomy for the (overwhelmingly Swedish-speaking) inhabitants of the Aaland Islands under Finnish sovereignty would in practice pursue the same objectives that would have otherwise been pursued through Aaland Islanders' independence by way of incorporation into Sweden.[36] In this sense, self-determination and autonomy (by means of extensive minority protection) mirrored, and yet reconfigured, one another. As the Commission of Jurists put it, "they have a common object – to assure to some national Group the maintenance and free development of its social, ethnical or religious characteristics". Tellingly, the Commission of Rapporteurs reinforced this idea by noting that the basic tenets of "justice and liberty" underpinning the "formula of self-determination" squarely applied "in a reasonable manner to the relations between States and the minorities they include". It stressed the "vague and general" nature of that formula, and noted that it had given rise "to the most varied interpretations and differences of opinion".

To some extent, it can be argued that the hybrid approach which was reflected in this case in response to the overlapping national desires of the time may have carried the seeds of future hybrid approaches to broadly similar ethno-cultural claims within a variety of modern legal (human rights) settings. While the drafters of the ICCPR erected a wall between the right of "all peoples" to self-determination in Article 1 and the rights of "persons belonging to" minorities in Article 27, and states rejected proposals for a right to autonomy or self-government under the 1992 United Nations Declaration on the Rights of Persons Belonging to National or Ethnic, Religious and Linguistic Minorities,[37]

---

36 *The Aaland Islands Question (On Jurisdiction)*, Report of the International Committee of Jurists, League of Nations Official Journal, Special Supplement No. 3 (1920); *The Aaland Islands Question (On the Merits)*, Report by the Commission of Rapporteurs, League of Nations Council Document B7 21/68/106 (1921).

37 F. Horn, 'Recent Attempts to Elaborate Standards on Minority Rights', in O. Bring and S. Mahmoudi (eds.), *Current International Law Issues – Nordic Perspectives, Essays in Honour of Jerzy Stucki* (Martinus Nijhoff Publishers, Dordrecht, 1994) p. 81, at p. 104. *Compare* the Document of the Copenhagen Meeting of the Conference on the Human Dimension of the CSCE, 29 June 1990, para. 35.

legal argumentation has continued to inform 'living' human rights practice in ways that have progressively exposed the interlocking nature of claims and the need for contextual assessments that often challenge strict rights typologies or group classifications.

It is in this sense that we can explain, for example, the United Nations Human Rights Committee's (HRC's) acknowledgment of the connection between self-determination and Article 27 in a number of cases, despite their otherwise formal, and repeatedly stated, separation under the Covenant.[38] The link has largely drawn upon participation of the group in decision-making and has appeared to intimate various degrees of control over that process, though not necessarily in the form of territorial autonomy. It arguably chimes with earlier views presented by the United Nations Secretary General on 'popular participation' in the mid-1980s where the right to self-determination and minority rights featured amongst the 'elements' of a seemingly emerging global right to participation.[39] In *Katangese Peoples' Congress v. Zaire*, the African Commission on Human and Peoples' Rights found a correlation between political rights and internal self-determination by indicating that self-determination may include, *inter alia*, "self-government, local government, federalism", as long as this accords with "the wishes of the people" and is fully compatible with the preservation of territorial integrity.[40] The Commission has taken a similar view in the specific context of 'indigenous' communities in the African continent by disaggregating the various forms or dimensions of self-determination (including self-government) in order to assess their compatibility with the African Charter on Human and Peoples' Rights (ACHPR).[41] Within the Inter-American system, the Inter-American Court of Human Rights has taken the lead in articulating land rights as a central pillar of indigenous autonomy within their traditional

38 Human Rights Committee, *The rights of minorities: General Comment No. 23*, 8 April 1994, UN GAOR, CCPR/C/21/Rev.1/Add.5; *Apirana Mahuika et al. v. New Zealand*, Comm. No. 547/1993, 27 October, 2000, UN Doc. CCPR/C/70/D/541/1993, para. 9.2; *Diergaardt v. Namibia*, Comm. 760/1997, 25 July 2000, UN Doc. CCPR/C/76/D/760/1997 (2000), para. 10.3; *Angela Poma Poma v. Peru*, Comm. No. 1457/2006, 27 March 2009, UN Doc. CCPR/C/95/D/1457/2006 (2009) (the case did not draw on Article 1 ICCPR per se, but did endorse key elements of participation linked to indigenous self-determination).

39 *Study by the Secretary-General on Popular Participation in its Various Forms as an Important Factor in Development and in the Full Realization of Human Rights*, UN Doc. E/CN.4/1985/10 (1984) p. 34.

40 Comm. No. 75/92 (1995), para. 4.

41 *Advisory Opinion of the African Commission on Human and Peoples' Rights on the United Nations Declaration on the Rights of Indigenous Peoples*, 41st session, Accra, Ghana, May 2007, paras. 23–24, 27, 35.

lands by exposing interlocking issues of non-discrimination, property, culture, and self-determination.[42] In several other cases, narrower or broader forms of autonomy for sub-national groups have been taken to be either the most obvious outcome, or one of the most desirable ones, or even the basis for a constitutional redefinition of the state.[43]

One may argue that much of this practice shows that autonomy may derive from certain interpretations of human rights norms rather than the existence of an international legal obligation on states to provide for autonomy arrangements under their own jurisdictions. Here again, this view's primary (and probably solely) concern is with whether or not a specific right to autonomy is available. What this practice reveals, if anything, is that human rights interpretation is or can be a complex exercise. For one thing, there might be circumstances in which autonomy appears to be the only way of implementing existing obligations. In a paper presented at the UN Working Group on Minorities in 2005, Marc Weller noted that, particularly in circumstances of ethnic conflict there will be a "strong presumption" that autonomy will be the only way of implementing existing minority rights norms. This seems to be reinforced by the fact that, not only has autonomy been repeatedly deployed in several states from various regions of the world, including hybrid peace agreements with significant self-determination/human rights features. The international community has also supported autonomy solutions in almost all ethnic conflicts, particularly in Central and Eastern Europe, calling upon

42 G. Pentassuglia, *supra* note 14, pp. 202–203.

43 For example, in the context of Quebec's autonomy, the Supreme Court of Canada noted that international law expects self-determination to be exercised within the framework of existing sovereign states, *supra* note 3, para. 122; the Arbitration Commission on Yugoslavia sought to reconcile sovereignty, self-determination and human rights by looking at minority protection and possible dislocations of power across national boundaries (European Community Arbitration Commission, *Opinion No. 2*, 11 January 1992, 31 *International Legal Materials* (1992) p. 1497); the FCNM Advisory Committee has unambiguously favoured autonomy arrangements in certain circumstances in order to secure more effective participation of minority members in decision-making, and it has recommended ways in which such arrangements should be designed under domestic law (*Commentary on The Effective Participation of Persons Belonging to National Minorities in Cultural, Social and Economic Life and in Public Affairs*, 27 February 2008, paras. 133–137; *see also supra* note 37); several multiparty (national/international) peace agreements have endorsed autonomy as a key form of group accommodation in the context of a more general reconfiguration of the state in divided societies: for discussion, *see* C. Bell, *On the Law of Peace: Peace Agreements and the Lex Pacificatoria* (Oxford University Press, Oxford, 2008) chs. 5,11.

the parties to negotiate in good faith on that basis.[44] On a separate front, the Inter-American Court of Human Rights has found that states parties are under an obligation to recognise indigenous customary law, and thus some form of legal pluralism, as essential components of the protection of indigenous land rights under the American Convention on Human Rights (ACHR). At the same time, autonomy issues or legal pluralism for particular ethno-cultural groups have been treated within other human rights frameworks as either permitted or required depending on context.[45]

The broader point here is that, regardless of the specific circumstances of each case, human rights norms have the capacity to validate autonomy arrangements, and that this capacity does not necessarily or automatically require or presuppose a distinctive right to that effect (however important such a right can be). Crucially, the focus tends to shift towards the *content* and *application* of the law in its various substantive and procedural or institutional manifestations, and whether or not they allow for narrower or wider margins of appreciation on the part of the state. If this reading is correct, then it also tells us that, while autonomy may involve specific considerations in relation to indigenous rights, autonomy as a human rights category ultimately operates as a cross-cutting dimension that has the potential of affecting a variety of human rights norms and a variety of groups.

2.4 *Autonomy across the Board: Cross-Cutting Dimensions*

2.4.1 Autonomy as Control over Decision-Making

One way, probably the best way, of illustrating the cross-crossing nature of autonomy within human rights discourse is by looking at the theme of participation in decision-making, particularly across the indigenous/minority classifications. On the one hand, the question of autonomy is widely regarded as integral to an overarching continuing (internal) relationship between the state and its political community, including a range of institutional possibilities short of secession.[46] At the same time, autonomy claims ordinarily seek to achieve some form of specific control over decision-making while still

---

44 M. Weller, 'Towards A General Comment on Self-Determination and Autonomy', UN Doc. E/CN.4/Sub.2/AC.5/2005/WP.5, 25 May 2005, pp. 13–16; C. Bell, *supra* note 43 (arguing that hybrid self-determination, including autonomy arrangements, from the Bougainville to the Belfast agreements, can be pursued as "the best application of the law in situations of intrastate ethnic conflict", *ibid.*, p. 225). *See also* below, Section 3.1.

45 H. Quane, *supra* note 12.

46 I shall further elaborate on this point in Section 3.

acknowledging the wider community. Autonomy thus becomes inextricably intertwined with rights to have a say, to shape up the process, or even to negotiate distinctive outcomes.

In the case of *Diergaardt at al v. Namibia* before the HRC, Mr Scheinin argued that the general rights of participation in Article 25 ICCPR may include forms of "local, regional or cultural autonomy" needed to comply with the requirement of effective participation of certain groups in decision-making.[47] Indeed, participation rights for national minorities and indigenous peoples feature prominently in international human rights instruments. While the interpretation of a typical minority right to participation contemplates autonomy as a possible, albeit not automatic, outcome of institutional processes within the state, the interpretation of a typical indigenous right to participation assumes autonomy – implicitly or explicitly – as its starting point.[48] However, on closer inspection, the circularity of the relationship between autonomy and participation in such texts could not be more striking. 'Effective' participation in decision-making may require forms of autonomy in the former case, yet autonomy itself is made dependent upon a process of 'effective' participation in the latter case. The UNDRIP's right to autonomy, for example, requires the group to engage in negotiations with the state (and vice versa) over the exact terms of its political status, its cultural autonomy and/or legal systems where they exist. This is not only dictated by the need to ensure that indigenous autonomy is generally consistent with the human rights of group members and non-members. It also signals the fact that the right to autonomy, as strong as it certainly is, can hardly amount to a bundle of unilateral entitlements to determine the position of the group vis-à-vis the state. Rather, its implementation should be measured against sustained efforts aimed to secure as much as possible the group's 'free, prior and informed consent'.[49]

General Comment 21 on the right to take part in cultural life in Article 15(1)(a) of the International Covenant on Economic, Social and Cultural Rights provides another example of these hybrid articulations of control over

47 Comm. 760/1997, 69th sess., July 25, 2000, UN Doc. CCPR/C/76/D/760/1997 (2000), Separate opinion by Mr Martin Scheinin.

48 UNDRIP, Articles 3–5. *See e.g. supra* note 43.

49 *See e.g.* UNDRIP, preambular paras. 18–19, Arts. 18, 19, 32(2), 38. For an interesting case of hybrid autonomy in a negotiating context involving the Sami communities in Finland, Norway, and Sweden, *see* J. Hamilton, 'Acknowledging and Accommodating Legal Pluralism: An Application to the Draft Nordic Saami Convention', in N. Bankes and T. Koivurova (eds.), *supra* note 4, p. 45. For addition comments, *see also* Section 2.5.

relevant decision-making processes. The General Comment addresses cultural rights in a broad sense and does not delve into the contours or permissibility of group-based cultural autonomy or legal pluralism as such. However, it does seek to bridge the gap between individual rights and group protection and, quite remarkably, recognises the "participation of persons belonging to minority groups, indigenous peoples or to other communities in the design and implementation of laws and policies that affect them" to be an integral part of the minimum core of the right to take part in cultural life, which should involve "their free and informed prior consent" when their "cultural resources [...].. are at risk".[50]

What these examples have in common is reasonably straightforward. They all refer to cases where standards on participation in decision-making have been employed within particular contexts but still derive from general concepts that do not presuppose or require specific group classifications. To the extent that autonomy and participation are inextricably linked to one another in human rights discourse through the inevitable prism of control over decision-making, autonomy comes into view (directly or indirectly) as a specific tool for specific forms of group accommodation, not as a devise for achieving group status precision.

2.4.2 Does Autonomy Need a 'People'?

Indeed, if the cross-crossing dimension of autonomy tends to be obscured by a primary concern with the existence of a direct international legal right for a tightly construed type of group, as illustrated by the right to autonomy under the UNDRIP, such a dimension is further side-lined by complex, yet arguably inconclusive, debates over whether the claimant qualifies as a 'people' under international law.

As previously implied, the rationale for this generally lies in the understanding of autonomy as a variant of self-determination short of independence, a variant which is often thought to continue to attract the legal requirement for the group concerned to establish itself as a 'people' for that, more limited, purpose. On its face, this approach seems to apply to the colonial context, to the extent that autonomy represents a viable, though possibly provisional, constitutional option involving the voluntary realignment of the entity with the metropolitan (colonial) state. However, such a case differs profoundly from a situation whereby a well-established sub-national group claims to be

50 Committee on Economic, Social and Cultural Rights, *Right of everyone to take part in cultural life: General Comment No. 21*, 21 December 2009, U.N. GAOR, E/C.12/GC/21, para. 55(e).

a people for purposes of self-determination within the state. For its part, autonomy in colonial and quasi-colonial circumstances has been rarely used or considered. More importantly, the modes of implementing the right to external self-determination in that context have ignored ethno-cultural considerations ('peoplehood' in that sense) to affirm priorities of 'national unity' and 'territorial integrity', as I discussed earlier on.

The 'peoplehood' argument is effectively a broader argument resting on the notion that autonomy as a form of internal self-determination requires the claimant group to be treated as a people entitled to it. This argument seems to have been rekindled by the Supreme Court of Canada's approach in the *Reference* case, and seemingly reinforced by flexible views of self-determination or self-government in a number of legal contexts where autonomy in its various forms appears to have been linked to a right of 'people' or 'peoples'. Here again, a more realistic assessment arguably conveys a more complex picture.

The gist of the Court's line of reasoning is that, because the right to self-determination is a human right, it cannot be a right of states, let alone nation states. Being as it is a right that accrues to a 'people' as opposed to a state, it "may include a portion of the population of an existing state". Arguing otherwise, the Court says, would make the right to self-determination "largely duplicative" and "would frustrate its remedial purpose".[51] Leaving the question of remedial secession aside,[52] there seems to be every reason to be skeptical about the actual reach of these comments for the purposes of our discussion. Rightly distinguishing the rights of states from the rights of individuals and groups (of which the right to self-determination is one) does not, in and of itself, tell us anything specific about the relationship between 'peoplehood' and autonomy. It is one thing to argue that the rights of groups are not the rights of states or governments, and it is quite another to derive from this any firm conclusions

51 *See supra* note 3, para. 124.

52 While the Court implied a connection between 'peoplehood' and remedial secession in response to a chronic failure to exercise internal self-determination, it can be doubted whether the existence of a distinct 'people' (as opposed to a minority, a generic population, or an institutional entity comprising several groups) is required in any assessment of remedial secession in international law. This is even more so if the unit in question includes individuals or groups who do *not* wish to secede or if that unit is subsumed into the colonial category of non-self-governing territory: on the latter case, *see* T. Franck, 'Post-modern tribalism and the right to secession', in C. Brölmann, R. Lefeber and M. Zieck (eds.), *Peoples and Minorities in International Law* (Kluwer Law International, Dordrecht, 1993) p. 3, at pp. 13–14; J. Crawford, *supra* note 7. For recent discussion, *see e.g. Chiragov and Others v. Armenia*, Application No. 13216/05, Judgment of 16 June 2015, Dissenting Opinions of Judge Gyulumyan and Judge Pinto de Alburquerque.

about the extent to which the term 'people' can reach out to particular groups as a matter of human rights law or indeed international law. All human rights – both individual and collective – accrue to entities other than the state within which they are enjoyed. In other words, all individuals and groups hold (or may hold) human rights because they are not states. While this disjunction – or non-state marker – lies at the very heart of international human rights law, it cannot be determinative of the personal scope of the right to self-determination other than by contrasting this right with the rights of states. This does not mean that self-determination may not benefit "a portion of the population of an existing state". It only means that the self-determination/human rights nexus as defined by the Court is not conclusive as to who is entitled to claim some form of autonomy within the state.

Quite remarkably, the Court itself indicated in no uncertain terms that determining the exact status of the French-speaking community of Quebec, or indeed of any other group within Quebec, as a 'people' was *not* necessary in the case at hand. Given that much of the judgment locates Quebec's autonomy within a wider process of internal self-determination to the benefit of all the parties concerned, including groups and individuals within, and that the very possibility of Quebec's secession might have prompted the Court to address that matter as it applied to the case,[53] such an agnostic view says more about the ambiguities of the peoplehood argument than it says about the substance of self-determination. In a language that essentially drew upon the 1970 United Nations Friendly Relations Declaration, the Court focussed instead on the "whole of the people or peoples resident within the territory" as a basis for proper constitutional (internal) arrangements. In the context of the judgment, this language does not seem to go far beyond an explicit, yet hybrid, acknowledgment of the coexistence of various groups or sub-national groups within the state and the requirement of complex constitutional conversations designed to achieve accommodation of that diversity, regardless of specific group classifications.

It is certainly true that autonomy for particular groups appears to have been linked to a right of peoples in particular legal contexts such as the ACHPR (in addition, of course, to the UNDRIP itself). Nonetheless, the evidence that this reflects an underlying general requirement of 'peoplehood' for autonomy claims within the state is rather thin. For one thing, the relative significance of

53 True, the Court ruled out remedial secession on human rights grounds in the case at hand, but it was unclear how that reconciled with the Court's prior silence as to who was entitled to remedial secession in the first place, and whether Quebec would have been entitled to remedial secession as a distinct 'people' or some other entity, had denial of access to government and gross human rights abuses been proven.

this practice must be fully appreciated in its own context. For example, what emerges from the recent jurisprudence of the African Commission on Human Rights is that the category of 'peoples' rights' – fairly unique to the African continent in international human rights law – has come to represent a typical entry point for consideration of group issues under the Charter, and that within that category, the treatment of sub-national groups has gradually come within the purview of this treaty. But other than these minimum baselines, the Commission's jurisprudence does not seem to reflect a coherent approach to the concept of 'people'. In fact, it has employed the concept fairly flexibly and in connection with a variety of legal meanings. In some cases, it has linked 'peoplehood' to the whole population of the state, or even the state. In other cases, it has discussed the possibility of self-government for a sub-national entity while declining to characterise the entity as a people under the Charter. In yet other cases, it has determined the existence of a 'people' but linked it primarily to remedial secession claims or to a modified idea of 'indigeneity' in the African context (one that can dispense with the requirement of aboriginality or 'priority in time'). This flexible line seems to have been confirmed by the African Court on Human and Peoples' Rights which has extended the protection of peoples' rights to "sub-state ethnic groups and communities" that are part of the state population, regardless of indigenous peculiarities.[54] It is very difficult to distil from all of these cases a consistent view of peoples' rights under the Charter, let alone an unqualified or autonomous right of peoples to autonomy or self-government. This is even more so in light of what appears to be an overall reluctance on the part of the Commission to preface discussions of group issues under the Charter with complex findings about the exact status of any particular group. Indeed, leading cases have deemed the status of the group irrelevant, suggesting the capacity of the Charter to protect a variety of minority groups, in line with the legislation and/or practice of several African states.[55]

---

54 *African Commission on Human and Peoples' Rights v. Republic of Kenya*, App. No. 006/2012, Judgment of 26 May 2017, para. 198. For the Commission's position, *see Katangese Peoples' Congress v. Zaire*, Comm. No. 75/92 (1995); *Centre for Minority Rights Development (Kenya) and Minority Rights Group International on behalf of Endorois Welfare Council v. Kenya*, Comm. No. 276/2003 (2009); *Kevin Mgwanga Gunme et al. v. Cameroon*, Comm. No. 266/2003 (2009). For reviews, *see e.g.* S.A. Dersson, 'The jurisprudence of the African Commission on Human and Peoples' Rights with respect to peoples' rights', 6 *African Human Rights Law Journal* (2006) p. 358; F. Viljoen, *International Human Rights Law in Africa* (Oxford University Press, Oxford, 2007) pp. 281–284. On the early conflation of 'people' and 'state', *see* below Section 3.1.

55 *See e.g. The Social and Economic Rights Action Center for Economic and Social Rights v. Nigeria*, Comm. No 155/96 (2001); *Malawi African Association and Others v. Mauritania*,

Similar quests for coherence within other areas of the international human rights framework seem to be equally futile. Take, again, the case of indigenous rights. While the UNDRIP recognises a right of indigenous 'peoples' to autonomy or self-government, the 1989 International Labour Organisation (ILO) Convention 169 on Indigenous and Tribal Peoples in Independent Countries spells out much of the substance of indigenous autonomy while openly decoupling 'peoplehood' from the right to self-determination in international law (and indeed a fully-fledged right to autonomy itself).[56] As noted, the Inter-American Court of Human Rights has endorsed indigenous legal pluralism through innovative readings of 'ordinary' civil and political rights. The HRC has deemed indigenous issues relevant to the implementation of Article 1 ICCPR, but so too has treated wider constitutional and political processes within the state as a whole.[57]

What this picture suggests is that, while it is possible for specific international (human rights) instruments to recognise certain groups as peoples in connection with issues of autonomy, this is far from necessary or automatic in any particular instance, and crucially, cannot have wider implications as a matter of international human rights law. In other words, tying indigenous autonomy or otherwise sub-national autonomy to the beneficiary of that autonomy being a 'people' in one context does not automatically imply an underlying general requirement of 'peoplehood' for all indigenous rights across the system, let alone a general requirement of 'peoplehood' for all autonomy claims made by ethno-cultural groups. This is further supported by the notion that, although the instrumental value of autonomy for the interests of such groups is widely acknowledged, the organisation of autonomy structures around the idea of exclusive or intolerant *ethnos* is not.[58] If anything, the reality of *non-colonial*

Comm. Nos. 54/91, 61/91, 98/93/, 164/97 à 196/97 and 210/98 (2000), para. 131. The *Ogiek* case (*supra* note 54) seems to suggest that the Court is likely to pursue a similar level of hybridity. For a recent survey of domestic law and policy in selected African countries, *see* ILO/ACHPR, Overview Report of the Research Project by the International Labour Organization and the African Commission on Human and Peoples' Rights on the Constitutional and Legislative Protection of the Rights of Indigenous Peoples in 24 African Countries (2009), at http://www.ilo.org/wcmsp5/groups/public/---ed_norm/---normes/documents/publication/wcms_115929.pdf, p. 1, at p. 20.

56 ILO Convention 169, Article 1(3); *see also* fifth preambular paragraph.

57 Human Rights Committee, *Concluding Observations of the Human Rights Committee: Canada*, U.N. GAOR, 65th session, 7 April 1999, UN Doc. CCPR/C/79/Add.105; Human Rights Committee, *General Comment No. 12: Article 1 (Right to Self-determination)*, 13 March 1984, at http://www.refworld.org/docid/453883f822.html, para. 4.

58 *See e.g.* The Lund Recommendations on the Effective Participation of National Minorities in Public Life (OSCE), 1999, Section III, paras. 14, 17 (Explanatory Note). *See also* Y. Ghai,

autonomy arrangements in various regions of the world shows that the overwhelming majority of those arrangements (actual or proposed) do not rest on a prior recognition of the group or entity in question as a people for purposes of international law, nor do adjudicators and policy-makers appear keen to make such determinations when an opportunity arises.[59]

2.5 *Existing Autonomy and Human Rights: A Two-Pronged Tale*

In the previous sections I have discussed the extent to which autonomy for certain ethno-cultural groups can attract legal protection under international human rights law, and the extent to which such protection necessarily entails a distinct right to it for tightly construed categories of 'peoples'. I have argued that a focus on right-holding and group status matters tends to obscure the variety of ways and contexts in which autonomy can be applied as well as some cross-cutting dimensions that defy strict group classifications in human rights practice.

But aside from the very place of autonomy against human right norms, it is clear that the operation of autonomy in practice can raise a host of overlapping, yet distinct, issues under international law which need to be equally valued as significant aspects of this debate. They are mainly concerned, not with whether autonomy can be extended to certain groups as a matter of human rights law, but rather with the question of whether autonomy can be protected *against withdrawal* once autonomous arrangements have been put in place and whether, conversely, autonomy can be *justified* in light of human rights standards.

'Participation as Self-Governance', in M. Weller (ed.), *supra* note 17, p. 613, at pp. 623, 627 (commenting on the tensions between democracy and ethnicity in autonomy arrangements).

59 M. Suksi, 'On the Entrenchment of Autonomy', in M. Suksi (ed.), *Autonomy: Applications and Implications* (Kluwer Law International, Dordrecht, 1998) p. 151, at p. 165 (noting that very few groups enjoying autonomy through domestic arrangements have been recognised as 'peoples' for such purposes, one exception to the rule being the 'Gagauz people' in Moldova). *Contrast*, for example, with the sui generis case of Greenland which is driven by the legacy of Danish colonialism (Act No. 473 on Greenland Self-Government, 12 June 2009). For adjudicators' reluctance to address group status matters in any significant international legal detail, in addition to the *Reference* case, *see e.g.* European Community Arbitration Commission, *Opinion No. 2*, *supra* note 43, p. 1497 (locating the position of the Bosnian Serbs around hybrid notions of 'population', 'minority' and 'ethnic group' for purposes of self-determination); *Accordance with International Law of the Unilateral Declaration of Independence in Respect of Kosovo* (Advisory Opinion), 22 July 2010, I.C.J. Reports 403, paras. 51, 56, 82, 89, 105, 109 (refraining from recognising the population of Kosovo as a people in international law).

When looking at the interstices of international legal practice, one can find more actual or potential levels of autonomy protection than one would expect given the lack of a freestanding entitlement to autonomy in international human rights law. There are at least three dimensions, or clusters of issues, that can be used here to illustrate the point. They revolve around the role of treaties, 'higher' domestic arrangements, and the impact of disproportionate measures. As experience shows, autonomy has often been linked to a treaty under which one of the parties undertakes the obligation to establish autonomy arrangements (usually on a territorial basis) for the benefit of a particular ethno-cultural sector of the population distinct from the state's majority. Where a treaty-based entrenchment exists, autonomy is not only a matter of legal obligation upon the state concerned, but also the subject of bilateral or multilateral (inter-state) concern designed to rule out the unilateral abolition of the autonomy arrangement by that state.

For example, the 1946 Treaty between Austria and Italy over South Tyrol (the province of Bolzano which was soon to become part of the wider Region of Trentino Alto-Adige), not only guaranteed autonomy for the German-speaking community of that area and consultation with the community about the forms such autonomy would take, but also effectively triggered a monitoring mechanism which precluded Italy from unilaterally withdrawing the arrangement over time. In the late 1950s, Austria raised the issue of implementation with the United Nations, and based on later parallel negotiations, the parties eventually agreed to refer future disputes over the scope of South Tyrolian autonomy to the International Court of Justice.[60] Similarly, the agreement reached in the early 1920s between Finland and Sweden over the Aaland Islands resulted in an arrangement (now deemed defunct) whereby the Legislative Assembly of the Aaland Islands could (through the Finnish government) complain about the implementation of Finnish autonomy legislation to the Council of the League of Nations (and possibly, through the Council, to the Permanent Court of International Justice).[61] Given the fairly widespread use of treaties to secure various forms of autonomy, protection

---

60 H. Hannum, *supra* note 6, pp. 432–440; G. Pentassuglia, *Minorities in International Law: An Introductory Study* (Council of Europe Publishing, Strasbourg, 2002) pp. 232–233.

61 The second League of Nations Commission appointed to consider the case on the merits even argued that the Aalanders would be entitled to a referendum on independence if Finland failed to uphold their rights. For discussion, *see e.g.* L. Hannikainen and F. Horn (eds.), *Autonomy and Demilitarisation in International Law: The Åland Islands in a Changing Europe* (Kluwer Law International, Dordrecht, 1997).

against the unilateral withdrawal of autonomy arrangements in this context should not be understated.[62]

I would argue that, in addition to this case, the very existence of domestic arrangements on autonomy interfaces with international human rights law in a number of important ways. The minimum baseline from which to assess such measures is typically provided by a human rights treaty clause that disallows the withdrawal of higher standards under domestic laws or other applicable international conventions on the basis that the treaty in question does not specifically require them.[63] In reality, human rights practice reveals a more complicated, yet again hybrid, picture. For one thing, such advanced measures, while external to the treaty on their face, may gradually operate as a trigger of expanded obligations under the treaty. The Inter-American Court of Human Rights, for instance, has dynamically found important levels of indigenous autonomy under the ACHR by drawing upon the respondent state's domestic legislation and international instruments as parts of a wider framework of interpretation.[64] On the other hand, domestic autonomy arrangements, where they exist, can provide a platform for implementing obligations that leave states with a wider margin of appreciation.

The case of the Serbian region of Vojvodina under the FNNM seems to support this point. Vojvodina is home to over 25 ethnic groups and the Hungarian-speaking community represents the largest national minority within it. The FCNM Advisory Committee was clear during its first cycle of monitoring that a recently passed law on Vojvodina's competences as an Autonomous Province was "a positive step in the implementation of Article 15 of the Framework Convention", which deals with the right of members of national minorities to participate in decision-making processes. But the Committee was also clear that any possible *revision* of existing territorial arrangements required a robust

---

62 For recent attempts to articulate and guarantee a multi-layered treaty settlement for the Sami community in Scandinavia, *see* N. Bankes and T. Koivurova (eds.), *supra* note 4. It is a different matter whether agreements signed by sub-national groups or entities with the states where they are located can be treated as international agreements of some kind. For discussion, *see* C. Bell, *supra* note 43, pp. 132–135.

63 For a discussion and critique in a different setting, *see* J. Lisberg, l'Does the EU Charter of Fundamental Rights Threaten the Supremacy of Community Law? Article 53 of the Charter: a fountain of law or just an inkblot? 4/01 *Harvard Jean Monnet Working Papers* (2001), at www.jeanmonnetprogram.org/papers/01/010401.htm.

64 G. Pentassuglia, 'Protecting Minority Groups Through Human Rights Courts: The Interpretive Role of European and Inter-American Jurisprudence', in A. F. Vrdoljak (ed.), *The Cultural Dimension of Human Rights* (Oxford University Press, Oxford, 2013) pp. 97–102.

consultation process with the minorities concerned.[65] This did not strictly prohibit the abolition of the autonomous regime by the central government but did imply that any such abolition, unless consented to by the local population, would very likely result in a breach of Article 15 participation rights.[66]

A similar argument can be replicated on a broader scale. It can be argued, for instance, that the existence of certain autonomy arrangements in fulfilment of constitutional or statutory laws, though may not be sourced back to a specific obligation under general human rights law, still provides a basis for implementing underlying, interlocking duties regarding internal self-determination within the wider political community, minority protection, or even basic requirements of inter-group equality. It is hard to see how, for instance, the legislative repeal of the autonomies of Quebec, the Aaland Islands, the Basque Country, the Faroes Islands, Greenland, Northern Ireland, Bougainville and many others, including those procedures that normally require consent or qualified majorities of the entity to enact changes to them, could be disentangled from the general requirement of securing 'meaningful access to government', including effective opportunities for control over decision-making for certain groups, under international human rights law.[67]

The possibility or implementation of such *negative* measures operates, at a minimum, as a valid indicator of whether or not the state is properly complying with its international obligations, that is, whether or not those measures are bound to have a disproportionate impact on the level of protection afforded under human rights norms.[68] In politically volatile scenarios, such a possibility may even trigger specific international legal obligations targeting expulsions, ethnic cleansing or gerrymandering. Article 16 FCNM, for instance,

---

65 ACFC/INF/OP/I(2004)002, 27 November 2003, para. 112 ("The Advisory Committee calls on the authorities to take the views of persons belonging to national minorities carefully into account in addressing this issue in the constitutional reform and other pertinent processes").

66 The matter here was one of granting more powers to the Province but the point applied a fortiori in the event of existing powers being abolished by the central government. In another case, the Advisory Committee warned that local reform was likely to curtail effective participation under Article 15: ACFC/INF/OP/II(2004)005, 9 December 2004, paras. 158–168. For examples under the ECHR, *see also* G. Pentassuglia, *supra* note 18, p. 11.

67 The implication of the *Reference* decision, for example, was that internal arrangements concerning Quebec informed the implementation of internal self-determination within Canada. This point thus stands regardless of any international legal obligations that may exist solely in the context of specific autonomies.

68 *See*, however, M. Suksi, *supra* note 29, pp. 164–5 (noting that specific self-determination remedies may be limited).

prohibits measures aimed to generate demographic changes within national minority areas, including the redrawing of administrative boundaries or forced evictions and expulsions. What generally transpires from international practice is that the *reinstatement* of autonomy regimes in broadly comparable circumstances is generally supported by the international community (as in the case of Kosovo's "substantial autonomy and self-government" under United Nations Security Council Resolution 1244 (1999)).[69]

What is equally undervalued in debates over autonomy is the fact that, while autonomy may or may not be a matter of right and may or may not be linked to the recognition of the group as a 'people', it is most certainly a matter of *relationships*, that is to say, it is an issue that necessarily requires an assessment of its impact on the rights of *others*, both *within* and *outside* the community concerned. The governing of competing rights-claims is integral to much of international human rights law and adjudication. However, what makes autonomy issues somewhat unique in this context is that, in addition to the articulation of basic spaces of freedom as discussed earlier, autonomy regimes ordinarily take the form of institutional structures, entities or otherwise bodies endowed with a measure of political and legal decision-making authority in the public sphere. So while the existence of autonomy can and should be thought to attract protection under human rights law, the sustainability of autonomy can only be achieved within a wider robust rights-based framework that accounts for the internal diversity and plurality of groups. It is precisely the relational dimension of self-determination that comes into view in the *Reference* case, where the Court articulated matters of internal governance, including Quebec's autonomy, by delving into the complex constitutional interplay of federalism, democracy, the rule of law and the protection of minorities. In this sense, recognising Quebec's Francophone population as a 'people' for purposes of international law (or even a 'people' amongst other 'peoples' within Quebec) would not have added anything specific or substantive to the general argument. The key point here is that autonomy for the benefit of certain sub-national groups does *not* involve unilateral rights to determine one's political and legal status within the wider polity or unbounded freedom within the group itself, however strong the relative position of the group (in terms of right-holding or status) can be.[70]

69 Though not necessarily a conclusive factor in terms of conflict resolution, it should be noted that the international support for robust autonomy regimes in Eastern Europe as a way of settling territorial disputes has often represented an attempt at reintroducing such regimes in a revised form. *See* discussion below, Section 3.1.

70 As noted, this point is valid in relation to the UDRIP as well.

What this relational dimension does bring into focus is instead, I would submit, the justificatory capacity of international human rights law vis-à-vis autonomy regimes. In the widely known disputes over Quebec's language policies in the 1990s initially turning on the exclusivity of the French language in a variety of activities, including outdoor commercial ones, adjudicators, including at one stage the HRC, were concerned with the question of whether the affected English speakers had been effectively deprived of their right to use the language of their choice in relation to those activities.[71] The legal and political controversy was not meant to contest the very existence of interferences or restrictions resulting from those policies – arguably the upshot of any autonomy regime – but rather whether they represented a fundamental denial of the rights of others (in this case, of English language users living in Quebec). The HRC recognised the legitimate aim of those policies but concluded that the implementation of those policies still required adjustments that would render them fully human rights compliant. This example broadly chimes, not only with the relational rationale firmly endorsed in the *Reference* case, but also with a wider strand of human rights practice, particularly judicial and quasi-judicial practice, which has frequently upheld the *overall legitimacy* of the group arrangements in question, such as special mechanisms of political representation, territorially-based language/education provisions or even statutory-based religious practices, while still seeking revisions and corrections of particular aspects of them.[72] In this sense, the justificatory (legitimacy-enhancing) ability of human rights discourse has less to do with the finding of an obligation upon states to grant autonomy and more to do with making sure that autonomy is in practice compatible with international human rights law.

This is not to suggest that all autonomy arrangements have unproblematically passed human rights scrutiny. Rather, the point here is that this sort of scrutiny works towards identifying the broad parameters within which, in circumstances of diversity and pluralism, those arrangements are required to operate. For example, in its 2003 judgment in *Refah Partisi and Others v. Turkey* the European Court of Human Rights famously dismissed as tout court incompatible with Article 14 ECHR a model of faith-based legal pluralism that would curtail individual freedom, would cover all fields of public and private law, and would deny

71 For general accounts and discussion, *see e.g.* Pentassuglia, *Minority Groups and Judicial Discourse in International Law: A Comparative Perspective* (Martinus Nijhoff Publishers, Leiden, 2009) pp. 130–131; J. Tully, *Strange Multiplicity: Constitutionalism in an Age of Diversity* (Cambridge University Press, Cambridge, 1995) pp. 168–171.

72 G. Pentassuglia, *supra* note 71, pp. 125–133; *id., supra* note 18, pp. 11–13.

the state the role of guarantor of individual rights.[73] Nevertheless, for all the criticism that it sparked, this decision could hardly entail the impermissibility of forms of cultural autonomy under the ECHR. The Court did not take issue with forms of faith-based legal pluralism in other cases, including exemptions from the general law for certain religious rituals or the implementation of religious court rulings, as long as the rights of the individual had been protected in those particular instances.[74] The *Refah Partisi* decision essentially reaffirmed that logic by implicitly signalling a number of criteria (freedom of choice; appropriate tailoring of decision-making authority; parallel secular remedies) against which forms of legal pluralism should be assessed on a case-by-case basis. This is also in line with other human rights regional and global trends that largely break down matters of legal pluralism (broadly understood) into sub-sets of issues focussing on the concrete operation of the regime and whether any internal reform that may be needed is being fostered by the state by encouraging an inclusive and participatory process within the community.[75] Interpretative judgments are of course amenable to challenge and calls for further review of the arrangements can be made in legal and political discourse. International human rights law does not have the capacity to generate ready answers to what are often complex domestic circumstances, but it can draw upon standards, indicators or other considerations typical of legal argumentation in order to test the viability of those arrangements and/or their need for contextual recalibration. Admittedly, there are cases where drawing the line between the enabling and disallowing role of international human rights law will be more difficult to achieve as the arrangements draw their force precisely from their being structurally open-ended settlements available for contestation and potential revision.[76]

Whether it comes into view as a space of freedom, a legal requirement or possibility, an international guarantee against domestic encroachments, or a legitimate and human rights compliant institutional devise, autonomy for

73 Applications Nos. 41340/98, 41342/98 & 41344/98, Judgment of 13 February 2003.

74 *See e.g. Jewish Liturgical Ass'n Cha'are Shalom ve Tsedek v. France*, Application No. 2741/95, Judgment of June 27 2000; *Serif v. Greece*, Application No. 38178/97, Judgment of 14 December 1999.

75 For a thoughtful review of human rights practice at regional and global levels, *see e.g.* H. Quane, *supra* note 12, p. 675, at pp. 687–702.

76 For examples of 'hard cases' and possible criteria, *see* G. Pentassuglia, *supra* note 14, pp. 308–316. For the complex question of comprehensive power-sharing agreements such as the Dayton Peace Agreement in Bosnia, *see e.g.* C. McCrudden and B. O'Leary, 'Courts and Consociations or How Human Rights Courts May Destabilize Power-sharing Settlements', 24 *European Journal of International Law* (2013) p. 477, at pp. 493–496; C. Bell, *supra* note 43, pp. 236–238.

ethno-cultural sub-national groups reproduces itself – almost invariably – as a means to an end, not an end in itself. It may or may not be linked to a particular right or a particular group status or a particular international standard and still be open to endorsement or challenge on separate grounds. At the level of rights and obligations, autonomy is always contextual and contingent upon a variety of factors – from group existence and claims to the boundaries of its protection under international human rights law and domestic law. As the multiple faces of autonomy expose legal complexities that are typically obscured by concerns with the establishment of direct rights to autonomy for tightly construed classes of 'peoples', they also reflect deeper conceptual and practical uncertainties about the 'contingency' of autonomy in overarching debates over self-determination and sovereignty, human rights, and the role of law. It is these more 'systemic' issues that I intend to address in the remainder of this chapter.

3 Autonomy within the International Legal System: Contingent, Not Inherent

3.1 *Autonomy and the Ambivalences of International Law Discourse*

In one sense, autonomy as a contingent project seems to be fuelled by at least two empirical challenges. On the one hand, it is widely acknowledged that different circumstances on the ground require different measures, and that although autonomy may work in some cases, it may well not work, or may even be counter-productive, in other cases. Crucially, the types of autonomy vary and are not necessarily exhausted by the model of territorial self-government which is built around a set of public powers, including legislative ones, assigned to a particular constitutional unit within the state which functions primarily for the benefit of a group that is predominately concentrated in the designated area.[77]

Indeed, models of so-called cultural (non-territorially-based) autonomy involving a measure of decision-making authority in narrowly tailored matters of special significance to the group's identity, have also proved viable in a number of cases in the past and some states have revived weaker or stronger versions of this model in their national legislation. Even so, questions have been

77 For discussion and comparisons, *see e.g.* H. Hannum, *supra* note 6; M. Suksi, *Sub-State Governance Through Territorial Autonomy: A Comparative Study in Constitutional Law of Powers, Procedures and Institutions* (Springer-Verlag, Heidelberg, 2011).

raised about the reach of this form of autonomy and the extent to which it can replace territorial solutions. In fact, it has been argued that in several cases where cultural autonomy can be a useful option the overall approach rests (or should rest) on a combination of territorial and non-territorial arrangements. This is because several (if not all) minority groups tend to live in certain parts of the state or are otherwise partly 'concentrated' and partly 'dispersed'.[78] More broadly, details of design, including content and modalities of power distribution, level of entrenchment, financial arrangements, as well as dispute settlement mechanisms, represent classic institutional factors on which the practical viability of autonomy depends.[79] It is thus no coincidence that international law has proved generally unable to provide specific guidance on the form of autonomy in any particular context.[80]

On the other hand, as I noted, autonomy tends to be seen as the preferred, or indeed the only option in particular conflict situations. Following a detailed review of the conflict-related practice developed under the auspices of the Organisation on Security and Cooperation in Europe (OSCE) and the United Nations throughout the 1990s, including the Kosovo crisis, Julie Ringelheim obverses, for example, that "these two institutions consider themselves entitled to support solutions of autonomy – even though they imply a restructuring of the country – when it is aimed at settling civil war".[81] She goes on to conclude that this signals an extensive interpretation of the scope of such institutions' action in those circumstances.

These are unquestionably very real challenges with a very real impact on day-to-day approaches. However, I would argue that, no matter how practically constraining these variables are, the contingency of autonomy in human rights discourse is fundamentally a function of the conceptual ambivalence of international law discourse towards autonomy solutions. Unsurprisingly, this ambivalence has largely played out in the context of self-determination.

---

78 M. Suksi, *supra* note 24, p. 82, at p. 114. For discussion, *see also* E. Nimni, A. Osipov and D. J. Smith (eds.), *The Challenge of Non-Territorial Autonomy* (Peter Lang, Bern, 2013).

79 These institutional variables are obviously on top of broader domestic and regional political factors that affect the sustainability of autonomy arrangements, including the timely handling of claims. *See e.g.* Y. Ghai, 'Introduction: Nature and origins of autonomy', in Y. Ghai and S. Woodman (eds.), *Practising Self-Government: A Comparative Study of Autonomous Regions* (Cambridge University Press, Cambridge, 2013) pp. 25–31.

80 *See e.g.* A. Cassese, *supra* note 2, p. 332.

81 J. Ringelheim, 'Considerations on the International Reaction to the 1999 Kosovo Crisis', 2 *Revue Belge de Droit International* (1999) p. 523.

This can be best illustrated by post-World War II and post-Cold War debates over ideas of sovereignty, democracy, and security. At one end of this scale are positions that have equated the right of self-determination with a right of the state. Commenting on the immediate aftermath of decolonisation in Africa, Hurst Hannum perceptively remarks that "Africa may simply be more honest that the rest of the world in admitting that self-determination *of the state* has replaced the theoretical self-determination of peoples".[82] This statist view post-independence effectively sought to realign the debate to the post-1945 legal view of self-determination as a matter of sovereignty free from external interference. Indeed, it chimed with the early United Nations articulation of self-determination as a means of furthering friendly inter-state relations – a legal (positivist) snapshot of an international system based on independent sovereigns.[83] From this perspective, hostility towards autonomy solutions is the logical consequence of governmental resistance to decentralisation of power, which is perceived as a threat to 'national unity' understood as the centralising imperative of the state and a firewall against potentially secessionist tendencies. It is no coincidence that early (postcolonial) approaches to the ACHPR's 'peoples' rights' often conflated the rights of peoples with the rights of states or governments.[84]

But just as the African Commission on Human and Peoples' Rights has eventually (and correctly) increasingly looked below the surface of the state to protect and accommodate the rights of sub-national groups under the ACHPR – a line now upheld by the Court –, so too international law has firmly entrenched a move from state to people by both insisting on the latter's right to self-determination in the context of decolonisation – as best articulated in the 1960 Declaration – and shifting the emphasis towards notions of 'representative government' and participation outside that particular context. Nevertheless, calls for equating internal self-determination with a distinct

82 H. Hannum, *supra* note 6, p. 47.

83 United Nations Charter, Articles 1(2) and 55. *See* G. Pentassuglia, 'State Sovereignty, Minorities and Self-Determination: A Comprehensive Legal View', 9 *International Journal on Minority and Group Rights* (2002) p. 303, at pp. 304–305.

84 *See e.g.* J. Crawford, 'The Rights of Peoples: 'Peoples' or 'Governments'? in J. Crawford (ed.), *The Rights of Peoples* (Oxford University Press, Oxford, 1988) p. 55. For an example of the lingering effects of this, *see e.g.* D. Bayir, 'Turkey, the Kurds, and the legal contours of the right to self-determination', 1 *Kurdish Studies* (2013) p. 5, at pp. 17–19; J. Summers, 'The Internal and External Aspects of Self-Determination Reconsidered', in D. French (ed.), *Statehood and Self-Determination: Reconciling Tradition and Modernity in International Law* (Cambridge University Press, Cambridge, 2015) p. 229, at p. 238.

'right to democracy' under international law – the right of a people to engage in meaningful decision-making within the state – have remained ambiguous given their somehow elusive empirical foundations and more crucially, the different ways in which the requirement of democracy can be articulated. Here again, autonomy solutions have been rejected or endorsed depending on the idea of democracy said to be emerging as part of the human rights canon. Proponents of narrow electoral views of democracy have emphasised general collective aspects of voting rights and internationally-backed processes of election monitoring rather than any requirement of allocating or reallocating decision-making power for the benefit of particular minority groups.[85] And yet, insofar as minority groups endemically manifest themselves as political minorities and come under pressure to conform to dominant cultural norms, a 'right to democracy' understood as a mere entitlement to liberal democracy does little to engage with such groups' claims, including claims to some form of political autonomy.[86] Although the 1970 United Nations Friendly Relations Declaration does not resolve these matters (and neither do other international instruments that draw upon the notion of internal self-determination), there are good reasons to believe that a fluid and broader conception of democracy can be derived from the interlocking impact of various human rights norms, including the ones that articulate equality and participatory standards for minority groups as an enriched version of representation within a general framework based on the rule of law.[87]

85 *See e.g.* T. Franck, 'The Emerging Right to Democratic Governance', 86 *American Journal of International Law* (1992) p. 46; G. Fox, 'The Right to Political Participation in International Law', 17 *Yale Journal of International Law* (1992) p. 539; G. Fox and B. Roth (eds.), *Democratic Governance and International Law* (Cambridge University Press, Cambridge, 2000). But *see also* United Nations Millennium Declaration, GA Res. 55/2, UN Doc. A/55/L.2 (2000), Section V, paras. 24–25.

86 For a thoughtful account, *see e.g.* S. Marks and A. Clapham, *International Human Rights Lexicon* (Oxford University Press, Oxford, 2005) pp. 61–70. From a different angle, *see also* D. Orentlicher, 'Separation Anxiety: International Responses to Ethno-Separatist Claims', 23 *Yale Journal of International Law* (1998) p. 1, at pp. 44–78 (cautioning that an unconditional and rapid focus on popular sovereignty might paradoxically support certain ethno-separatist claims and/or entrench ethnic divisions while a strong civic culture is still in the making).

87 *See e.g.* the United Nations Secretary General's Study cited *supra* note 39; G. Pentassuglia, *supra* note 14, pp. 274–278; it is worth noting here that in the *Reference* case the Supreme Court of Canada did take a complex view of democracy that embraced robust participatory standards, including forms of self-government.

However, placing the normative spotlight on democratic regimes has typically generated controversy over the content and boundaries of such regimes – from minimalist universal requirements of non-discrimination and electoral rights to ambitious and contextual projects of constitutional restructuring. To the extent that a focus on democratic governance aligns with traditional accounts of human rights, it also generates tensions with efforts to vest rights in particular minority communities.[88] More importantly, a focus on the content of domestic arrangements within a particular institutional human rights-based framework, together with assessments of the various decision-making models that are available, have often obscured central questions relating to the legitimacy of the broader political community within which group claims, including autonomy claims, are made. There is little evidence in international law, however, that claiming autonomy as a 'people' endowed with an 'inherent' right to self-determination can in itself operate as a helpful or necessary ingredient of this debate, though it might perhaps prove of some legal significance within particular contexts for particular purposes.

At the opposite end of this scale of ambivalence is what I might call the security approach to autonomy. As I mentioned, there is some kind of consensus amongst international organisations and in expert analyses that autonomy is one of the most appropriate ways of settling territorial disputes – a constructive alternative to secession and thus state fragmentation. This position has been reinforced in cases where the group concerned used to enjoy some form of autonomy that was subsequently, and abruptly, removed due to changing political circumstances.[89] In one sense, this approach seems to restate the aforementioned line of reasoning, namely that autonomy may prove the best way of securing a host of human rights pertaining to members of minority groups, most notably rights to participate in decision-making. In this context, autonomy (and a fortiori, its reinstatement) would result from good faith negotiations that both the government

88 The point can also be made from a moral or political perspective. A modified version of the approach to democracy, including the 'equalising effect' of autonomy regimes, is defended, for example, by A. Patten, *supra* note 30, p. 120.

89 For discussion, *see e.g.* M. Weller and S. Wolff (eds.) *Autonomy, Self-Governance, and Conflict Resolution: Innovative Approaches to Institutional Design in Divided Societies* (Routledge, London, 2005); S. Spiliopoulou Åkermark (ed.), *The Åland Example and Its Components: Relevance for International Conflict Resolution* (The Åland Islands Peace Institute, Mariehamn, 2011); R. Lapidoth, *Autonomy: Flexible Solutions to Ethnic Conflicts* (US Institute of Peace Press, Washington DC, 1997).

and the legitimate group representatives would be legally required to undertake.[90] In another sense, though, international support for autonomy solutions in states torn by armed conflict places pragmatic considerations of stability rather than normative concerns at the very centre of this approach. The prevention of ethnic conflict or its further escalation is what, for example, has led the OSCE to support high levels of autonomy in such areas as Nagorno-Karabakh (Azerbaijan) or Transnistria (Moldova), despite the complexities of the territorial claims involved and their hybrid ('ethno-territorial') connotation. Crucially, what many of these cases have in common is not only the fact that the territories have enjoyed some level of autonomy in the past, but also the recognition by the international community of the group's *factual control over the area* or otherwise a situation on the ground which is nearly impossible to ignore, involving significant *loss of life* or at least strong potential for it.

One can safely argue that in times of war the logic of the institutional approach to autonomy replicates at its core the traditional logic of international law vis-à-vis secession. While there is no freestanding right to secession under international law, the 'fact' of a successful secession against the will of the central government will be processed by the international legal order in ways that can govern the consequences arising from it. The principle of 'effectiveness' is not necessarily a trump card for securing statehood under these circumstances, but what is important to stress here is that its logic is fundamentally the logic of *fait accompli* whereby international law's clearly hostile, yet deregulatory, approach to unilateral secession can be overtaken by new political and military realities on the ground, and can possibly become entrenched by some degree of international recognition.[91] Similarly in cases where autonomy is being seen as a solution to an ongoing ethnic conflict, the international community tends to be exceptionally vocal in response to new 'facts' on the ground – the reality of territorial control and/ or loss of life often coupled with the abolition of previous forms of autonomy – and, conversely, more cautious and tentative (though not necessarily hostile) where these circumstances have not (or have never) been met.

---

90 J. Ringelheim, *supra* note 81, pp. 527–528; C. Bell, *supra* note 43, ch. 11.

91 T. Christakis, 'The State as a 'primary fact': some thoughts on the principle of effectiveness', in M. Kohen (ed.), *Secession: International Law Perspectives* (Cambridge University Press, Cambridge, 2006) p. 138. As a matter of positive international law, it is doubtful that this approach has been radically altered by scholarly sympathies for the notion of remedial secession in response to a state's endemic failure to generate a 'representative government' in the sense of the 1970 Declaration.

The consequent asymmetry in fostering autonomy solutions then becomes a reflection of *realpolitik*, not human rights law.

The upshot of these underlying ambivalences is that autonomy, whatever the model, is deemed either unacceptable in the name of overly statist priorities, or in tension with conventional democratic procedures and the equal rights of individuals, or a necessary evil to prevent or stop the outbreak of ethnic violence – perhaps a necessary step on the road to 'normal' statehood.[92] As these tensions variably impact the language and scope of international human rights law, they also raise the question of whether there is a better way to explain the role of autonomy in human rights discourse, not only from the perspective of human rights norms and their practical working (the focus of Section 2), but also in terms of its broader function within an international legal system of which human rights law is a key counterpoint.

3.2 *The Contingency of Autonomy and the Shaping of Sovereignty*

When stepping back from issues of legal detail one would find it difficult to deny that the protection of minority rights, including indigenous rights, runs deeper than mainstream accounts of human rights seem to suggest. While the legal entrenchment of those rights within the wider international human rights framework has been repeatedly affirmed, their deep intertwining with the allocation and reallocation of sovereign authority within the international legal order has been often missed or underplayed. Traditional views of human rights focus on the role of minority cultures within a universal code of human rights standards that values (at least in principle) cultural differences across the wide spectrum of human identity. What is less commonly analysed, though, is the close interaction between the protection of groups like 'national minorities' and 'indigenous peoples' and the ways in which sovereignty manifests itself in international law.[93]

---

92 For an illustration of this conundrum in the context of the Dayton Agreement, *see* the European Court of Human Rights' decision in *Sejdić and Finci v. Bosnia and Herzegovina*, Applications Nos. 27996/06 and 34836/06, Judgment of 22 December 2009, Dissenting Opinion of Judge Bonello. *See also* McCrudden and B. O'Leary, *supra* note 76; and the chapter by Padraig McAuliffe in this volume.

93 A strand of scholarship has drawn attention in different ways to this 'systemic' dimension. *See e.g.* P. Macklem, *supra* note 2, chs. 5–7; S. Krasner and D. Froats, 'Minority Rights and the Westphalian Model', in D. Lake and D. Rothchild (eds.), *The International Spread of Ethnic Conflict: Fear, Diffusion, and Escalation* (Princeton University Press, Princeton, 1998) p. 227; C. Reus-Smit, *Individual Rights and the Making of the International System* (Cambridge University Press, Cambridge, 2013) pp. 97–105; J. Nijman, 'Minorities and Majorities', in

The terms of this interaction can be traced back to the articulation of sovereignty that the international legal system entrenches and the implications of that sovereignty's continuing (internal) exercise, rather than the universal value of identity or cultural affiliations alone.[94] The several allocations and reallocations of sovereign authority that have been buttressed by international law throughout history through treaty settlements, special acquisition doctrines, acts of independence, or otherwise ex post-facto validations, have been constantly punctuated by efforts to mitigate the effects of those redistributions on groups who found themselves within wider political communities with which they had little or no affiliation. From the Westphalia settlement, to the Versailles and League of Nations settlement, to the rise of indigenous rights post-decolonisation, to more recent attempts to govern the demise of the USSR and Yugoslavia and other processes of state reconfiguration, the mitigating impact of these multi-layered regimes of group protection says more about the structural impact of international law than it says about the universality of cultural difference per se. It does point to a series of 'pathologies' or 'anomalies' that arise upon several recalibrations of sovereign power and the deployment of those norms as a way to not only limit and correct, but also (re-)define 'Westphalian sovereignty'.[95] And to the extent that the 'anomaly'

B. Fassbinder and A. Peters (eds.), *The Oxford Handbook of the History of International Law* (Oxford University Press, Oxford, 2012) p. 100; R. Kuppe, 'The Three Dimensions of the Rights of Indigenous Peoples', 11 *International Community Law Review* (2009) p. 103.

94 For excellent discussion, *see* P. Macklem, *supra* note 2, p. 48 (noting for example, that minority rights are meant "to mitigate injustices associated with the kinds of recalibrations of sovereign power that international law treats as possessing international legal force"). For an earlier articulation of aspects of this tension in human rights discourse from a jurisprudential perspective, *see* G. Pentassuglia, *supra* note 71, pp. 248–256.

95 N. Berman, '"But the Alternative is Despair": European Nationalism and the Modernist Renewal of International Law', 106 *Harvard Law Review* (1993) p. 1792, at pp. 1872–1873 (commenting on the role of international law in shaping 'national' statehood at Versailles, and the role of the international community in the Aaland Islands case evidenced by the solutions favoured by the Rapporteurs: "[m]inority protection was no one-shot affair like a plebiscite; it effected the permanent embroidering of the sovereign into the fabric of the international legal community"). For a review of the historical link between sovereignty and minority protection, *see* J. Nijman, *supra* note 93. For a reading of Opinion No. 2 of the so-called Badinter Commission as an attempt to redefine the nature of sovereignty in former Yugoslavia, *see* C. Bell, *supra* note 43, pp. 225–226. *See generally* European Community Declaration on Yugoslavia and the Declaration on the Guidelines on the Recognition of New States in Eastern Europe and in the Soviet Union, 16 December 1991, 31 *International Legal Materials* (1992) p. 1485; *Report of the Secretary General on the International Conference on the Former Yugoslavia*, *ibid.*, p. 1549.

is dynamically projected into the future of the state, it speaks to a concept of internal self-determination as a legal context within which that type of group protection, in its multiple articulations and iterations, must be achieved.[96]

In this sense, the contingency of group protection is not solely a matter of practical implementation or a function of military or political realities, but derives from distinctive sovereign redistributions and distinctive conditions for 'just' social and political orders. This explains the tension within traditional human rights discourse when it comes to developing specific positive obligations for the benefit of minority groups and/or a pro-active approach to issues that affect the constitutional organisation of the state.[97] Pragmatism, for its part, is unable to explain possibilities of legal or institutional differentiation or asymmetries within the state in ways other than crude deference to political stability or conflict resolution, or even the intentional or unintentional forging of sovereign inequalities.[98]

Autonomy is deeply intertwined with these narratives and legal dimensions. For one thing, international human rights law does provide varying (and ever expanding) degrees of protection for the cultural interests of minority groups. It begins by protecting a space of pluralism and non-discrimination that fits more accurately into a classic code of human rights standards – a space that can translate into 'thin' forms of personal autonomy through private law structures while enabling the legitimate articulation of group identities and

96 M. Koskenniemi, *supra* note 10, pp. 247–249 (noting that self-determination "both supports and challenges statehood" in the sense that the anomalies primarily linked to the creation of states have been gradually contained by the "anti-statist character of self-determination" built around group protection within the territorial state). *See* more broadly, G. Pentassuglia, 'Self-Determination, Human Rights, and the Nation-State: Revisiting Group Claims through a Complex Nexus in International Law', 19 *International Community Law Review* (2017), forthcoming.

97 On some of these tensions, *see e.g.* G. Pentassuglia, *supra* note 14, pp. 291–292. After all, the idea that the cultural distinctiveness of minority groups would progressively disappear within wider national communities was frequently voiced in the distant and not-so-distant past. *See e.g.* A. Anghie, 'Nationalism, Development and the Postcolonial State: The Legacies of the League of Nations', 41 *Texas International Law Journal* (2006) p. 447.

98 *See e.g.* J. Nijman, *supra* note 93, p. 115 (noting the built-in asymmetries in legal obligations regarding minority protection in the Versailles settlement). N. Berman, 'The International Law of Nationalism: Group Identity and Legal History', in D. Wippman (ed.), *International Law and Ethnic Conflict* (Cornell University Press, Ithaca and London, 1998) pp. 36–44 (elaborating on the active role of international law in entrenching or rejecting cultural projections relating to 'nations', 'minorities' and 'persons belonging' to them in Europe and beyond, including partly the League Mandate system).

claims.[99] But as the focus shifts away from these traditional human rights dimensions towards a core claim to ticker levels of legal and political authority within the state, the relationship between autonomy and international human rights law becomes tense and, as noted, ambivalent.

On the one hand, important (yet often neglected) substantive elements of the autonomy debate have been endorsed in human rights practice, in addition to the most obvious articulation of an indigenous right to autonomy under the UNDRIP. At the same time, international human rights law tends to fall back on an overarching requirement of good faith negotiations between the group and the state as part of a continuing relationship between the state and the wider political community. Internal self-determination in international law effectively provides the context for intercultural conversations – 'multilogues' to borrow from James Tully – over the nature of the state and the legitimacy of its authority, that is, over the very terms of that relationship.[100]

If this reading is correct, then the contingency of autonomy for certain ethno-cultural groups does not reflect a debate over what is inside or outside international human rights law (or an alleged irreconcilability of individual and collective interests), nor is it only a function of the vagaries of practical circumstances and variety of autonomy models. Instead, it is linked to the normative question of whether or not autonomy can and should rebut the presumption of authority and viability of existing arrangements within the state. As long as we see autonomy (and the field as a whole) as primarily designed to mitigate the impact of certain group-related pathologies that arise from the very allocation and reallocation of sovereign authority actively pursued or validated by international law, autonomy in human rights discourse can only, relatedly, serve the purpose of remedying or offsetting those pathologies, that is, certain forms of majoritarian domination or oppression that have emerged (or might emerge) as a result of that process. Exclusion from state-formation in its various forms and/or unequal access to government, systematic attempts at forced assimilation into a singularly defined 'national' identity and/or coercive measures involving state-sponsored violence, the abolition of previous levels of self-government, or a combination of these, represent the most obvious threats faced by the groups claiming some measure of 'thick' autonomy on a territorial or non-territorial basis. Historically, some of these pathologies have been 'cured' (at least partially) upon the very creation or enlargement of

99 *See supra* Section 2. For examples drawn from human rights jurisprudence, *see* G. Pentassuglia, *supra* note 18.

100 G. Pentassuglia, *supra* note 14, pp. 271–280. J. Tully, *supra* note 71.

a state, or even fuelled attempts to mitigate the impact of empires.[101] Others, such as the exclusion of indigenous communities from the acquisition of sovereign power or otherwise decision-making authority, have been addressed retrospectively, especially in the face of continuing threats and challenges faced by the group. In a significant number of other cases, the pathologies have remained unresolved.

What is important for present purposes is not whether autonomy regimes are put in place in any particular case. It is instead the fact that the contingency of such regimes depends, not simply upon issues of practical implementation, model design or one's conception of democracy, but upon deeper normative concerns regarding the extent to which the group has been affected by certain distributions of sovereign power buttressed by the international legal order and the parallel role of human rights as an internal substantive and procedural counterpoint. Given the largely reciprocal relationship between this type of group protection and sovereignty in international law, such normative concerns cannot be reduced, or made dependent upon, exclusive considerations of stability or perennial (yet inconclusive) quests for evidence of 'peoplehood' in the context of self-determination. Rather, they speak to the need to address some of the most typical pathologies, imbalances, or otherwise injustices affecting group identities that are (directly or indirectly) of international law's own making.

Seen through the prism of sovereignty, human rights law both enables the pursuit of autonomy as part of a series of institutional possibilities within the state (regardless of the potential remedy of remedial secession in the event that those possibilities are endemically lacking) and contributes to shaping up the legal boundaries of autonomy arrangements by articulating the relational dimension of such arrangements within the group and the larger political community. While this legal framework cannot *ipso facto* determine the outcome of the internal process, prejudge the options available regardless of empirical conditions and circumstances, let alone secure irreversible legal closure, it does help capture the key issues involved and how norms and practice ought to relate to them. More specifically, it seeks to distinguish claims (such as claims to autonomy) that are ultimately a call for enhancing or rebuilding the legitimacy of state sovereignty in its most foundational sense from claims (such as claims to non-discrimination or general cultural protection) that

101 For historical precedents and theoretical discussion in relation to imperial times, *see e.g.* K. Kössler, 'Conclusions: Beyond the Illusion of Ethno-culturally Homogenous Territory', in T. Malloy and F. Palermo (eds.), *supra* note 12, pp. 254–255; J. Tully, *supra* note 71, pp. 145–152.

only question the scope of particular forms of state power over individuals and groups within a jurisdiction the overall legitimacy of which is *prima facie* presumed.[102]

4 Conclusions: Group Autonomy between the Interstices and Structure of International Law

This chapter has sought to address the question of whether a right to autonomy for particular ethno-cultural groups is (or ought to be) available under international law, particularly in the context of the right to self-determination. The core thesis or structure of argument in this regard is defined by matters of right-holding and group status. It generally claims that, consistent with United Nations self-determination practice, the group concerned constitutes, or can be treated as, a 'people' (or a 'nation') entitled to territorial autonomy as part of an 'inherent' or 'universal' international legal right to (internal) self-determination. The gist of this line, whatever its distinctive outlook, lies in the legal reshaping of the language of 'peoplehood' and/or in grounding practical attempts to contain the 'anti-statist' potential of self-determination through distinctive rights to self-government. The twenty-year struggle of indigenous communities to be recognised as 'peoples' entitled to the right to self-determination under the UNDRIP epitomizes this sort of concern. In this chapter, I have pursued an alternative and more complex line of reasoning by contending that autonomy may or may not be a matter of right; it may or may not involve territorial control; it may or may not benefit an entity recognised as a 'people' (let alone a 'nation'); and it may or may not be based on international law. I have argued that, while there is a clear need for international human rights law to engage constructively with group claims to autonomy, there is much more to the story than free-standing rights, territorial exclusivity or distinct peoplehood (or nationhood).

---

102 For a broadly similar point on the question of sovereignty in the context of indigenous rights, *see e.g.* R. Kuppe, *supra* note 93, pp. 111–118. In this sense, the argument assumes the legal existence of states and looks at the issue of governmental legitimacy as a function of concrete interventions of international law, with their legacies of inclusion and exclusion, rather than a matter to be solved or framed in purely theoretical terms, let alone through semantic or ideological shortcuts. It is of course a different matter how each of those interventions should be characterised and whether autonomy can be an appropriate solution in any particular case. For a broader argument, see G. Pentassuglia, *supra* note 96.

The analysis has developed along two complementary trajectories. At the level of legal standards and practice, I have sought to disaggregate the autonomy debate into a number of elements or dimensions that draw upon emerging hybrid forms of group protection within the wider framework of international human rights law. They generally defy strict distinctions between the individual and the group in human rights discourse and show autonomy, not as a 'quick fix' to be endorsed by law and implemented by states, but as a project contingent upon a variety of factors – from group existence and claims to the boundaries of its protection under international human rights law and domestic law. By emphasising autonomy as a space of freedom, a legal requirement or possibility, an international guarantee against domestic encroachments, or a legitimate and human rights compliant institutional devise, I have sought to expose the complex multidimensionality of the autonomy debate from a human rights perspective that is typically obscured by preoccupations with the establishment of direct, 'primordial' legal rights to autonomy for tightly construed classes of 'peoples'. I have looked at autonomy essentially as a bundle of legal and policy issues rather than a problem to be solved through ready-made and generally applicable rights.

In so doing I have also exposed deeper tensions surrounding the 'contingency' of autonomy in human rights discourse against overarching debates over self-determination, sovereignty, and the role of law. I have argued that, while autonomy as a contingent institutional possibility can be said to be a function of conceptual ambivalences in international human rights law that are fuelled by statist, moral or *realpolitik* priorities, and that those ambivalences can be partly reinforced by genuine complications of autonomy design and implementation in particular domestic contexts, autonomy issues call above all for an assessment of the very pathologies or anomalies that need to be addressed within the framework of the state. There is no evidence, though, that a focus on "supposedly timeless or historical or primordial rights"[103] is a helpful or necessary ingredient of this debate, whatever significance it may have in particular legal settings. Rather, I have argued that the question of autonomy in human rights law should be addressed in the context of a larger story about the way in which the international legal system actively partakes in the articulation of sovereign authority and the extent to which human rights law – as an integral part of that system – can remedy or offset whatever majoritarian domination or oppression has resulted (or might result) from that articulation.

---

103 H. Hannum, *supra* note 6, p. 503.

Some serious group-related pathologies relating to the very nature and/or competing visions of the state and its political community represent the most obvious or familiar candidates for a remedy in the form of territorial or non-territorial autonomy. Other pathologies boil down to more general cultural recognition deficits that require positive rights to equality and bespoke identity protection – an active role in the reshaping of 'national identity' – instead of autonomy as a discrete regime or device.[104] What is important here is that minority groups are treated as very concrete by-products of certain allocations and re-allocations of sovereign power rather than abstract or 'natural' images or configurations of cultural difference throughout the world.

Although this framework does not dictate the specific outcome of the internal process, it arguably contributes to closing the gap between seemingly unconditional rights and the legally crude role of effectiveness or political realities by providing a better, more principled explanation of debates over the re-allocation or dislocation of power through various forms of minority protection or indigenous rights, including complex self-determination regimes in international law and constitutional law.[105] Crucially, it works towards a human rights framework that has the capacity to value and distinguish certain ethno-cultural group claims from the plethora of claims made by individuals and groups, on the basis of their significance relative to the interface between sovereignty and international law-making.[106]

---

104 For discussion of the claims involved and their impact on human rights categories, *see* G. Pentassuglia, *supra* note 14, especially pp. 274, 277, 280 (commenting on the question of self-government versus other human rights claims).

105 These debates tend to be conducted either in isolation from one another (the indigenous literature on autonomy being the most obvious example of this), or from the descriptive perspective of institutional design, or from some other particular vantage point, as I have noted. Many of these debates are oblivious to the complex role of international legal history and what it means, or has meant, to contemporary human rights-based group accommodation disputes.

106 More broadly (though largely implicitly), this line of reasoning also intimates something of a framework for assessing claims that transcend, in whole or in part, the politics of definition that largely absorbs debates over international legal claims made by 'national minorities', 'indigenous peoples' or other socio-cultural entities that view themselves as 'peoples' or 'nations'. In this sense, it differs from those arguments that seek to capture commonalities amongst certain groups and/or the varied elements of protection but still leave the origins of such commonalities or diverse levels of protection unexplained. *See e.g. supra* note 7.

CHAPTER 5

International Law, Ethno-Cultural Diversity and Indigenous Peoples' Rights: A Postcolonial Approach

Felipe Gómez Isa

> *In the past, indigenous peoples were living peacefully in their homelands, in harmony with nature. Then came 'civilization' ... They conquered the land, we lost our homes, our sacred sites, our agricultural areas, our hunting fields, our fishing waters. They called it development, we called it destruction ... They thought civilization, we lost our cultures, our language, our religion. They subjected us to their laws ... It has been going on for more than 500 years. And it still goes on.*[1]

1 Introduction

The international legal system has a contradictory and somewhat paradoxical nature as far as indigenous peoples are concerned. While traditional international law played a highly significant role in the dramatic history of the conquest of indigenous peoples, the usurpation of their sovereignty, and the dispossession of their lands, territories and resources, post-1945 international law has been increasingly used by indigenous peoples as a privileged avenue for framing their claims as human rights, calling for reparation of the historical injustices perpetrated against them, and fostering the recognition of their ethno-cultural diversity. The main aim of this chapter is to shed light on the function of international law as a legitimizing tool of colonialism and cultural imperialism in all its forms, thus paving the way for the physical annihilation and cultural alienation of indigenous peoples worldwide. The structural oppression still suffered by indigenous peoples has been defined by Latin American postcolonial theorists as the *coloniality of power*. Against this background, we will explore the potential of contemporary international law and international institutions to become tools of emancipation instead of sources of neo-colonial attitudes and practices.

1 Statement of Max Ooft, Organization of Indigenous Peoples in Suriname, UN Doc. E/CN.4/Sub.2/1995/24, para. 54.

 | DOI 10.1163/9789004328785_007

2 Early Legal Scholars and Natural Law

Pioneers of international law such as Francisco de Vitoria (1486–1547), Bartolomé de las Casas (1484–1566) and Hugo Grotius (1583–1645)[2] considered the Indians 'discovered' by Christopher Columbus as international legal subjects. These scholars defended the position that "indigenous peoples' societal structures constituted distinct polities that possessed political rights under international law".[3] As a consequence, Vitoria rejected both the authority of the Spanish Crown and the authority of the Pope[4] to acquire title over indigenous lands. Therefore, the Indians were regarded as "true owners of their lands".[5] The only legitimate title to enter into relations with the Indians was the *ius communicationis*,[6] the right to travel and trade with the Indians, and the right to preach the Catholic faith. All these rights were derived from core principles of natural law. But if the Indians interfered in the efforts to develop these activities, the Spanish Crown could resort to 'just war' and conquest. According to Anaya, "the theory of just war ... provided enduring support for patterns of colonization and empire that exerted control over indigenous peoples and their lands".[7]

---

2 A deep analysis of the main Grotian ideas on colonialism can be found in E. Keene, *Beyond the Anarchical Society: Grotius, Colonialism and Order in World Politics* (Cambridge University Press, Cambridge, 2002).

3 M. Ahrén, *Indigenous Peoples' Status in the International Legal System* (Oxford University Press, Oxford, 2016) p. 8.

4 Pope Alexander VI granted land title to Spain by virtue of his Bull *Inter Caetera*, adopted on 3 May 1493. Incredibly, this Papal Bull has not been officially revoked so far. On 4 May 2016, a delegation of eleven indigenous leaders from the US and Canada, in the framework of an indigenous march to Rome, asked Pope Francis I to revoke it and to "Shout out the Lie that a man can be considered as less than human purely because he does not worship at the same altar as other men from other land", available at *The Long March to Rome*, http://longmarchtorome.com/ (accessed 17 January 2017). On the influence of this Papal Bull on the evolution of international law, see K. B. Vera, 'From Papal Bull to Racial Rule: Indians of the Americas, Race, and the Foundations of International Law', 42 *California Western International Law Journal* (2011) pp. 453–472.

5 S. J. Anaya, *Indigenous Peoples in International Law* (Oxford University Press, Oxford, 2004) p. 17.

6 J. A. Carrillo Salcedo, 'Aportaciones de Francisco de Vitoria a los fundamentos filosóficos de los derechos humanos', in A. Mangas (ed.), *La Escuela de Salamanca y el Derecho Internacional en América. Del pasado al futuro* (Asociación Española de Profesores de Derecho Internacional y Relaciones Internacionales, Salamanca, 1993) p. 52.

7 *See* S. J. Anaya *supra* note 5, p. 19.

The truth is that the Spanish Crown "used the Catholic faith as the principal justification of its conquest".[8] This is well illustrated by the introduction of the so-called *Requerimiento* in 1513. The Requerimiento was a statement to be announced to the Indians before military hostilities could be legally launched. It basically *required* Indians to acknowledge "the Church as the Ruler and Superior of the whole world" and the Papal donation to the Spanish Crown of all territories they discover.[9] Additionally, the native Indians should allow the Catholic faith to be taught to them.[10] If they resisted, the Requerimiento threatened the Indians with the eloquent words that follow:

> [I]f you do not this or if you maliciously delay in doing it, I certify to you that with the help of God we shall make war against you…, we shall take you and your wives and your children and shall make slaves of them …; and we shall take away your goods and shall do to you all the damage that we can …; and we protest that the deaths and losses which shall accrue from this are your fault …[11]

Obviously, the Indians did not fully understand the real meaning of the formula used in the Requerimiento.[12] Therefore, it became a legal formalism to justify the conquest and the war against those who resisted,[13] in other words an act of profound hypocrisy. Some years later, Bartolomé de Las Casas strongly criticized these forms of evangelization, since the Catholic faith can only be

8 J. Gilbert, *Indigenous Peoples' Land Rights under International Law. From Victims to Actors* (Transnational Publishers, Ardsley, 2006) p. 7.

9 *See supra* note 4.

10 A detailed analysis of the Requerimiento can be found in L. Hanke, 'The Requerimiento and its Interpreters', 1 *Revista de Historia de América* (1938) pp. 25–34.

11 An English translation of the original document in Spanish can be found in L. Hanke, *The Spanish Struggle for Justice in the Conquest of America* (University of Pennsylvania Press, Philadelphia, 1949) p. 33.

12 As pointed out by Amber Ferris, "the observance of the proper application of The Requirement varied depending on the expedition. Some conquistadors read this in a 'grotesquely absurd' way while others took pains to make sure the natives understood what they were hearing", A. Ferris, 'Bartolome de las Casas Revisited', Seminar Paper Presented to the Department of History, Western Oregon University, in partial fulfillment of the requirements for the degree of Bachelor of Science in History, 2009, p. 17, available at http://www.wou.edu/history/files/2015/08/Amber-Ferris-HST-499.pdf (accessed 17 January 2017).

13 M. Segura Ortega, 'El Derecho de Indias', in G. Peces-Barba and E. Fernández (dirs.), *Historia de los Derechos Fundamentales. Tránsito a la Modernidad, Siglos XVI y XVII* (Dykinson, Madrid, 1998) p. 719.

preached by peaceful means and through persuasion.[14] But what Las Casas never questioned was the colonization process itself as a legitimate way to christianise the Indians.[15]

Although the Indians were considered as legitimate owners of their lands according to basic principles of natural law, in practice the Spanish Crown opened the door to dispossession by the *conquistadores* through the institution of the *Encomienda*. The encomienda was the institution that articulated the master-servant relationship between the colonists and the Indians in the very first phase of the colonization process,[16] and served both the religious interests of the Crown and the economic purposes of the conquistadores.[17] By virtue of it, the King distributed land and commended Indians (*repartimiento*[18]) to the settlers (*encomenderos*) for compulsory labour. In return, "the encomenderos were obliged to provide religious instruction for the Indians and to protect them".[19] The encomienda was conceived as a form of serfdom that did not give actual ownership of the Indian workers to the encomenderos, but "in practice it differed little from slavery".[20]

The so-called Spanish School of International Law, based on the Aristotelian and Thomist idea of the natural sociability and rationality of all human beings, defended the essential humanity and freedom of the Indians in the context of the Spanish conquest of the Americas.[21] The ideas of Vitoria and Las Casas paved the way to the consideration of the Indians as full human beings in need of care and protection.[22] All men, including the Indians, given that they

---

14 B. De las Casas, *De unico vocationis modo omnium gentium ad veram religionem* (*On the Only Way of Attracting All Peoples to the True Religion*), 1540.

15 R. Mesa, 'Bartolomé de las Casas, Maestro contemporáneo', in A. Mangas (ed.) *supra* note 6, p. 79.

16 One of the deepest analyses of the Encomienda system is to be found in S. Zavala, *La Encomienda Indiana* (Junta para la Ampliación de Estudios, Madrid, 1935). *See* also R. Himmerich y Valencia, *The encomenderos of New Spain, 1521–1555* (University of Texas Press, Austin, 1991).

17 R. Sánchez Domingo, 'Las Leyes de Burgos de 1512 y la Doctrina Jurídica de la Conquista', 28 *Revista Jurídica de Castilla y León* (2012) p. 25.

18 M. Segura Ortega *supra* note 13, p. 719.

19 L. Hanke, *supra* note 11, p. 19.

20 S. J. Anaya *supra* note 5, p. 35. Along the same lines *see* T. J. Yeager, 'Encomienda or Slavery? The Spanish Crown's Choice of Labor Organization in Sixteenth-Century Spanish America', 55 *The Journal of Economic History* (1995) pp. 842–859.

21 J. B. Scott, *The Spanish Origin of International Law: Francisco de Vitoria and his Law of Nations* (Clarendon Press, Oxford, 1934).

22 P. G. Carozza, 'From Conquest to Constitutions: Retrieving a Latin American Tradition of the Idea of Human Rights', 25 *Human Rights Quarterly* (2003) p. 291.

are made "in the image and likeness of God", must be regarded as *equal* and free[23] according to sacred principles of natural law.[24] But, unfortunately for indigenous peoples, the conquest of the Americas did not follow the teachings of these precursors of contemporary international human rights law.[25]

3 The Peace of Westphalia and Beyond

The Peace of Westphalia (1648) changed the nature and scope of the emerging international legal system, and consecrated the state as the unique international legal subject. Accordingly, peoples and other ethno-cultural entities had no place in international law whatsoever. In sharp contrast with Vitoria and Grotius, international law held that "indigenous peoples do not constitute international legal subjects".[26] This significant shift has been explained very illustratively by Paul Keal. In his view:

> [A]s the expansion of Europe proceeded international law became simultaneously more universal and exclusionary. It aspired to universal application, but excluded primitive societies from its community ... It was partly a result of the gradual eclipse of natural law as international law evolved into the positive law of relations between states.[27]

International law became a very powerful instrument of European expansionism and imperialism.[28] Since its inception, given the role played by the main European powers in its creation and the subordinate position of indigenous peoples and other non-Western countries and societies, international law

23 This is one of the main differences between Aristotle and Las Casas, since the Greek philosopher defended slavery as in conformity with natural law. On the influence of Aristotle on Las Casas *see* G. L. Huxley, *Aristotle, Las Casas and the American Indians* (Royal Irish Academy, Dublin, 1980).

24 C. del Arenal, 'La visión de la sociedad mundial en la Escuela de Salamanca', in A. Mangas *supra* note 6, p. 33.

25 F. Gómez Isa, 'The First Cry for Justice in the Americas-From Antonio de Montesinos to the Laws of Burgos (1512)', in M. Suksi *et al* (eds.), *First Fundamental Rights Documents in Europe. Commemorating 800 Years of Magna Carta* (Intersentia, Antwerp, 2015) p. 101.

26 *See* M. Ahrén *supra* note 3, p. 14.

27 P. Keal, *European Conquest and the Rights of Indigenous Peoples: The Moral Backwardness of International Society* (Cambridge University Press, Cambridge, 2003) p. 108.

28 A. Anghie, *Imperialism, Sovereignty and the Making of International Law* (Cambridge University Press, Cambridge, 2004).

could be characterised as a hegemonic discourse and a source of domination.[29] Along the same lines, Elvira Pulitano has referred to traditional international law as "quintessentially Eurocentric".[30] Indigenous peoples were not only excluded from international law-making, but also from the realm of 'civilization'. Using the binary category 'civilized vs. non-civilized', international law became an ideological tool to justify oppression, dispossession and marginalization of those that did not conform to the standard established by European states. The international legal order turned into a 'civilized' system of "construction of *otherness*",[31] thus legitimizing land appropriation through the concept of *terra nullius*,[32] political subordination, and cultural annihilation of those that did not deserve to be considered as civilized. Since then, the 'civilizing mission' to save non-European peoples from ignorance and backwardness has been one of the core aspirational principles of international law.[33]

---

29 B. Rajagopal, *International Law from Below. Development, Social Movements and Third World Resistance* (Cambridge University Press, Cambridge, 2003).

30 E. Pulitano, 'Indigenous rights and international law: an introduction', in E. Pulitano (ed.), *Indigenous Rights in the Age of the UN Declaration* (Cambridge University Press, Cambridge, 2012) p. 4.

31 *See* P. Keal *supra* note 27, p. 21.

32 As defined by Lindley, *terra nullius* is "a tract of territory … not subject to any sovereignty – either because it has never been so subject or, having once been in that condition, has been abandoned- in which case the sovereignty over it is open to acquisition by a process analogous to that by which property can be acquired in an ownerless thing", M. F. Lindley, *The Acquisition and Government of Backward Territory in International Law: Being a Treatise on the Law and Practice Relating to Colonial Expansion* (Negro University Press, New York, 1969) p. 10.

33 This is the essence of some provisions found both in the *General Act of the Berlin Conference* (1885) and in the *Covenant of the League of Nations* (1919). According to Article VI of the General Act of the Berlin Conference, "all the powers exercising sovereign rights or influence in the aforesaid territories bind themselves to watch over the preservation of the native tribes, and to care for the improvement of the conditions of their moral and material well-being … They shall … protect and favour all religious, scientific, or charitable institutions and undertakings created and organized for the above ends, or which aim at instructing the natives and *bringing home to them the blessings of civilization* …" (emphasis added). In the same vein, Article 22 of the Covenant of the League of Nations provided the following: "to those colonies and territories which as a consequence of the late war have ceased to be under the sovereignty of the States which formerly governed them and which are inhabited by *peoples not yet able to stand by themselves* under the strenuous conditions of the modern world, there should be applied the principle that the well-being and development of such peoples form a *sacred trust of civilization* …" (emphasis added).

Postcolonial scholars[34] have underlined that, in spite of the formal end of colonialism both in the American continent in the eighteenth century and in Africa and Asia in the twentieth century, most indigenous peoples still suffer the pervasive influence of what Eve Darian-Smith calls "new forms of colonialism"[35] that lead to "soft imperialism" over sites of former colonial control.[36] As has been critically emphasized by Antony Anghie, "imperialism has always been part of the international system",[37] therefore colonial relations still dominate the global relations between the North and the South,[38] and the internal relations between dominant societies and indigenous peoples within the boundaries of nation-states that emerged from the processes of decolonization.

An illustrative example of the continuation of colonial relations *vis-à-vis* indigenous peoples is the application of the rule of *uti possidetis*. According to this international legal principle, the borders drawn by colonizers should be maintained during and after the process of decolonization.[39] The main consequence of this policy was that the new states "had the same borders as the former colonies, and indigenous peoples continuously enjoyed no rights over their traditional territories".[40] In the case of Africa, the straight lines drawn by the colonial powers at the Berlin Conference in 1884 "cut right through the heartlands of very distinct linguistic and ethnic groups, creating problems that

34 E. W. Said, *Orientalism* (Penguin, London, 1978); G. C. Spivak, *A Critique of Postcolonial Reason* (Harvard University Press, Cambridge MA, 1999).

35 E. Darian-Smith, 'Postcolonial Theories of Law', in R. Banakar and M. Travers (eds.), *An Introduction to Law and Social Theory* (Hart Publishing, Oxford, 2013) p. 247.

36 K. Nkrumah, *Neo-Colonialism: The Last Stage of Imperialism* (International Publishers, New York, 1966).

37 A. Anghie, 'The Evolution of International Law: colonial and postcolonial realities', 27 *Third World Quarterly* (2006) p. 749.

38 On the role that International Financial and Trade Institutions such as the International Monetary Fund (IMF), the World Bank (WB) or the World Trade Organization (WTO) play in the maintenance of colonial relations between the North and the South aiming at the imposition of a neoliberal global order, *see* D. Fidler, 'A Kinder, Gentler System of Capitulations? International Law, Structural Adjustment Policies, and the Standard of Liberal, Globalized, Civilization', 35 *Texas International Law Journal* (2000) pp. 387–413; B. S. Chimni, 'International Institutions Today: An Imperial Global State in the Making', 15 *European Journal of International Law* (2004) pp. 1–37.

39 M. N. Shaw, 'The Heritage of States: The Principle of *Uti Possidetis Juris* Today', 67 *British Yearbook of International Law* (1997) pp. 97–151.

40 *See* M. Ahrén *supra* note 3, p. 19.

persist to the present day".[41] In practice, decolonization and emergence of new independent states did not make any meaningful difference for indigenous peoples; on the contrary, they continued experiencing oppressive and exclusionary colonial relations, particularly as regards their lands and territories.

The continuation of colonial and imperial relations as applied to indigenous peoples in Latin America has given rise to the concept of *coloniality of power*.[42] This concept influences not only power relations, but also the production and reproduction of knowledge,[43] and the construction of subjectivities and collective identities. As highlighted by a distinguished indigenous scholar, "while colonialism is the territorial occupation by coercive means..., coloniality refers to the imposition of the Western cultural imaginary",[44] an advanced form of cultural imperialism.[45] Coloniality of power implies that indigenous peoples are still in a situation of vulnerability and symbolic domination through the internalization of the logics of the coloniality of power. As a consequence, most legacies of colonialism still prevail in the relations between indigenous peoples and dominant sectors of society. The most influential consequence of the coloniality of power is the colonization of minds and hearts of subaltern groups such as indigenous peoples.[46] In this process of naturalization of

41 S. Wiessner, "Indigenous self-determination, culture, and land: a reassessment in light of the 2007 UN Declaration on the Rights of Indigenous Peoples", in E. Pulitano *supra* note 30, p. 36. A critical account of the influence of the principle of *uti possidetis* in today's Africa can be found in M. Mutua, 'Why Redraw the Map of Africa: A Moral and Legal Inquiry', 16 *Michigan Journal of International Law* (1995) pp. 1113–1176. *See also* S. R. Ratner, 'Drawing a Better Line: *Uti Possidetis* and the Borders of New States', 90 *American Journal of International Law* (1996) pp. 590–624.

42 *See* the seminal work by A. Quijano, 'Colonialidad y Modernidad/Racionalidad', in H. Bonilla (comp.), *Los conquistados. 1492 y la población indígena de las Américas* (Tercer Mundo-Libri Mundi, Bogotá, 1992) pp. 437–447. *See also* E. Dussel, *1492. El Encubrimiento del Otro: hacia el Origen del Mito de la Modernidad* (Plural Editores-UMSA, La Paz, 1994); W. Mignolo, 'El desprendimiento: pensamiento crítico y giro descolonial', in C. Walsh, A. García Linera y W. Mignolo (eds.), *Interculturalidad, Descolonización del Estado y del Conocimiento* (Ediciones del Signo, Buenos Aires, 2006) pp. 9–20.

43 *See* B. de Sousa Santos (ed.), *Another Knowledge is Possible: Beyond Northern Epistemologies* (Verso, London, 2007).

44 P. Garzón López, *Ciudadanía Indígena. Del multiculturalismo a la colonialidad del poder* (Centro de Estudios Políticos y Constitucionales, Madrid, 2016) p. 279.

45 I. M. Young, *Justice and the Politics of Difference* (Princeton University Press, Princeton, 1990); A. Martínez de Bringas, *La cultura como derecho en América Latina. Ensayo sobre la realidad postcolonial en la globalización* (Universidad de Deusto, Bilbao, 2005).

46 S. Castro-Gómez, *La poscolonialidad explicada a los niños* (Universidad Javeriana de Bogotá, Bogotá, 2005) p. 59.

domination, education and law play a remarkable role; they form a "constitutive link to the coloniality of power".[47]

4 Contemporary International Law: a New Approach to Indigenous Peoples

4.1 *The League of Nations and the International Labour Organization (ILO)*

The League of Nations (1919) began to pay attention to the situation of indigenous peoples after First World War, and opened some limited spaces for indigenous advocacy before the League.[48] According to Article 23.b) of the Covenant of the League of Nations, the members of the League committed to "undertake to secure just treatment of the native inhabitants of territories under their control". Against this background, the ILO was the body that, paradoxically, focused on the needs of indigenous peoples basically in terms of working and living conditions. This increasing attention to the marginalized situation of indigenous peoples was permeated by a paternalistic approach, since international law and international institutions had the 'civilizing mission' of caring and protecting them. As has been expressed by Luis Rodríguez-Piñero, one of the leading experts in this field:

> [I]ndigenous peoples entered into international law through the backdoor of international developmental policy, at a time when the persistence of indigenous cultures was regarded as a major hindrance to the 'development' and 'national integration' of the countries where these peoples had become cloistered.[49]

---

47 C. Walsh, *Interculturalidad, estado y sociedad. Luchas (de)coloniales de nuestra época* (Universidad Andina Simón Bolívar, Quito, 2009) p. 167.

48 In 1923, one indigenous representative of the Six Nations (the Iroquois Confederacy) travelled to Geneva to submit a petition to the League of Nations against Canada. According to Singel, this example of indigenous advocacy "set in motion a series of developments that slowly advanced the recognition of indigenous peoples' rights in international law", W. T. Singel, 'New Directions for International Law and Indigenous Peoples', 45 *Idaho Law Review* (2009) p. 510.

49 L. Rodríguez-Piñero, *Indigenous Peoples, Postcolonialism and International Law. The ILO Regime (1919–1989)* (Oxford University Press, Oxford, 2005) p. 332.

In line with this approach, the first international treaty adopted by the ILO in 1957[50] to deal specifically with indigenous peoples was largely based on an assimilationist paradigm.[51] As stated in Article 2 of the Indigenous and Tribal Populations Convention (Convention No. 107, 1957):

> Governments shall have the primary responsibility for developing co-ordinated and systematic action for the protection of the populations concerned and their *progressive integration* into the life of their respective countries (emphasis added).[52]

This integrationist paradigm was modified with the adoption of Convention No. 169 on Indigenous and Tribal Peoples by the ILO in 1989 in order to replace the former ILO Convention. As stated in the preamble of this Convention:

> [T]he developments which have taken place in international law since 1957, as well as developments in the situation of indigenous and tribal peoples in all regions of the world, have made it appropriate to adopt new international standards on the subject with a view to removing the *assimilationist orientation* of the earlier standards (emphasis added).

Irrespective of the lack of a significant participation of indigenous peoples in the drafting process of the ILO Convention 169, we must acknowledge that it marked a turning point in the history of the legal recognition of indigenous peoples as true subjects of rights under international law. In Carpenter and Riley's view, while ILO Convention 169 "failed to meet certain aspirations in terms of both process and content, it was still a relatively progressive instrument for its time".[53] We must acknowledge that, in spite of its poor ratification

50 27 states ratified this Convention. Since the adoption of ILO Convention 169, Convention 107 is no longer open for ratification. However, it is still in force in 18 countries that have not yet ratified Convention 169.

51 P. Thornberry, *Indigenous Peoples and Human Rights* (Manchester University Press, Manchester, 2002) pp. 329–333; J. M. Salgado, *Convenio 169 de la OIT sobre Pueblos Indígenas* (Universidad Nacional del Comahue, Neuquén, 2006) pp. 29–30.

52 Besides, ILO Convention No. 107 refers to indigenous "populations" rather than peoples. The recognition as true peoples and nations is one of the main claims of the global indigenous movement.

53 K. A. Carpenter and A. R. Riley, 'Indigenous Peoples and the Jurisgenerative Moment in Human Rights', 102 *California Law Review* (2014) p. 190.

record,[54] it has had a "tremendous effect in contemporary international and domestic practice".[55]

4.2 *The United Nations*

Post-Second World War international law recognized two core principles that have been of utmost importance to the struggle of indigenous peoples for recognition as distinct peoples in need of specific and qualified protection. The first principle relates to the purpose of the then-nascent United Nations of "promoting and encouraging respect for human rights and for fundamental freedoms for all without distinction as to race, sex, language, or religion".[56] The second principle affirms the right of peoples to self-determination,[57] a principle that paved the way for the second process of decolonization after the 1960s.[58] These two principles served as the theoretical frame through which

---

54 As of January 2017, 22 states have ratified ILO Convention No. 169 (Argentina, Plurinational State of Bolivia, Brazil, Central African Republic, Chile, Colombia, Costa Rica, Denmark, Dominica, Ecuador, Fiji, Guatemala, Honduras, Mexico, Nepal, Netherlands, Nicaragua, Norway, Paraguay, Peru, Spain and Bolivarian Republic of Venezuela), available at http://www.ilo.org/dyn/normlex/en/f?p=NORMLEXPUB:11300:0::NO:11300:P11300_INSTRUMENT_ID:312314:NO (accessed 18 January 2017).

55 *See* L. Rodríguez-Piñero *supra* note 49, p. 342.

56 Article 1.3 of the United Nations Charter (1945).

57 Article 1.2 of the United Nations Charter establishes as one of the purposes of the UN "to develop friendly relations among nations based on respect for the principle of equal rights and *self-determination of peoples* …" (emphasis added).

58 As stated by the *Declaration on the Granting of Independence to Colonial Countries and Peoples*, GA Res. 1514 (XV), 14 December 1960, "All peoples have the right to self-determination; by virtue of that right they freely determine their political status and freely pursue their economic, social and cultural development". The conventional proclamation of the right of peoples to self-determination is to be found in common Article 1 of the two UN Human Rights Covenants adopted in 1966. The problem with this decolonization process is that, as Siegfried Wiessner explains, "the choice as to the political future of colonized peoples was not given to the individual peoples conquered, but to the inhabitants of territories colonized by European conquerors, within the borders drawn by the colonizers". The colonial powers used the Roman legal category of *uti possidetis* to maintain the borders that were delineated by them at the Berlin Conference of 1884, S. Wiessner *supra* note 41, p. 36. As a consequence of this interpretation of the right to self-determination limited to the colonial context, indigenous peoples were not considered as potential beneficiaries of such a right. One of the most difficult issues during the process of negotiation of the UNDRIP was precisely the incorporation of the right of indigenous peoples to self-determination. Article 3 of the UNDRIP does ultimately recognize this controversial right, a right that has to be interpreted in light of Articles 4 a 46.1 of the Declaration. As James Anaya has stressed, "reflecting the state of contemporary

indigenous peoples articulated their main claims in the 1970s and 1980s.[59] International law, particularly international human rights law, became a very powerful discursive resource for indigenous peoples to advance their demands both domestically and at international fora. In Rhiannon Morgan's view, based on social constructivism as a theoretical framework of analysis, "the global indigenous movement is just one example of a movement that has grasped the transformative, dynamic potential lodged in the discourse of human rights, drawing on its manipulability and malleability to foster the reform of human rights".[60] At the same time, and as part of the process of empowering indigenous peoples, the United Nations has since the 1970s been increasingly receptive to claims by indigenous peoples,[61] opening institutional spaces and avenues for their participation and the advancement of their demands.[62] Indigenous

---

international law in relation to this principle as well as the demands of indigenous peoples themselves, the affirmation of self-determination in the Declaration is deemed compatible with the principle of territorial integrality and political unity of States", *Report of the Special Rapporteur on the situation of human rights and fundamental freedoms of indigenous people, S. James Anaya*, UN Doc., A/HRC/9/9, 11 August 2008, para. 37. *See* the illuminating reflections on the 'remedial dimension' of both self-determination and indigenous rights by G. Pentassuglia in this volume

59 On the so-called 'indigenous emergence' during the 1970s and 1980s, *see* A. Brysk, *From Tribal Village to Global Village. Indian Rights and International relations in Latin America* (Stanford University Press, Stanford, 2000). *See also* S. Martí i Puig, "Emergencia indígena y política en América Latina tras la Década de los Pueblos Indígenas", in F. Gómez Isa and S. Ardanaz Iriarte (eds.), *La plasmación política de la diversidad. Autonomía y participación política en América Latina* (Universidad de Deusto, Bilbao, 2011) pp. 165–178.

60 R. Morgan, *Transforming Law and Institution. Indigenous Peoples, the United Nations and Human Rights* (Ashgate, Farnham, 2011) p. 43.

61 A very lucid analysis of the increasing involvement of the UN in indigenous issues by one of the key players within the Organization can be found in A. Willemsen-Diaz, "How Indigenous Peoples' Rights Reached the UN", in C. Charters and R. Stavenhagen (eds.), *Making the Declaration Work. The United Nations Declaration on the Rights of Indigenous Peoples* (IWGIA, Copenhagen, 2009) pp. 16–31.

62 A number of bodies were created to deal specifically with indigenous issues (Working Group on Indigenous Peoples; Working Group on a Draft Declaration on indigenous peoples' rights; Permanent Forum on Indigenous Issues; Special Rapporteur on the rights of indigenous peoples, and Expert Mechanism on the Rights of Indigenous Peoples). The General Assembly of the UN also proclaimed two consecutive UN Decades on Indigenous Peoples (1994–2003, and 2005–2014). The UN Permanent Forum on Indigenous Issues has recently called for a Third International Decade of the World's Indigenous Peoples. In its view, "over the course of the two Decades, we have seen some progress … However, we need to ensure and reinvigorate momentum to genuinely implement the UN Declaration … A Third Decade can provide a framework and consolidate clear milestones for

peoples used the United Nations as a mobilizing structure to increase visibility of their marginalized position and to pursue some strategic goals in terms of recognition and protection.[63] In a sense, the period saw a very promising process of *decolonization* of both international law and the United Nations.[64] This process has allowed indigenous peoples to transform from mere victims to actors, and from objects of protection to subjects of rights,[65] thus opening the door to their acquisition of some forms of international legal personality.[66]

The culmination of this legal and institutional development was the creation of the UN Permanent Forum on Indigenous Issues in 2000, a unique body in which states and indigenous representatives participate on an equal footing,[67] and the adoption of the United Nations Declaration on the Rights of Indigenous Peoples (UNDRIP) in 2007. As the Committee on the Rights of Indigenous Peoples of the International Law Association (ILA) has affirmed, all these developments demonstrate that "indigenous persons and peoples are

---

the achievement of the UN Declaration…", *A Third International Decade of the World's Indigenous Peoples*, UN Doc., United Nations Permanent Forum on Indigenous Issues, Dalee Sambo Dorough, Chairperson, 7 November 2014, in http://www.un.org/esa/socdev/unpfii/documents/Communication-UNPFII%20Chair-3decade.pdf.

63 I. Bellier and M. Préaud, 'Emerging Issues in indigenous rights: transformative effects of the recognition of indigenous peoples', 16 *The International Journal of Human Rights* (2012) pp. 474–488.

64 Post-1945 international law and institutions have been used by the West (itself an imagined community) to construct and impose a new set of rational truths based on particular values, norms and socio-political organizations that have been defined as universal. Post-colonial studies have demonstrated that international law and institutions, among many other structures of power, were used by the West to maintain its hierarchies and modes of domination. Indigenous peoples' struggles have aimed to decolonize both the theory and practice of the "ideological-institutional complex" known as international law. On this challenging processes *see* the illuminating essay by S. Pahuja, *Decolonizing International Law. Development, Economic Growth and the Politics of Universality* (Cambridge University Press, Cambridge, 2011).

65 F. Gómez Isa, 'Indigenous Peoples: from objects of protection to subjects of rights', in A. Brysk and M. Stohl (eds.), *Expanding Human Rights. 21st Century Norms and Governance* (Edward Elgar Publishers, Cheltenham, 2017) pp. 55–74.

66 D. S. Dorough, 'The Significance of the Declaration on the Rights of Indigenous Peoples and Its Future Implementation', in C. Charters and R. Stavenhagen (eds.) *supra* note 61, p. 265. *See also* A. Meijknecht, *Towards International Personality: The Position of Minorities and Indigenous Peoples in International Law* (Intersentia, Antwerp, 2001).

67 A description of the process that led to the creation of the PFII and its main functions in L. García-Alix, *The Permanent Forum on Indigenous Issues* (IWGIA, Copenhagen, 2003).

back not only as fully entitled holders of individual human rights, but as collective actors with distinct rights and status under international law".[68]

4.3 *The UNDRIP*

The adoption of the UNDRIP in 2007 by the UN General Assembly was the culmination of a challenging process initiated in the 1980s in which indigenous peoples themselves were the main driving force.[69] The adoption also reflects the deep aspirations of the world's indigenous peoples and their confidence in international law and human rights law as powerful tools to modify entrenched patterns of domination and exclusion that have affected indigenous peoples since colonial times.[70] To a great extent, the UNDRIP is an attempt to repair historical wrongs suffered by indigenous peoples.[71] As established by the UNDRIP in its Preamble, "indigenous peoples have suffered from *historic injustices* as a result of, inter alia, their colonization and dispossession of their lands, territories and resources, thus preventing them from exercising, in particular, their right to development in accordance with their own needs and interests"[72] (emphasis added).

The adoption of the UNDRIP in 2007 is the result of more than 20 years of intense and controversial negotiations in which indigenous peoples and their close allies achieved very significant levels of participation. Undoubtedly, the

68 International Law Association, *Rights of Indigenous Peoples*, Report of the Hague Conference (2010) p. 2, available at http://www.ila-hq.org/en/committees/index.cfm/cid/1024 (accessed 2 February 2017).

69 I. Bellier, 'Retour sur la négotiation de la Déclaration des Droits des Peuples Autochtones: reconnaître le principe d'égalité pour avancer des interprétations pragmatiques', in S. Pessina Dassonville, *Le statut des peoples autochtones. A la croisée des savoirs* (Karthala, Paris, 2012) pp. 73–96.

70 H. P. Glenn, 'The Three Ironies of the UN Declaration on the Rights of Indigenous Peoples', in S. Allen and A. Xanthaki (eds.), *Reflections on the UN Declaration on the Rights of Indigenous Peoples* (Hart Publishing, Oxford, 2011) p. 174.

71 F. Gómez Isa, 'Repairing Historical Injustices: Indigenous Peoples in Post-Conflict Scenarios', in G. Oré Aguilar and F. Gómez Isa (eds.), *Rethinking Transitions. Equality and Social Justice in Societies Emerging from Conflict* (Intersentia, Antwerp, 2011) pp. 265–300.

72 Para. 5 of the Preamble. In James Anaya's view, this preambular paragraph of the Declaration "stresses the essentially remedial purpose of the instrument. Far from affirming special rights per se, the Declaration aims at repairing the ongoing consequences of the historical denial of the right to self-determination and other basic human rights affirmed in international instruments of general applicability", *Report of the Special Rapporteur on the situation of human rights and fundamental freedoms of indigenous people, S. James Anaya*, UN Doc., A/HRC/9/9, 11 August 2008, para. 36.

way in which this process was conducted, together with its highly positive outcomes, will come to influence international norm-creation exercises in other areas of international law in general, and international human rights law in particular. H. Patrick Glenn situates the Declaration within a broader international law movement. In his view, the Declaration "would represent not simply a use or application of international law, in novel circumstances, but a major shift in the nature and direction of international law itself".[73] Indigenous peoples are having an increasing role in international law-making. In this sense, Aponte Miranda has emphasized that "the ability of a traditionally marginalized community to succeed in strategically facilitating the recognition of an international legal identity and substantive reconstitution of human rights precepts is a unique phenomenon that merits attention".[74]

Under traditional international law, the sources for the emergence of law have been primarily treaties and customary law. Accordingly, the creation of international rules was a predominantly state-led process. Contemporary international law-making has become a much more complex, dynamic and, sometimes, contradictory process, with a number of norms, ranging from hard law conventions to soft law instruments, and with a multiplicity of actors participating. Nevertheless, as the long delay in the process that led to the adoption of the UNDRIP clearly shows, "the political will of states remains crucial to the law-making activities of non-state actors".[75] But in spite of the centrality of the state in the process of creation of international law, the progressive participation of a myriad of actors (both state and non-state actors)[76] in international norm-creation processes is one of the key features of contemporary international law-making. This can be precisely illustrated by the example of indigenous peoples. They have employed "a multi-layered approach to international human rights law-making that includes participation in both informal

---

73 H. P. Glenn *supra* note 70, p. 174. A very similar position has been expressed by Will Kymlicka, for whom the Declaration can be seen "as a victory for international law itself", W. Kymlicka, 'Beyond the Indigenous/Minority Dichotomy?', in S. Allen and A. Xanthaki (eds.) *supra* note 70, p. 183.

74 L. Aponte Miranda, 'Indigenous Peoples as Lawmakers', 32 *University of Pennsylvania Journal of International Law* (2010) p. 205.

75 A. Boyle and C. Chinkin, *The Making of International Law* (Oxford University Press, Oxford, 2007) p. 49.

76 A reflection on the role that non-state actors play in contemporary international law can be found in J. d'Aspremont (ed.), *Participants in the International Legal System. Multiple perspectives on Non-State Actors in International Law* (Routledge, London, 2011). *See also* M. Noortmann and C. Ryngaert (eds.), *Non-State Actor Dynamics in International Law. From Law-Takers to Law-Makers* (Ashgate, Farnham, 2010).

mechanisms of knowledge production and norm-generation as well as more formal decision-making structures".[77]

This new legal scenario has led to a necessary flexibilization of the methods for the making of international law, which had been rooted in legal positivism and Article 38.1 of the Statute of the International Court of Justice (1945).[78] Soft law is now a well-established legal category,[79] and contemporary international law has to accommodate it within the varied processes for creating and implementing international norms in which non-state actors, including indigenous peoples, are key participants. Stephen Allen has described this process as a "de-formalization of international law itself".[80] In a sense, we can argue that the contemporary international legal system is becoming more *liquid*, to use the metaphorical term coined by philosopher Zygmunt Bauman.[81]

4.4 *Increasing Participation of Indigenous Peoples*

As already seen, indigenous peoples participated very actively in all stages of the process leading to the adoption of the UNDRIP.[82] Since the creation of the UN Working Group on Indigenous Populations (WGIP) in 1982 by what was then the Sub-Commission on Prevention of Discrimination and Protection of Minorities (the Sub-Commission),[83] and the decision in 1985 to adopt a draft Declaration on the rights of indigenous peoples, followed by the creation of the Working Group on the Draft Declaration (WGDD) in 1995, the meaningful participation of the global indigenous movement has become one of the key features of the lengthy process of negotiation and adoption of the UNDRIP.[84]

77 L. Aponte Miranda *supra* note 74, p. 207.

78 A. D'Amato, 'International Soft Law, Hard Law, and Coherence', 8 *Northwestern Public Law Research Paper* (2008) pp. 1–31.

79 S. Lagoutte, T. Gammeltoft-Hansen, and J. Cerone (eds.), *Tracing the Roles of Soft Law in Human Rights* (Oxford University Press, Oxford, 2016).

80 S. Allen, 'The United Nations Declaration on the Rights of Indigenous Peoples and the Limits of the International Legal Project', in S. Allen and A. Xanthaki (eds.) *supra* note 70, p. 244.

81 Z. Bauman, *Liquid Modernity* (Polity, Cambridge, 2000).

82 A. Xanthaki, *Indigenous Rights and United Nations Standards: Self-Determination, Culture and Land* (Cambridge University Press, Cambridge, 2007) p. 102.

83 UN Doc., ECOSOC Resolution 1982/34, 7 May 1982.

84 I. Bellier, 'Les peuples autochtones aux Nations Unies: un nouvel acteur dans la fabrique des normes internationales', 54 *Critique Internationale* (2012) pp. 61–80.

At the time of the creation of the WGIP, a body composed of five independent experts, only NGOs with consultative status before the UN Economic and Social Council (ECOSOC) could participate as observers in the meetings of the working groups created by the Sub-Commission. This was an obstacle for indigenous organizations wanting to participate in the WGIP, since almost no indigenous organization had consultative status before the ECOSOC at that time. The first Chair-person of the WGIP, Asbjorn Eide, took a decision that was to have significant consequences for the process of institutionalizing indigenous participation at the UN bodies dealing with indigenous issues. He opened up the working group to indigenous representatives, thus effecting a dramatic change in the tradition of participation of NGOs in working groups. Although this decision met with some objections, he received strong support by Theo Van Boven, Director of the UN Human Rights Center. As Eide has lucidly explained:

> [T]o fulfil the mandate of reviewing developments concerning indigenous populations and to work towards developing the corresponding standards, there was a need to have the best possible experts present, and the best experts were the indigenous representatives themselves.[85]

The same dilemma was faced by the WGDD when it was created in 1995 by the then UN Commission on Human Rights (CHR)[86] aimed at adopting a draft Declaration on the rights of indigenous peoples. Indigenous peoples' representatives were concerned about the strict rules on NGO participation established by the CHR, and lobbied extensively to gain similar spaces for participation to those existing within the WGIP. While not meeting the degree of openness that characterized the WGIP, indigenous organizations also had the chance to participate significantly throughout the negotiation process. In Rhiannon Morgan's view:

> [D]uring the drafting of the UNDRIP, indigenous representatives succeeded in pressing for unprecedented levels of inclusiveness and participation, allowing not only for the extensive input of indigenous

85 A. Eide, 'The Indigenous Peoples, the Working Group on Indigenous Populations and the adoption of the UN Declaration on the Rights of Indigenous Peoples', in C. Charters and R. Stavenhagen (eds.) *supra* note 61, p. 34.

86 UN Doc., UN Commission on Human Rights, Resolution 1995/32, 3 March 1995.

> perspectives as to the content of their rights but also some degree of control over decision-making processes.[87]

The truth is that indigenous peoples' representatives and organizations benefited immensely from this democratic culture of openness, and since then have occupied an increasing number of spaces within UN bodies dealing with indigenous issues. The increasing participation of civil society movements and other transnational actors in the "state-centric system of international law has itself been part of the democratisation trend" of contemporary international law-making.[88] Ultimately, we can defend the position that participation of indigenous peoples in those spaces that take decisions that affect them has become a well-established principle of international law.[89] As a corollary of the right to self-determination[90] and autonomy,[91] the right of indigenous peoples to participate in those decisions affecting them has already been recognised by ILO Convention 169,[92] the UNDRIP,[93] and the jurisprudence of a number of UN treaty-bodies such as the UN Committee on the Elimination of Racial Discrimination (CERD).[94] This position, which I fully share, has led Boyle and Chinkin to defend that "there is now a principle, backed by supporting state

---

87 R. Morgan *supra* note 60, p. 41. This process did not count on support from the US. In its view, "this process was unfortunate and extraordinary in any multilateral negotiating exercise and sets a poor precedent with respect to UN practice", United States, 'Observations of the United States with respect to the Declaration on the Rights of Indigenous Peoples: Explanation of Vote by Robert Hagen, U.S. Advisor, on the Declaration on the Rights of Indigenous Peoples, to the UN General Assembly', 13 September 2007.

88 See A. Boyle and C. Chinkin *supra* note 75, p. 43.

89 R. Morgan *supra* note 60, p. 113.

90 UNDRIP, Article 3.

91 UNDRIP, Article 4.

92 According to Article 2.1, "Governments shall have the responsibility for developing, *with the participation of the peoples concerned*, co-ordinated and systematic action to protect the rights of these peoples and to guarantee respect for their integrity" (emphasis added). *See also* Arts. 5.c), 6.1, 6.2, 7.1, 7.2, 15.2, 17.2, 22, and 23.

93 As proclaimed in Article 18, "indigenous peoples have the right to participate in decision-making in matters which would affect their rights, through representatives chosen by themselves in accordance with their own procedures, as well as to maintain and develop their own indigenous decision-making institutions".

94 The CERD called upon States parties to "ensure that members of indigenous peoples have equal rights in respect of effective participation in public life and that no decisions directly relating to their rights and interests are taken without their informed consent", *CERD General Recommendation XXIII*, UN Doc., A/52/18, Annex V, 18 August 1997, para. 4 d).

practice, that rights of indigenous peoples cannot be determined without their participation and consent".[95]

As a clear manifestation of the increasing relevance of indigenous peoples' participation in international spaces, the UN itself is leading a promising process of consultations to reflect about ways and means to foster the participation of indigenous peoples in those bodies that take decisions affecting them. Based on relevant provisions of the UNDRIP[96] and on the Outcome Document of the World Conference on Indigenous Peoples (2014),[97] the UN Secretary-General[98] and the UN General Assembly have sponsored a process of consultations with all relevant stakeholders to develop specific measures to enable the participation of indigenous peoples' representatives and institutions in UN bodies.[99] Although the process is still evolving, "most responses have in principle indicated the need for enhanced forms of participation for indigenous peoples in UN bodies affecting them".[100] Additionally, there was "considerable (but not uniform) support expressed for a separate category of participation in the UN, including in the General Assembly, for indigenous peoples".[101] Against the background of this emerging consensus, the consultations are focusing now on procedures for indigenous peoples' meaningful participation,

95 A. Boyle and C. Chinkin *supra* note 75, p. 50.

96 *See* note 93.

97 According to paragraph 33, UN member states committed "to considering, at the seventieth session of the General Assembly, ways to enable the participation of indigenous peoples' representatives and institutions in meetings of relevant United Nations bodies on issues affecting them, including any specific proposals made by the Secretary-General in response to the request made in paragraph 40 below", *Outcome document of the high-level plenary meeting of the General Assembly known as the World Conference on Indigenous Peoples*, UN Doc., A/RES/69/2, 22 September 2014.

98 *See* the background document, *Ways and means of promoting participation at the United Nations of indigenous peoples' representatives on issues affecting them*, UN Doc., 2 July 2012.

99 To assist in the implementation of the mandate, the President of the General Assembly appointed two Advisors from member states (Mr. Kai Sauer, from Finland, and Ms. Martha Ama Akyaa Pobee, from Ghana), and two Advisors from indigenous peoples (Ms. Claire Charters and Mr. James Anaya).

100 *Compilation of views on possible measures necessary to enable the participation of indigenous peoples' representatives and institutions in relevant United Nations meetings on issues affecting them, and of good practices within the United Nations regarding indigenous peoples' participation*, UN Doc., A/70/990, 25 July 2016, p. 4.

101 *Ibid.*

criteria for the eligibility of indigenous peoples' representatives, nature and membership of the body to determine eligibility, and the process to obtain accreditation.

5 Conclusions

Indigenous peoples have used contemporary international law and international institutions as close allies in their struggle for recognition and for the elimination of historically-rooted patterns of subjugation, dispossession and cultural assimilation. As part of this evolution, indigenous peoples have become subjects of rights under international law rather than objects of protection. Soft law norms have played a major role in this process, contributing significantly to the transformation of the dynamics of international law, and paving the way for its flexibilisation, de-formalisation and, ultimately, democratisation. The UNDRIP, adopted in 2007 by the UN General Assembly "as a standard of achievement to be pursued in a spirit of partnership and mutual respect",[102] must be seen as the culmination of a long and difficult journey in which indigenous peoples themselves and their representatives have been the driving force and key participants. Ultimately, the UNDRIP can be considered as a hybrid document, given that incorporates both universal human rights and indigenous views on dignity and human rights.

Fully aware of these significant achievements, postcolonial scholarship has put on the table the thought-provoking category of coloniality of power. This concept has served to shed light on the structural forms of oppression that still affect the daily life of most indigenous peoples in the world, especially when it comes to their lands, territories and natural resources. The former UN Special Rapporteur Rodolfo Stavenhagen referred to the "implementation gap"[103] as the main challenge so that international law and human rights law become sources of emancipation instead of sources of new forms of economic, social, cultural, and epistemological domination.

---

102 UNDRIP, Preamble, para. 24.

103 *Report of the Special Rapporteur on the situation of human rights and fundamental freedoms of indigenous people, Mr. Rodolfo Stavenhagen*, UN Doc., E/CN.4/2006/78, 16 February 2006, para. 83.

CHAPTER 6

Indigenous Peoples and Intergenerational Equity as an Emerging Aspect of Ethno-Cultural Diversity in International Law

Malgosia Fitzmaurice

1 Introduction

This chapter takes an unusual approach to ethno-culturalism and diversity in relation to indigenous peoples. The approach suggested in this chapter is based on a philosophical theory of intergenerational equity and how it may be applied to indigenous people's ethno-cultural diversity. Therefore, it is necessary first to analyse the theory of intergenerational equity. The next step will be its application to indigenous peoples within the context of ethno-cultural diversity. The theory of intergenerational equity, as it will be explained, analyses the relationship between generations in relation to obligations of environmental nature concerning the preservation of the planet. Are these obligations universal or, due to the special ethno-cultural character of certain groups of people, are there any exemptions from this universal obligation? Therefore, this chapter is based on a different premise to that of the majority of scholarly writings, which analyse the right to the enjoyment of environment and natural resources from the viewpoint of indigenous peoples, due to their special relationship with the environment.

This chapter's hypothesis is different: do indigenous peoples have the obligation to protect the environment for future generations; or are they exempted from this obligation due to their ethno-culturalism? This question will be analysed in relation to the general obligation to protect the environment and exemplified by a particular case of indigenous (aboriginal) whaling. This issue has a broader aspect within a discourse of cultural pluralism; and the link between indigenous peoples' rights to human rights and general international law, i.e. a 'relational' approach to the 2007 United Nations Declaration of Rights of Indigenous Peoples (UNDRIP).[1] This chapter will deal with the concept of

1 *See* on this subject G. Pentassuglia, 'Ethnocultural Ethnicity and Human Rights: Legal Categories, Claims, and the Hybiridity of Group Protection', VI *The Yearbook of Polar*

 | DOI 10.1163/9789004328785_008

intergenerational equity; intergenerational equity, protection of the environment and the rights of indigenous peoples; ethno-cultural diversity and indigenous peoples; whaling and the ethno-cultural diversity of indigenous peoples (including a controversial example of the Makah peoples whaling); and finally aboriginal whaling and intergenerational equity.

2 The Concept of Intergenerational Equity

Intergenerational equity directly links successive generations to environmental issues. As explained by Brown-Weiss, who introduced and elaborated this concept, the use of our natural resources raises at least three kinds of equity problems between generations: depletion of resources for future generations; degradation in the quality of resources; and discriminatory access to use and benefit from resources received from past generations.[2]

There is a multitude of ways in which the depletion of natural resources may occur. The present generation may deplete a more expensive natural resource, thus making it unavailable (or available only at higher price) for future generations. Natural resources may also be exploited by the present generation in ignorance of their potential economic importance. In some cases the present generation may exhaust certain natural resources by destruction of areas of high biological diversity. Depletion of resources may reduce the diversity of resources available for adapting to climate change and the destruction of forests can result in an increase of global greenhouse emissions.[3] Degradation of the quality of the environment also poses questions of equity. The quality of the natural environment (globally and locally) has certainly deteriorated, especially in the last 50 years. Pollution, which degrades many components of

---

Law (2015) p. 251; H. Quane, 'Legal Pluralism and International Human Rights Law: Inherently Incompatible, Mutually Reinforcing of Something in Between?', 36 *Oxford Journal of Legal Studies* (2013) p. 1.

2007 United Nations Declaration on the Rights of Indigenous Peoples, adopted 13 September 2007, by affirmative vote of 143 States, 4 against (the United States; Canada; Australia; and New Zealand), 11 abstentions (Azerbaijan; Bangladesh; Bhutan; Burundi; Colombia; Georgia; Kenya; Nigeria; Russia; Samoa; Ukraine), at www.un.org/esa/socdev/unpfii/documents/DRIPS_en.pdf.

2 E. Brown-Weiss, 'Implementing Intergenerational Equity', in M. Fitzmaurice, D. Ong and P. Merkouris (eds.), *Research Handbook on International Environmental Law* (Edward Elgar Publishing, Cheltenham, 2005). *Ibid., In Fairness to Future Generations* (United Nations University and Transnational Publishers, Tokyo, 1989).

3 E. Brown-Weiss, 'Implementing Intergenerational Equity', *supra* note 2, p. 101.

the environment (such as marine areas, the atmosphere, fresh water, soil, and land), affects both the uses that future generations can make of the environment and the cost of doing so.[4]

Every generation has the right to use the environment and natural resources. The main problem is finding a balance between the respective rights of the present generation and future generations, taking into account such factors as poverty, which may prevent certain communities from securing an equitable share in their legacy.[5] Intergenerational equity is formed on the basis of two relationships: the relationship between generations and that between the human species and the natural system. Humans bear the main responsibility for the preservation of the natural system. The notion of equality is at the core of the legal framework connecting generations, in their care and use of the natural system. The concept of intergenerational equity is based on a notion of a partnership between generations themselves and between natural systems and generations. The present generation holds the natural environment in trust for future generations and is also its beneficiary with the right to use it. Each generation has an obligation to pass the natural environment on to future generations in a state no worse than comparable to that when it had received it from the past generations.[6]

Brown-Weiss distinguished three elements of the principle of intergenerational equity: conservation of diversity of natural and cultural resources (or comparable option); conservation of environmental quality (or comparable quality); and equitable or non-discriminatory access to the earth and its resources. The first principle (conservation of diversity) means that each and every generation has an obligation to conserve the diversity of natural and cultural resources so as not to restrict the options available to future generations to meet their own needs and satisfy their own values. Conservation of quality means that every generation must maintain the quality of the natural environment so it can be passed on to future generations in no worse condition than inherited from past generations. Equitable access means that each generation has a non-discriminatory right to access and benefit from the natural environment.[7] These principles should themselves meet three criteria. First, they should encourage equality among generations, by introducing balance in the use of natural resources, i.e., using natural resources in a manner not exclusionary to future generations, on the one hand; and not imposing undue burdens upon the present generation, on the other hand. Secondly, the present

4 *Ibid.*

5 *Ibid.*, p. 102.

6 *Ibid.*, p. 102

7 *Ibid.*, p. 103.

generation should not interfere with or attempt to predict the values of future generations, but rather should offer flexibility to future generations with regard to how to pursue their own goals and aims. Third, these principles should be sufficiently clear as to be applicable in different social and legal systems.[8]

The rights of future generations and the notion of keeping our planet in trust for future generations are not entirely new ideas. Multilateral Environmental Agreements (MEAS) and soft law documents drafted many years ago include, at least in the preamble, the invocation of future generations.[9] The question of intergenerational equity has also been the subject of national and international case law. The classic case concerning the application of this principle is the 1993 *Minors Oposa* claim,[10] where an action was filed by several minors, represented by their parents, against the Philippines' Department of Environment and Natural Resources in order to cancel existing timber licence agreements in the country and to stop issuance of new ones. The claim alleged violation of the constitutional rights to a balanced and healthful ecology and to health (sections 16 and 15, Article II of the Constitution) and of the concept

8 *Ibid.*

9 *See*, for example, the International Convention on the Regulation of Whaling (ICRW). It states as follows: "1 Recognising the interest of nations of the world in safeguarding for future generations the great natural resources represented by whale stocks ..."; Convention on International Trade in Endangered Species of Wild Fauna and Flora: "Recognising that wild fauna and flora in their many beautiful and varied forms are an irreplaceable part of the natural systems of the earth which must be protected for this and generations to come ..."; 1979 Bonn Convention on the Conservation of Migratory Species of Wild Animals, 19 *International Legal Materials* (1980) p. 15: "Aware that each generation of man holds the resources of the earth for future generations and has an obligation to ensure that this legacy is conserved and, where utilised, is used wisely ..."; 1979 Convention on the Conservation of European Wildlife and Natural Habitats, *Official Gazette of the Council of Europe* p. 104: "Recognising that wild flora and fauna constitute a natural heritage of aesthetic, scientific, cultural, recreational, economic and intrinsic value that needs to be preserved and handed on to future generations ..."; Principle 2 of the 1972 Stockholm Declaration on the Human Environment, 11 *International Legal Materials* (1972) p. 1416: "The natural resources of the earth including the air, water, land, and fauna and especially representative samples of natural ecosystems must be safeguarded for the benefit of present and future generations through careful planning or management, as appropriate"; Principle 3 of the 1992 Rio Declaration on Environment and Development 31 *International Legal Materials* (1992) p. 874: "The right to development must be fulfilled so as to equitably meet developmental and environmental needs of present and future generations".

10 *Minors Oposa v. Secretary of the Department of Environment and Natural Resources* (*DENR*), Supreme Court of the Philippines, 30 July 1993, 33 *International Legal Materials* (1994) p. 173.

of intergenerational equity (the petitioners represented others of their generation as well as generations yet unborn). Finding for the petitioners, the Court stated that even though the right to a balanced and healthful ecology is recognised under the Declaration of Principles and State Policies of the Constitution and not under the Bill of Rights, it does not follow that it is less important than the rights noted in the latter. The Court upheld both bases for the claim and stated that the petitioners enjoyed standing on behalf both of themselves and of future generations as "the minors' assertion of their right to a sound environment constitutes, at the same time, the performance of their obligation to ensure the protection of that right for the generations to come".

It must be mentioned, however, that national courts have not always been willing to apply this concept. In Pakistan, for example, this concept has not been applied in any case.[11] Furthermore, in Bangladesh in the 1997 case of *M. Farooque v Bangladesh and Others*,[12] the petitioners submitted that they were representatives not only of their own generation but of generations to come, relying on the *Minor Oposa* claim. The Court, however, rejected this argument, stating that in the Philippines minors had *locus standi*, since the Constitution of the Philippines grants the fundamental right to a clean environment, but that this did not exist in Bangladesh.

The concept of intergenerational equity has also been applied in international case law. In the ICJ, Judge Weeramantry has been a great supporter of this concept, for example in the *Nuclear Test II* case.[13] The Court itself dealt with this issue in the *Nuclear Weapons Advisory Opinion* in the following way:[14]

> The use of nuclear weapons could constitute a catastrophe for the environment. The Court also recognizes that the environment is not an abstraction but represents the living space, the quality of life and the very health of human beings, including generations unborn. The existence of the general obligation of States to ensure that activities within their

---

11 For discussion of the case law in certain other developing countries, *see* J. Razzaque, 'Human Rights and the Environment: the National Experience in South Asia and Africa', Joint UNEP-OHCHR Expert Seminar on Human Rights and the Environment, 14–16 January 2002, Geneva; Background Paper No 4.

12 *M. Farooque v Bangladesh and Others* (1997) 9 *DLR* (AD) 1.

13 *Request for an Examination of the Situation in Accordance with paragraph 63 of the Court's Judgement of 20 December 1974 in the Nuclear Tests (New Zealand v. France) Case*, Order of 22 September 1995, I.C.J. Reports 317, Dissenting Opinion of Judge Weeramantry.

14 *Legality of the Threat or Use of Nuclear Weapons,* (Advisory Opinion) 8 July 1996, I.C.J. Reports 226, para. 29, p. 249.

> jurisdiction and control respect the environment of other States or of areas beyond national control is now … 'the use of nuclear weapons would be a serious danger to future generations. Ionizing radiation has the potential to damage the future environment, food and marine ecosystem, and to cause genetic defects and illness in future generations.'[15]

There are some other examples of the mentioning of this concept before the ICJ. In the *Gabcikovo-Nagymaros Project* case the Court also referred to future generations:

> Owing to new scientific insights and to a growing awareness of the risks for mankind – for present and future generations – of pursuit of such interventions at an unconsidered and unabated pace, new norms and standards have been developed, set forth in a greater number of instruments during the last two decades.[16]

One of the most important aspects of the Brown-Weiss's articulation of the concept of intergenerational equity was the suggestion of the appointment of an ombudsman representing the interests of future generations. Initially, at the global level, this idea appeared to be quite far-fetched, if not completely unworkable at the time.

At the national level certain States set up special organs whose function is the representation of such interests. In 1993, the government of France established a Council for the Rights of Future Generations, whose task was to consider issues related to nuclear power. This body lapsed, however, when France resumed nuclear testing in the Pacific.[17]

Another example is Israel, where the Knesset established a Commission for Future Generations, though this body is also now defunct. Its function was to assess draft Bills that were of particular relevance for future generations within the area of the environment, natural resources, development, health, the economy, planning and construction, education, quality of life, technology and all matters which were determined by the Knesset's Constitution, Law and Justice Committee as having particularly important consequences for future generations. In practice the Commission dealt with protecting children.[18] It operated

15 *Ibid.* para. 36, p. 244.

16 *Case Concerning the Gabcikovo-Nagymaros Project (Hungary v. Slovakia)*, 26 September 1997, I.C.J. Reports 7, para. 140, pp. 77–78.

17 E. Brown-Weiss, 'Implementing Intergenerational Equity', *supra* note 2, p. 110.

18 *Ibid.*, p. 110

from 2001 until 2006. The Commission regulated matters, which were of special interest to future generations, providing parliament with recommendations on bills and secondary legislation. The Commission had "powers to examine each legislative act wherever there is a suspicion of possible prejudice to future generations".[19] The Commission performed four basic functions: "To give opinions regarding bills brought ... that are of concern to future generations"; "[t]o give opinions regarding secondary legislation and regulations ... that are of concern to future generations"; "[t]o provide parliament ... with recommendations on any matter the Commissioner [head of the commission] considers to be of importance to future generations"; and "[t]o provide the members of the parliament with advice on matters that are of special interest regarding the future generations."[20] The Commissioner had the authority to review any prospective primary or secondary legislation and participate in all top-level debate on the legislation. The Commissioner had his right to access relevant information: The Knesset Commissioner for Future Generations may request from any organization or body being investigated ... any information, document or report ... in the possession of that body and which is required by the Commissioner for the implementation of his tasks; the aforesaid body will give the Commissioner the requested information. [21]

S. Shoham and N. Lamay wrote that: "[t]he Commission preferred to consider future generations as the next baby to be born tomorrow morning, a definition that relates to the immediate future generation, consisting of currently existing children".[22] Regrettably, the Commission has ceased to exist in 2006 because it was argued that the Commission was unnecessary, ineffective and wasted public funds.[23]

In 2008 the Hungarian Parliament enacted legislation establishing an Ombudsman for Future Generations (so-called 'the Green Commissioner' or 'Ombudsman') which was vested with broad powers, including advising the

---

19 M. Fitzmaurice, *Contemporary Issues in International Environmental Law* (Edward Elgar Publishing, Cheltenham, 2009) p. 151.

20 As cited in: 'Models for Protecting the Environment for Future Generations Science and Environmental Health Network The International Human Rights Clinic at Harvard Law School', at www.sehn.org/pdf/Models_for_Protecting_the_Environment_for_Future_Generations.pdf p. 18

21 *Ibid.*

22 S. Shoham and N. Lamay, 'Commission for Future Generations' in, J. C. Tremmel (ed.), *Handbook of Intergenerational Justice* (Edward Elgar Publishing, Cheltenham, 2006) p. 52.

23 Common Ground News Service, at www.commongroundnews.org/article.php?id=25099&lan=en&sid=1&sp.

Parliament on the impact of certain legislation on future generations and intervening to enjoin activities that could have a detrimental impact on future generations. As of 2012 the office of the Future Generations Ombudsman has been abolished and it was incorporated into the Office of the Commissioner for Fundamental Rights, together with the Office of the Parliamentary Commissioner for Civil Rights, the Office of the Parliamentary Commissioner for the National and Ethnic Minorities Rights.[24] The Green Ombudsman is a consultative body to the Parliament regarding environmental legislation. It may initiate proceedings at the Constitutional Court or intervene in court litigations in the interest of future generations and the enforcement of the right to a healthy environment. However, ombudspersons in Hungary have no authority to issue binding and enforceable resolutions. Nonetheless, the office contributed to the identification of possible solutions of environmental conflicts. The Green Ombudsman also participates in on-going discussions related to the general issues of environmental policy and environmental law and regularly contributes to the legislative process by issuing proposals.[25]

The Finnish Parliamentary Committee for the Future generates dialogue with the Government about problems concerning the future whilst forwarding possible solutions. One of its responsibilities is to prepare Parliament's response to the Government's Report on the Future during each electoral period. The themes covered in the parliamentary term 2007–2011 included climate change and in 2011–2015 included sustainable growth, which according to some entails questions of intergenerational equity.

The Canadian Commissioner of the Environment and Sustainable Development, appointed by the auditor general, "provides parliamentarians with objective, independent analysis and recommendations on the federal government's efforts to protect the environment and foster sustainable development".[26]

It has to be said that at national level the initial enthusiasm for the representation of the interests of future generations has been greatly reduced, as several of the bodies representing future generations have been abolished or their powers diminished. Resent practice indicates, there are not many (if at all) new examples of special organs established at the national level in order to protect interest of future generations.

---

24 *See* details at www.jno.hu.

25 Dr Marcel Szabó, Deputy-Commissioner for Fundamental Rights, Hungary, 'The Way Forward: Protecting Future Generations through the Institution of Green Ombudsman', at www.futurejustice.org/blog/guest-contribution/an-example-guest-post.

26 *Supra* note 20.

However, at the international, universal level of the United Nations, there were several proposals for the establishing of the Ombudsperson for Future generations. In the preparation to the RIO + 20, a coalition of Civil Society and the Major Group Youth/Children have introduced the idea for the establishment of 'Ombudspersons for Future Generations' at global, national and local level, in order to advocate "sustainable development as envisaged and defined by the Brundtland Commission: – to enhance the well-being and prospects of present and future generations to meet their needs, serve as an auditor at the heart of governments and deal with citizens' complaints".[27]

The following were criteria for Effective Representation of Future Generations: each Ombudsperson for Future Generations needs to be designed in accordance with local or national legal and cultural reality. Sustainable Development Councils, in States when where they exist, should be mandated to act as the Representative for future generations. The Ombudsperson and its staff should be independent and not hold another governmental post that would influence their freedom of reasoning nor should they have any interests in commercial sectors. The office should be established on the principles of legitimacy and should enjoy large public support from civil society. The selection process of the actual Ombudsperson should be designed to guarantee broad support and citizens should have the direct access to submit and to receive information. In order to enjoy and increase trust, the office should be based on the principle of transparency, i.e. clear mandate to access all information, especially early in the policy-making process. It should maintain open relationships with all stakeholders during investigations and should report regularly about its work in a format that is accessible to all citizens. Such an office should also have some authority; the 'shadow of enforcement' for a more effective intervention.[28]

There are several national Constitutions which refer to the rights of future generations.

The 2010 Constitution of Kenya, currently in operation, makes multiple references to future generations. The preamble of the Constitution states "We the people of Kenya ... respectful of the environment, which is our heritage, and determined to sustain it for the benefit of future generations". Articles 42, 69, 70 and 201 make further references to the rights of future generations. The

---

27 Dr M. Göpel, Director Future Justice, World Future Council, 'Ombudspersons for Future Generations as Sustainability Implementation Units', at www.stakeholderforum.org/fileadmin/files/SDG%204%20Ombudspersons%20for%20Future%20Generations%20Thinkpiece.pdf.

28 *Ibid.*, p. 13.

Argentinian Constitution Article 41, Clause 1 states "All inhabitants are entitled to the right to a healthy and balanced environment ... *productive activities shall meet* present needs without endangering those of future generations; and shall have the duty to preserve it". The Constitution of Poland Article 74, clause 1, states "Public authorities shall pursue policies ensuring the ecological security of current and future generations". Article 20 of the German Constitution states: "Mindful also of the responsibility to ward future generation, the State shall protect the natural bases of life by legislation and, in accordance with law and justice, by executive and judicial action, all within the framework of the constitutional order". The Constitution of South Africa includes both the right to a clean environment and generational justice. In 2015, in Wales, the Well-being of Future Generations (Wales) Act was enacted. It is based on the sustainable development concept. Interestingly, it also established the Office of Future Generations Commissioner for Wales in order to promote the needs of future generations by monitoring and reporting on the extent to which the public bodies take into account objectives of the sustainable development principle and well-being of future generations. The Commissioner reviews the policy of public bodies in this respect.[29]

It might be concluded from the literature that the concept of intergenerational equity features very prominently in international environmental law; it may be even said that it is a leading concept. However, its precise normative content and practical application remain ambiguous. It is unclear whether it has acquired the normative content of a principle, or remains merely a concept, or perhaps a philosophical theory (as to which, see below). Attempts to invoke it before national courts have largely proved unsuccessful; and before international courts and tribunals intergenerational equity has not acquired a great prominence. Its ambiguous legal content also raises questions of legal standing before courts and tribunals.

3 Intergenerational Equity, Protection of the Environment and the Rights of Indigenous Peoples

3.1 *Introduction*

In protecting the rights of future generations the theory of intergenerational equity does not differentiate between indigenous and non-indigenous peoples;

29 Well-being of Future Generations (Wales) Act 2015, at www.legislation.gov.uk/anaw/2015/2/part/1/enacted.

it appears that such an obligation is of a universal character. It may be reminded that in environmental law there is a well- entrenched principle of common but differentiated responsibilities the gist of which is that there is a difference between the implementation of environmental obligations by developed and developing countries due to the difference in the levels of development. There does not seem to be an equivalent principle in relation to obligations deriving from intergenerational equity:

> It may be said that one predominant assumption in present-day international legal and political discourse is that indigenous peoples, when permitted to participate, can make a significant contribution to the sustainability of the global environment, based on their traditional knowledge and practices relating to the environment.[30]

However, such a generalized approach does not reflect all possible situations. As it was explained:

> The environmental practices of indigenous peoples vary greatly across communities and regions, and just as we need to reject offensive stereotyped assessments of historically colonized populations, so today we must eschew romantic generalizations of indigenous peoples that overlook areas of ambivalence.[31]

It may also be added that indigenous peoples among themselves may have differences of opinions concerning environmental goals and economic priorities. Since they "are often the most economically disadvantaged segment of society, pressures upon indigenous communities to develop ways of alleviating their plight can cause "profound schisms" among their members".[32]

Therefore, it may be observed that not all environmental practices of indigenous peoples are compatible with environmental conservation and are thus also not reconcilable with the tenets of intergenerational equity. There were instances where indigenous peoples resisted the establishment of national parks and other conservation initiatives. Their cultural and religious activities

---

30 L. Heinämaki, 'Protecting the Rights of Indigenous Peoples-Promoting the Sustainability of the Global Environment?', 11 *International Community Law Review* (2009) p. 67.

31 B. J. Richardson, 'Indigenous Peoples, International Law and Sustainability', 10 *Review of European Community and International Environmental Law* (2001) p. 4.

32 *Ibid.*

conflict with environmental legislation, in particular in relation to the protection of endangered wildlife.[33]

3.2 *Ethno-cultural Diversity and Indigenous Peoples*

Central to the rights of minorities and indigenous peoples is Article 27 of the International Covenant on Civil and Political Rights (ICCPR):[34]

> In those States in which ethnic, religious or linguistic minorities exist, persons belonging to such minorities shall not be denied the right, in community with the other members of their group, to enjoy their own culture, to profess and practise their own religion, or to use their own language.

The construct of this Article was subject to some criticism as being rather vague. General Comments 21 and 23 of the Human Rights Committee (HRC) were instrumental in the clarification of this Article in relation to minority rights.[35]

The HRC's case-law contributed to further understanding of the rights of indigenous peoples. There are several instruments and General Comments, which relate directly to such rights. For example, in 2000 the United Nations Sub-Commission on the Promotion and Protection of Human Rights approved and revised the United Nations Draft Principles and Guidelines on the Protection of the Cultural Heritage of Indigenous Peoples,[36] which were based on the premise of a separate legal regime for the protection of indigenous heritage.[37] These Principles take a comprehensive approach to the definition

---

33 L. Heinämaki, *supra* note 30, p. 37.

34 International Covenant on Civil and Political Rights 999 *United Nations Treaty Series* 171, entered into force Mar. 23, 1976; A. Yupsanis, 'Article 27 of the ICCPR Revisited- The Right to Culture as a Normative Source for Minority/Indigenous Participatory Claims in the Case of Human Rights Committee,' 26 *The Hague Yearbook of International Law* (2013) p. 359.

35 General Comment 21, at www1.umn.edu/humanrts/gencomm/hrcom21.htm; General Comment 23 at www1.umn.edu/humanrts/gencomm/hrcom23.htm last accessed 21; A. Yupsanis, *supra* note 34, at pp. 361–364, 364–370.

36 UN Economic and Social Council (ECOSOC), Commission on Human Rights, Human Rights of Indigenous Peoples: Report of the Seminar on Draft Principles and Guidelines for the Protection of the Heritage of Indigenous Peoples, UN Doc.E/CN.4/Sub2/2000.26, 19 June 2000, at www.refworld.org/docid/3b00f28018.html.

37 S. Wiessner and M. Battiste, 'The 2000 Revision of the United Nations Draft Principles and Guidelines on the Protection of the Heritage of Indigenous People', 13 *St. Thomas Law Review* (2000) p. 383; S. Wiessner, 'Culture and Rights of Indigenous Peoples', in

of indigenous heritage which includes all artifacts, cultural expressions – such as works of art, music, dance and ceremonies, traditional knowledge, human remains and burial grounds. The 1989 169 International Labour Organization (ILO) Indigenous and Tribal Peoples Convention[38] has implications for the cultural rights of indigenous peoples, as it grants indigenous peoples control over their legal status and guarantees their right to ownership of land and possession of the total environment they occupy or use.[39]

General Comment 21 of the Committee of the International Covenant on Economic, Social and Cultural Rights (ICESCR) refers directly to the right to culture of indigenous peoples in paragraphs 36 and 37. Paragraph 36 is of particular importance as it states that indigenous peoples enjoy collective rights:

> To ensure respect for their right to maintain, control, protect and develop their cultural heritage, traditional knowledge and traditional cultural expressions, as well as the manifestations of their sciences, technologies and cultures, including human and genetic resources, seeds, medicines, knowledge of the properties of fauna and flora, oral traditions, literature, designs, sports and traditional games, and visual and performing arts. States parties should respect the principle of free, prior and informed consent of indigenous peoples in all matters covered by their specific rights.[40]

In its Preamble, the UNDRIP states that "Indigenous people possess collective rights which are indispensable for their existence, well-being and integral development as peoples". It should, however, be mentioned that the collective character of indigenous peoples' rights (including cultural rights) is somewhat controversial. The legal integrity of collective rights of indigenous peoples, as opposed to their individual rights, is not universally accepted. However, the UNDRIP is unequivocal about this. Several views were expressed that such a collective right is vital for their self – realization and survival as a societal group.[41] It may be said that indigenous peoples constitute a prototype of an

---

A. Vrdoljak (ed.), *Cultural Dimension of Human Rights. Collected Courses of the Academy of European Law* (Oxford University Press, Oxford, 2013) pp. 117–156, 135–138.

38 1989 ILO Convention No. 169 Concerning Indigenous and Tribal Peoples in Independent Countries, 1650. *United Nations Treaty Series* 383, entered into force on 1 April 1999.

39 Articles 1–19.

40 General Comment 21, *supra* note 35.

41 *See e.g.* the '... shift away from positivist, state dominated dialogue toward a more inclusive framework that is much more responsive to the ideals enshrined in the Charter of the United Nations ... has created [for indigenous peoples] a space for them to move an

organic group of human beings, who aspire to lead the same way of life and to spend their entire life together. At present, such peoples frequently lead lives in self-defined broadly autonomous communities, sharing similar beliefs, and most importantly their attachment to land, on which they were the original dwellers. Therefore, a collective spiritual relationship to their land is what separates them out from other surrounding groups, and, often, they are denominated as minorities within an overall outsider state.[42]

The right to culture based on dignity is also a cornerstone of the approach adopted in relation to indigenous peoples, as enshrined in Article 15 of the UNDRIP[43] that provides that:

> Indigenous peoples have the right to the dignity and diversity of their cultures, traditions, histories and aspirations which shall be appropriately reflected in education and public information.

The cultural rights of indigenous peoples have to be approached and understood in harmony with the fundamental rights underlying the Declaration, as part of the whole nexus of indigenous rights. Therefore, such rights have to be viewed together with the right of self-determination (Article 3),[44] and the right to autonomy or self government in matters relating to their internal and local affairs and to financing their autonomous function.[45] It must be noted that

---

agenda of promoting and encouraging respect for their human rights within this formal international organization, including the collective rights to their culture, their land, and self-government as an essential part of their individual self-realization'. International Law Association, The Hague Conference 2010, Rights of Indigenous Peoples, Professor S. Wiessner Chair, Dr F. Lenzerini (Italy), Rapporteur, p. 3.

42 S. Wiessner, 'Culture and Rights of Indigenous Peoples', *supra* note 37, at pp. 124–125.

43 *See also* Article 11: "1. Indigenous peoples have the right to practice and revitalize their cultural traditions and customs. This includes the right to maintain, protect and develop the past, present and future manifestations of their cultures, such as archaeological and historical sites, artefacts, designs, ceremonies, technologies and visual and performing arts and literature".

44 Article 3: "Indigenous peoples have the right to self-determination. By virtue of that right they freely determine their political status and freely pursue their economic, social and cultural development".

45 Article 4: "Indigenous peoples, in exercising their right to self-determination, have the right to autonomy or self-government in matters relating to their internal and local affairs, as well as ways and means for financing their autonomous functions". See also Article 46 (1). See also other Articles which are of importance: participatory right in decision – making (Article 18); obligation of States to consult; and to obtain "free, prior and informed"

indigenous peoples' right to culture is interlinked with their rights to land and natural resources (Articles 25 and 26). Their special relationship with land and nature distinguishes them from other types of social minority. Of importance are also the UNDRIP provisions that prohibit their forced assimilation (Article 8 (1)), genocide (Article 7(2)), and their relocation and forced displacement (Article 10).[46]

The cultural rights of indigenous peoples are also set out in the UNDRIP Articles 12 to 14. Article 12 grants the right to practice and revitalize indigenous peoples' right to traditions and culture,[47] Article 13 concerns the indigenous peoples' right to practice their spiritual and religious traditions,[48] and Article 14 refers to indigenous peoples' intangible heritage.[49]

General Comment 21 of ICESCR promotes free, prior and informed consent regarding culture. This is further strengthened by paragraph 36 of General Comment 21 that states that:

---

consent to legislative acts which may affect indigenous peoples (Articles 19, 32 (2); the rights to improve their social and economic conditions (Articles 17, 21, 22, 24); rights to development (Article 23);the right international cooperation (Articles 26, 39, 41. 42); rights to redress and reparation (Articles 8(2), 28).

46 S. Wiessner, "Culture and Rights of Indigenous Peoples", *supra* note 37, p. 143.

47 Article 12: "Indigenous peoples have the right to practise and revitalize their cultural traditions and customs. This includes the right to maintain, protect and develop the past, present and future manifestations of their cultures, such as archaeological and historical sites, artefacts, designs, ceremonies, technologies and visual and performing arts and literature, as well as the right to the restitution of cultural, intellectual, religious and spiritual property taken without their free and informed consent or in violation of their laws, traditions and customs".

48 Article 13: "Indigenous peoples have the right to manifest, practise, develop and teach their spiritual and religious traditions, customs and ceremonies; the right to maintain, protect, and have access in privacy to their religious and cultural sites; the right to the use and control of ceremonial objects; and the right to the repatriation of human remains. States shall take effective measures, in conjunction with the indigenous peoples concerned, to ensure that indigenous sacred places, including burial sites, be preserved, respected and protected".

49 Article 14: "Indigenous peoples have the right to revitalize, use, develop and transmit to future generations their histories, languages, oral traditions, philosophies, writing systems and literatures, and to designate and retain their own names for communities, places and persons. States shall take effective measures, whenever any right of indigenous peoples may be threatened, to ensure this right is protected and also to ensure that they can understand and be understood in political, legal and administrative proceedings, where necessary through the provision of interpretation or by other appropriate means".

> States parties must … take measures to recognize and protect the rights of indigenous peoples to own, develop, control and use their communal lands, territories and resources, and, where they have been otherwise inhabited or used without their free and informed consent, take steps to return these lands and territories.[50]

This obligation has a clear link with rights of indigenous peoples where free, prior and informed consent is one of the fundamental rights accorded to them. In that respect, should the government of a State Party take measures that affect the cultural rights of indigenous peoples within their territory, it should do so with

---

50 General comment No. 21 also states as follows: "1. Cultural rights are an integral part of human rights and, like other rights, are universal, indivisible and interdependent. The full promotion of and respect for cultural rights is essential for the maintenance of human dignity and positive social interaction between individuals and communities in a diverse and multicultural world. 2. The right of everyone to take part in cultural life is closely related to the other cultural rights contained in Article 15: the right to enjoy the benefits of scientific progress and its applications (Art. 15, para. 1 (b)); the right of everyone to benefit from the protection of moral and material interests resulting from any scientific, literary or artistic production of which they are the author (Art. 15, para. 1 (c)); and the right to freedom indispensable for scientific research and creative activity (Art. 15, para. 3). The right of everyone to take part in cultural life is also intrinsically linked to the right to education (Arts. 13 and 14), through which individuals and communities pass on their values, religion, customs, language and other cultural references, and which helps to foster an atmosphere of mutual understanding and respect for cultural values. The right to take part in cultural life is also interdependent on other rights enshrined in the Covenant, including the right of all peoples to self-determination (Art. 1) and the right to an adequate standard of living (Art. 11). 3. The right of everyone to take part in cultural life is also recognized in Article 27, paragraph 1, of the Universal Declaration of Human Rights, which states that "everyone has the right freely to participate in the cultural life of the community…", *supra* note 41.
General Comment 23 *inter alia*, includes the following statements: "1. Article 27 of the Covenant provides that, in those States in which ethnic, religious or linguistic minorities exist, persons belonging to these minorities shall not be denied the right, in community with the other members of their group, to enjoy their own culture, to profess and practise their own religion, or to use their own language." The Committee observes that this article establishes and recognizes a right which is conferred on individuals belonging to minority groups and which is distinct from, and additional to, all the other rights which, as individuals in common with everyone else, they are already entitled to enjoy under the Covenant; and para. 6.2. "Although the rights protected under article 27 are individual rights, they depend in turn on the ability of the minority group to maintain its culture, language or religion. Accordingly, positive measures by States may also be necessary to protect the identity of a minority and the rights of its members to enjoy and develop their culture

the free and informed consent of those groups likely to be affected by any such measure. This right is enshrined in Article 19 of the UNDRIP. It states as follows:

> States shall consult and cooperate in good faith with the indigenous peoples concerned through their own representative institutions in order to obtain their free, prior and informed consent before adopting and implementing legislative or administrative measures that may affect them.

This duty is also confirmed by the ILO Convention No. 169 in Art. 6(2).

It may be said that the indigenous peoples' right to participation is "a core principle and right under international human rights law".[51] Cowan reminds that in 1997 the Committee on the Elimination of Racial Discrimination (CEDR) urged States to "ensure that members of indigenous peoples have equal rights in respect of effective participation in public life and that no decisions directly relating to their rights and interests are taken without their informed consent".[52] The right of participation of indigenous peoples has evolved into the most fundamental right in relation to indigenous peoples. At the national level, UNDRIP distinguishes between State-wide 'external' participation and local 'internal' participation. External participation is reflected in Article 25 of the ICCPR. It is recognised as a group right by the UNDRIP, exercised by indigenous peoples collectively:[53]

> Internal participation is the 'extra dimension' of participation that provides the essential element of empowerment in UNDRIP: meaningful participation in decision-making about indigenous peoples' local affairs

and language and to practise their religion, in community with the other members of the group. In this connection, it has to be observed that such positive measures must respect the provisions of articles 2.1 and 26 of the Covenant both as regards the treatment between different minorities and the treatment between the persons belonging to them and the remaining part of the population. However, as long as those measures are aimed at correcting conditions which prevent or impair the enjoyment of the rights guaranteed under article 27, they may constitute a legitimate differentiation under the Covenant, provided that they are based "on reasonable and objective criteria", *supra* note 41.

51 A. Cowan, 'UNDRIP and the Intervention: Indigenous Self – Determination, Participation, and Racial Discrimination in the Northern Territory of Australia', 22 *Pacific Rim Law & Policy Journal* (2013) p. 247, at p. 291.

52 The Committee on the Elimination of Racial Discrimination (CERD), General Recommendation No XXIII on Indigenous Peoples (Aug. 18, 1997), U.N. Doc. A/52/18. Annex V, para. 4 (d), cited in A. Cowan, *supra* note 51, p. 291.

53 A. Cowan, *supra*, note 51, p. 292.

> and interests. The right to participation embodied in UNDRIP is broader than simply political participation, requiring both the internal and external elements of participation combined, as fundamental prerequisites for self-determination.[54]

Article 25 of the ICCPR guarantees the right of individual indigenous persons to participate in political processes. In many States, including those with a democratic government, indigenous peoples do not always enjoy an effective right of participation in the decisions that affect them.[55] Cowan argues that "[a]t its lowest level, the right to participation in decision-making corresponds to a basic duty on states to consult with indigenous peoples before making decisions about issues that affect their interests" ... "[at] its highest level (short of full secession and independence), the right to participation amounts to internal autonomy or self-government as provided in Article 4 of UNDRIP".[56]

The right to free, prior and informed consent was also confirmed by the HRC in the case of *Àngela Poma Poma v. Peru* which stated that in the case of the imposition of measures which would substantially compromise or interfere with the culturally economic significant activities of the members of a minority or indigenous community, free, prior and informed consent is necessary.[57] Of great relevance is also *the Saramaka People v. Suriname* in which the Inter-American Court of Human Rights confirmed that in the event of large-scale development or investment projects which are bound to have a major impact on the community's way of life and subsistence economy, the requirement of effective participation must take place in the form of free, prior, and informed consent to the relevant measures. Therefore 'mere' consultation is considered to be inadequate in order to properly engage the community.[58]

There are additional cases in which the HRC reaffirmed the right to culture of indigenous peoples, in the context of the application of the ICCPR. For

---

54 *Ibid.*

55 *Ibid.*

56 *Ibid.*, pp. 293–94.

57 *Àngela Poma Poma v. Peru* HRC, Comm. No. 1457/2006, 27 March 2009, UN Doc. CCPR/C/95/D/1457/2006 (2009) para. 7.6.

58 *The Saramaka People v. Suriname*, IACtHR (2007) Series C, No 172, Judgment of 28 November 2007. *See* in depth on this G. Pentassuglia, 'Protecting Minority Groups through Human Rights Courts. The Interpretive Role of European and Inter-American Jurisprudence', in A. Vrdoljak (ed.), *supra* note 37, pp. 80–81.

example in the *Kitok v. Sweden*[59] and *Ominayak v. Canada*[60] cases, the HRC interpreted the cultural guarantees under Article 27 of the ICCPR to extend to economic and social activities that the indigenous group relied upon.[61] It is, however, important to note that such a right of indigenous peoples to cultural diversity is neither unlimited nor absolute; rather, it is subject to a balancing act by the State authorities, as is the case of other human rights, such as the right to privacy. Therefore, as the HRC observed in the *Lansmänn and Others v. Finland*, the interests of the wider society must be taken into account.[62] In other decisions, such as the *Hopu & Bessert v. France*,[63] the HRC explained that the cultural rights of indigenous peoples are not derived only from Article 27 of the ICCPR but also from its other Articles such as 17 and 23, dealing with the right to privacy and family life.

The cultural rights and the recognition of traditional knowledge were confirmed by several other international instruments relating to environmental protection, such as Rio +20 which stated that:

> We recognize that the knowledge, innovations and practices of indigenous peoples and local communities make an important contribution to the conservation and sustainable use of biodiversity, and their wider application can support social well – being and sustainable livelihoods.[64]

Provisions concerning indigenous peoples are also contained, for example, in the 1992 Convention on Biological Diversity (Articles 8j and 15) and Principle 22 of the 1992 the Rio Declaration on Environment and Development.

From the general state of human rights law and the practice of human rights bodies concerning the right to culture (and also in general multiculturalism) it would appear that indigenous peoples enjoy the right to whaling so long as

---

59 *Kitok v. Sweden CCPR*, Comm. No. 197/1985, 27 July 1988, Supp. UN Doc. CCPR/C/33/D/197/1985.

60 *Ominayak, Chief of Lubicon Lake Band v. Canada*, Comm. No. 267/1984, Report of the Human Rights Committee, U.N.GOAR, 45th Sess., Supp. No. vol., 2, p. 1.

61 S. J. Anaya, 'International Human Rights and Indigenous Peoples: The Move Toward the Multicultural State', 21 *Arizona Journal of International& Comparative Law* (2004) pp. 9–34, 29.

62 *Lansmänn and Others v. Finland*, Comm. No. 511/1992, 8 November 1994, U.N. Doc.CCPR/C/52/D/511/1992.

63 *Hopu&Bessert v. France*, Comm. No. 549/1993, 29 December 1997, U.N. Doc. CCPR/C60/D/549/1993/Rev.1.

64 Report of the United Nations Conference on Sustainable Development (2012), A/CONF.216/16, Annex, para. 39.

it is a *bona fide* expression of their traditional way of life and their traditional use of natural resources. According to Kymlicka, in the case of indigenous peoples, however, there has been a trend towards a greater recognition of customary law and self-governing rights, without any retreat or backlash. This trend culminated in the adoption of the 2007 UNDRIP. Nonetheless, certain indigenous practices have been viewed as culturally conservative and restricting upon individual freedoms due to their overly communitarian and/or traditionalist character,[65] and as expressing a desire for cultural isolationism.[66] Some argue that, inadvertently, social conservatism, traditionalism, and isolationism are elevated to 'sacred obligations' in order to silence, manage or otherwise 'delegitimize' group members who want to change such practices.[67] After all, indigenous groups are not immune from inevitable social change within their own communities, and a regime of collective rights—while unquestionably progressive given that it safeguards the cultural identity and relative autonomy of groups surrounded by outsider dominant cultures—should not lend itself to intra-community oppression when its principal overall purpose is to resist domination and oppression from forces extraneous to the group, such as the State and the dominant culture that envelops such ethnic groups. Therefore, the participation of indigenous peoples' is important. Likewise, the indigenous peoples' rights guaranteed by the UNDRIP should be compatible with general human rights of other stakeholders, both within and outside the community.

In contrast, other views emphasize that, unlike Western attitudes towards nature (recognized as self-destructive and unsustainable), indigenous peoples and their practices may, in the same context, often offer inspiration and guidance.[68]An apposite illustration of the contentious nature of the issue of indigenous (aboriginal) whaling and of the lack of clarity as to what defines 'aboriginal cultural whaling' is the case study of the Makah Indians (State of Washington, USA) (see Section 3.3).

It has been argued that the fact that the legal status of indigenous peoples has been widely recognized by the international community, somehow gives rise to the 'responsibility' on the part of such peoples to uphold the rule of

65 W. Kymlicka, *Multicultural Odysseys: Navigating the New International Politics of Diversity* (Oxford University Press, Oxford, 2007) p. 149.

66 W. Kymlicka, *Multiculturalism and Citizenship: A Liberal Theory of Minority Rights* (Oxford University Press, Oxford, 2001) p. 103.

67 W. Kymlicka, *supra* note 65, p. 149.

68 W. Kymlicka, *supra* note 66, p. 121. *See also* A. Xanthaki, 'Multiculturalism and International Law: Discussing Universal Standards', 32 *Human Rights Quarterly* (2010) p. 21.

international law.[69] It would appear that animal welfare theorists might be permissive of indigenous whaling, for example they might support Inuit small-scale whaling as ecologically sound, given that they only kill the bare minimum necessary for their subsistence.[70]

The right to self-determination, when extended to indigenous peoples, means that indigenous peoples should be free to decide on the development of their culture. This should not, however, under any circumstances mean that indigenous peoples are free to engage in environmentally dangerous practices. If they are to be subjects of international law, they must necessarily be bound by the same environmental principles – such as the sustainability requirement – as States.[71] It was pointed out that indigenous peoples' commitment to ecologically sustainable living is not a trade-off in return for self-determination, but a necessary requirement for their own future wellbeing.[72] It may be said that in general, indigenous peoples have a well-known sustainable relationship with nature, and depict themselves as its guardians.[73] It must be stressed, however, that indigenous whaling should in principle conform, if not to animal rights approaches, at least to animal welfare approaches, that is to say, to ensure that pain and suffering are minimized. There are no inherent guarantees that indigenous whaling would not be exploited by commercial interests. As Gillespie persuasively argues:

> Many historical records and contemporary practices have combined to show specific indigenous cultures as being the antithesis of environmental sustainability. This has become increasingly apparent as certain indigenous cultures have apparently exchanged their supposed belief system for financial rewards ... Certain commentators have taken this even further than questions of political economy, and have challenged the idea of indigenous communities as suitable examples of livelihoods overall. ... This is *not* to suggest that no indigenous communities are exemplars of environmental sustainability. Rather, the point is that no generic claims can be based suggesting that all indigenous cultures are environmentally benign.[74]

---

69 R. L. Barsh, 'Indigenous Peoples,' in D. Bodansky, J. Brunnée and E. Hey (eds.), *The Oxford Handbook of International Environmental Law* (Oxford University Press, Oxford, 2006) p. 850.

70 L. Heinämäki, *supra* note 30, p. 66.

71 *Ibid.*, p. 66.

72 B. J. Richardson, *supra* note 31, p. 3.

73 L. Heinämäki, *supra* note 30, pp. 67–68.

74 A. Gillespie, 'The Ethical Question in Whaling Debate,' 9 *The Georgetown Int'l Environmental Law Review* (1997) p. 363.

According to some views, exempting aboriginal (Inuit) peoples from the trade ban on seal hunting, and at the same time, from presumably, the requirements of animal welfare is demeaning to them and even racist as it depicts them as 'noble savages', in contrast to more developed non-indigenous seal hunting communities, to which the ban and animal welfare requirements apply.[75] There have been a number of cases in which the HCR has clarified the rights of indigenous peoples regarding Article 27 of ICCPR,[76] addressing, in particular, the issue of the use of modern technology within traditional indigenous hunting activities. Thus, in the 1992 *Länsman* case, the HCR stated that modern practice adopted by indigenous peoples did not prevent them from invoking Article 27 of the ICCPR.[77] This was confirmed in the *Apirana Mahuika* case, where it was stated that the right to enjoy one's culture cannot be determined in the abstract, but has to be placed in context. In particular, Article 27 of the ICCPR does not only protect traditional means of livelihood of minorities, but allows also for adaptation of those means to modern way of life and its ensuing technology.[78]

The 169 ILO Convention links cultural identity of indigenous peoples with environmental protection, which is already indicted in its Preamble, which stresses "… the distinctive contribution of indigenous and tribal peoples to the cultural diversity and social and ecological harmony of humankind and to international cooperation and understanding". Articles 4 and 7 deal with the environmental rights of indigenous peoples.[79] The UNDRIP also recognises in

---

75 N. Sellenheim, 'Policies and Influence. Tracing and Locating the EU Seal Product Trade Regulation,' 17 *International Community Law Review* (2015) p. 3, at p. 33.

76 *See e.g.* HRC, *Ilmari Länsman et al. v. Finland*, Comm. No. 511/1992, 26 October 1994, UN Doc. CCPR/C/57/1; *Jouni E. Lansman et al v. Finland*, Comm. No. 671/1995, 30 October 1996, UN Doc. CCPR/C/58/D/671/1995.

77 *Jouni E. Lansman et al v. Finland*, para. 9.3.

78 *Apirana Mahuika et al v. New Zealand*, Comm. No. 447/1993, 27 October 2000, UN Doc. CCPR/C/70/D/547/1993, para. 9.4.

79 Article 4: 'Special measures shall be adopted as appropriate for safeguarding the persons, institutions, property, labour, cultures and environment of the peoples concerned.
2. Such special measures shall not be contrary to the freely-expressed wishes of the peoples concerned.
3. Enjoyment of the general rights of citizenship, without discrimination, shall not be prejudiced in any way by such special measures'.
Article 7: 'The peoples concerned shall have the right to decide their own priorities for the process of development as it affects their lives, beliefs, institutions and spiritual wellbeing and the lands they occupy or otherwise use, and to exercise control, to the extent possible, over their own economic, social and cultural development. In addition, they shall

the Preamble that "respect for indigenous knowledge, cultures and traditional practices contributes to sustainable and equitable development and proper management of the environment". Article 25 further states that environmental protection is not only a right but also a duty of indigenous peoples.[80] The most interesting part of this Article is that it holds responsible indigenous peoples towards future generations in respect to the protection of the environment.

3.3 *Whaling and the Ethno-cultural Diversity of Indigenous Peoples*

The question of intergenerational equity is particularly important in relation to whaling as the Preamble of the International Convention for the Regulation of Whaling (ICRW)[81] states as follows: "Recognizing the interest of the nations of the world in safeguarding for future generations the great natural resources represented by the whale stocks ..."

In light of a special ethno-cultural position of indigenous peoples, a question may be posed whether their activities are in conformity with the spirit of intergenerational equity or whether their special status exempts them from adhering to it in their activities. There is no better example illustrating this dilemma than indigenous whaling.

The ICRW does not include any special provision regulating aboriginal subsistence whaling. However, the Schedule to the Convention (which is an integral part of the Convention), recognises its special position by excluding it from the definition of commercial whaling and the provisions relating to

---

participate in the formulation, implementation and evaluation of plans and programmes for national and regional development which may affect them directly.
2. The improvement of the conditions of life and work and levels of health and education of the peoples concerned, with their participation and co-operation, shall be a matter of priority in plans for the overall economic development of areas they inhabit. Special projects for development of the areas in question shall also be so designed as to promote such improvement.
3. Governments shall ensure that, whenever appropriate, studies are carried out, in co-operation with the peoples concerned, to assess the social, spiritual, cultural and environmental impact on them of planned development activities. The results of these studies shall be considered as fundamental criteria for the implementation of these activities.
4. Governments shall take measures, in co-operation with the peoples concerned, to protect and preserve the environment of the territories they inhabit'.

80 Article 25: "'Indigenous peoples have the right to maintain and strengthen their distinctive spiritual relationship with their traditionally owned or otherwise occupied and used lands, territories, waters and coastal seas and other resources and to uphold their responsibilities to future generations in this regard". *See* also Article 29 UNDRIP.

81 International Convention of the Regulation of Whaling 161 *United Nations Treaty Series* 72, entered into force on 10 November 1948.

this type (commercial) of whaling. In 1979, the International Whaling Commission (IWC) Anthropology Panel adopted an unofficial definition of "subsistence whaling" as comprising:

> The personal consumption of whale products for food fuel, shelter, clothing, tools, or transportation by participants in the whale harvest;
> (2) the barter, trade, or sharing of whale products in their harvestable form with relatives of the participants in the harvest, with others in the local community or with persons in locations other than the local community with whom local residents share familial, social, cultural or economic ties. A generalised currency is involved in this barter and trade, but the predominant portion of the products from each whale is ordinarily directly consumed or utilised in their harvested form within the local community; and
> (3) the making and selling of handicraft articles from whale products, when the whale is harvested for the purposes (1) and (2).[82]

"Aboriginal (subsistence) whaling" was again defined in 1981, this time by the IWC's technical Committee Working Group on Development of Management Principles and Guidelines for Subsistence Catches of Whales by Indigenous (Aboriginal) Peoples, as comprising whaling conducted for "purposes of local aboriginal consumption carried out by or on behalf of aboriginal, indigenous or native people who share strong community, familial, social and cultural ties related to a continuing traditional dependence on whaling and on the use of whales".[83] These definitions are very problematic. For instance, the interchangeable use of the terms 'aboriginal', 'native' and 'indigenous' is in itself confusing, as in many indigenous communities these carry different meanings. For example, doubts have been raised as to whether whaling in Greenland can qualify as aboriginal.

The 1979 definition of "subsistence use of whale products" coined by cultural anthropologists is more restrictive as to the area in which the distribution of whale products is permitted and does not recognise the distribution of whale products that involve cash, as in aboriginal subsistence whaling.[84] It

82 Report of the Panel Meeting of Experts on Aboriginal Subsistence Whaling, Special Issue 4 (IWC, Cambridge) p. 7.

83 G.P. Donovan, 'Aboriginal/Subsistence Whaling (with special reference to the Alaska and Greenland fisheries), Reports of the International Whaling Commission – Special Issue' 4 (1982) pp. 79–86.

84 H. Hamaguchi, 'Aboriginal Subsistence Whaling Revisited', 84 *Senri Ethnological Studies* (2013) pp. 81, 86.

may be added that the report proposing the definitions was not very consistent as it said that in some cases products are distributed to and used by communities away from the coastal areas where whaling is actually conducted, and in some areas the practice of trading to meet subsistence need has emerged. Further, the IWC ad hoc Working Group stated that it was arguable whether there is a difference in principle between the sale of whale products in order to buy essential goods and the direct exchange of whale products for such goods. According to Hamaguchi this is indicative of the fact that even the ad hoc Working Group's definition did not completely deny for all cases the extensive distribution of whale products or their distribution involving cash.[85]

At the outset, confusion has resulted from the lack of any conclusive definition of what constitutes 'commercial' whaling, which makes it difficult to differentiate between 'aboriginal' and 'commercial' whaling. The *ad hoc* Working Group attempted to distinguish between commercial and aboriginal whaling. These two forms were considered to be different in respect of two elements: management and catching. The main objective of the management of aboriginal subsistence whaling was to maintain individual stocks at the highest possible level, and the main purpose of aboriginal subsistence whaling was to fulfil nutritional and cultural needs. The main objective of commercial whaling on the other hand was to maximise yields from individual stocks, and the main purpose of catching whales commercially was to sell their products. Hamaguchi observes that "these differences indicate that aboriginal subsistence whaling prioritizes quality (the cultural aspect) and commercial whaling prioritizes quantity (the economic aspect)".[86]

The term 'indigenous' is one that grew in prominence, especially after the adoption of the UNDRIP, as a means of describing aboriginal peoples in an international context. However, it may have contentious connotations since internationally, and in the United Nations context, it may define groups primarily in relation to their colonisers.[87]

According to the IWC, the objectives in regulating aboriginal subsistence whaling are as follows: (i) to ensure that the risk of extinction is not seriously increased (this being the objective with the highest priority); (ii) to enable harvests in perpetuity and appropriate to cultural and nutritional requirements; (iii) to maintain stocks at the highest net recruitment level (which is when the

85 *Ibid.*, p. 86.

86 *Ibid.*

87 Strategic Alliance of Broadcasters for Aboriginal Reflection, *Key Terminology Guidebook for Reporting on Aboriginal Topics*, at www.sabar.ca/wp-content/uploads/2012/06/SABAR-Glossary-English-Final.pdf>.

population is at its maximum sustainable yield level), and, if they fall below that, to ensure they move towards it.[88]

In general the IWC has identified four specific whaling operations as qualifying for the status of aboriginal subsistence whaling, and therefore permitted: (i) minke and fin whales (formerly also humpback whales) in Greenland; (ii) humpback whales in the Lesser Antilles (specifically at the island of Bequia, St. Vincent and the Grenadines); (iii) bowhead whales (and formerly also gray whales) in the US (Alaska); and (iv) gray and bowhead whales in Russia (Chukotka).[89] Whaling by Makah Indians is one of the most controversial cases of aboriginal whaling. It has been the subject of much discussion at the IWC and was also the subject of many legislative regulations and legal debates within the US. It still, however, remains controversial in a number of respects:

(i) it is an instance of a claim (there are others) to resume aboriginal whaling after a period during which, for different reasons, the practice had been abandoned; in this case, a claim by the Makah Indians to resume whaling after a 70 year hiatus;
(ii) there were also doubts whether their whaling was purely aboriginal subsistence whaling or was also commercial;
(iii) the claim raised questions concerning the ethical nature of the resumption of aboriginal whaling;
(iv) it also raised the issue as to whether aboriginal whaling constitutes a cultural exemption.[90]

---

88 *See* J.G. Cooke, 'A Review of Some Implications of Environmental Variability for the Management of Baleen Whale Populations, at www.researchgate.net/publication/255592686_The_influence_of_environmental_variability_on_baleen_whale_sustainable_yield_curves.

89 The IWC indigenous quotas allocated for 2014–2018, agreed at IWC 54, at http://uk.whales.org/issues/aboriginal-subsistence-whaling:
The number of fin whales struck from the West Greenland stock in accordance shall not exceed 19 in each of the years 2015, 2016, 2017 and 2018.
The number of minke whales from the Central stock shall not exceed 12 in each of the years 2015, 2016, 2017 and 2018.
The number of minke whales struck from the West Greenland stock shall not exceed 164 in each of the years 2015, 2016, 2017 and 2018.
The number of bowhead whales struck from the West Greenland shall not exceed 2 in each of the years 2015, 2016, 2017 and 2018.
The number of Humpback whales struck off West Greenland shall not exceed 10 in each of the years 2015, 2016, 2017 and 2018.

90 L. Heinamaki, *supra* note 30, pp. 46–52.

In general, the US first incorporated the IWC's regime into domestic law in the 1971 Pelly Amendment to the Fisherman's Protective Act of 1967. On the basis of this amendment, when the Secretary of Commerce determines that the nationals of a foreign country are diminishing the effectiveness of an international fishery conservation programme (such as the IWC's programme), the Secretary shall certify this fact to the President. The President then has the discretion to ban importation of fishing products from the offending country. For example, President Barack Obama informed the US Congress on 15 September 2011 of his decision not to apply trade measures to Iceland for commercial whaling in defiance of the IWC ban on such activity.[91] The US also governs aboriginal whaling by Alaska Natives via the Marine Mammal Protection Act (MMPA) and the Endangered Species Act (ESA).

Whaling by aboriginal peoples is allowed under US law to the extent that it is approved by the IWC.[92] The ICRW limits how many bowhead or gray whales aboriginal groups may harvest. However, no domestic law restricts harvest numbers on whales except specific regulations under the ESA or MMPA (provided the harvest is for non-wasteful subsistence use).[93] The Makah Indian tribe is the only indigenous group in the US with a treaty specifically reserving the right to hunt whales. According to the US Supreme Court ruling in *US v. Dion*, a treaty right cannot be extinguished by the absence of the exercise of this right.[94] For the Makah, the inclusion of this right in a treaty means that, even if no whales are taken, the right remains enforceable (providing that the treaty is still in force and the right has not been abrogated).

The Makah indigenous people live in the State of Washington and traditionally hunted for gray whales for centuries (commencing 1,500 years ago).[95] They ceded certain lands to the US on the basis of the 1855 Treaty of Neah Bay between the Makah and the US government. This treaty also guaranteed their rights to hunt for seals and whales and to fish in a reservation they were

---

91 Humane Society International, 'Iceland, Whaling and the Pelly Amendment', at www.hsi.org/issues/whaling/facts/iceland_whaling_and_pelly.html.

92 J. Firestone and J. Lilley, 'Aboriginal Subsistence Whaling and the Right to Practice and Revitalize Cultural Traditions and Customs', 8 *Journal of International Wildlife Law and Policy* (2005) pp. 197–200.

93 *Ibid.*, pp. 197–200.

94 US Supreme Court, *US v. Dion*, 476 U.S. 734 (1986) (cited in J. Sepez, 'Treaty Rights and the Right to Culture, Native American Subsistence Issues in US Law', 14 *Cultural Dynamics* p. 143, at p. 150).

95 J. J. Brown, 'It's in Our Treaty: the Right to Whale' (2002), at http://nativecases.evergreen.edu/collection/cases/its-our-treaty-whaling.html .

relocated to. Around the turn of the 20th century, the Makah people voluntarily ceased hunting for gray whales due to the depletion of their stocks, caused mainly by commercial hunting. The absence of hunting for whales had an adverse impact on the economy of the Makah people. When the eastern Pacific gray whale was removed from the endangered species list in 1994, the Makah tribe began preparations to resume hunting, as they alleged, for nutritional and cultural reasons in consultation with the National Marine Fisheries Service.[96] They also claimed that the resumption of whaling would enable them "to instil in the tribe the values traditionally associated with whaling".[97] However, the plan to resume this activity after a 70-year hiatus was met with fierce opposition in the IWC and in the US Congress; and also by some of the Makah indigenes themselves (acting as observers at the meeting of the IWC). The Makah people argued that the resumption of whaling had not been supported by all Makah people. Furthermore, due to the change in the IWC policy (following the bowhead crisis)[98] from one of a general exemption for aboriginal subsistence to one based on the requirement of 'needs', the Makah Indians' rights to aboriginal whaling were not automatically granted by the IWC[99] and the IWC initially decided that the Makah request did not fulfil the requisite conditions (i.e., subsistence needs and continuing traditional dependence) for aboriginal subsistence whaling.

In 1997, the US government brought the case before the IWC for a second time on behalf of the Makah. This time, however, the US submitted a joint request together with the Russian Federation (which was acting on behalf of

96 J. Sepez, *supra* note 94, p. 149.

97 J. Firestone and J. Lilley, *supra* note 92, p. 185.

98 In the 1970s bowheads were considered an endangered species. At the height of the bowhead crisis, the IWC adopted Resolution 1979-4 on 'Bering Sea Bowhead Whales' (Report of the International Whaling Commission 30; 31st IWC Meeting 1979):
'THE COMMISSION INTENDS that the needs of the aboriginals of the United States shall be determined by the Government of the United States of America. This need shall be documented annually to the Technical Committee, and shall be based upon the following factors:
1. importance of the bowhead in the traditional diet,
2. possible adverse effects of shifts to non-native foods,
3. availability and acceptability of other food sources,
4. historical take'.
5. the integrative functions of the bowhead hunt in contemporary Eskimo society, and the risk to the community identity from an imposed restriction on native harvesting of the bowhead; and
6. to the extent possible, ecological considerations'.

99 J. Sepez, *supra* note 94, pp. 149 *et seq.*

the Chukotka people). It was in fact a trade-off between the US and the Russian Federation. The US argued the case for the resumption of Makah whaling on the basis of the rights granted by the 1855 Treaty of Neah Bay. The IWC agreed to this renewed request and set the limit of 620 catches for the period 1998 to 2002. Their resumption of hunting, however, was strongly objected to by environmental NGOs, which contended that, after the resumption of hunting for whales, the Makah people would engage in commercial activities by selling meat to Japan (allegations which were strongly denied by the Makah people).[100]

The opponents of the resumption of whaling further argued that whaling was not necessary for subsistence of the Makah, noting that they had lived for a long period of time without whale meat. Again, the Makah opposed this contention, insisting that whale meat was a necessary part of their subsistence, despite the almost 100-year break.[101] There was also opposition to the argument that the resumption of whale hunting would contribute to the cultural revitalisation of the Makah. In this respect, the Makah argued that resumption of whaling would enable them 'to instil in the tribe the values traditionally associated with whaling'.[102] Opponents of the Makah's proposed hunt also felt that if the Makah claim were accepted, other claims would be made on the same basis. Additionally, some argued that such whaling would give a boost for Norwegian and Japanese claims for support of their own whaling traditions.

Opposition to the Makah Indians' resumption of whaling was also based on environmental grounds. For example, two NGOs[103] wrote to the US Department of Commerce (DOC) and to the National Oceanic and Atmospheric Administration (NOAA) stating that their departments had breached the National Environmental Policy Act (NEPA) because they authorised Makah whaling without first applying NEPA or making an Environment Impact Statement (EIS) and Environmental Assessment (EA). In response, a draft EA was issued and a new agreement between NOAA and the Makah was entered into; and the NOAA issued a final EA indicating a finding of 'No Significant Impact'.[104]

---

100 M. Weinbaum, 'Makah Native Americans vs. Animal Rights Activists', at www.umich.edu/~snre492/Jones/makah.htm

101 J. Firestone and J. Lilley, *supra* note 92, p. 186.

102 *Ibid.* p. 185.

103 'Australians for Animals' and 'BEACH Marine Protection'.

104 J. Firestone and J. Lilley, *supra* note 92, p. 198.

The coalition opposed to the resumption of whale hunting by Makah Indians is led by the Sea Shepherd Society; altogether, approximately 250 animal welfare organisations and 27 conservation organisations are involved. Some of these organisations filed a suit in the US courts. The decision of the Court stated that the EA was made too late in the decision-making process.[105] The NOAA had to abandon the agreement with the Makah in the light of the Court's decision. In 2001 a new draft EA was issued; and the same year the NOAA established the quota of five landings of gray whales for 2001 and 2002. This decision was again challenged by the anti-whaling lobby.[106] The dispute in essence was over the localised effect on the whole whale population in the area of the hunt. The Court required a full application of the EIS protocol in the light of the ambiguity and uncertainty in this respect, i.e., regarding the failure of the EIS to address fully the effect of the whaling permit on other Native Americans that might wish to hunt, and also of the effect on other IWC members.

According to other court decisions, the situation concerning the Makah whale hunting rights has still not yet been resolved.[107] The claim of the Makah tribe was supported by some scholars[108] who were of the view that Makah should not be deprived of their right to hunt whales. The latest decision of the US government is to scrap a seven-year-old draft environmental study on the impact of Makah tribal whaling and write a new impact statement in light of substantial new scientific information. The new information is that the gray whales which the tribe wants to hunt off the Washington coast may need to be managed separately from the overall gray whale population that migrates up and down the West Coast.[109]

Arguably, one of the causes of the unresolved situation concerning the Makah tribe's right to hunt gray whales is the concern over environmental

105 *Metcalf v. Daley* 214 F.3d 1135 (9th Cir. 2000). On this and other Makah-related cases (*Anderson v. Evans* 314 F.3d 1006 (9th Cir. 2002) and *Anderson v. Evans*, 371 F.3d 475 (9th Cir. 2004).

106 *Anderson v. Evans*, *supra* note 105.

107 J. Firestone and J. Lilley, *supra* note 92, pp. 201–207.

108 J. Sepez *supra* note 94, pp. 143–159.

109 This decision is based on a study by Canadian scientists (Tim Frazier and Jim Darling) who state that a separate, genetically distinct Pacific Coast Feeding Group of about 200 whales regularly feeds in areas that include waters between northern California and south-eastern Alaska during the summer and autumn. *See* P. Gottlieb, 'Restart of whaling study disappoints Makah chairman, Peninsula News', at www.peninsuladailynews.com/article/20120525/news/305259989/restart-of-whaling-study-disappoints-makah-chairman.

issues; and, indeed, in this case environmental considerations (the preservation of gray whales stocks) clashed to some extent with the right to cultural diversity. It would, however, be both imprudent and simplistic to attempt to draw general conclusions based on this single case. According to the US courts, environmental obligations were not fully implemented, therefore it can be said that the right of the Makah people was overruled on the basis of a legal technicality (the failure to correctly apply EA), rather than on any informed discussion balancing the right to cultural diversity (whaling) and obligations stemming from the duty of environmental protection. The question thus arises, what would the outcome of the case have been if the application of the EA had been properly followed? It is possible that, if there had been a favourable result concerning the EA, the quotas allocated to the Makah peoples would have been unchallenged. In conclusion, it can be said that there is support in various conventions, soft law instruments and practice of the IWC for indigenous subsistence whaling based on the right to cultural diversity. On the other hand, there is also a very persuasive and large opposition, led particularly by civil society, which finds requests by States to increase aboriginal whaling quotas by the IWC harmful for the preservation of whale stocks. During the 2012 meeting of the IWC, the Danish delegation walked out in protest against the refusal by the Commission to increase the quotas of humpback whales for Greenland's Inuit peoples and refused to accept any aboriginal quotas at all.[110] As noted above in the context of US litigation, the same conflicts can exist in national law.

In the view of this author, aboriginal whaling will remain contentious due to the growing importance of environmental issues (especially protection of biodiversity) and the very strong position of civil society.

A detailed analysis of aboriginal whaling leads to the conclusion that it is equally problematic and involves its fair share of contentious issues that are questions of law and issues of ethics. The lack of agreement as to the definitive content of the term 'aboriginal whaling' and the ongoing disputes regarding the number of whale stocks open to aboriginal whaling result in the inability of the IWC to manage and regulate aboriginal whaling effectively and consistently.

Various views on this type of whaling vary from rather adverse to aboriginal whaling (or at least its current regulation by the IWC), to overly enthusiastic (professing that aboriginal whaling trumps whale welfare).

110 *See* details at www.tumblr.com/tagged/international%20whaling%20commission.

3.4 *Aboriginal Whaling and Intergenerational Equity*

The next question which is posed is whether aboriginal whaling is reconcilable with the objectives of intergenerational equity.

It must be noted that two other types of whaling provided for in the ICRW i.e. commercial whaling and extended scientific whaling have been considered that, as drafted in the Convention, are no longer reconcilable with the present notions regarding the protection of biodiversity. Commercial whaling has been subject to the moratorium on whaling (i.e. so – called 'zero quotas') and the scientific whaling, conducted by Japan, was significantly limited following the Judgment of the International Court of Justice in the *Whaling in the Antarctic* case.[111] Therefore it may be stated that the only type of whaling which is still quite widely practised and which is characterised by the expanding quotas of allocated whales, is aboriginal whaling.

A view may be expressed that such a whaling activity does not conform easily with the spirit of intergenerational equity and its principles: conservation of diversity of natural and cultural resources; conservation of environmental quality; and equitable or non-discriminatory access to the earth and its resources, which are based on a premise that each and every generation has an obligation to conserve the diversity of natural and cultural resources so as not to restrict the options available to future generations to meet their own needs and satisfy their own values.

Aboriginal whaling has to be viewed a well in the context of general obligations deriving from international environment law. As it was argued, notwithstanding indigenous peoples' right to cultural identity, there is a general and uncontested obligation to protect the environment, which is universally accepted. There is also an issue of humane methods of hunting whales, which is part and parcel of a broader issue of animals' rights. The use of traditional methods of killing whales by indigenous peoples whaling is a very sensitive issue and of great concern. In traditional practices, pain and suffering are often inflicted despite good intentions. Deaths on average take between thirty and sixty minutes. In 2003, in Greenland the average time for the minke whale to die was fourteen minutes and the average time for a fin whale was 114 minutes. The worst case was 740 minutes. The same concerns were expressed regarding primary killing of small cetaceans. In 1977 the IWC adopted a Resolution which urged aboriginal subsistence whaling to reduce suffering of whales. This request mainly originated from Japan stemming from a desire for equity in the

111 *Whaling in the Antarctic* (*Australia* v. *Japan: New Zealand intervening*), Judgment, I.C.J. Reports (2014) p. 226.

IWC.[112] According to Harrop "there is a clash of moral interests in this area".[113] On the one hand there is the desire to rectify past injustices and the view that their cultural life should respected; on the other hand, there is moral pressure to secure humane killing.[114]

The cruelest method was the use of the so-called 'cold harpoon' on smaller whales such as minke whales. Alaskan Inuit presently use penthrite projectiles (small grenades). But as Stoett observes:

> An intense ethical question arises regarding the aboriginal hunts: The more traditional-style hunts were almost certainly agonizing affairs for the whales involved, involving hours of bleeding. Today's aboriginal whaler has recourse to shotguns and other technically expeditious devices, minimizing the pain and suffering of the captured whale; yet again when does a traditional hunt end and modern one begin?[115]

The contemporary approach of the IWC to the use of technology follows the stand adopted by the HRC, one of the reasons being that the modern means of killing are more humane (even though, it must be noted, many such modern methods also cause increase in depletion of whale stocks).[116] However, this is not a uniformly accepted position as the HRC acknowledgement of the evolving life style of indigenous peoples and also their permissible use of modern technology, is seen as by certain States as an contentious issue within the IWC:

> Increased use of technology is another potential issue. Improved technology makes whaling safer, more efficient and more humane, but it may be seen by some to compromise aboriginal authenticity. The world has undoubtedly changed since 1946 when the Convention was written, but for some this may be difficult to accept in the context of indigenous whaling,

112 S. R. Harrop, 'From Cartel to Conservation and on to Compassion: Animal Welfare and International Whaling Commission', 6 *Journal of International Wildlife and Policy* (2003) p. 79, at p. 95.

113 *Ibid.*

114 *Ibid.*

115 P. Stoett, 'Of Whales and People-Normative Theory, Symbolism and the IWC,' 8 *Journal of Wildlife Law and Policy* (2005) p. 151, at pp. 175, 170.

116 Report of the Panel Meeting of Experts on Aboriginal/Subsistence Whaling, *supra* note 98; *See also* R. R. Reeves, 'The Origins and Character of "Aboriginal subsistence" Whaling: a Global Review,' 32 *Mammal Review* (2002) p. 71, at p. 98.

> even when the result of technological advance is a quicker and more humane killing method. For others, use of the more traditional technology is seen as a problem for the opposite reasons.[117]

Therefore, as the practice of the IWC indicates, what it understands under culture and the method of aboriginal (subsistence) whaling is not entirely clear and perhaps not always in line with the jurisprudence of the HRC. The difficulties of placing whaling within the culture of indigenous peoples also result partly from general confusion as to what is understood by culture.

4 Concluding Remarks

The above-analysed indigenous (aboriginal) whaling which is an expression of their ethno-cultural identity is a complex question which straddles international law, human rights law, ethics and indigenous peoples' law. The relationship of indigenous peoples with the environment is complicated; it cannot be defined by stating the obvious, namely that they have a special link with the environment, a statement which has become almost a cliché. That is of course not to deny that indigenous peoples do have a special relationship with land, the environment, and natural resources, and that this relationship forms a part of their cultural identity. However, the whole relationship is far more complex, as it was stated, since cultural identity does not exempt from preserving the environment for future generations and from the participation in its protection. Therefore, it would appear that extensive indigenous whaling is at odds with the spirit of intergenerational equity and the general obligation of the environmental protection (which includes the protection of natural living resources).

The view of the present author is that indigenous whaling *per se* should not be eliminated, as it is an expression of their cultural identity but the number of species allocated by the IWC should be limited. The current practice is in fact the opposite, as the number of allocated whales is expanding. There are views expressed by some of the authors that although the status of indigenous peoples still evolves, they enjoy already a privileged position as quasi-state actors. They are more than a part of the wider trend towards NGO participation in policy discussions and programme implementation.[118] To this

---

117 IWC, at http://iwc.int/aboriginal.

118 R. L. Barsh, *supra* note 69, p. 850.

extent, the organisations and authorities of indigenous peoples have the same responsibility to respect all internationally agreed rights and principles as the States of their residence.[119] Participation, as it was stated, is a crucial element which affects the relationships between the group; the State and the manner of conducting affairs within the group and the international community.

In the view of the present author, the direct participation of indigenous peoples in the whaling discourse, both nationally and internationally (within the framework of the IWC), would lead to more satisfactory results concerning whaling. Such a participation would at least result in an informed dialogue. As it stands at present, the official discussion on indigenous quotas within the IWC are conducted by States (on behalf indigenous communities) with some (unofficial) input by civil society. At the State level, there is also a marked lack of joint discussion between indigenous comminute itself (as evidenced by the Makah peoples whaling) and in a wider context between States and all interested stakeholders.

Another issue is the method of whaling. Intergenerational equity, as explained by Professor Brown – Weiss, includes the well-being of animals as well. The traditional method of hunting them is a matter of great concern as it causes unnecessary suffering. Neither the ICRW links indigenous whaling with traditional methods of hunting nor the HRC introduces the prohibition of modern way of living by indigenous peoples. It may be suggested that the introduction of new methods of whaling within the indigenous communities, can benefit from participation, including a debate within the community and also between the State and the community. As it stands at present, there is a marked lack of meaningful debate and the issue of modern v. traditional methods of whaling is a source of constant tension and also misunderstandings.

In light of this, it would be a better practice to abandon the method causing suffering and to switch to more modern methods, which would be also more compatible with general environmental law obligations and the spirit of the concept of intergenerational equity. Therefore, it may be said that despite the great contribution of indigenous peoples to the protection of the environment, certain practices, are not entirely compatible with the tenets of intergenerational equity and may even be not fully acceptable as good environmental practices.

---

119 *Ibid.*

PART III

Ethno-Cultural Diversity, Migration, and Intersectionality

CHAPTER 7

Ethno-Cultural Diversity and Human Rights in an Era of Mass Migration: Human Rights Issues in the Balance between Separate Provision and Integration for Settled Immigrant Communities

Tom Hadden

1 Introduction

The current focus on the control of migration conceals the equally important issue of how to treat the growing settled immigrant communities that have migrated from one country – or ethnic-culture – to another.

The main legal focus in recent years has been on the physical protection and treatment of migrants while they move from place to place and then on the legal status and rights of individuals, whether as irregular or unlawful entrants, those seeking asylum, those seeking to join families or relatives already established, those facing deportation, those accepted as refugees or granted temporary residence or citizenship. This is obviously an important and often the primary concern of many human rights lawyers and activists seeking to assist the increasing numbers of migrants fleeing from conflicts and economic deprivation throughout the world and hoping to establish themselves and build new lives in more prosperous European countries.

There has been rather less focus on human rights requirements and prohibitions in respect of practical provision for the different categories and generations of immigrants who have attained some measure of stability, whether temporary or permanent, in a particular country. Some of the most important areas in which human rights issues as well as those of making temporary or more permanent practical provision arise are employment, social services and policing, housing, education, and participation in local and national government. Underlying many of these are the more general issues of cultural accommodation and various forms of integration. This sets against each other two categories of claims and rights, those of individual immigrants and their communities to practise and maintain their distinctive languages and cultures and those of national populations and their governments to develop and implement policies designed to foster greater integration between different settled

 | DOI 10.1163/9789004328785_009

communities and avoid the tensions stemming from 'parallel living' that often develop in areas where there is a high level of immigrant settlement. This will involve an attempt to clarify and give some specificity to a wide range of often confused and confusing terms: multi-culturalism, inter-culturalism, integration and assimilation.[1]

From a human rights perspective this raises some important and difficult issues. Some of the most significant that this chapter will address are:

- the balance between making provision to recognise and accommodate the cultures of these new immigrant communities and the objective of integrating them with the established population in their new national home;
- the extent to which positive action is permissible with a view not only to dealing with past discrimination but also to promote integration between separate communities;
- the tension between the rights of individual immigrants and those of their communities;
- the tension between the rights asserted by first, second and later generations of individuals in settled immigrant communities;
- the relevance to all these issues of the size and concentration of immigrant communities and the distinction between them and long-established 'national minorities'.

2 Some Facts and Figures

The extent and significance of these issues can be gauged by setting out some facts and figures on the scale and nature of migration into some major European states and their increasing ethno-cultural and communal diversity.

In the United Kingdom the census of 2011 reported that the 'indigenous' 'White British' population had declined to 80.5%, that those of Indian/Pakistani/Bangladeshi background had increased to 5.2% and those of Black

1 There is a huge literature on all these issues and terms: for an overview of some of the terminology, *see* N. Meer, T. Modood and R. Zapata-Barrero, *Interculturalism and Multiculturalism: Debating the Dividing Lines* (Edinburgh University Press, Edinburgh, 2016) at https://edinburghuniversitypress.com/book-multiculturalism-and-interculturalism.html; and for current approaches to integration, *see* Institute of Strategic Dialogue, 'Integration: What Works?', at http://migrantforum.org.uk/wp-content/uploads/2013/10/Integration_Report.pdf.

Caribbean/African background had increased to 3.3%.[2] These figures, of course, conceal huge local and regional variations. In Newham in London roughly one third of the population and in Bradford in Yorkshire roughly 40% was of Indian/Pakistani/Bangladeshi background. And in some parts of Lambeth and Wandsworth in London over 50% is of Black Caribbean/African background. Smaller concentrations of communities with Turkish, Somali, Chinese, Kurdish and many other ethnic group backgrounds can readily be identified. There is a general tendency for minority ethnic communities to cluster together for linguistic, educational, religious and general mutual support. And it is often in areas of this kind that tensions between the 'indigenous' and migrant populations are likely to arise. Pervasive feelings among migrants of discrimination and of police oppression linked to the confidence stemming from force of numbers have led to serious disorders and rioting in Toxteth, Tottenham, Brixton and Oldham. And the increasing numbers in immigrant communities have contributed to a widespread perception that more stringent controls are needed, as evidenced in the Brexit vote.

In France similar patterns have been recorded of high levels of immigration, substantial increases in second generation populations and their concentration in major cities. The French census of 2013 reported that the total number of non-European first and second generation migrants constituted just over 11% of the total population, of which 5.7% were of Maghreb (North African) origin, and 2.3% of Sub-Saharan African origin; more than half of both groups were classed as second generation descendants.[3] The concentration of many of these in 'le banlieu' in Paris and elsewhere, long experience of discrimination and exclusion and communal solidarity have led to frequent rioting and confrontations with the police and also to growing support for anti-immigration political parties.

In Germany under a series of bilateral treaties with Turkey and other states there has been an equally large influx of immigrant workers (*Gastarbeiter*) and their dependants. Out of a total population of some 82m some 20% have been classified as from an immigrant background. Until recently most of these have

---

2 Figures compiled from the Office for National Statistics Census 2011 at https://www.ons.gov.uk/census/2011census; for a more general commentary, *see* T. Cantle & E. Kaufman, 'Is Segregation Increasing in the UK?', (Open Democracy, London, 2016), at https://www.opendemocracy.net/wfd/ted-cantle-and-eric-kaufmann/is-segregation-on-increase-in-uk.

3 Figures compiled from Institut National de la Statistique et des Etudes Economiques, *Portrait Social 2016*, pp 150–51: Ch. 2.3 Immigres et descendants d'immigres, which includes a general commentary on the history and patterns of immigration, at www.lgdj.fr/france-portrait-social-edition-2016-9782111512962.

been of Turkish or European origin: some 3m (3.7%) have been recorded as of Turkish, 1.5m (1.9%) Polish, 1.2m (1.5%) Russian and 0.85 (0.9%) Italian backgrounds with substantial numbers from most other European countries.[4] But in contrast to the position in Britain and France a higher proportion of these (8% of the total population) have not as yet been granted citizenship and thus remain as formally temporary residents, as opposed to second generation members of migrant families who have been born in Germany and are thus entitled to citizenship. More recently the more welcoming governmental response to large flows of mainly Muslim refugees from the Middle East and Africa has also resulted in increasing opposition among the 'indigenous' population to the growing number of 'alien' migrant settlement.

3 Differential Responses

There is a wide range of different policies that states can adopt – and have adopted – in response to these pattern and concerns. In very general terms it is possible to identify a kind of continuum or spectrum within which these may be described and assessed, as suggested in Table 7.1.

At one end might be placed a policy of rejection or exclusion or the grant of only temporary residence with a view to retaining some kind of national or ethnic purity, or more recently to reducing the inflow of migrants by erecting barriers to entry. Where this is not practical, notably where large numbers have already entered or are regarded as essential for economic development or to maintain services, there may be a policy of assimilation, requiring or expecting incoming migrants to adopt the language and culture of the established population. An example of required assimilation might be the policy of Ataturk in Turkey in respect of the Kurdish population: requiring all children to attend state schooling in Turkish and prohibiting the use of the Kurdish language.[5] Encouraged assimilation might be exemplified by the policy of the founding fathers of the United States of America in promoting a common American identity by providing schooling for all in English

4 Figures from the German Federal Statistical Office (destatis.de), at https://www.destatis.de/DE/Publikationen/Thematisch/Bevoelkerung/MigrationIntegration/AuslaendBevoelkerung.html?nn=68748.

5 Though the Kurds are not migrants the Turkish government has pursued a policy of assimilation since they were incorporated in Turkey in the 1920s; *see generally* D. McDowall, *A Modern History of the Kurds*, (I B Tauris, 3rd ed., London, 2004).

TABLE 7.1 *The spectrum of approaches to the treatment of immigrant communities*

Rejection	Assimilation	Formal Equality	Integration	Multicultural	Separation
Exclusion, expulsion or lack of effective recognition	Forced or encouraged adoption of national culture	Equal citizenship for all; protection from all forms of discrimination	Acceptance/ fostering of diversity, interaction and balanced participation	Promotion of distinctive identities, separate provision in some spheres	Separate communal provision, autonomy in some spheres
Fences in some EU states; Roma in Europe	Kurds in Turkey; Europeans in USA	Equality/ Secularity in France	Prevailing European approach	Canada; Britain in the 1980s?	Belgium

with regular acts of respect for the national flag and anthem without prohibiting other private schools or languages.[6]

A central position would be occupied by policies of treating all citizens and all other lawful residents as formally equal without recognizing any cultural or ethnic differences. This is likely to be combined with action to deal with the various forms of discrimination that typically emerge between long established and incoming populations. A model or example might be the concept of French citizenship through which all those entitled, whether as indigenous or as immigrants from French colonies, are treated as formally equal; this has usually been combined with a denial of the existence of minorities, though with elements of assimilation in respect of policies over any recognition of the Breton and Basque languages.

The next position on the spectrum might be policies of integration designed to combine a recognition of diversity with measures to encourage members of all ethnic or cultural communities to enjoy and practise their cultures while engaging and contributing on an equal basis in the economic and political spheres. In a series of papers for the UN Working Group on Minorities and elsewhere Asbjorn Eide described this approach as a distinction between equality in the common political realm (the 'demos') and cultural diversity in the

6 For this policy, *see* M. Vile, *The Presidency: American Historical Documents* (Chambers, Edinburgh, 1974).

ethnic realm (the 'ethnos').[7] This is likely to be accompanied by measures to encourage equal and proportional involvement of members of every community in economic and political activity and fair support for distinctive cultural activity. This form of integration is currently the prevailing governmental policy in most European states.

Towards the other end of the spectrum might be what are often referred to as policies of multiculturalism designed to facilitate, encourage or formally recognise the enjoyment and expression of many different cultures and languages. The term multiculturalism, however, is widely used and misused to refer to rather different approaches. For some the term encapsulates a form of integration that combines formal and practical equality for members of all communities in the public sphere while celebrating and giving equal status to the expression of many different cultures. For others multiculturalism means a regime under which all cultures are treated in exactly the same way without reference to established national values and therefore undermines social cohesion. It is often argued that this was the dominant policy in Great Britain during the 1980s and 1990s, though with more recent moves towards the encouragement of integration with a concept of 'British identity' and 'British values'.

The final position on this spectrum is separation, whether within the state by various forms of separate administrative provision in education or other services, the development of regional or functional autonomy, as for example in Belgium, or ultimately the creation of a new state or amalgamation with another by an act of self-determination or by force of arms. It should be added that this is less likely to be the outcome in respect of immigrant as opposed to national minorities.

It will immediately be obvious that this simple spectrum conceals a much more complicated picture in which different elements of policy and different political objectives are usually combined. The current predominant approach might be described as a combination of encouraged integration – a weak form of assimilation – with continuing recognition and accommodation of cultural and linguistic diversity, often referred to as integration with respect for diversity. As will be seen, however, within the concept of integration there are further variations, notably the concept of an interculturalism that envisages a constructive dialogue between different cultures[8] and perhaps also the evolution

7 Commentary on the UN Declaration on the Rights of Persons Belonging to National or Ethnic, Religious and Linguistic Minorities, UN Doc. E/CN.4/Sub.2/AC.5/2001/2.

8 For an elaboration of this approach, *see* N. Meer *et al.*, *supra* note 1.

of a new combined identity and culture which may in Darwinian terms be a stronger hybrid of its component parts.

4 The Development of State Integration Programmes

Most major European countries and the European Union have produced policy statements, programmes, objectives and monitoring systems to promote various forms of integration. These typically focus on a separation of different aspects of modern life in some of which the objective is integration or voluntary assimilation and in others voluntary and officially recognised diversity. In most forms of employment and economic activity the objective is usually that of ethnic blindness, fair participation in all sectors and ever increasing economic equality. In housing and locational planning it is usually to avoid the development of exclusive ethnic areas in major cities and towns and to encourage ethnic mixing. In education the picture is more mixed, with some acceptance of separate religious schooling and therefore considerable ethnic separation combined with linguistic integration and some form of nationally conceived curriculum. In politics there is usually encouragement for proportional representation in major parties and governmental positions linked with discouragement for the growth of exclusively ethnic parties. And in culture there is general support, and often state funding, for the flowering of ethnic traditions. But there have been substantial differences in the way in which these objectives have been approached as can be seen from a comparison of developments in Britain, France and Germany.

In Britain the approach to integration has been influenced by two major semi-official reports. The Cantle report *Community Cohesion*,[9] published in 2001 following serious confrontations in Oldham between the White and Asian communities, identified the dangers of what was called 'parallel living' by communities which lived in separate districts, attended separate schools, saw themselves in competition with each other for resources and territory and were ready – and encouraged by some political activists – to confront each other physically. It recommended action to reverse this degree of separation by establishing shared schools in neutral areas and other initiatives to promote contacts across the communal divide. The Singh Commission on

9 *Community Cohesion: A Report of the Independent Review Team* (Home Office, London, 2001), at http://dera.ioe.ac.uk/14146/1/communitycohesionreport.pdf; for an updated version, *see* T. Cantle, 'Parallel Lives', in N. Johnson (ed.), *Citizenship, Cohesion and Solidarity* (Smith Institute, London, 2008).

Cohesion and Integration: Our Shared Future,[10] established in 2006, analysed the issues on a more general basis throughout England and Wales and recommended a broader and more flexible set of strategies: the identification of particular less affluent urban and rural areas at risk; the development of active local authority strategies based on mapping and communal consultation; the provision of courses in English for Speakers of Other Languages (ESOL); the promotion of a sense of shared citizenship through programmes to introduce immigrants to British values, customs and systems of government; and the establishment at a national level of formal citizenship ceremonies for those who meet the criteria for permanent establishment. Most of these were formally accepted by the national government but the severe cutbacks on local authority budgets has undermined their delivery. And the failure to develop an effective strategy to counteract the separatist impact of the growth of faith schools has left a substantial gap in the system. The latest governmental review on progress in integration[11] has reiterated the lack of progress in many areas and focused attention on problems, particularly within some Muslim communities, in respect of economic deprivation, communal separation, lack of proficiency in English and denial of women's rights; it has repeated earlier recommendations on the need to discourage segregation and educate migrants in British values and suggested that all new entrants should be expected to commit to integration.[12]

Policy in France has been heavily influenced by the republican principle that all citizens must be treated with strict equality and a consequent reluctance to accept that different policies can legitimately be adopted for distinct ethnic, religious or cultural groups or even to collect statistics on a racial or ethnic basis.[13] The obvious problems with this approach eventually led to the creation of a series of administrative agencies designed to encourage the growing populations of immigrants to accept the French conception of citizenship.

10 Commission on Integration and Cohesion, *Our Shared Future* (2007), at www.integrationandcohesion.org.uk

11 *The Casey Review: a review into opportunity and integration*, (Department for Communities and Local Government, 2016), at https://www.gov.uk/government/publications/the-casey-review-a-review-into-opportunity-and-integration.

12 For a summary and critique of recent British policies, *see* O. Jensen and B. Gidley, *The Politics of Mainstreaming Immigrant Integration Policies: case study of the United Kingdom* (COMPAS, Oxford, 2014).

13 The account that follows is based on a report by Angeline Escafre-Dublet, *Mainstreaming Immigrant Integration Policy in France: Education, Employment and Social Cohesion Initiatives* (Migration Policy Institute Europe, Brussels, 2014).

The current structure established in 2007 is controlled by the National Office for Immigration and Integration (DIAC – Direction de l'accueil, de l'intégration et de la citoyennité) and administered in major cities by the Agency for Social Cohesion and Equal Opportunity (Acse – Agence pour la cohésion et l'égalité des chances). DIAC administers programmes for education in the French language and culture for newly arrived immigrants during their first five years during which they are expected to sign a Reception and Integration Contract (Contrat de l'accueil et d'intégration). Acse is responsible for measures to deal with discrimination and disadvantage formally for the whole population but in practice mainly for immigrants. It works with city authorities to identify and provide additional resources for designated 'priority neighbourhoods' and schools and also for the award of 'diversity labels' for employers and bodies that meet approved criteria. It is hard to assess the efficacy of these programmes, not least due to the continuing reluctance to collect statistics on a racial or ethnic basis. But the terminology used for the various agencies highlights the focus on shared and equal citizenship.

In Germany policy was for many years based on the acceptance of 'guest workers' (Gastarbeiter) with an essential temporary status and thus a presumption that there was no need for any permanent integration.[14] Measures until 2000 were mainly concerned with the management of this form of temporary migration to fulfil the demands of the labour market. The first serious focus on longer term integration came with a formal policy report in 2001[15] followed eventually by a new immigration law[16] in 2005 which formalised earlier *ad hoc* programmes for courses in the German language and institutions. The new law established a Federal Office for Migration and Refugees (*Bundesamt für Migration und Fluchtlinge*) and a National Integration Plan (*Nationaler Integrationsplan*). This provided for federally based integration courses covering the German language, civilisation and culture for new arrivals and counselling for those finding it difficult to gain access to the German labour market and social systems. Measures have also been developed to promote integration in the labour market, notably by recognising foreign qualifications and by new

---

14 The account that follows is based on a report by Petra Bendel, *Coordinating Immigrant Integration in Germany: mainstreaming at the federal and local levels* (Migration Policy Institute Europe, Brussels, 2014).

15 The Independent Commission on Immigration (Unabhängige Kommission Zuwanderung, 2001), at http://www.bmi.bund.de/cae/servlet/contentblob/123148/publicationFile/9076/Zuwanderungsbericht_pdf.pdf.

16 M. Schmid-Druner, 'Germany's New Immigration Law: A Paradigm Shift?', 8 *European Journal of Migration and Law* (2006) p. 191.

legislation prohibiting discrimination by private sector employers. Similar approaches have been developed at a provincial level in each Land for action on language education, access to employment and social integration. Much has also been done on all these fronts by non-governmental civil society organisations and churches. But there are continuing concerns over differences in levels of education and employment between native Germans and young persons from an immigrant background, leading some Lander to attempt to reduce the highly competitive nature of the tripartite education system. The continuing administrative tensions between federal and provincial authorities and the dispersed nature of the various programmes and initiatives has been a significant features of the German response to immigration and integration. And the popular and political reaction to the open door policy of the government during the recent migration crisis has caused additional difficulties in the implementation of integration policies.

At a wider European level the focus has been on broader recommendations. In 2004 the European Commission produced a rather general set of *Common Basic Principles for Immigrant Integration Policy*[17] emphasising the need for action on employment, education in the language and culture of host states, equality of access to public services, the promotion of interaction with national populations, participation in the democratic process, acceptance of diversity in religions and cultures in accordance with human rights and regular monitoring of progress. This was followed up with a *Common Agenda for Integration.*[18] But since the Commission has no direct competence in a sphere that remains the exclusive responsibility of Member States, its main practical contribution has been through a series of funding initiatives in support of state action. Somewhat more detailed recommendations for action in a range of areas has been provided by the OSCE High Commissioner for National Minorities in *The Ljubljana Guidelines on Integration of Diverse Societies*,[19] based on its previous Recommendations and Guidelines on the human rights and treatment of established national minorities.

---

17 Adopted at the Legal and Home Affairs European Council on 19 November 2004, at http//www.consilium.europa.eu/ueDocs/cms_Data/docs/pressData/en/jha/82745.pdf (full text and commentary at pp. 15–24).

18 https://ec.europa.eu/migrant-integration/#zoom=100; *see* also the recent updated Action Plan on the Integration of Third-country Nationals of 2016 (European Commission COM(2016) 377).

19 Published in November 2012, at www.osce.org/HCNM.

5 Human Rights Requirements and Standards

With the exception of the *Ljubljana Guidelines* and general references to discrimination, few of these policy documents make much detailed reference to human rights standards. And it is not entirely clear which of the various schematic approaches or specific policies within them outlined above are required, permitted or ruled out under human rights conventions or standards.

The starting point for an assessment of this kind must be the requirement in the Universal Declaration and other major conventions that all individuals are to be treated equally without discrimination on a wide range of grounds:

> Everyone is entitled to all the rights and freedoms set forth in this Declaration, without distinction of any kind, such as race, colour, sex language, religion, political or other opinion, national or social origin, property, birth or other status. Furthermore, no distinction shall be made on the basis of the political, jurisdictional or international status of the country or territory to which a person belongs ...[20]
>
> All persons are equal before the law and are entitled without any discrimination to the equal protection of the law. In this respect the law shall prohibit any discrimination and guarantee to all persons equal and effective protection against discrimination on any ground such as race, colour, sex, language, religion, political or other opinion, national or social origin, property, birth or other status.[21]
>
> The enjoyment of the rights and freedoms set forth in this Convention shall be secured without any discrimination on any ground such as sex, race, colour, language, religion, political or other opinion, national or social origin, association with a national minority, property, birth or other status.[22]

This may seem straightforward despite some minor but significant variations in the formulations. But, none of them differentiate explicitly between direct and indirect discrimination which is increasingly relied on in this sphere.[23] Nor do they explain the complexities that arise when some differentiation is arguably necessary or justifiable.

---

20 Universal Declaration of Human Rights (UDHR), 10th December 1948, Article 2.

21 International Covenant on Civil and Political Rights (ICCPR), 16th December 1966, Article 26.

22 European Convention on Human Rights and Fundamental Freedoms, 3rd September 1953, Article 14.

23 Though none of these instruments refer directly to this distinction some of the recent case-law of the UN Human Rights Committee and the European Court of Human Rights

The distinction between direct and indirect discrimination is particularly important as much racial and ethnic and religious discrimination is not explicit but concealed behind unexpressed motives and apparently non-discriminatory rules and practices. For this reason many more recent national and European Union laws explicitly include indirect discrimination, covering laws or practices that are apparently non-discriminatory but may have a disproportionate and unjustified impact on protected populations, as for example the European Equality Directives and the British [Single] Equality Act 2010[24] based on it:

> Indirect discrimination shall be taken to occur where an apparently neutral provision, criterion or practice would put persons of a racial or ethnic origin at a particular disadvantage in comparison with other persons unless that provision, criterion or practice is objectively justified by a legitimate aim and the means of achieving that aim are appropriate and necessary.[25]

This formulation puts a heavy emphasis on what is justified by a legitimate aim and proportionate means. It is reflected in the specific limitations in respect of some of the rights protected under the European Conventions on Human Rights. The rights to respect for family life, freedom of religion, expression and association may be curtailed in the interests of such societal interests as public order, national security and the rights of others as long as they are provided by law and justified in a democratic society.[26] And discrimination in respect of all these rights is governed by the test established in the *Belgian Linguistic* case on the right for parents to secure education for their children in conformity with their religious or philosophical convictions without discrimination, that any

relies on indirect effects as a form of discrimination, as for example in *DH and others v The Czech Republic* Application No. 57325/00, Judgment of 13 November 2007 (disproportionate allocation of Roma children to special schools held to be indirectly discriminatory on racial grounds, clarifying the law and reversing the Chamber judgment); nonetheless the lack of clarity on the issue has led the European Union and national legislatures to introduce their own more precise definitions, as discussed below.

24 Section 19 of the Equality Act 2010 follows the wording of the Directive on a wider range of protected groups though with a slightly altered formulation in respect of provisions, criteria or practices that would put members of a protected group 'at a particular disadvantage that cannot be shown to be a proportionate means of achieving a legitimate aim'.

25 Racial Equality Directive 2000/43/EC, 19th June 2000, Article 2(2)(b).

26 Articles 8, 9, 10 and 11.

differential treatment must be justified on objective and reasonable grounds.[27] A pertinent example in the field of immigration is the recent Supreme Court decision in the *Bibi* case arising out of the requirement imposed by the British Government on the spouses of British citizens to secure a pre-entry language qualification in English before seeking to enter the UK.[28] It was held that the requirement was potentially a discriminatory breach of the right to respect for family life under article 8 of the European Convention but was justified on the ground of its planned contribution to the objectives of integration and social cohesion:

> The evidence therefore leads to the conclusion that the rule does have a legitimate aim (or a series of aims all linked to the promotion of integration and with it the larger aim of social cohesion) and that the aim is sufficiently important to justify interference with the fundamental right to respect for family life.[29]

These qualifications on the prohibition of racial or ethnic discrimination and the more general limitations on important individual human rights and by extension those asserted by members of immigrant communities clearly leave a good deal of flexibility for governments in devising and implementing measures to promote various forms of integration.

The more specific human rights conventions and declarations designed to protect minority communities, though they are usually formulated in terms of their individual members, are also limited and qualified. The most general is Article 27 of the ICCPR which prohibits states from denying the right of members of minorities, in community with the other members of their group, "to enjoy their own culture, to profess and practise their own religion or to use their own language". The interpretation and application of this article by the UN Human Rights Committee, however, has been focused mainly on social and economic issues for indigenous minorities rather than those of immigrant communities.[30] And it has been concerned more with private practice and enjoyment of cultural traditions and their prohibition than state provision, notably in education and other public services.

---

27 (1968) 1 EHRR 252.

28 *R (Bibi) v Secretary of State for the Home Department* [2015] 1 Weekly Law Reports 5055.

29 *Ibid. per* Baroness Hale, at p. 5074.

30 See the detailed analysis in G. Pentassuglia, 'Ethnocultural Diversity and Human Rights: Legal Categories, Claims and the Hybridity of Group Protection', VI *The Yearbook of Polar Law* (2015) pp. 250–317.

The more recent UN and OCSE declarations and the European Framework Convention on the Protection of National Minorities (FCNM) though they are not effectively binding[31], set out more detailed obligations and prohibitions in each sphere of state provision. But they also include specific provisos and exemptions in respect of these obligations. In the Copenhagen Document of the OSCE of 1990 the commitment "to create appropriate local or autonomous administrations corresponding to the specific historical and territorial circumstances of such minorities" is qualified by the phrase "in accordance with the policies of the State concerned". In the UN Minorities Declaration of 1992 the commitment in Article 4.2 "to take measures to enable persons belonging to minorities to express their characteristics and to develop their culture, language, religion, traditions and customs" is qualified by the phrase "except where specific practices are in violation of national law and contrary to international standards". As discussed further below, this provision has had most impact in cases where ethnic practices affecting younger generations, such as forced marriages and female genital mutilation, have been made criminal offences.[32] And in the FCNM the obligation in Article 5 "to promote the conditions necessary for persons belonging to national minorities to maintain and develop their culture, and to preserve the essential elements of their identity, namely their religion, language, traditions and cultural heritage" and "to refrain from policies or practices aimed at assimilation of persons belonging to national minorities against their will" is qualified by the phrase "without prejudice to measures taken in pursuance of their general integration policy"; and the obligation in Article 13 to "recognise that persons belonging to a national minority have the right to set up and manage their own schools" is qualified by the phrase "within the framework of their education systems" and the proviso that "this right shall not entail any financial obligation". These provisions, like the formal limitations and flexible interpretations of the main human rights conventions, clearly provide considerable scope for state policies designed to encourage if not to require integration.

An additional issue on which there are conflicting views is whether and on what criteria newly immigrant communities are to be regarded as minorities or

31 Council of Europe, Framework Convention for the Protection of National Minorities, February 1995; the Convention is formally binding on States parties but is in practice quite flexible and lacks an effective adjudication or enforcement mechanism.

32 Forced marriage is prohibited under the UDHR, Article 16, the ICCPR, Art. 23(3) and the ECHR, Article 12; it was made a criminal offence in the UK under the Forced Marriages (Civil Protection) Act 2007; female genital mutilation was made a criminal offence under the Prohibition of Female Circumcision Act 1985. Neither has been effectively enforced.

'national minorities' for the purposes of these human rights obligations. There is a significant difference in the wording of the UN conventions and declarations, which refer to all 'ethnic, linguistic or religious minorities', and those of the OSCE and the Council of Europe in which all the obligations are restricted to what are termed 'national minorities' which some argue do not include immigrant minorities.[33] The general approach in Europe has been that special rights should be accorded only to long established minorities, whether historically resident populations that have ended up on the 'wrong' side of a border or traditionally distinctive indigenous populations within a state or states, such as the Saami in Scandinavia or the Roma in many states. There has been a corresponding reluctance in many European states, notably in France and Germany, to accept that immigrant communities are entitled to the same special rights. This raises the question of how long it takes for an established immigrant community, many of whose members may have been accepted as citizens, to qualify as a national minority, an issue that has been studiously avoided in the Ljubljana Guidelines.

There is a closely related issue on whether and to what extent the number of persons and their concentration in a particular area is relevant to their status as a minority. This is particularly important in relation to linguistic and educational recognition in states in which there are very large numbers of relatively small and widely scattered immigrant communities: how far are states required to adopt formal measures to recognise and provide for their languages in public spheres or in educational curriculums. The FCNM, for example, grants specific linguistic rights in Article 14 only in areas where there is an historic concentration of persons speaking an established minority language and sufficient demand. This is a different issue, it should be noted, from that of protection from discrimination which applies to every individual member of a relevant minority. It may also apply not only to direct but also to indirect discrimination covering laws and practices which seem unobjectionable but which in practice have a differential impact on a minority or group to which the individual belongs.

6 Permissible Positive Action

A final and particularly significant issue in human rights law is the extent to which it is permissible to take positive action to deal not only with communal inequality or to achieve balanced representation but also to foster integration

33 The broader international approach has been adopted both in General Comment 23 on Article 27 by the Human Rights Committee, UN Doc. CCPR/C/21/Rev.1//Add.5 (1994), para.5.2 and in the Commentary on the UN Minorities Declaration, *see supra* note 7, paras. 8–11.

in ways that may constitute direct or indirect discrimination. The formal standards on this differ under the main conventions and at universal and Europeans levels.

Under the Universal Declaration and the International Covenants there is no reference to positive action, so that all these issues must be dealt with under general limitation or accommodation clauses and ad hoc adjudications on state policies and practices. The position under the Convention on the Elimination of All Forms of Racial Discrimination (CERD)[34] is somewhat clearer in that there is specific provision in Article 1(4) that special and concrete measures to ensure full and equal enjoyment of human rights by certain racial groups and their members shall not be deemed racial discrimination, though these measures are not to lead to the maintenance of separate rights for different racial groups after the objectives have been achieved. There is a similar provision in Article 4 of the Convention on the Elimination of Discrimination against Women (CEDAW)[35] stating that temporary special measures aimed at accelerating *de facto* equality between men and women shall not constitute discrimination. The corresponding provision in Article 8(2) of the UN Declaration on Minorities states only that measures taken by States to ensure the effective enjoyment of the rights in the Declaration shall not *prima facie* be considered contrary to the principle of equality in the Universal Declaration. But it is not clear whether these various provisions extend to positive action designed to foster greater integration as opposed to more effective individual or communal equality.

There is a similar range of provisions in the Council of Europe system. Under the ECHR there is no provision for positive action, but the limitations on specific rights in respect of national concerns over public safety, public order or the rights of others may be interpreted to afford a wide margin of appreciation for proportional measures in national law. And measures that might otherwise be considered discriminatory may be justified on objective and reasonable grounds in pursuit of a legitimate aim, as outlined above. Under the FCNM there is a more general provision in Article 4(3) stating that "adequate measures adopted where necessary to promote in all areas of economic, political and cultural life full and effective equality between persons belonging to a national minority and those belonging to the majority shall not be considered to be an act of discrimination". Here too there is a lack of clarity on whether full and effective equality extends to measure to promote integration.

---

34 UN Convention on the Elimination of All Forms of Racial Discrimination, 4th January 1969.

35 Convention on Elimination of all Forms of Discrimination against Women, 18th December 1979.

Within the European Union there is somewhat greater clarity on positive action. Under Article 52 of the EU Charter of Fundamental Rights limitations that are "necessary and genuinely meet objectives of general interest recognised by the Union or the need to protect the rights and freedoms of others" are acceptable. It is clearly arguable that the promotion of integration has been formally recognised as such.[36] Under Article 5 of the EU Race Directive[37] there is specific authorisation with a view to securing full equality in practice for Member States "to maintain or adopt specific measures to prevent or compensate for disadvantages linked to racial or ethnic origin". In the field of employment, in which the provisions of the Framework Equality Directive and the resulting case-law, are even more complex, the European Court of Justice has adopted a generally flexible approach:

> Under EU law, the Member States, and where appropriate the social partners at national level, enjoyed broad discretion in their choice, not only to pursue a particular aim in the field of social and employment policy, but also in the definition of measures capable of achieving it.[38]

On all these issues there is clearly a considerable degree of flexibility on what is and what is not permitted in pursuit of state policy objectives. But there is also a more general lack of clarity on what those policy objectives should be and in particular on the balance between giving priority to the expression and long-term retention of minority cultures and languages and the pursuit of greater cohesion and integration. The more political European and national codes of practice, such as the Ljubljana Guidelines or the UK Commission on Integration and Cohesion, are even less specific and tend to recommend well-meaning measures to promote integration while respecting diversity without setting out any very clear account of what is and what is not required or permissible under human rights law and practice in this context. There is little focus, for example, on the distinction between national and immigrant minorities or on the implications of the right not only not to be assimilated against your will but also not to be treated as a member of a minority against your will[39] in respect of different generations of immigrant communities.

---

36 As in the *Common Basic Principles for Immigrant Integration Policy* adopted in 2004; *see supra* note 17.

37 Council Directive on Equal Treatment between Persons Irrespective of Racial or Ethnic Origin, 2000/43/EC of 29 June 2000.

38 *Palacios de la Villa v Cortefiel Servicios SA*, Case C-411/05, 16 October 2007.

39 UN Minorities Declaration, Art 3(2); FCNM, Articles 3(1) and 5(2).

The more general question for state policy is how to achieve an appropriate balance between the preservation of ethnic distinctiveness and the acceptance or encouragement of cultural integration and mixing. There is a significant difference for this purpose between the various forms of multi-culturalism, inter-culturalism and integration. Multiculturalist approaches tend towards the preservation of distinctive languages, cultures and even physiological characteristics. Interculturalist approaches can also allow for the preservation of those distinctive characteristics, for example through intercultural education through which children and their parents learn about and accept diversity, but may also facilitate or encourage the melding of cultural and physiological differences through interaction and intermarriage. Integrative approaches tend towards various degrees of assimilation. The impact of human rights in this sphere may be thought of as primarily preservationist and backward looking while state policy may be thought of as potentially more forward looking. This is not a matter of choice between two incompatible approaches, but rather of providing a broader perspective in which both preservation and hybridisation are accepted and valued.

The most productive approach, as already indicated, may therefore not be to search for an overall prescription in human rights principles or even a series of absolute red lines but to discuss an acceptable balance between cultural recognition or accommodation and measures to promote longer term integration and cohesion in each of the many different fields of activity in which migrant communities and individual migrants are engaged.

7 Some Key Areas of Concern

7.1 *National and Non-National Minorities*

A good starting point may be to abandon the questionable distinction drawn in the European conventions and documents between national and non-national minorities or communities. In simple terms this may be seen and experienced as in itself discriminatory on racial or ethnic grounds. A better approach may be to focus not only on the long-established and indigenous nature of so-called 'national minorities' but also on the size or concentration of any migrant community as a guide to the way in which their rights are to be recognised or accommodated. It seems clear that long-established 'national' minorities have a stronger claim to the protection of their language than newly-arrived migrants. But both may sensibly be required to learn and be able to use the dominant national language, except perhaps in formally bi-lingual states like Belgium and Canada. But large and concentrated immigrant communities are also entitled to greater special recognition and accommodation in most spheres. Size and numbers may matter as much as length of settlement. Members of more scattered and less numerous communities may have to be content with their rights as individuals. How these various categories of peoples or communities are to be distinguished cannot of course be prescribed in terms of precise numbers or measurable degrees of concentration. One of the objectives of integration, however, is to encourage dispersal and mixing as well as to discourage any of the specially recognised aspects of particular minority cultures, such as barriers to inter-marriage, that may stand in the way of social and economic and national cohesion. In that sense the promotion of integration involves an acceptance that some dispersal and mixing while respecting some elements of diversity is often preferable to maintaining and protecting cultural and physical separation on a long term basis.

7.2 *Generational Issues*

Another significant issue that is relevant across the board is that of generational differences. This is indirectly recognised in some of the minorities instruments in the provision that it is a matter of choice to belong or not to belong to a minority and that no disadvantage shall result for any member of a minority from exercising or not exercising any special rights.[40] But it may be equally important to recognise the generational differences within immigrant communities. There is a natural tendency for first generations to cling together for religious and linguistic reasons, for second generations to move away from restrictive cultural traditions and for third and subsequent generation to prefer to be treated in the same way as the general population. Some obvious examples are the reaction against arranged marriages by second and later generations from the Indian subcontinent and the rejection of restrictions on the activities of women and modern forms of socialisation by young people. On the other hand some practices, such as the wearing of a headscarf by Muslims or a pendant cross by Christians, may be welcomed or accommodated as inoffensive badges of identity while others, such as the wearing of a full burka may be more problematic. In Britain the approach to such issues has generally been quite flexible, distinguishing between situations in which distinctive dress is accepted and others, such as complying with rules on school uniforms[41] or

---

40 FCNM, Article 3.1; a leading case of an individual right to be treated as a member of a minority under Article 27 of the ICCPR is *Lovelace v Canada* Communication No. 24/1977, UN Doc. CCPR/C/13/D/24/1977.

41 *R (Begum) v Denbigh High School Governors*, [2007] 1 AC 100 (ban on a full covering jilbab in a school in which agreed forms of Muslim dress were permitted held compliant).

giving evidence in court, in which reasonable regulation is accepted. In France and some other countries a ban on the wearing of headscarves in schools and universities has been accepted as compliant with human rights standards.[42] The tendency in some human rights adjudications to regard minority communities as uniform and to ignore generational differences is to be resisted.

7.3 *Employment*

The sphere of employment and other forms of economic activity is one in which the principle of equality generally takes precedence over the recognition and accommodation racial, religious, ethnic or gender difference. But there are two aspects to equality: the right of each individual to be treated fairly and without discrimination and the emerging claim for each major racial, ethnic and gender group to fair participation at every level of employment and economic activity.

The initial and established principle in human rights terms has been the prohibition of discrimination at the point of recruitment or promotion or service delivery. Though there is some difference in the main conventions on the list of prohibited grounds the primary focus was on the reasons why the individual applicant or consumer has been treated. The extension in many systems from this form of direct discrimination, in which it is the intention or mindset of those responsible that is at issue, to indirect discrimination introduces a wider focus in which it is the impact of prescribed or established criteria on the group to which the applicant belongs that is at issue. This clearly involves a consideration of communal rather than merely individual impact, though it is usually dependent on complaints by individuals. And in formal terms at least it results in individual compensation, though often also in more general changes in the practices and assumptions that lay behind the discriminatory results. The right not to be treated as a member of a minority against your will, however, should perhaps not extend to a bar on data collection on ethnic identity which is generally regarded as essential to the monitoring of progress towards genuine equality in many spheres.[43]

---

42 *Leyla Sahin v Turkey*, Application No. 44774/98, Judgment of 10 November 2005 (a general ban on headscarves held compliant).

43 This has been a contentious issue in France, where there is a reluctance to monitor ethnic origin *supra* note 13, and in Northern Ireland where a proposal that the Bill of Rights provided for in the Good Friday Agreement should incorporate article 3.1 of the FCNM was regarded by some as an illegitimate interference with the policy objective of monitoring progress on communal equality.

The increasing focus on fair participation by members of different gender, religious, racial, ethnic and other recognised communities in various economic sectors raises somewhat different issues. Policies and practices designed to achieve a better balance in economic participation may range from outreach measures to encourage applications from members of underrepresented communities to the introduction of preferential treatment for applicants at the point of selection or service delivery. Some of these can run counter to the individual rights of members of over-represented communities, typically national populations, and to that extent are clearly discriminatory. As already indicated, it is not always clear what positive or corrective measures of this kind are permissible under different human rights regimes or whether they may legitimately be authorised and implemented on a compulsory as well as a voluntary basis. But it is also clear that feelings of lack of balance in employment and communal exclusion from positions of power or influence are important factors in the development of alienation and possible radicalisation among members of immigrant communities. Some positive measures of this kind may therefore be essential to an effective integration programme. It is becoming clear that the underlying objective in this sphere is to achieve an integrated and representative workforce at every level in the economic sphere. And it is not always clear that judges in human rights or constitutional courts are best placed to decide on how best to achieve that goal.

7.4 *Social Services and Policing*

The approach to the delivery of social services and also policing follows a slightly different set of objectives to a similar integrative position. The underlying principle is that those delivering state services to individual migrants or their communities should reflect and be representative of those communities. This does not typically result in the separatist conclusion that services should be delivered only by members of the same ethnic or religious background as those they deal with. That runs counter to the general conception of public services set up to serve the whole community. But it is also generally accepted that those working with individuals or communities from diverse non-nationals backgrounds or cultures should as far as possible know about and operate with understanding and respect for those differences. There is no binding obligation in this field other than the bar on discrimination. But there is widespread acceptance that the best means of ensuring that understanding and respect is that there should be sufficient representation of those diverse backgrounds at all levels of the state agencies.

This principle of representative diversity is most clearly set out in respect of policing in the UN Code of Conduct for Law Enforcement Officials which states that all law enforcement agencies should be "representative of and responsive and accountable to the community as a whole".[44] The tendency of police forces to be predominantly recruited from dominant 'national' populations has commonly been a major cause of friction between the police and immigrant communities. But there is also strongly held and concerted opposition to the idea that separate police services or units should be established to enforce the law and maintain public order in areas with significant immigrant communities. This has led to sustained efforts in most countries to ensure more balanced recruitment and promotion whether by non-discriminatory 'outreach' measures or in some cases, as in Northern Ireland, to the formal exemption of police recruitment from general prohibitions of any form of discrimination.[45]

7.5 *Housing*

The major concern on housing and location for incoming migrants is the impact on community relations of the concentration of immigrant or other ethnic communities in particular areas. The tendency of newly arrived immigrants to congregate in areas near to their churches, mosques or schools is to be expected. And many of the most recent refugees and migrants entering Britain and other European states are seeking to join relatives and associates already established there. The location of individuals or families without such links under government sponsored or internationally negotiated settlement schemes tends towards wider dispersal though it often poses greater local resistance. The policy issue is whether governments or local authorities can or should plan for or provide incentives for mixing or integration of communities, given the extensive evidence that it is regular contact in daily life that helps to minimise the development of communal antagonisms.[46]

There is little direct guidance on these issues in human rights documents, other than the general prohibition of discrimination on racial, ethnic, religious or linguistic grounds. Most European governments have adopted policies of dispersal for recently arrived refugees, despite the desire of most migrant to live

44 Adopted by General Assembly Resolution 34/169 of 17 December 1979.

45 A specific negotiated exemption from EU discrimination law was thought to be necessary for this purpose and was included in Article 15.1 of Council Directive 2000/78 of 27 November 2000 (Framework Employment Directive); for a more detailed review of policy and practice in this area see T. Hadden, 'Policing for Shared Societies: An Institutional Approach to Reform', in M. Fitzduff (ed.), *Public Policy for Shared Societies: A Comparative Approach*, (Palgrave Macmillan, London, 2013) pp. 75–95.

46 The evidence on the extent and impact housing segregation in the UK is summarised in the Cantle, Singh and Casey reports, *see supra* notes 9–11.

in areas where others from their home countries are established and some resistance from communities into which substantial number of immigrants have been located. Apart from the clear human rights principle of respect for family life and extensive case-law in respect of family reunification there does not appear to be any binding obligation on this issue. Nor is there much clarity on whether local authorities or housing associations are entitled to adopt positive action but potentially discriminatory allocation schemes designed to promote mixed multi-ethnic housing. If such a policy is adopted with a view to what is arguably a legitimate objective of promoting social cohesion and supported by credible evidence that it is likely to work it could be justified under the established case-law of the European Convention on Human Rights. But it is less clear whether there is any way in which private sector landlords or estate agents can legitimately be encouraged or required to pursue similar objectives. This is an area in which there is a high level of flexibility for national governments to adopt and legislate for any reasonable and proportionate housing and location policy.

7.6 *Education*

Policy and practice in education raise different and often more difficult issues in that control of schooling a key factor both in the development of a shared national identity and also in the preservation of distinctive religious, linguistic or ethnic cultures. In this sphere the human rights principles point in different directions. The starting point is the well-established right of parents to choose the type and content of education for their children in accordance with their religious or philosophical convictions.[47] But this cuts across the equally well-established principles that states are not required to fund school systems other than those provided by the state but that if they provide funding for separate religious or ethnic schools they should not discriminate between them.[48] One approach that has been adopted in the United States and France is to provide funding only for common state schools and to refuse any state funding for alternative private religious or other distinctive or exclusive schools. In Britain the approach has traditionally been to fund both local authority common schools and some Christian and Jewish schools and more recently some independent academies, while retaining a right of 'opting out' from any specifically religious classes.[49] This has led to pressure to provide equivalent

47 International Covenant on Economic, Social and Cultural Rights (ICESCR), Article 13.3; ECHR, Protocol 1, Article 2.

48 FCNM, Article 13.

49 Currently provided in England and Wales under the School Standards and Framework Act 1998, s. 71; there are equivalent provisions in other jurisdictions.

funding for newer and often exclusive Muslim schools despite concerns about their separatist impact. Given the more general concern that separate faith schools may contribute to communal separation and distrust a major issue is thus whether states are permitted to provide financial or other incentives for shared or common schooling

The fundamental problem in this area is that the prevailing human rights approach is in practice likely to lead to educational separation as opposed to the objective of ensuring mutual respect and tolerance between members of all communities.[50] One response is to require all schools through a statutory national curriculum to provide non-denominational religious and cultural education for all children with a view to fulfilling the general human rights obligation to provide education that "shall enable all persons to participate effectively in a free society, promote understanding, tolerance and friendship among all nations and all racial, ethnic or religious groups".[51] But this may not be effective or appropriately delivered in schools that are exclusively or predominately attended by children from a single ethnic or religious community. An alternative approach, promoted in both Northern Ireland and the Irish Republic where most schools are provided or controlled by religious bodies, is to argue that there is a human right for parents, and perhaps also older children, to insist on the provision of integrated or integrating schools for all who want them.[52] There are further generational issues over the extent to which and the age at which children or young persons can assert a right independently of their parents to choose shared or integrated schooling. Second and third generation immigrant children and young persons may prefer to opt for common schools provided they are willing and able to provide an appropriate integrating environment that respects all forms of ethnic and cultural diversity. A better and more generally applicable stance may be to argue that where segregated religious schools are already established states are entitled to provide more favourable financial and other incentives for integrated schooling.

50 The Advisory Committee on the FCNM has stated that 'the core task is to organise the education system in a way which allows for interaction between persons from various groups in order to encourage mutual understanding and tolerance while at the same time ensuring successful maintenance and development of the elements of the identities of members belonging to various groups'; *Commentary on Education*, ACFC/25DOC(2006)002, p. 16.

51 UDHR, Article 26.2; ICESCR, Article 13.1.

52 C. Moffat, 'Education Rights in Divided Societies: A Right to Integrated Education in Northern Ireland', 2 *Socio-Legal Studies Review*, (2013) pp. 23–54; A. Mawhinney, 'Freedom of religion in the Irish primary school system: a failure to protect human rights?', 3 *Legal Studies* (2007) p. 379.

There are additional issues in respect of separate linguistic schooling and 'mother tongue' education. This is more strongly asserted in the UN Minorities Declaration[53] than the European Framework Convention in which support for education in or through separate non-national languages is restricted to areas in which sizeable linguistic minorities are long established.[54] And there are strong reasons for insisting on education in the dominant national language since an inability to understand or speak it is a significant barrier to integration in employment and other spheres.[55] Support for 'mother tongue' primary and secondary education has come initially from educational practitioners and researchers and has been discussed in some human rights documents.[56] But it poses major practical problems, particularly for schools in places where there are many different linguistic communities in multi-linguistic cities or regions.

These conflicting human rights considerations suggest that a flexible approach to educational policies may be preferable to one in which key strategic decisions are left to be determined in human rights courts.

7.7 *Language*

Language is one of the most salient and contested aspects of cultural diversity. It is one that is accorded some of the most detailed provisions in human rights conventions and declarations. But it is also one in which the importance of integration is usually recognised by the acceptance of priority status for a nationally dominant language or languages over those of immigrant communities.

The clearest human rights provision is the right under Article 27 of the ICCPR for members of linguistic minorities to use their own language in community with other members. In Europe under Article 10 of the FCNM there is an obligation on states parties to 'endeavour to ensure as far as possible the conditions which would make it possible to use the minority language in relations between those persons and the administrative authorities' in areas inhabited by them traditionally or in substantial numbers if requested and meeting a real need; and also under Article 14 to permit education in such areas in or through the minority language. But these rights and obligations are balanced by a clear proviso in Article 14.2 that they 'shall be implemented without prejudice to the learning of the official language or teaching in this language'. These provisions, however, are directed primarily at long-established and concentrated national minorities who are being granted a kind of right to the preservation

53 UN Minorities Declaration, Article 4.3.

54 FCNM, Article 14.

55 As in the national policies outlined above and the Bibi case, *supra* note 28.

56 The issue is extensively discussed in the *Commentary on Education, supra* note 50.

of their language. The same is not so clear in respect of the languages of dispersed minorities and of immigrants. The commentary on the UN Minorities Declaration makes this clear and emphasises that the children of isolated or new minorities "have a great need to learn to use the language of the country of immigration as quickly and effectively as possible".[57] And, as has been seen, this has been extended in recent state integration programmes to all incoming migrants by providing for and in some cases requiring attendance at classes designed to equip them to live and work in the wider national community.

Further complications arise in countries where there is an ongoing conflict over the status and use of two or more established languages, as for example in Belgium, Canada and Wales.[58] The approach of constitutional and human rights courts on such matters has generally been to accept that state governments have a right to determine and regulate the circumstances in which different languages are given official status in public administration and in education, though formal prohibitions on their use in private and in voluntary schooling are ruled out.[59] Overall it may be concluded that in the drafting of human rights conventions and declarations and in court rulings on state legislation a very large degree of freedom has been afforded to states to give special and positively discriminatory status to formally recognised national languages and that this is especially the case in respect of measures to encourage linguistic integration.

7.8 *Cultural Accommodation*

This is the area in which human rights standards and litigation have been most influential. The main human rights conventions and documents set out in the clearest terms that members of ethnic, religious and linguistic communities or minorities are not only to be protected from discrimination on those grounds but also have the right to enjoy and express their identities and

57 Commentary on the UN Minorities Declaration, paras. 63–64

58 In Belgium detailed legislation prescribing the exclusive use of Flemish and French for official purposes in Flanders and Wallonia and bilingualism in Brussels was approved by the European Court of Human Rights in the *Belgian Linguistic* case, *supra* note 27; in Canada the ban in 'Bill 101' on the use of English in shop signs in Quebec was held to be an unlawful restriction of freedom of expression by the Canadian Supreme Court in *Ford and others v Attorney General of Quebec* [1988] 2 S.C.R. 712 but the general pro-French provisions of the Bill have been maintained with a few amendments under the 'notwithstanding' clause in the Canadian Constitution; in Wales the use of the Welsh language has been regulated in detail under the Welsh Language Act 1993.

59 This is a highly contested and complex legal area which cannot be fully discussed in this context; for a detailed analysis of these and other language disputes *see* F. de Varennes, *Language, Minorities and Human Rights* (Martinus Nijhoff, The Hague, 1996).

cultures.[60] The issue for states is how far these rights extend in both the public and the private spheres and how far there is an obligation to alter established laws and practices to accommodate those identities and cultures.

The case-law from different countries has been quite variable, notably on the issue of the Muslim headscarf and other forms of dress.[61] In the most recent decision by the European Court of Human Rights it was held that the Swiss authorities could insist on Muslim girls sharing in mixed gender swimming lessons with a view to facilitating their successful social integration according to local customs and mores despite religious objections by their parents:

> By giving precedence to the children's obligation to follow the full school curriculum and their successful integration over the applicants' private interest in obtaining an exemption from mixed swimming lessons for their daughters on religious grounds, the domestic authorities had not exceeded the considerable margin of appreciation afforded to them ... in compulsory education.[62]

There has been more debate and action in France and Germany on banning the fully covering burka[63] than in Britain where the recent focus has been on the illegitimacy of the expression of Christian values in commercial settings.[64] But in other contexts there has been a shift in recent years away from the view that public bodies cannot express or recognise any religious symbols or festivals[65] towards

---

60 *Supra* note 30.

61 For some leading cases *see supra* notes 41 and 42.

62 *Osmanoglu & Kocabas v Switzerland*, Application No. 29086/12, Judgment of 10 January 2017; as the judgment is reported only in French the quotation is taken from the official Registry summary in English.

63 Action has been taken or proposed by legislation rather than human rights litigation; the ban by some local authorities in France on bathing in Muslim dress (the 'burkini' case) was overturned by the Conseil d'Etat on the ground of excess of power without a rational basis, decision on cases 402742 and 402777 of 26 August 2016.

64 UK courts have generally given clear preference to the prohibition of discrimination in any commercial setting even where it allegedly infringes the Christian commitment of service providers, as in the provision of bed and breakfast accommodation for gay couples (*Bull & Bull v Hall & Preddy* [2013] UKSC 73), or the icing of a cake with a pro-gay marriage slogan (*McArthur & Ashers Baking Co Ltd v Lee* Northern Ireland Court of Appeal 24 October 2016).

65 The leading case is *Lautsi v Italy*, Application No. 30814/06, Judgment of 18 March 2011, in which the display of crucifixes in state schools in Italy was held to be a legitimate expression of its Christian tradition.

an acceptance that reasonable recognition of both Christian and non-Christian practice is a better approach to diversity. The wider issue is whether and if so what incentives or pressure towards the promotion of national as opposed to separate communal cultures are permissible. States have generally been granted a wide margin of appreciation, for example in respect of recognition and acceptance of particular national constitutional traditions, such as state religious institutions in Britain and Norway or secularity in France. There is a similar flexible approach to the corresponding accommodation or support for migrant communities in language, arts, media, street and personal names and other spheres[66] or, as discussed above, of requirements to learn the national language as a means to foster social and economic integration.

7.9 *Participation in Government*

There is growing pressure on political parties and governments to achieve balanced representation of women and ethnic minorities. The established international human rights standard is that members of national or ethnic, religious and linguistic minorities are entitled to 'effective participation' in decisions at national or regional levels concerning them.[67] But this is qualified in the UN Declaration by the phrase 'in a manner not incompatible with national legislation'. And there is little clarity on what constitutes 'effective participation'. The guidance from the Council of Europe Expert Committee ranges from measures to ensure that voting systems and electoral boundaries do not make it difficult for members of minorities to secure election and provision for reserved seats, to separate arrangements for consultation with minority representatives and various forms of regional, local or functional autonomy.[68] But there appears to be little enthusiasm for the establishment or supportive measures for exclusively ethnic or religious parties and a preference for inclusive and integrated representation within established political parties. In two major political cases which have been widely criticised the European Court of Human Rights has prioritised the rights of individuals over those of communal or religious communities: it has ruled that the Turkish Constitutional Court could legitimately ban an allegedly exclusive and separatist religious party on

66 The extensive range of acceptable policies is reviewed in detail in the *Ljubljana Guidelines*, *supra* note 15, and in S. Holt and Z. Machnyikova, 'Culture in Shared Societies' in M. Fitzduff, *supra* note 45.

67 UN Minorities Declaration Article 2.3; FCNM, Article 15.

68 Advisory Committee on the Framework Convention for the Protection of National Minorities, *Commentary on the Effective Participation of Persons belonging to National Minorities in Cultural, Social and Economic Life and in Public Affairs*, ACFC/31DOC(2008)001.

the ground that it threatened the secular basis of the state and curtailed the political freedom of individual citizens;[69] and also that the provisions of the Bosnian Constitution providing for separate ethnic eligibility and voting for representation in the House of Peoples infringed the individual human rights of Jewish and Roma citizens.[70] There is an equal lack of clarity in human rights terms on what measures are permissible or prohibited in respect of the selection of candidates, such as women-only or ethnic-only short lists or other forms of positive action.[71]

As in the other spheres discussed above, it is difficult to resist the conclusion that human rights law, soft law standards and court adjudications have generally allowed a very large margin of appreciation to states to develop and implement their own approaches to the balance between individual rights and measures to facilitate or promote various forms of integration or inter-cultural development.

8 Conclusions

The conclusion to this chapter will already be clear. It is that the highly general formulations in human rights conventions and instruments are not always helpful in resolving the difficult policy judgments and choices that governments and others must make in responding both to the claims of the increasing number and diversity of migrant communities and the concerns of their more established 'national' populations. Nor is it clear that lawyers and judges are best qualified to deal with the wide range of social and economic issues that arise in deciding how far to give priority to measures designed to foster integration or to promote inter-cultural mixing or to measures to preserve and promote cultural differences. The complexity of these policy options

69 *Refah Partisi v Turkey*, Applications Nos. 41340/98, 41342/98 and 41344/98, Grand Chamber Judgment of 13 February 2003.

70 *Sejdic & Finci v Bosnia & Herzegovina*, Applications Nos. 27996/06 and 34836/06, Judgment 22 December 2009; the decision has been widely criticised as an infringement of the carefully constituted power-sharing structures agreed at the Dayton Peace Accords, *see* C. McCrudden and B. O'Leary, *Courts and Consociations: Human Rights versus Power-Sharing* (Oxford University Press, Oxford 2013).

71 In the UK women-only short lists have been authorised by legislation after a court ruling that they infringed the law on equality and non-discrimination (*Jepson & Dyas-Elliott v Labour Party* [1996] IRLR 166) in the Sex Discrimination (Election Candidates) Act 2002 and the Equality Act 2010, s 105; the exemption has recently been renewed to 2030.

TABLE 7.2 *The range of accommodation and integration policies in different spheres*

	Blind Equality	Fair participation	Positive Action	Integration	Formal recognition	Separate provision	Autonomy
Employment	Preferred approach	Increasingly an objective	Generally accepted	In some sectors	Generally not accepted	Only in some religious areas	Only in some religious areas
Social Services	Preferred approach	An objective in staffing	Generally accepted	Programmes for change over time	OK for services Not for staffing	OK for service delivery	Only in very limited spheres
Policing	Required for service delivery	Increasing an objective	Generally accepted	Programmes for change over time	Generally not accepted	Generally not accepted – same justice for all	Not accepted – same justice systems for all
Housing	Allocation by need	Possible special points schemes	Possible action to secure balance	Acceptable on voluntary basis	Generally not in public housing	Generally not in public housing	Only in private sector
Education	Common schools	Balanced enrolment	Bussing to secure balanced rolls?	Integrated schools	Funding for faith & linguistic schools	State provision of faith/linguistic schools	Private sector faith & ethnic schools
Language	National only	State services in many languages	State funded language classes	Induction classes required	Multiple official languages	Single language regions or areas	Free choice of any accepted
Culture	No account of ethnic content	Equal allocation of funding	Special funding for diversity	Not usually needed	Acceptable	Block grants for ethnic sectors	Block grants for ethnic sectors
Government	Democratic voting for all	Pressure for balance in all appointments	Acceptable for selection of candidates	Reserved seats	Separate ethnic parties not generally approved	Separate voting/ reserved seats	Functional or local autonomy

and an indication of current thinking of what may be most appropriate and acceptable is set out in the accompanying Table 7.2.[72]

Human rights courts have thus perhaps been wise to refrain from active involvement in this area. Human rights standards and adjudications have a role in assessing the legitimacy and rational basis of differing policies and their impact and setting some limits to clearly discriminatory programmes. They are less obviously appropriate for dealing with the constant and inevitable changes in the political, economic and social conditions under which policy must be made. This is partly due to the fact that human rights concepts and principles are generally more attuned to the preservation of established values and practices, both of 'indigenous' national populations and of the initial generations of migrants. They are less attuned to the accommodation and provision for ongoing and future changes as later cohorts of migrants become more integrated in a developing and hybridising culture. Social scientists and policy-makers are perhaps more attuned to dealing with social change and the interaction of individual and communal concerns and aspirations. So it may be better to focus academic research and political action not only on the interpretation of human rights instruments but also on the policies that are best suited to deal with conflicting and emerging societal demands and needs.

---

72 For an earlier attempt to analyse and tabulate the different considerations that may arise in different spheres *see* J. Levi, 'Classifying Cultural Rights', in I. Shapiro and W. Kymlicka, *Ethnicity and Group Rights* (New York University Press, New York 1997).

CHAPTER 8

Minorities-within-Minorities Frameworks, Intersectionality and Human Rights: Overlapping Concerns or Ships Passing in the Night?

Dolores Morondo Taramundi[1]

1 Introduction

It is increasingly common to find ethno-cultural diversity discussed as, or from the perspective of, human rights. Yet, for a long time, the human rights angle was not the preferred perspective to discuss ethno-cultural claims, which were generally framed as minority rights issues and translated into forms of protection for particular groups and group rights.

International minority rights documents pre-date the Universal Declaration of Human Rights and follow the logic of guaranteeing the collective interests of those particular groups, assuming that the rights of their members would be fully realised within the collective cultural rights of the group. Traditionally, these collective rights have offered protection for minority groups to speak their minority language, to practice their minority religion or to maintain particular forms of customary laws or other traditional practices that were alien to the majority society of the states in which they lived.

After the Second World War, with the Universal Declaration of Human Rights and the development of international human rights standards, international law had to make room for a different subject, the individual human being, who could claim rights 'against' the state. States, once the primary rights-holders in international law, became now bounded, not only by the rights of other states, but by the rights of a different type of subject: their own citizenry.[2] In this sense, human rights are commonly understood as a limitation on the sovereignty of the state, especially when international standards of human rights become part of domestic constitutions and legislation. Since

1 An earlier version of this work was discussed at the Conference "Ethno-cultural Diversity and Human Rights: Tacking Stock – Looking Ahead", held at the University of Liverpool in May 2016. The research on which it is based received funding from the European Union's Seventh Framework Programme (FP7/2007-2013) under grant agreement n° 316796.

2 A. Cassese, *I diritti umani oggi* (Laterza, Roma, 2005) p. 25.

 | DOI 10.1163/9789004328785_010

'minority rights' instruments were already considered a constraint for the action of the state (and the social majority) in which those minority groups were living, they could be considered, from this perspective, similar to human rights. They were a distinct and *sui generis* form of human rights whose differences drove the discussion on 'minority rights' to peripheral debates of human rights issues, separated and self-centred. On the other hand, mainstream human rights scholarship paid little attention to the 'minority group' condition as such, burdened as it was with the riddles of the long-lasting debate on individual or collective entitlements in human rights law.

In the last decades, however, there has been a growing interest in ethno-cultural diversity from the perspective of human rights.[3] I shall not attempt to discuss here how this has affected the literature on minority rights and traditional approaches to minority groups' protection. Rather, I will focus on a recurring topic of the discussion of ethno-cultural claims protection whenever the focus is opened beyond minority rights instruments, namely, the position of the so-called internal minorities or 'minorities within minorities'.

The riddles around the particular position of, and the forms of injustice suffered by, groups that can be identified as minorities within minorities were a topic for, sometimes heated, discussion in the late 1990s and during the 2000s in Canada and the United States. The enduring interest of this discussion is that some of the issues which were raised therein might be found in current debates over the management of cultural and religious pluralism in Europe. There are some differences between the older American debates and their newer European counterparts. The growing multiculturality of European societies is generally attributed to migration movements and globalised cultural change, whereas in the American debates the role attributed to *ab origine* ethno-cultural differences is much more prominent.[4] This has also resulted in

3 *See e.g.* G. Pentassuglia, 'The Strasbourg Court and Minority Groups: Shooting in the Dark or a New Interpretive Ethos?', 19 *International Journal on Minority and Group Rights* (2012) p. 1; G. Pentassuglia, 'Ethno-cultural Diversity and Human Rights: Legal Categories, Claims and the Hybridity of Group Protection', VI *The Yearbook of Polar Law* (2014) p. 250.

4 This distinction is empirically very debatable, of course. American debates have also dealt with the accommodation of cultural and religious practices of migrant groups. However, the discussion was very much influenced by the claims of Aboriginal groups and long-standing minority religious communities (as the Amish or the Mormons in the United States). On the other hand, European debates are driven mostly by the accommodation claims of religious communities of migrant origin (although many times the members of these communities have been citizens of the state for generations). Cultural pluralism is so linked to migration in European political discourse that even the case of the European minority *par excellence*, the Roma, has emerged mainly due to their mobility from Central and Eastern Europe to

the American debates mostly discussing the requirements and scope of liberalism, whereas the European debates are more distinctively related to human rights claims and equality and antidiscrimination issues.

There are however common traits that make it appropriate for us to look back at the Canadian and US experiences with minorities-within-minorities treatment. Firstly, obviously, we are speaking very often about the very same groups and practices. The European experience is somehow more limited and understudied, but most of the examples that have ignited the debate in Europe might find precedents in Canada or the USA. Examples abound: treatment of second or further wives of polyginous marriages in migrant communities in France or the UK; application of Islamic rules to marriage or inheritance through Private International Law; homosexual persons employed by religious associations or churches; children in Roma communities or religious families. Secondly, we can find concurring arguments in both debates. The most prominent example is the argument of consent, which plays a fundamental role in the definition of the right to exit in American debates and is also at the centre of the discussion in European debates such as the face-veil bans in France or Belgium, for example.[5] Thirdly, there is already a degree of overlapping of the two debates, with some authors serving as a bridge between them.[6]

It can be safely concluded, thus, that the minorities-within-minorities framework is re-emerging in Europe under slightly modified names (i.e., vulnerable groups within minorities). Current debates in Europe give a prominent role to human rights and equality issues, but these intermingle with arguments of (more) multiculturalist origin. I shall follow Anne Phillips' advice in taking equality as the defining concern for framing minorities-within-minorities

---

Western Europe after the enlargement of the EU (*see* T. Magazzini, 'Cultural Institutions as a Combat Sport: Reflections on the European Roma Institute', 2 *The Age of Human Rights Journal* (2016) p. 50).

5 D. Morondo Taramundi, 'Women's oppression and face veil bans: A feminist assessment', in E. Brems (ed.), *The Experiences of Face Veil Wearers in Europe and the Law* (Cambridge University Press, Cambridge, 2014) p. 218.

6 T. H. Malloy, 'Standards to Eliminate Compounded Discrimination: The Case of the Intersectionality of "Minorities within Minorities" Or, why Universal Legal Standards Must Engage with the Concept of Culture', in K. Henrard (ed.), *Double Standards Pertaining to Minority Protection* (Martinus Nijhoff Publishers, Leiden / Boston, 2010) p. 259; C. Baldwin, 'Do Vulnerable Groups within Ethnic, Religious or Linguistic Minorities need Special Standards?', in *ibid.*, p. 243; M. Malik, 'Minorities and Law: Past and Present' 67 *Current Legal Problems* (2014) p. 67.

cases.[7] What I want to argue is that, when we look at it from the point of view of critical approaches to equality, the minorities-within-minorities framework shows some limitations in terms of human rights and, paradoxically, in terms of the analysis of the collective dimension of human rights involved in minorities-within-minorities cases. These critical issues appear explicitly when we cross-examine minorities-within-minorities cases from a relevant perspective in antidiscrimination theory, i.e., intersectionality or the interaction of different axes of discrimination and inequality.

The chapter will therefore proceed as follows: I shall first briefly outline the different approaches to 'minorities within minorities' and how these approaches have evolved and transformed themselves in current discussions about ethnocultural diversity and its treatment in Europe, particularly in relation to the so-called 'new minorities'. Secondly, I shall assess two main critical issues in relation to the minorities-within-minorities framework when we look at them from the perspective of human rights and equality or non-discrimination principles. Finally, I shall introduce some contributions resulting from feminist theory and critical approaches to antidiscrimination law in relation to intersectionality which might shed some light on those critical issues.

2 Framing Problems and Interests in 'Minorities within Minorities' Debates

In multicultural states, minority groups might advance claims for measures (in terms of rights or public policy) intended to protect their cultures against the dominant majority culture and thus to create the conditions in which the practice of their culture is made possible or socially normalised. Avigail Eisenberg has noticed an expanding trend, among policy-makers and courts, whereby rights are interpreted in light of different dimensions of identity, such as culture, nation or language.[8]

At the same time, there are members of minority groups who might seek the protection of the state against some of those very same cultural practices because they find them oppressive or because they think these practices violate

7 A. Phillips, 'Dilemmas of Gender and Culture: the Judge, the Democrat and the Political Activist', in A. Eisenberg and J. Spinner-Halev (eds.), *Minorities within Minorities. Equality, Rights and Diversity* (Cambridge University Press, Cambridge, 2004) p. 113, at p. 118.

8 A. Eisenberg, 'À la défense des droits culturels: une réponse à Jean Leclair', 41 *Recherches Amerindiennes au Quebec* (2012) p. 112. *See also* G. Pentassuglia, 'The Strasbourg Court', *supra* note 3, in particular p. 19 *et seq.*

some right they would enjoy, and for which they would have the protection of the state, if they were members of the majority (or rather, if they were not members of the minority group). These conflicts and tensions are generally known as minorities-within-minorities cases.[9]

2.1 *Early Warnings amidst Discussions of Liberal Multiculturalism*

Scholarly literature on 'minorities within minorities' has been growing since the controversial intervention by Susan Moller Okin in 1997, *Is multiculturalism bad for women?*, where she pointed out that, under certain conditions, autonomy rights granted to minority groups under multicultural policies in liberal states could pose risks of tension or conflict with the principle of sex equality professed by the very same liberal states.

Before that however, and although there had been an intense debate over multicultural policies especially in Canada and in the United States, the specificity of intra-group power dynamics and the resulting condition of some subgroups within minorities had not raised significant concern. This was not for want of attention paid to the question of equality in the debates on multiculturalism and in its policies or arrangements. Equality is widely considered a "constitutive element of multiculturalism";[10] yet, equality inquiries among multiculturalists put the focus on inter-group equality and the disadvantage suffered by minorities in the public arena. Inter-group inequality is attributed to the lack of recognition or public acknowledgement of minority cultures which leads to cultural assimilation patterns which, in turn, disadvantage cultural minorities' members. For liberal multiculturalists, equality between communities is generally pursued through policies aimed at promoting cultural diversity. This is the logics followed by the kind of special minority rights advocated, for example, by Will Kymlicka in *Liberalism, Community and Culture*: cultural community rights, separate representation or self-government rights have mainly the aim of curbing homogenisation and protecting diversity.[11]

Multicultural equality debates thus focused on the relationship and the interaction between two distinct sets: the majority, which was identified with a political entity (the liberal state), and the minority (or various minorities),

9 M. Pinto, 'The Right to Culture, the Right to Dispute, and the Right to Exclude: A New Perspective on Minorities within Minorities', 28 *Ratio Juris* (2015) p. 521; A. Eisenberg and J. Spinner-Halev, *supra* note 7.

10 G. Mahajan, 'Can Intra-Group Equality Co-exist with Cultural Diversity? Re-examining Multicultural Frameworks of Accommodation', in A. Eisenberg and J. Spinner-Halev, *supra* note 7, p. 90.

11 W. Kymlicka, *Liberalism, Community and Culture* (Clarendon Press, Oxford, 1989).

which were considered as collectives (communities) formed outside (and in many cases before) the state.[12] Internal power dynamics and the question of equality for individual members of minority groups were not considered essential for defining that relationship.[13]

This question drastically took on a visible role within the discourse on multicultural policies by the end of the 1990s. Leslie Green[14] first gave a name to this concern about intra-group power dynamics and their relationship to multicultural policies in liberal states. Some mechanisms to protect minority groups from majorities, he argued, "make it more likely that those minorities are able to oppress *their own internal minorities*".[15]

Green used a wide array of examples of such internal minorities, from Aboriginal women in patriarchal bands, homosexuals in the Evangelical Church or English native speakers in Quebec. In 1997, two years after Green's essay and in a very similar line of argument, Susan Moller Okin published her controversial essay '*Is multiculturalism bad for women?*',[16] which focussed more specifically on the possibilities of a conflict between some mechanisms of multicultural policies and the continuation of women's subordinated status within cultural minority groups.

Both Green's and Okin's work can be considered an early diagnosis of a concern that would later develop, in the work of other scholars, into more detailed analysis and different kinds of proposals on how to solve the issue.

Green's analysis concentrated on the arguments used for denying internal minorities the kind of rights that liberal multiculturalism recognised to minority groups. These minority rights comprise for Green both individual and collective rights, or rather rights that protect both individual and collectively

12 Meital Pinto makes this distinction when she leaves some participatory goods (such as trade union activity and collective bargaining) outside the scope of group rights: "This is because unions and corporations are artificial entities that do not exist before the law recognizes them as such. Cultures on the other hand do not need an official legal status in order to be recognized by society as such". M. Pinto, *supra* note 9, p. 9.

13 Gupreet Mahajan has, in fact, highlighted the parallelism between foreign countries and minority groups in Kymlicka's reluctance to "interfere with internal affairs". *See* G. Mahajan, *supra* note 10, p. 99.

14 L. Green, 'Internal Minorities and their Rights', in J. Baker (ed.), *Group Rights* (University of Toronto Press, Toronto, 1995) p. 257.

15 *Ibid.*, p. 257, italics added.

16 S. M. Okin, 'Is Multiculturalism Bad for Women?', *Boston Forum Review*, 1997. Almost contemporaneously she published the more elaborated 'Multiculturalism and Feminism: Some Tensions', 108 *Ethics* (1998) p. 661.

bounded interests.[17] Internal minorities are generally denied the recognition of individual and collective minority rights within their own minority groups on two grounds: internal minorities have a right to exit the group (which minority groups do not have in relation to the wider society) and the protection of internal minorities against their groups would weaken already weak groups. For Green, neither of these reasons was enough to justify the exclusion of members of internal minorities from the protection of the state.[18]

Whereas Green contrasted the liberal theory's failure to protect internal minorities against the standard which liberal theory itself established for minority rights (the problem of the 'double standard'),[19] Okin's argument extended the liberal state's responsibilities by unveiling a patriarchal bias of that state which sustained minority women's vulnerability to their communities' gendered and discriminatory practices.[20]

For both Okin and Green, the possibilities of tension and conflict between some multicultural policies and the rights of some individuals and groups in those minorities are serious, with "significant consequences for the relationship between liberalism and minorities".[21] For Green this depended upon the fact that, contrary to the commonplace description of liberals as atomistic individualists, overlapping social groups are the "most significant constituents of civil society" to modern liberalism because it is through such associations that

---

17 Green distinguished between rights that people have *even when* they are in the minority and rights that they have *because* they are minority members. The former is an antidiscrimination clause – members of the minorities are not granted any specific right but the guarantee that they will not be excluded from what Green calls "individuated interests" which are generally recognised to other individuals; the latter are rights that protect collective interests. These, too, are not as such related solely to minorities. However, "membership in some minority groups – for instance certain ethnic, national, cultural, or religious communities – is bound up with significant collective interests of this kind. In such cases, in addition to the usual individual rights (…) there are further special rights to powers and resources needed for the existence of the group". Green considers these special powers and minority cultural rights as an ex-ante compensation which makes the continued enjoyment of membership and individual rights possible. L Green, *supra* note 14, pp. 259–260.

18 *Ibid.*, pp. 264–268.

19 *Ibid.*, p. 262.

20 I have discussed Okin's argument, its legacy for current European debates and its limitations in D. Morondo Taramundi, 'Is multiculturalism bad for women, still? Persisting dilemmas in cultural and religious accommodation in Europe', in I. Handzlik and Ł. Sorokowski (eds.), *Found in Multiculturalism. Acceptance or Challenge?* (Peter Lange, Frankfurt am Main, 2014) p. 141.

21 L. Green, *supra* note 14, p. 269.

people "find value and meaning in their lives".[22] For Okin, the state's failure to protect minority women was in continuation with its neglect of the so-called private sphere which resulted in the state's siding up with those in power within the communities.[23]

It must be noticed that both authors are sceptical about what, at the time, was considered the main solution to the problems faced by internal minorities, namely the right to exit or to leave the group. Not only could exiting a group be empirically difficult or almost impossible in the case of ascriptive identities as well as psychologically wrenching, the fact that leaving the group was proposed as a solution for those who claim to suffer injustices from which they would be protected by the state if they were not members of a minority, signalled something more serious in relation to liberalism and its theory of justice.[24]

2.2 *Assuming the Paradox of Multicultural Vulnerability*

Especially Okin's intervention was largely read in terms of establishing a dilemma, or rather two: a 'feminism vs. multiculturalism' dilemma for scholars and activists, and a dilemma 'your rights or your culture' for minority women. Despite a growing literature on multicultural dilemmas which has addressed 'internal minorities' other than women,[25] most of the ensuing literature spans around the 'feminism vs. multiculturalism' dilemma worldwide (with a variation 'feminism vs. antiracism' in Europe).[26]

Although the alleged dichotomy 'multiculturalism vs. feminism' caused much criticism, by the mid-2000s there was a large body of multicultural theorists addressing the issue of women's rights within minority groups. Among this second wave,[27] it was accepted that there was a tension between accommodating cultural differences and protecting historically disadvantaged groups within those cultural groups. As Anne Phillips noted, this expanding literature on 'minorities within minorities' did not necessarily took issue with

22 *Ibid.*, p. 258.

23 S. M. Okin, 'Replay', in J. Cohen, M. Howard and M. C. Nussbaum (eds.), *Is Multiculturalism Bad for Women?* (Princeton University Press, Princeton, 1999) p. 115, at p. 121.

24 Indeed, Green argues that "it is no part of a liberal theory that justice can be secured merely by providing for exit. If a certain social structure is unjust, it cannot become just merely by becoming avoidable". *See* L. Green, *supra* note 14, p. 266.

25 *See e.g.* M. Pinto, *supra* note 9, or M. Mookherjee, 'Minority Rights', *The Encyclopedia of Political Thought* (2014) p. 2386.

26 C. Delphy, 'Antisexisme *ou* antiracisme? Un faux dilemma' 25 *Nouvelles Questions Féministes* (2006) p. 59.

27 The distinction in waves of scholarship addressing the problems of minority women's rights is discussed in A. Shachar, 'The Puzzle of Interlocking Power Hierarchies: Sharing

the principles of multiculturalism but rather with the question of who carries the costs of multicultural arrangements.[28]

Ayelet Shachar led the way to these new analyses, calling the phenomenon "the paradox of multicultural vulnerability":

> Well-meaning accommodation policies by the state, aimed at levelling the playing field between minority communities and the wider society, may unwittingly allow systematic maltreatment of individuals within the accommodated minority group – an impact, in certain cases, so severe that it nullifies these individuals' rights as citizens. I term this phenomenon the paradox of multicultural vulnerability.[29]

It should be noted that Shachar restricts these paradoxes to "systemic intragroup practices that adversely affect a particular category of group members"[30] which leaves out of the analyses some internal minority cases where violations might be considered incidental or resulting from specific personal interests.[31]

To these cases (which might all be considered 'genuine and tragic conflict' in Green's sense), the second wave of multicultural scholars proposed solutions which have been divided broadly into those which tend more towards stressing the values of liberalism, and others which put higher emphasis on finding solutions through democratic processes (even if they do not lead to liberal solutions).[32]

---

the Pieces of Jurisdictional Authority' 35 *Harvard Civil Rights-Civil Liberties Law Review* (2000) p. 385, at pp. 389 and 399.

28 A. Phillips, *Multiculturalism Without Culture* (Princeton UniversityPress, Princeton, 2007), p. 12; *see also* A. Shachar, *supra* note 27; and M. Malik, 'El derecho a la igualdad: Resolviendo conflictos de igualdad y derechos humanos. La experiencia británica' 45 *Anales de la Cátedra Francisco Suárez* (2011) p. 109.

29 A. Shachar, *supra* note 27, p. 386.

30 *Ibid.*, and *also* at p. 393.

31 For example, Pinto recalls the cases of French speaking Quebecer parents who wanted their children to attend schools teaching in English, which were restricted to the English speaking minority (M. Pinto, *supra* note 9, pp. 530–533). Although, this particular group of parents may be construed as a minority within the French speaking minority in Canada (in the sense they are fewer), there is nothing in the case which shows "systemic intragroup practices" towards that group in their enjoyment of language or cultural rights in general.

32 *See* S. M. Okin, 'Multiculturalism and Feminism: No Simple Question, No Simple Answers', in A. Eisenberg and J. Spinner-Halev, *supra* note 7, p. 67, at p. 69. It is important to notice Okin's remark that – although each of these approaches might have their usefulness – they both exert some degree of coercion (and not only liberal approaches, as it is often assumed) since most traditional *nomoi* groups tend to be neither liberal nor democratic (*Ibid.*, p. 87).

Most of the solutions in the liberal trend are aimed at fine-tuning the right to exit. Different criteria have been developed to assess the minorities-within-minorities cases[33] but the rationale behind remains very much as it was: if there is a right to exit, discriminatory or subordinating practices falling short of extreme forms of violence should be allowed under the protection of minority cultures.

Yet, the right to exit is closely related to the dilemma 'your rights vs. your culture', and thus many authors have gone beyond the limitations imposed by the liberal framework,[34] which they deem trapped by the 'right to exit' solution, in search of more attractive arrangements for these vulnerable groups. Thus, solutions have been proposed which seek transformative accommodation processes, through the involvement of minority authorities and communities which – it is expected – would drive those group authorities to interact with wider society norms and values and reduce subordinating internal norms and practices. Ayelet Shachar, for example, has developed the idea of multicultural jurisdictions,[35] as a process of devolution of power to *nomoi* groups'

---

33 For example, Marilyn Friedman's idea of consent by which "cultural practices that violate women's rights are nevertheless justified when the women in question want to live under those practices and choose to do so voluntarily". That consent, nonetheless, should be supported by three conditions (acceptable array of alternatives, freedom from coercion and manipulation, and early developed capacities to critical decision making) so hard to obtain that the proposal might be deemed closer to abstract models of theoretical rational consensus than to the democratic approaches that we shall see next. *See* M. Friedman, *Autonomy, Gender, Politics* (Oxford University Press, Oxford, 2003), p. 182. Avigail Eisenberg has also developed a set of conditions under which discriminatory minority practices should be assessed: jeopardy condition (whether the failure to accommodate those practices could jeopardize communities and their ability to function), validation condition (whether those practices are validated by those who adopt them through meaningful and uncoerced choice) and safeguard condition (which assesses how harms or risks of harm which result from cultural and religious practices are mitigated). This structured assessment would help decision-makers to refrain from relying on their own subjective biases and/or on mandates which suit the values of mainstream groups but fail to consider minority values. A. Eisenberg, 'How Should Public Institutions Assess Religious Identity?', in G. Calder and L. Beaman (eds.), *Poligamy's Rights and Wrongs: Perspectives on Harm, Family, and Law* (UBC Press, Toronto Vancouver, 2014) p. 46.

34 With this, I do not mean that they are illiberal but that they put the stress on issues (such as collective dimensions or deliberative processes) which are neglected by mainstream liberal theories.

35 A. Shachar, *supra* note 27, p. 399. The focus on jurisdiction in Shachar is concerned more with the institutional grounding for multicultural concerns than with the rights discourse or legal aspects of jurisdiction itself.

authorities. Monique Deveaux[36] or Anne Phillips[37] have insisted on deliberative approaches as a better way of addressing value conflicts, developing models of inter-cultural dialogue and cooperation which place greater emphasis on the political and social contexts in which minorities-within-minorities cases occur and on the extended participation of minorities-within-minorities groups instead of relying on cultural groups' 'spokesmen'.

These trends in minorities-within-minorities debates find also a continuation in the approach taken nowadays in Europe to similar cases. In her insightful analysis of "minority legal orders" in the UK, carried out in the midst of the controversy over the Archbishop of Canterbury's speech about religious jurisdictions, Maleiha Malik[38] assessed several approaches to the relations between the normative orders of religious and cultural groups and liberal states. Whereas current debates are generally restricted to a binary choice between prohibition or permissive non-interference, Malik explores the strengths and weaknesses of transformative accommodation, cultural voluntarism, or mainstreaming, as ways of responding to demands for recognition of group membership and cultural practices while, at the same time, protecting the rights of vulnerable groups within minority groups.[39]

2.3 *New Perspectives on 'Minorities within Minorities': Collective Dimensions*

By the end of 2000s, the debate on 'minorities within minorities' was spinning around 'hard choices'. As we have seen with the scholars in the previous Section, most positions conceived minorities-within-minorities cases as a clash between two incommensurable or conflicting rights (collective right to culture vs. individual right to equality or freedom) and most of the solutions consisted in either pondering around the right to exit or proposing to abandon the rights framework altogether, to embrace forms of 'negotiation' or political processes that would lead to joint forms of governance which, it is imagined, would simultaneously protect the minority culture (and the self-esteem of their members who see themselves as autonomous) and safeguard basic rights of the so-called vulnerable members. The latter, more complex and inclusive

36 M. Deveaux, 'A Deliberative Approach to Conflicts of Culture', 31 *Political Theory* (2003) p. 780.

37 A. Phillips, *supra* note 7.

38 M. Malik, *supra* note 6. That essay was based on a 2012 research, *see* M. Malik *Minority Legal Orders in the UK: Minorities, Pluralism and the Law* (The British Academy, London, 2012).

39 *Ibid.*

theoretical proposals appear, nonetheless, as fraught with practical difficulties for their implementation as the hypothetical right to exit, and nor do they guarantee that in the short term existing cases and the prevailing condition of subordinated groups within minority groups would benefit at all.[40]

In the last few years, though, some authors have advanced 'new perspectives' on the issue which highlight the collective dimensions implied in the position of the minorities within minorities and reclaim the rights discourse and the centrality of the principle of equality.

Meital Pinto, for example, from whom I have borrowed the expression 'new perspectives', offers an account of minorities-within-minorities cases which reclaims the rights discourse highlighting the participatory nature of the good protected by the right to culture of minority groups.

According to the participatory nature of culture, Pinto distinguishes two kinds of minorities-within-minorities cases. A first group, where minorities-within-minorities members challenge and revise internal prominent norms of their cultures, and a second group, where minorities-within-minorities members try to advance "external interests" they might have, such as economic interest or advancement in the larger society.[41] Only this second kind of cases represents for Pinto a tension between the collective right to culture of the minority group and the individual right to equality or freedom of a member of a minority within that minority group. In the first set of cases, where minorities-within-minorities members challenge cultural norms, cases would be better discussed in terms of the right to culture of those minority members, the right to revise values and norms of the minorities-within-minorities members and the right to exclude of the majority-within-minorities members. Pinto takes up Leslie Green's considerations on how to think about minority rights as collective rights. Green had distinguished two ways of understanding collective rights: we might think of them as rights that have a collective right-holder, i.e., only a group acting through its leadership can claim or make decisions regarding that right; or we might think of collective rights as rights that protect interests that are collectively shared by all group members rather than separately by each individual.[42]

40 *See e.g.* Y. Sezgin, 'How to Integrate Universal Human Rights into Customary and Religious Legal Systems?', 60 *Journal of Legal Pluralism* (2010) p. 5.

41 M. Pinto, *supra* note 9, pp. 522–523.

42 L. Green, 'Two Views of Collective Rights', 4 *Canadian Journal of Law and Jurisprudence* (1991) p. 315; M. Pinto, *supra* note 9, p. 525. *See also* P. Jones, 'Human Rights, Group Rights, and Peoples' Rights', 21 *Human Rights Quarterly* (1999) p. 80.

3 Paradoxes and Dilemmas in the Minorities-within-Minorities Frameworks

Internal minorities and minorities-within-minorities cases described thus far resonate very much with the acknowledgement of the multidimensional character of inequality and discrimination experiences, which has occupied European antidiscrimination scholars since the introduction in 2000 of the European Union directives expanding the field of antidiscrimination law.[43]

The recuperation of the rights discourse which can be appreciated in authors like Pinto or Malloy also brings the two debates, multiculturalism and antidiscrimination, closer. This, in turn, makes it possible to draw insights from one another, which might prove useful in the treatment of complex inequality cases.

Looking from the vantage point of antidiscrimination theory at the way minorities-within-minorities debates frame issues of multiple disadvantage or discrimination, there are two particularly critical points which deserve further attention. Firstly, the dilemmatic character of the framework, and secondly, its limitations for capturing the whole range of collective dimensions involved in these conflicts. The current section is dedicated to the discussion of these two aspects.

3.1 *Minorities-within-Minorities Frameworks as Dilemmatic*

As we have seen, most of the literature analysing minorities-within-minorities cases by mid-2000s had come to think of these cases as a sort of dilemma and, in general, avoided or even explicitly recommended to avoid discussing them in terms of rights. It is also the dilemmatic character of the minorities-within-minorities frame which explains that the scholarly effort devoted to the possibility and conditions of the right to exit became, and has remained, a central point of the debate: depending on whether or not there is a proper or effective right to exit, group rights covering practices that fall short of human rights standards can be upheld or not in liberal states.

The dilemmatic character of these cases is, to my mind, closely linked to the two basic ways in which they have been constructed and the interests involved have been conceptualised. One is based on the premise that culture is a good and a good deserving protection; the other is tied to the presentation of the

43 Council Directive 2000/43/EC implementing the principle of equal treatment between persons irrespective of racial or ethnic origin [2000] OJ L 180/22 (Race Directive); and Council Directive 2000/78/EC establishing a general framework for equal treatment in employment and occupation [2000]OJ L303/16 (Framework Directive).

members of the groups suffering from oppressive or harmful norms and practices as a 'minority', which limits the ability of these frameworks to apprehend the collective dimensions involved.

Culture is, admittedly, one of the most elusive terms in social sciences debates in general, and specifically in 'minorities within minorities' discussions. Anne Phillips has warned to be cautious when dealing with "invocations of culture, for this is a term that lends itself readily to cultural essentialism, cultural reification, and the dissemination of cultural stereotypes".[44] The idea that cultures can be understood as "neatly wrapped packages" that mark them out from all others is highly congenial, according to Phillips, to cultural spokesmen – usually male – who want to claim particular practices as definitive of their culture;[45] but it might be also adopted by majority members who, for various reasons, exaggerate the "otherness" of cultures they see as different from their own.

In these discussions, culture is understood as a good, a collective good and for some a participatory good. The fact that culture is a good is also the reason that we find that it is protected by domestic provisions and international standards, including human rights standards. It can be hardly debatable that we are formed and developed through language; that we understand ourselves and make sense of the world around us through cultural artefacts; that we live in groups and societies and interact with other individuals through social norms and institutions. Exclusion from these, and other, cultural dimensions or mistreatment and misrecognition of one's cultural endowments might put individuals in positions of disadvantage, marginalisation, social and economic exclusion, maimed self-perception and so on.

Yet, if culture is a good, and a good deserving protection, how should we consider and assess those instances where practices, norms or values appear or are deemed to be oppressive or harmful by some (within or from outside the culture in question)? Are oppressive practices not cultural?[46] Or if their

---

44 A. Phillips, *supra* note 7, p. 123.

45 *Ibid.*

46 This is for example the position adopted by the wider (majority) society in relation to the oppressive or harmful practices of their own culture: they are hardly ever assessed in cultural terms, they might be considered individual behaviour (for example, violence against women has been explained for a long time as the behaviour of deviant individuals) or belonging to the idiosyncrasy of determined social groups (which were attributed specific 'sub-cultures', like the poor, the youth, or particular 'urban tribes'). Feminist theory or critical race theory have struggled to show the structural character of patriarchy or racism in our societies, their intertwined manifold expressions in different aspects of our cultures

cultural meaning and significance is established, should we regard them as not being oppressive?[47]

Minorities-within-minorities cases show the difficulty in confronting the relationship between culture and power dynamics. Power dynamics are generally (not only in minority cultures) codified, socialised and transmitted through values and norms, cultural practices and their related societal arrangements. Human rights and antidiscrimination laws exist precisely to modify, more or less successfully and effectively, (some or parts of) those power dynamics *within the culture that upholds them*. It is *because* our societies are, for example, racist and produced societal arrangements (from slavery to segregation, discriminatory exclusion from goods and services, subordinated positioning in the labour market, etc.) which fitted with ideas about racial superiority of whites over non-whites that alternative cultural artefacts (of which legal norms are only a part) had to be produced.

Human rights standards or antidiscrimination laws were designed and adopted to address (and transform) societal arrangements which were considered unfair, harmful, oppressive following the claims and struggles of certain groups who did not consider that the societal arrangements, cultural practices, norms or values of their societies treated them fairly enough.[48] Antidiscrimination norms have also been resisted by other groups and individuals who might have had vested interests in keeping societal arrangements as they were, or who thought that traditional arrangements produce security and stability and these are goods not to be risked lightly at the whim of individuals or groups.

The relationship between power and culture needs therefore better clarification than what minorities-within-minorities frames offer. These tensions – in terms of political dynamics and struggles – within groups which try to define themselves on an ethno-cultural basis is a point generally avoided in multicultural discussions, which focus on the relations (also in terms of power dynamics) between majority (state) and minority groups. One of the most problematic

---

and their related societal arrangements. *See e.g.* K. Crenshaw, N. Gotanda, G. Peller and K. Thomas (eds.), *Critical Race Theory: The Key Writings that Formed the Movement* (The New Press, New York, 1995) *or* C. MacKinnon, *Feminism Unmodified: Discourses on Life and Law* (Harvard University Press, Cambridge Mass., 1987).

47 This type of *aut-aut* choices has played a fundamental role, for example, in the discussion on the face veil bans in Europe and the resulting 'feminism vs. anti-racism' stalemate. See D. Morondo, *supra* note 5.

48 Norberto Bobbio argued that human rights are historical, that is, that they appear gradually in times characterised by "struggles for new liberties against old powers". *See* N. Bobbio, *L'età dei diritti* (Einaudi, Torino, 1990) p. XIII.

ways, from the point of view of antidiscrimination law, to avoid debating how internal tensions shape culture and cultural difference or distinctiveness is the claim of incommensurability.[49] Incommensurability claims generally stop the discussion – values used in the assessment of power dynamics (such as freedom or equality) or concepts to describe them (such as oppression or domination) are ruled out as ethnocentric or non-neutral. Incommensurability has been warned against also from multicultural perspectives[50] as it tends to present minority and majority cultures in terms of irreconcilable differences or minority cultures as necessarily divergent from human rights values (such as sex equality). Yet, even if avoiding 'incommensurability' language and seeking transformative dynamics of joint governance (between minority and majority groups) that would preserve group rights and cultural autonomy while, at the same time, protecting the members of vulnerable groups, these authors still recommend that the position of the members of the minorities within minorities are not treated through human rights or antidiscrimination law approaches, but rather through schemes of power distribution between majority and minority groups which might – at best – contain some safeguards for 'vulnerable groups'. For Maleiha Malik, for example, the problem in cases of dress codes, intimate relationships or the choice of religious fora for family dispute resolution is not whether they are unequal or discriminatory; these practices do not belong to the jurisdiction of human rights law or constitutional law and they are thus outside the scope of antidiscrimination law.[51] I think that this is not due to the fact that the cultural practices in question (for example, sex discriminatory rules regarding divorce, child custody or inheritance) are in any way different from sex discriminatory rules regarding the same issues in European legal systems, which disappeared under the pressure of equality claims. The suggestion to move minorities-within-minorities issues outside the realm of human rights and antidiscrimination law is dictated precisely by the recognition of a conflict of norms in which both of them cannot be had simultaneously.[52]

49 A. Eisenberg, *Reasons of Identity: A Normative Guide to the Political & Legal Assessment of Identity Claims* (Oxford University Press, Oxford, 2009), ch. 5; P. Shah, 'Transnational Family Relations in Migration Contexts: British Variations on European Themes', 7 *RELIGARE Working Paper* (2011), at http://www.religareproject.eu/system/files/Religare%20WD%20No%207%20Shah%20on%20Transnational%20family%20relations.pdf.

50 A. Phillips, *supra* note 28; M. Malik, *ibid.*

51 M. Malik, *ibid.*, p. 126.

52 This is expressed forcibly by Okin when she comments on the negotiations towards South African Customary Marriages Act. After such a long disregard of customary law by the

The solution proposed is therefore to move outside the law and treat it as a political conflict, pressing maybe for greater participation of vulnerable groups in decision-making or to limit the conflict to singular cases, looking for safeguards and solutions when, and if, they arise.

3.2 *Limitations for Analysing Collective Dimensions*

Beside the dilemmatic character of the minorities-within-minorities frames, there is a second critical issue, especially when those frames are used to analyse cases regarding family law and women's human rights. I shall argue that, beginning with the very expression 'minorities within minorities', this frame is misleading and obscures the collective dimensions involved in the disputes.

As noted by Anne Phillips, the expression 'minorities within minorities' suggests both parallels and potential collision.[53] But is there any real parallelism between the two uses of the term 'minority' in that expression? The analysis of most minorities-within-minorities cases starts exactly from the realisation that measures intended to protect ethno-cultural and religious groups might have the effect of limiting the protection of the rights of some of their members. One of the uses of 'minority' in the expression refers to minority groups which, as discussed earlier, are generally understood as a collective, a 'micro body politic' which identifies itself as distinct from and preceding (not constituted by) the political organisation of the larger society, the State. The other use of 'minority' is clearly different from this. This second use of 'minority' refers to *minorities within*, they exist thus as parts or sub-groups of the minority group. Differently from the relationship between the minority group and the State, minorities within minorities do not have an independent or preceding existence from the minority group. They are not conceived as organised (political) collectives.[54] In fact, in this second meaning, the expression 'minorities within' has been frequently substituted by other expressions such as vulnerable groups or historically disadvantaged

---

apartheid regime, "if the customary laws were so much transformed at the moment of their recognition as to become non-sexist, they might appear never to have been recognized". S. Okin, *supra* note 32, p. 81.

53 A. Phillips, *supra* note 7, p. 113.

54 Some members of this group might, eventually, organise themselves with a political intention, to defend what they come to consider shared interests within the minority group. In some minorities-within-minorities cases, these organised members of the internal minority have played an important role, such as women's groups in the negotiations of the Customary Marriages Act in South-Africa.

groups and individuals. In most cases, these 'minorities' are not even distinctive of the minority group[55] but the very same groups which are oppressed and disadvantaged in the larger society (women, children, LGTBI, disabled, dissenters, those with a different ethnic origin). They are, in fact, categories of individuals created by axes of discrimination or oppression rather than groups which *define themselves* on the possession of any given characteristic.

This way of understanding the internal minorities as categories of individuals rather than groups emerges clearly when we examine minorities-within-minorities cases which are frequently presented as conflicts between a group right or interest and an individual right or interest. Classic examples are Audrey Martinez claiming before the courts that her tribe's sex discriminatory norms about membership excluded her[56] or Shah Bano resorting to state laws in India to counterweigh the effects of the application of her group's divorce norms.[57] Most of the scholars from the second wave who address these cases have concerned themselves with finding a way out of the dilemma which would preserve group rights while, at the same time, protecting vulnerable individuals. In her analysis of *Santa Clara Pueblo* v. *Martinez* case, Ayelet Shachar suggests a solution by which the tribe's compelling interest in the demarcation of its boundaries is recognised and therefore Audrey Martinez is not granted a possessory right to tribal communal lands "if no other 'outsiders' were permitted to own a share in such lands. However, other distributive remedies could have been provided for the excluded children", for example educational or loan funds.[58] In the very controversial aftermath of the *Shah Bano* judgment, the Indian Government passed a law to stop Muslim women from getting access to the legal remedy under State law which had protected Ms. Shah Bano against the application of her group's norms (so that the group rights would be protected from state (judicial) interference). At the same time, the law established that the women who would be left destitute by the future application of the group's norms[59] had to be given support by the Muslim community or by their own families.

---

55 There are cases of oppressed groups which have, generally, no counter-part; for example, twin siblings in U'wa or Hitnu indigenous communities in Colombia (and their mothers, who are sterilised after giving birth) or people with albinism in some parts of Africa.

56 *Santa Clara Pueblo* v. *Martinez*, 436 U.S. 49 (1978).

57 *Mohammad Ahmed Khan* v. *Shah Bano Begum and Others* (AIR 1985 SC 945).

58 A. Shachar, 'Group Identity and Women's Rights in Family Law: The Perils of Multicultural Accommodation', 6 *The Journal of Political Philosophy* (1998) p. 285.

59 A. Phillips, *supra* note 7, pp. 128–129; C. Baldwin, *supra* note 6, pp. 249–250.

However, and independently of the fact that, at times and in certain contexts, pragmatic solutions might be the best option, why should the state strive to protect a series of individuals rendered vulnerable also, although not only, by the norms and practices which the state itself is *protecting from* the application of the principle of equality?

Some of the new perspectives on minorities within minorities have tried to address this issue by conceptualizing cultural rights as the right to a participatory good. Minorities-within-minorities cases are thus re-framed as the right of minorities-within-minorities individuals to revise their (minority) culture and the right of the majority within the minority group to oppose this right and exclude the minority-within-minority members from the minority culture. This conceptualisation establishes 'culture' not as something that minorities possess and through the possession of which they can be identified (a reified notion of culture), but as something which is produced by the participation of all members of the minority group. Even if framing minorities-within-minorities cases in this way has, therefore, a great advantage in that it allows for the expression of different positions and interests in relation to any given cultural practice or arrangement, there is still something missing. Meital Pinto makes the example of an ultra-orthodox Jewish community (a minority group in Israel) with an ethnic discriminatory practice.[60] Here, it is clear that the majority within the minority is excluding the minority from equal access to cultural rights (religious studies in a religious school) and that the latter might claim their right to access their own culture. It is also hard to see what could be the right invoked by the majority to oppose the minority's right to their (minority) culture.[61]

Yet, many minorities-within-minorities cases do not concern exclusion from access to culture but the attribution of subaltern positions or restrained possibilities within the group through recognisable cultural practices (such as gender discriminatory divorce norms, condemnation of homosexual activity, the guiding function of parents over children). In these cases, contrary to Pinto's example, it is hard to see what is the "right to revise one's own culture" and in what sense this way of framing the conflict is any way different from those political struggles that authors like Anne Phillips or Monique Deveraux tried to channelled through democratic deliberative processes. These processes, as we have said, might not have a happy solution for those claiming against the

60 Beit Yaakov case (*Noar KeHalacha Association* v. *Ministry of Education* [2009] HCJ 1067/08). *See* M. Pinto, *supra* note 9, p. 528 *et seq.*

61 *See also*, G. Pentassuglia, *Minority Groups and Judicial Discourse in International Law: A Comparative Perspective* (Martinus Nijhoff Publishers, Leiden / Boston 2009), particularly ch. 4.

practices of their group and might even increase the pressure on vulnerable groups to appear loyal to their group or be blamed for losses in the minority group-state relationship.[62]

The result is thus an unhappy choice. The liberal individualistic outlook on minorities-within-minorities cases misses that collective dimension which the approach through democratic deliberative processes manages to grasp. Yet, in order to facilitate or even make the deliberative process possible, the democratic approach lets go of protected interests (such as sex equality or the best interest of the child) which in any democracy are generally shielded from decisional processes. In fact, we said at the very beginning that human rights standards (and the principle of equality) cast themselves as limits to what the state can (decide to) do.

4 Intersectionality: Potential Contributions to the Debate

'Minorities within minorities' debates resonate strongly with debates on antidiscrimination law which were prompted by a similar circumstance: the realisation that inequality and discrimination is not experienced equally by everyone within any given category (women, Blacks, disabled, children). Over the past few years, minority rights scholars and antidiscrimination lawyers have crossed their paths in debates over specific minorities-within-minorities cases.[63] Moreover, the limitations of the minorities-within-minorities framework described in the section above bear resemblance to some of the difficulties encountered by critical approaches to antidiscrimination law as well. For that reason, I shall argue that minorities-within-minorities 'dilemmas' could be illuminated by some discussion and developments in the field of antidiscrimination law aimed at addressing similar problems. This is particularly the case with the discussion around the concept of intersectionality, which we will see next.

62 Anne Phillips makes the example of the referendum on self-government of Canadian Indian councils and the position of the Native Women's Association of Canada. *See* A. Phillips, *supra* note 7, pp. 126–127.

63 C. Baldwin, *supra* note 6; T. H. Malloy, *supra* note 6; E. Brems, *supra* note 5; M. Malik, *supra* note 6. Part of this discussion, in relation to European human rights law, has also been subsumed into debates over vulnerable groups, *see e.g.* L. Peroni and A. Timmer, 'Vulnerable Groups: The Promise of an Emerging Concept in European Human Rights Convention Law', 11 *International Journal of Constitutional Law* (2013) p. 1056.

4.1 *Minorities within Minorities, Multiple Discrimination and Intersectionality*

Among the various criticisms which critical theories have levelled against the liberal concept of equality, there is one about its one-dimensionality. International instruments and domestic constitutions enshrine provisions proclaiming the principle of equality which is normally accompanied by an antidiscrimination clause. This clause establishes a list of grounds, which might be exhaustive or non-exhaustive, on the basis of which discrimination (or unfair distinction) is prohibited. For a long time, the grounds on the list were merely juxtaposed. It is still mostly so. The development of specific international instruments addressing discrimination grounds individually, such as the Convention for the Elimination of Racial Discrimination or the Convention for the Elimination of All Forms of Discrimination Against Women, has reinforced this feature.

Feminist legal scholars have criticised the one-dimensionality of antidiscrimination law since the 1980s.[64] At the international level, this translated into a number of declarations, such as paragraph 46 of the Beijing Platform for Action which recognises "that women face barriers to full equality and advancement because of such factors as their race, age, language, ethnicity, culture, religion or disability, because they are indigenous women or because of other status".[65] The Committee on the Elimination of Racial Discrimination asserted in 2000 that:

> [R]acial discrimination does not always affect women and men equally or in the same way. There are circumstances in which racial discrimination only or primarily affects women, or affects women in a different way, or to a different degree than men.[66]

64 In the USA, this criticism was also directed to the 'identity politics' of the social movements struggling against single-ground discrimination (primarily, feminism and antiracist groups). *See e.g.* N. Lacey, 'Legislation against Sex Discrimination: Questions from a Feminist Perspective', 14 *Journal of Law and Society* (1987) p. 411, *and* K. Crenshaw, 'Demarginalizing the Intersection of Race and Sex: A Black Feminist Critique of Antidiscrimination Doctrine, Feminist Theory and Antiracist Policy', 140 *University of Chicago Legal Forum* (1989) p. 139.

65 UN Report of the Fourth World Conference on Women, Beijing Declaration and Platform for Action, A/CONF.177/20/Rev.1, 1996.

66 Committee on the Elimination of Racial Discrimination, General Recommendation No. 25(2000), para. 1.

Progressively, also the Committee on the Elimination of All Forms of Discrimination against Women, the Committee on Social, Economic and Cultural Rights or the Committee against Torture have recognised multiple discrimination and intersectionality.[67] Subsequent instruments have included specific references to multiply-burdened sub-groups within the instrument's mandate.[68]

At the European level, two new antidiscrimination directives were adopted to combat discrimination on the grounds of ethnic and racial origin, religion and belief, sexual orientation, disability and age,[69] thereby expanding the existing prohibition of discrimination on grounds of sex and the norms on discrimination on grounds of nationality. Although there was only a fleeting reference to multiple discrimination in the recitals of these directives, this concept has gained considerable ground in European scholarship, and has appeared useful for the identification of vulnerable social groups which might be classified as minorities within minorities.[70]

Intersectionality is the name given by Kimbelé Crenshaw in 1989 to the analysis that matched the multidimensional character of discrimination experiences.[71] In these almost forty years intersectionality has become an almost obligatory reference for scholars and activists studying oppression experienced by minority women and minorities within minorities. This remarkable development is even more astonishing if we consider the broad awareness of the confusion around the notion and the function of intersectionality. Some have seen a causal relation between the ambiguity (and therefore the versatility) of

67 Committee on the Elimination of All Forms of Discrimination Against Women, General Recommendation No. 25 (2004), para. 12; Committee on Economic, Social and Cultural Rights, General Comment No. 16 (2005), para. 5; Committee Against Torture, General Comment No. 2 (2008), para. 22.

68 UN Convention on the Rights of Persons with Disabilities (2006) or the UN Declaration on the Rights of Indigenous Peoples (2007).

69 Council Directive 2000/43/EC implementing the principle of equal treatment between persons irrespective of racial or ethnic origin [2000] OJ L 180/22 (Race Directive) and Council Directive 2000/78/EC establishing a general framework for equal treatment in employment and occupation [2000]OJ L303/16 (Framework Directive).

70 F. Rey Martinez, 'La discriminación múltiple, una realidad antigua, un concepto nuevo', 84 *Revista Española de Derecho Constitucional* (2008) p. 251. On a note of caution about the possibility of expanding the notion of intersectionality in EU antidiscrimination law, D. Schiek, 'Revisiting intersectionality for EU anti-discrimination law in an economic crisis – A critical legal studies perspective', 2 *Sociologia del Diritto* (2016) p. 23.

71 K. Crenshaw, *supra* note 64. *See also* K. Crenshaw, 'Mapping the Margins: Intersectionality, Identity Politics, and Violence against Women of Colour', 43 *Stanford Law Review* (1991) p. 1241.

intersectionality and its expanding scholarly success.[72] Not all the scholarship appreciates this ambiguity, though, and in the last few years we have seen a growing number of critical interventions which call for an urgent reconsideration of the way in which intersectionality is understood in social sciences.[73]

Among the studies on intersectionality, this notion is understood predominantly, though not exclusively, as a way of conceptualizing identity and experiences of oppression.[74] This way of understanding intersectionality places the focus of attention on the 'intersectional subject', identified through the use of ever 'finer' categories (i.e. Women/Black women/Working-class Black women/ Working-class Black women with disabilities, etc.). Most scholarship agrees that intersectional subjects find themselves in particular positions of marginalization, which are neglected by dominant (anti-racist or feminist) identity politics. These subjects speak with a "special voice"[75] or have a "unique experience of discrimination",[76] which would constitute "a theoretical added value"[77] in order to understand or penetrate the systems of oppression.

Yet, whereas Crenshaw posited intersectionality as an instrument for correcting and improving identity politics, its incorporation into European antidiscrimination law seems to yield opposite results. The multiplication of the inequalities envisaged by European antidiscrimination law and the extension of gender equality policies have led to a reinforcement of identity politics and not to overcoming them: the question of which categories one belongs to (or is considered to belong to) is even more relevant since some categories are protected, and the protection offered to the different categories is unequal.

This result in antidiscrimination law and policies is particularly relevant for minorities-within-minorities groups because it has been said to foster dynamics which might have a direct effect on them. Indeed, the competition among discriminated groups, which is fuelled by the reinforcement of identity

---

72 K. Davis, 'Intersectionality as Buzzword', 9 *Feminist Theory* (2008) p. 67.

73 J. Nash, 'Re-thinking Intersectionality', 89 *Feminist Review* (2008) p. 1; J. Conaghan, 'Intersectionality and the Feminist Project', in E. Grabham, D. Cooper, J. Krishnadas and D. Herman (eds.), *Intersectionality and Beyond: Law, Power and the Politics of Location* (Routledge-Cavendish, Abingdon, 2009) p. 21; C. MacKinnon, 'Intersectionality as Method: A Note', 38 *Signs* (2013) p. 1019.

74 J. Nash, *supra* note 73.

75 M. Matsuda, 'Looking to the Bottom: Critical Legal Studies and Reparations', 22 *Harvard Civil Rights-Civil Liberties Law Review* (1987) p. 323, at p. 324.

76 S. Fredman, 'Double Trouble: Multiple discrimination and EU law', 2 *European Anti-Discrimination Law Review* (2005) p. 13.

77 J. Nash, *supra* note 73, p. 8.

politics, encourages groups both to highlight their differences from the wider society and to put pressure on their internal minorities not to express dissent which might jeopardise their claims.

In a recent interview,[78] Kimberlé Crenshaw reflected on the success of intersectionality and raised a note of caution about intersectional engagement as distinct from the "mass uptake of the term":

> [M]uch of intersectionality's initial critique was directed toward the overall structure and ideological infrastructure of anti-discrimination law. In particular, law's investment in a limited conception of what constitutes discrimination and how it is substantiated leaves in place an overall structure of the work place and various markets that permit only modest reforms.[79]

It has been argued that the development of intersectionality as an investigation into the complexity of the nature of identity and its (mis-)representation transformed the initial concern for the structures of power (such as the law) and neglects the modes of interaction of oppression and privilege. To investigate such interactions and structures goes beyond, or rather, is a qualitatively different action from extending a simple model:

> In this sense, one could say that intersectionality researchers are indeed (still) adding categories to each other, extending one simple model in search of incomplete information 'as if a more difference-sensitive, sophisticated scheme could solve the crisis of representation or the problem of categorization all together'.[80]

There is, in fact, an alternative understanding of intersectionality as an analytical perspective whose goal is not the construction, representation or protection of intersectional subjects, but the identification and eventually transformation of the interaction of axes or systems of oppression of subordinated groups. This second perspective, I shall argue next, could bring some light to the 'dilemmas' of minorities-within-minorities frameworks.

---

78 B.G. Bello and L. Mancini, 'Talking about Intersectionality: Interview with Kimberlé W. Crenshaw', 2 *Sociologia del Diritto* (2016) p. 11.

79 *Ibid.*, p. 18.

80 M. Carbin and S. Edenheim, 'The Intersectional Turn in Feminist Theory: A Dream of a Common Language?', 20 *European Journal of Women's Studies* (2103) p. 233, at p. 239 (quoting Randi Gressgård).

4.2 *Intersectional Perspectives on Minorities-within-Minorities Cases*

Notwithstanding the fact that intersectional perspectives and minorities-within-minorities share the same sociological problem as a subject matter, intersectional engagement with minorities-within-minorities cases is still very limited, the preferred approach being, as we have seen, still that of conflicting rights. Cases on which intersectionality has been given some role could be roughly divided into two groups. On the one hand, we have cases of minorities within minorities which feature processes of simple cumulative disadvantage; on the other hand, cases where experiences of cumulative disadvantage respond to the conflicting modes of interaction of systems of oppression.

The first group of cases was the phenomenon identified by Crenshaw, multiply-burdened subjects placed at the margins of both identity politics and equality policies. In her famous example, *DeGraffenreid* v. *General Motors* case, Black female employees were made redundant as a result of a seniority criterion: since discriminatory employment patterns have led to Black women entering the firm after both Black men and white women, they lost their employment first. Yet they could claim neither racial discrimination nor sex discrimination because the dismissal pattern did not affect Black men or white women, it affected just Black women as a combination of both race and sex.[81]

At the level of the Council of Europe or the European Union, this perspective has been frequently used for identifying specific vulnerabilities and needs of protection. The Committee of Ministers of the Council of Europe, for example, has made a number of recommendations on compound forms of vulnerability of elderly migrants[82] or migrant children,[83] especially if unaccompanied.[84] Also the European Union has used this approach to multiple or compound disadvantage in the Reception Directive, for example, for establishing special protection mechanisms for vulnerable persons within refugee groups, such as women who are pregnant or

81 K. Crenshaw, *supra* note 64.

82 Recommendation of the Committee of Ministers to Member State son reducing the risk of vulnerability of elderly migrants and improving their welfare CM/Rec(2011)5, of 25 May 2011.

83 Recommendation of the Committee of Ministers to Member States on strengthening the integration of children of migrants and of immigrant background CM/Rec(2008)4, of 20 February 2008.

84 Recommendation of the Committee of Ministers to Member States on life projects for unaccompanied migrant minors CM/Rec(2007)9, of 12 July 2007.

breastfeeding, unaccompanied minors or victims of sexual violence and human trafficking.[85]

This same perspective can be found in minorities-within-minorities cases. For example, in *Bhe and Others v Magistrate*[86], the South African Constitutional Court had to decide on the claim of the two minor and extra-marital daughters of an intestate deceased father who, under customary law, were not considered heirs to their father. Under customary law, these children suffered the compounded effects of being both female and extra-marital children.

This way of looking at intersectionality has advantages for minorities within minorities because it identifies and brings to the fore the needs and interests of groups which are not normally considered representative either of their minority (ethnic, cultural or religious) group nor of the wider social group with which they share other characteristics (women in general, children in general, the elderly in general, etc.). This was the initial concern to which intersectionality gave a voice: under equality policies at the time, it seemed that all Blacks were men and all women were white, leaving Black women at the margins of both state action and movements' concerns. Under multicultural policies too, this perspective has the effect of curbing the impulse to think that the interests of every individual within the group is covered by the interests of the group as such or by the interests expressed by those who represent the group. Thus, Roma inclusion policies or migrants' integration policies must diversify their offer in terms of rights, programmes and instruments to match a variety of those groups at the margins. They might need to listen to and respond to more voices, not only within the minority group but also to listen to them across groups.[87]

At the European Court of Human Rights this sort of cases of compound disadvantage regarding minorities within minorities has been considered mostly in terms of the heightened vulnerability of the groups in question. In *B.S. v. Spain*, the European Court of Human Rights was called by third intervening

85 Directive 2013/33/EU of the European Parliament and of the Council of 26 June 2013 laying down standards for the reception of applicants for international protection, OJ L 180, 29.6.2013, p. 96–116, Articles 21–25.

86 *Bhe and Others* v *Khayelitsha Magistrate and Others* (CCT 49/03) [2004] ZACC 17; 2005 (1) SA 580 (CC); 2005 (1) BCLR 1 (CC) (15 October 2004).

87 In fact, sometimes solutions for minority women imply that the minority condition is mainstreamed into general women's policies (for example, in the case of gender violence this has the effect of avoiding the ethnicisation of sexism); or, reversely, that women's needs are mainstreamed into the general policy for the minority group, so they will not appear as a particular (vulnerable or special) group (for example, recommendations on refugee women).

parties to consider explicitly the intersectional effect of the various characteristics of the claimant which placed her in a particularly disadvantaged position. The Court, although acknowledging this cumulative effect created by sex, race, migrant status and engagement in sex work, did so in terms of "the applicant's particular vulnerability inherent in her position as an African woman working as a prostitute".[88]

The second sort of cases presents a more complex form of interaction of different axes of discrimination and oppression because they do not only create a compound effect on the intersectional subject but they also present conflicting dynamics which might affect the way in which protection mechanisms are successfully deployed. These conflicting dynamics might arise from the interaction of different normative systems or from internal contestation of the group's norms. This is the sort of intersectionality cases which resemble more closely the minorities-within-minorities dilemmas described in the previous sections.

It is worth noting that the identity approach to intersectionality yields dilemmatic results in these cases too, just as the minorities-within-minorities framework. Let us consider, for example, the attempts of Christine Delphy and the journal *Nouvelles Questions Féministes* to overcome the paralysis of French feminists at the time of the law on 'ostensible religious symbols'. Christine Delphy argued that the so-called 'feminism vs. anti-racism' dilemma that kept French feminists silent regarding the law banning the Islamic scarf from secondary public schools was a false dilemma. Paraphrasing the work of Black feminism, she argued that this dilemma could only be sustained on the condition that "individuals oppressed by racism were all men, or in other words, this hypothesis [the dilemma] could not be understood unless it was considered that women in this group were not subject to the racist regime"[89] Notwithstanding this awareness of the interaction of oppression systems, Delphy's argument ultimately rested on a unidirectional view of interaction, which corresponded to the experience of the identified intersectional subject: the veiled Muslim woman. Since in the identity approach to intersectionality, the intersectional subject and her distinctive experience have a particular theoretical added value, those aspects of the interaction of the systems of oppression that escape the experience or interests of that intersectional subject are not taken into account in the analysis of the dilemma. In this case, Delphy's analysis

88 *B.S.* v. *Spain*, Application No. 47159/08, Judgment of 24 July 2012, par. 62; *see also, Muñoz Diaz* v. *Spain*, Application No. 49151/07, Judgment of 8 December 2012; *Oršuš and Others* v. *Croatia*, Application No. 15766/03, Judgment of 16 March 2010; *D.H. and Others* v. *The Czech Republic*, Application No. 57325/00, Judgment of 13 November 2007.

89 C. Delphy, *supra* nota 26, p. 70.

eschewed the gendered character of the practice of veiling and long-held feminist concerns over the continuum between gender discrimination and gender violence or the role of the family in gender discrimination. These concerns were doubted and silenced especially as intersectional issues, that is, as cases where patriarchal practices within a community combine with, and are reinforced by, the oppression (sexist and racist) from the main society. Instead of "targeting the forces that create the result",[90] these approaches to intersectionality resolve the dilemma by accommodating their static products.

Since the minorities-within-minorities framework and the identity approach to intersectionality have this problem in common, it might be argued that future discussions in intersectionality studies aimed to overcome this dilemma might be of interest for 'minorities within minorities' scholarship.

As it has been said earlier, the identity approach to intersectionality is not favoured by all authors. For many authors, intersectionality is best understood as an analytical perspective on the interaction of the systems of oppression, on the collective dimensions of discrimination, which would prevent those conceptualisations of intersectionality which dissolve political identities (such as women or Black) into individualities (every single woman with her unique interaction of identity traits), or reinforce one system of oppression in the fight against another.

This perspective could thus be applied to minorities-within-minorities cases which show those characteristics, such as *Santa Clara Pueblo* or *Sha Bano*. In both cases, we have particular individuals claiming that the application of the customary or religious norms of their groups caused harm to them. Audrey Martinez is excluded from tribal membership through a sex discriminatory norm and Sha Bano is left destitute through the application of sex discriminatory divorce rules. In both cases, the dilemma appears when the state is asked to uphold those sex discriminatory practices and protect them from the application of the principle of equality, in the name of respect for group difference and cultural diversity. The dilemmas are read then from the point of view of the conflict, as a contrast between feminist claims (in these cases) and multiculturalist or anti-racists claims. However, if we look at the interaction of the systems of oppression (sex-gender system and racism), the conflict is murkier than a binary choice. The state action which consists in protecting something (minority rules or practices) from the principle of equality between women and men could be seen as consistent with the patriarchal bias of the majority society itself. In this case, there is no contraposition or choice, but rather a

90 K. MacKinnon, *supra* note 73, p. 1023.

collaboration of majorities' patriarchal bias and minorities' patriarchal practices. This emerged clearly in the aftermath of the *Sha Bano* judgement, where the (leadership of the) minority group and the state agreed to protect the minority sex discriminatory rules from further interference of the principle of equality by specific legislation.[91]

If these are the dynamics at play, where patriarchal bias and practices within and outside the minority group might combine, where racial prejudice is offered compensation, not through anti-racist legislation, but through the vulnerabilisation of internal minorities, some of the proposals to solve the paradox of multicultural vulnerability miss the point, because they fail to see the collective dimensions of the singular cases of oppression.

If we look at the imbrications of power in those systems instead of looking at the individual positions that result from those interactions we might understand that in minorities-within-minorities cases we are not facing a dilemma: vulnerable members of the group do not want to choose between their culture and their rights, and in fact they are not given the choice. Vulnerable groups (or rather, groups rendered vulnerable) are claiming their rights to contrast power dynamics within their minority groups. And, on many occasions, they are not being given the chance to do so because the state is refraining from supporting those rights. This approach to intersectionality draws our attention towards structures and state action. It has been useful in the critique of the shortcomings of antidiscrimination law and it might be useful in the assessment of minorities-within-minorities cases only if we cling to the interaction between the systems of oppression (the collective dimensions of oppression and discrimination) to avoid that one oppressive system is reinforced in the fight against the other(s).

5 Conclusions

In this chapter I have examined an enduring question regarding ethno-cultural diversity protection and human rights, i.e. the position of internal minorities or minorities within minorities.

Minorities-within-minorities cases did attract some attention in US and Canadian debates on multiculturalism in liberal societies in the late 90s and during the first half of the 2000s. However, they were generally considered as 'dilemmas' or 'hard choices' where liberal states could not protect at the same

91 A. Phillips, *supra* note 7, pp. 128–129; C. Baldwin, *supra* note 6, pp. 249–250.

time the cultural rights of minority groups and the rights to freedom and equality of some of their members who deemed some of those cultural norms or practices oppressive or discriminatory. Solutions to these dilemmas consisted in either ensuring that minorities-within-minorities individuals had a right to exit the group or engaging minority groups in political deliberative processes in search of transformation. However, neither type of solution could guarantee the protection of those human rights that members of internal minorities claimed.

This kind of problematic cases and the difficulties encountered to solve them resemble very closely cases of multiple and intersectional discrimination, which have occupied European antidiscrimination scholars for some time now. Similarly to minorities-within-minorities approaches in the US and Canadian debates, some of the discussion on intersectionality has also faced 'dilemmas' and 'hard choices' which I have argued are due to the dilemmatic way of posing the conflict and to the limited ability of both minorities-within-minorities frameworks and intersectionality approaches based on the experiences of intersectional subjects to understand the collective dimensions of the human rights at stake in these cases, especially in the case of sex equality.

Finally, a different approach to intersectionality has been suggested, based on the analysis of the interaction of the systems of oppression, which has contributed to the clarification of the dilemmatic aspects of intersectional issues in European antidiscrimination law and could also be useful in addressing minorities-within-minorities cases.

PART IV

Ethno-Cultural Diversity, Conflict, and Peacebuilding

CHAPTER 9

Ethno-Cultural Diversity and Conflict: What Contribution Can Group Rights Make?

Chris Chapman[1]

Nothing is more likely to disturb the peace of the world than the treatment which might in certain circumstances be meted out to minorities.[2]

As far as he was concerned, there were plenty of peoples but no nations. Moreover there was now a spate of barely comprehensible decrees and orders from the government concerning kid-gloved treatment of the 'national minorities', one of Herr von Trotta's least favoured expressions. To his mind, 'national minorities' was nothing more than the collective form for 'revolutionary individuals'.[3]

1 Introduction

The history of group rights has always been closely linked to the search for stability, from the limited freedoms for religious minorities conceded by the Ottoman Empire, and in the Treaty of Westphalia that marked the end of the 17th Century wars of religion in Europe, through to the flurry of activity that saw new international minority rights standards and mechanisms in the 1990s, hoping to take the sting out of ethnic tensions after the collapse of the USSR and Yugoslavia. However that history has in part been one of the same mistakes being repeated over and over again. After reviewing some of the main issues, controversies and recent developments, I will present an overview of the main intra-state conflicts between 2007 and 2013, categorising them in terms of the role played by inter-group tensions, and violations of minority

1 The views expressed in this chapter are solely those of the author and do not necessarily represent those of Amnesty International.

2 Woodrow Wilson, statement to Paris Peace Conference, 31 May 1919, cited in J. Morsink, "Cultural Genocide, the Universal Declaration, and Minority Rights", 21 *Human Rights Quarterly* (1999) p. 1009.

3 J. Roth, *The Radetzky March* (Granta, London, 2002) p. 252 (translation from the German by M. Hofmann).

 | DOI 10.1163/9789004328785_011

rights and indigenous peoples' rights by states. The aim is to demonstrate the prevalence of conflicts which are driven by factors relating to group rights, and the need for governments – and for the actors who intervene, either to try to mediate an end to conflicts, or to guide the post-conflict transition, such as inter-governmental organisations (IGOs) – to develop better tools for accommodating ethno-cultural diversity and preventing conflicts that arise from failures of the accommodation of group rights.

2 State-building and the Recognition of Ethno-Cultural Diversity

Bangladesh, 1971. Shortly after the country had fought for and won its independence from Pakistan, a delegation of indigenous peoples from the Chittagong Hill Tracts (CHT) met with Sheikh Mujibur Rahman, the new Prime Minister. They wanted autonomy and to have their identity expressly recognised in the new Constitution that was to be drafted. "Mujibur rejected the demands, advising the Hill people to adopt the new, nationalist Bengali identity. Mujibur backed his advice with a threat to effectively marginalize [the Hill peoples] by sending Bengalis into the region."[4]

The irony was that two of the main issues over which Bangladesh had fought its war of liberation with Pakistan, were representation of the Bengali people in the national parliament, and recognition of the Bengali language. The new government appeared unable – or unwilling – to see how the two situations mirrored each other. In the following year, the new constitution "focused on a distinctive Bengali identity, language and culture".[5] Shortly afterwards, CHT leader Manabendra Narayan Larma addressed parliament: "You cannot impose your national identity on others. I am a Chakma not a Bengali. I am a citizen of Bangladesh, Bangladeshi. You are also Bangladeshi but your national identity is Bengali … [the indigenous peoples] can never become Bengali."[6]

M.N. Larma would go on to establish the Parbattya Chattagram Jana Sanghati Samity (PCJSS), a political party aiming to represent the interests of the Hill peoples. The Dhaka government increased the army presence in the CHT, and sent ethnic Bengalis to settle there, creating significant demographic changes.

4 A. Mohsin, *The Chittagong Hill Tracts, Bangladesh: On the Difficult Road to Peace* (Lynne Rienner, Boulder, 2003) p. 22; citing interview with Ananta Bihari Khisha, a member of the Hill delegation.

5 Amnesty International, *Pushed to the Edge: Indigenous Rights Denied in Bangladesh's Chittagong Hill Tracts* (Amnesty International, London, 2013) p. 15.

6 A. Mohsin, *supra* note 4.

As tensions between central government and the Hill peoples increased, the PCJSS formed an affiliated armed movement, the Shanti Bahini, and an armed conflict began which lasted until the signing of the Chittagong Hill Tracts Peace Accord of 1997. The Accord provided, among other things, for regional autonomy under a system of Hill Councils, in which indigenous peoples would play a leadership role, and a Land Commission to resolve disputes between indigenous peoples and ethnic Bengali settlers (or in some cases the army). To date, almost 20 years later, the Land Commission has not resolved a single case, and no elections to the Hill Councils have been held.[7] Some temporary army posts have been dismantled, but the army is still ubiquitous and its role in administering the region is unchallenged.[8] Access for journalists and human rights researchers is tightly controlled – a government memorandum requires all foreign visitors to the region to apply for special permission, and even Bangladeshis must seek permission to hold meetings.[9] The signing of the Peace Accord, and the ratification of ILO Convention 107 on Indigenous Peoples, appeared to indicate a will to move towards a policy of accommodating the concerns of different ethnic communities, but the last decade has seen that progress rolled back, for example in a change of policy in 2010 to one of denial of the existence of indigenous peoples in the country.

The failure to implement the agreement is arguably partly due to changing power dynamics – notably India withdrawing its support to the CHT insurgent movement. Unfortunately, this failure by the central government to respect the commitments it made, only gives weight to the perception that the only way to achieve concessions is by force of arms.

The story of the Chittagong Hill Tracts illustrates a problematic attitude to state-building – particularly in states that have newly gained independence. The temptation for majority-led governments to resist the cultural and political aspirations of minorities and indigenous peoples (MIPS) appears in some cases to have been hard to resist.[10] In countries with functioning democracies,

---

7 Parbatya Chattagram Jana Samhati Samiti, *A Brief Report on Implementation of the CHT Accord* (PCJSS, Rangamati, 2016) p. 28.

8 BBC radio documentary, *Bangladesh's Hidden Shame* (2016), at http://www.bbc.co.uk/programmes/p03wzrv4.

9 Amnesty International, *Government memorandum restricting access to Chittagong Hill Tracts poses serious human rights concerns* (2015), at https://www.amnesty.org/en/documents/asa13/2625/2015/en/.

10 *See* for example Z. Eyadat, 'Minorities in the Arab World: Faults, Faultlines and Coexistence' in W. Kymlicka (ed.), *Multiculturalism and Minority Rights in the Arab World* (Oxford University Press, Oxford, 2014) p. 82.

politicians may find themselves challenged by an opposition that appeals to – or tries to incite – the baser fears and prejudices of the majority, especially in countries with a history of ethnic conflict. To face down that challenge, governments may be tempted to "put on the iron trousers", in the words of former Haitian President Paul Magloire, even when the claims of MIPs have been voiced peacefully. What I will try to show in this chapter, is that this approach has not resulted in more stable entities, and that governments of fragile states, and the IGOs and other international actors who attempt to support them in tackling internal tensions, need to consider more constructive and collaborative approaches to the challenges of ethno-cultural diversity.

3 Do Group Rights Promote or Undermine State Stability? A Debate that Continues to this Day

In August 2016, the World Bank (WB) published its revised Environmental and Social Framework (ESF), after almost four years of consultations with donor and borrower governments, civil society and community representatives. The ESF lays down a set of safeguards with the aim of protecting communities and the environment from being adversely affected by the projects the WB funds. The debates surrounding the safeguard relating to indigenous peoples have been particularly fraught. These debates are reflected in its new title – previously known simply as "Operational Policy 4.10 – Indigenous Peoples", it now bears the name "Indigenous Peoples/Sub-Saharan African Historically Underserved Traditional Local Communities".

A number of African governments had objected strongly to the use of the term "indigenous peoples". In a meeting of African members of the World Bank Board (the board is made up of lender and borrower governments), the representative of Ethiopia stated "that Ethiopia as well as other African countries had expressed their strong opposition to the use of the term "indigenous peoples" since it could be a source of tension and social instability".[11] Another delegate expanded on this point:

> The Minister of Finance from Namibia said that [...] his country liberated itself from a system of apartheid that was based on racial discrimination under the pretext of preserving racial diversity. Hence, to put in place

11 Meeting of African Governors of the World Bank Group and the International Monetary Fund (27–28 August, 2015, Luanda, Angola): Fourth Session: Update and Review of the World Bank's Safeguard Policies – Statements by Delegates

> safeguards for specific groups of people within a unitary state based on inclusive approaches and equality of opportunity would "come very close to a system that is oppressive like apartheid".

Such a framework "would amount to discriminating against the majority". Finally he urged the WB to exercise care "when attempting to define a certain group as indigenous within a country where national boundaries were drawn up in an artificial manner by colonial powers" and concluded that "'divide and rule' should never be allowed and the proposed standard may open the door for that".[12]

It is to be noted that the speakers made clear appeals to the sense of responsibility of officials of the Bank – historically an institution dominated by Western, industrialised countries – for injustices from the colonial period. The WB unquestionably has a responsibility to exercise due diligence and ensure that its projects "do no harm", in all parts of the world, and that responsibility is owed primarily to communities, who are most directly, and often adversely affected by projects – rather than to governments. This is particularly the case when the issue is viewed from a human rights perspective, within which individuals, not governments, are rights-holders. These communities, including Africa's indigenous peoples, organised and pressed the Bank very vocally to maintain standards and terminology that are in line with international standards.

What, in human rights terms, are the consequences of the change in terminology? In terms of the actual substance of the protections offered by the safeguard, there are some advances and some steps back when compared to OP 4.10. The new safeguard requires that borrowers obtain the *free, prior and informed consent* (FPIC) of indigenous peoples before implementing projects which affect their land or cultural heritage – using the language of the United Nations Declaration on the Rights of Indigenous Peoples, rather than the vaguer "broad community support" used in OP 4.10. However the FPIC requirement applies to a narrower range of situations; in OP 4.10, all projects affecting indigenous peoples require their broad community support. More importantly, with the introduction of the ugly, clumsy compromise term, "Sub-Saharan African Historically Underserved Traditional Local Communities", a negative precedent has been created, potentially violating the right of indigenous peoples to self-identify, and weakening the link between the Bank's policies and international law.

---

12 *Ibid.*

Of more interest for the subject of this chapter, however, is the question of why the terminology used, rather than the substance of the rights, was so important. At the same meeting in Angola, the Ethiopian delegate stated that "the concerns of the African caucus are not simply an argument about terminology on paper but rather something which could and has had negative and violent consequences." The terminology that eventually proved acceptable to the African caucus indicates that these governments are more comfortable with a narrative of addressing under-development ("historically underserved communities") than identifying communities with distinct identities which are the subject of specific human rights frameworks. If anything, this category is arguably broader, creating an obligation to apply the World Bank safeguards to a larger number of communities, but that may be precisely the point. Clearly concerned that acknowledging the existence of a specific category of communities who are protected by safeguard policies will create tensions with other sectors of the population ("discriminating against the majority"), the governments concerned, if challenged on this domestically, can point to the new terminology and argue that any under-developed community would benefit.

Another objection to the application of group rights in conflict prevention and management processes, is based on the argument that human rights are non-negotiable, and therefore unsuited to conflict processes, particularly conflict resolution, which is about negotiation and compromise.[13] A modern application of this argument, specifically to minority rights, is found in the objection of Brendan O'Leary and Christopher McCrudden to the *Sejdić and Finci v. Bosnia and Herzegovina* (BiH) case before the European Court of Human Rights.[14] Sejdić and Finci are, respectively, a Roma and a Jew who took the case to challenge ethnic discrimination in the Dayton Peace Agreement, which brought an end to the conflict in BiH. Dayton is a consociational political arrangement which provided for power-sharing among the main ethnic communities – Bosnians, Serbs and Croats – in particular reserving a number of high-level political positions for their representatives, expressly excluding those who do not wish to identify with the three communities, for example Jews, Roma, or those who identify as being of mixed ethnicity. The Court ruled in favour of Sejdić and Finci, finding that Dayton was discriminatory. O'Leary and McCrudden's main objections to the ruling are, firstly, that an

13 R. Manikkalingam, 'Is there a tension between human rights and conflict resolution? A conflict resolution perspective' (Latin American Research Centre, Calgary, 2006) p. 4.

14 *Sejdić and Finci v. Bosnia and Herzegovina*, Applications Nos. 27996/06 and 34836/06, Judgment of 22 December 2009.

agreement that was negotiated by conflict parties to end a conflict should only be unwound by those same parties, otherwise it risks tipping the situation back into conflict, and the aim of avoiding violent conflict must take priority over all others;[15] secondly, that the ruling makes no mention of the fact that Dayton was not submitted to referendum in Bosnia, in the same way that, for example, the Belgian consociational arrangements were. They argue that by appearing to consider the question of popular support irrelevant, the Court weakens the case for maintaining arrangements that have such support – as the Belgian ones do. Finally by issuing a judgment that will almost certainly be ignored by the state – in fact it must be ignored, they argue, for reasons of self-preservation – the Court risks undermining its own legitimacy.

Given the horrific violence of the Bosnian war, and the fact that Dayton was successful in bringing it to an end, O'Leary and McCrudden's arguments certainly demand respect. To tackle them would probably require an entirely separate analysis, and I will not attempt to do it, and I certainly do not challenge the fundamental assertion that avoiding a return to conflict in Bosnia must be a compelling concern of all actors involved. I would only wish to raise some questions for consideration as this debate continues. Could smaller minorities, not associated with belligerent parties, have been given a seat at the table at Dayton? Was their exclusion from its political arrangements a necessary price to pay for peace? Might the inclusion of smaller minority groups at the negotiating table help to create a different dynamic, less focused on a confrontational, bipolar dynamic between the main belligerents? Does the demand for their inclusion now in the country's delicate power-sharing arrangements risk tipping the country back into conflict, or has the passage of time created a different dynamic? Are there creative solutions to the problem of effective political participation of different sectors of the population in Bosnia, and might representatives of smaller communities be well-placed to propose those solutions? Finally, if only the parties to the original agreement have the right to renegotiate it, what incentives are there for them to do so? Certainly, in Lebanon, similar arrangements which set in stone political power-sharing arrangements between religious denominations have remained in force for decades, many years after demographic changes have called into question the fairness of the arrangement. All of these questions are essentially speculative, and I do not claim to have the answers, but they go to the heart of issues surrounding modalities for the inclusion in peace processes of minorities who

15 B. O'Leary and C. McCrudden, *Courts and Consociations: Human Rights Versus Power-Sharing* (Oxford University Press, Oxford, 2013) p. 148.

have not been associated with one of the belligerent parties, and I argue that they warrant further research.

On one question, however, I would venture to be more forthright; if international courts must find violations of human rights and issue rulings only when they can be sure the government will accept them, that will turn them into an irrelevance even more surely than the indignity of being ignored.

4 Assimilation vs. Identity Promotion

There is no doubt that group rights can be seen negatively by majority populations. This is usually because they are wrongly seen as privileges, rather than what they are, which is a framework for ensuring that a specific group of people can benefit from the same rights as the rest of the population (in the same way that there is a specific regime for refugees, children, women, migrant workers, *inter alia*). But we should view with scepticism attempts by governments to use this argument to resist group rights claims. It does not necessarily follow that affirmative action in favour of such groups leads to conflict. Improvements to the lot of marginalised sectors of society are almost always resisted in the first instance – in fact extraordinary levels of violence are often the response when hitherto suppressed peoples take a stand and demand rights, thus threatening the privileges that majorities had previously enjoyed, as can be seen in the case of Dalits in India, or Afro-Americans in the USA during the period of the civil rights movement. In the end, in most cases, a process of awareness-raising produces social change, often resulting in widespread acceptance, and a feeling that it has been a scandal that this group of people had to suffer injustices for so long before something was done about it.

While it is often thought that the reason there are no minority rights provisions in the Universal Declaration of Human Rights (UDHR), is because of the claim that minority rights concerns were exploited by Hitler as an excuse to invade Germany's neighbours (ostensibly, to protect German minorities), the drafting history of the UDHR shows that, probably more importantly, there was strong resistance by Latin American and North American states, who were "wedded to their respective policies of assimilation".[16] This position parallels that of the nascent state of Bangladesh referred to above – the aim of the state being the promotion of a unified, homogeneous national identity. Finally, going further back in time, as Pentassuglia argues in his chapter of

16 J. Morsink, *supra* note 2, p. 1009.

this volume, the same thinking permeated the Versailles Peace Conference of 1919 – that is, the notion that minorities would progressively be assimilated and the minority rights protection regimes that Versailles established would be temporary.

It is likely no coincidence that the states most opposed to inclusion of minority rights in the UDHR were those of the Americas. These are states that are based on immigration, and on the colonisation of indigenous peoples. The original (Indigenous) culture of the territory is not valued or promoted. Therefore a new identity has to be forged based on the peoples who have colonised the territory. An undifferentiated hodge-podge of the various identities of the immigrating peoples would not be acceptable – a clearly defined national identity is usually needed to which citizens can be called upon to express their allegiance. Therefore some kind of over-arching identity is proposed (in the case of most of the countries of the Americas, some kind of vaguely defined 'European culture') and all others are expected to melt into it. Milton Gordon, one of the leading theorists of assimilation in the USA, whose influential work *Assimilation in American Life* was published in 1964, described the 'seven stages of assimilation' thus:[17]

Stage of assimilation	**Results in:**
Cultural or behavioral assimilation (acculturation)	Change of cultural patterns to those of host society
Structural assimilation	Large scale entrance into the cliques, clubs and associations of the host society on the primary group level
Marital assimilation (amalgamation)	Large scale intermarriage
Identificational assimilation	Development of a sense of peoplehood based exclusively on the host society
Attitude receptional assimilation	Absence of Prejudice
Behavior receptional assimilation	Absence of Discrimination
Civic assimilation	Absence of value & power conflict

17 H.L. DeBose and L.I. Winters, 'Dilemma of Biracial People of African American Descent', in H.L. DeBose and L.I. Winters (eds.), *New Faces in a Changing America: Multiracial Identity in the 21st Century* (Sage, London, 2003) p. 133.

Based on a number of interviews with "officials of intergroup relations and intragroup communal life organizations in the United States",[18] Gordon concluded that people reacted negatively to the expression of a different identity by others, and that this will inevitably lead to conflict. The only solution is to bring about a reduction in the expression of such identities, by, over time, assimilating those identities into the national one. His view is very far from the sentiment of Woodrow Wilson, with which this chapter began.

It might be argued that the assimilationist approach is specifically designed as a response to the dilemma of states based on immigration, but the fact that these countries opposed the inclusion of minority rights in the UDHR implies a belief that the approach had universal applicability. And the reality is that even in the USA, 50 years after the publication of Gordon's book, identities are expressed as strongly as ever, in particular, but not only, by Native and Afro-Americans. In fact, levels of inter-ethnic violence have surely reduced when compared to the period of the civil rights movement. So it is worth challenging the assumption that it is the expression of difference, per se, that contributes to increased tensions, as opposed to other factors such as the government response to expression of this sort (in particular the existence of a framework for management of diversity based on human rights and rule of law guarantees), or the instrumentalisation of group rights claims by either minority or majority leaders, or both. An argument has also been made – drawing on the example of India – for the crucial importance of strong civic structures for the management of inter-ethnic tensions in a non-violent manner.[19]

5 An Overview of the Evidence

Faced with the resistance of the proponents of the assimilationist model – Bangladesh, Ethiopia, Namibia and others – it is worth taking a look at the evidence in favour of the accommodation / integration model.[20] This can

---

18 M.M. Gordon, *Assimilation in American Life: The Role of Race, Religion and National Origins* (Oxford University Press, Oxford, 2010) p. 9.

19 A. Varshney, *Ethnic Conflict and Civic Life: Hindus and Muslims in India* (Yale University Press, New Haven, 2002).

20 An excellent summary of this evidence is provided in G. McDougall, *Report of the United Nations Independent Expert on minority issues to the General Assembly: Effective promotion of the Declaration on the Rights of Persons Belonging to National or Ethnic, Religious and Linguistic Minorities*, UN Doc. A/65/287 (2010).

be seen in the development of international law (reflecting beliefs and assumptions of states), historical developments, and academic studies.

At the international level, there is a long history of the development of norms and agreements enshrining group rights as a reaction to conflict driven by ethnic, religious or linguistic divisions – or the imminent threat of such conflict:

> The Treaties of Westphalia [...] which brought to an end the religious wars of the 17th Century, provided religious minorities with certain limited guarantees of freedom of belief, and the right to participate in decision-making in matters affecting them. Furthermore, the treaties, which were signed by the Holy Roman Empire, France and Sweden, set a precedent for the subjecting of minority rights protections to international guarantees.[21]

This trend continued in the 20th Century, with the minority treaties of the League of Nations period between the two world wars, which were concluded in order to calm the fears of minorities 'created' by the redrawing of boundaries after World War I.[22] Most importantly for the current international group rights framework, the early 1990s saw a flurry of activity. New standards and mechanisms emerged at both global and regional levels to protect and promote the rights of minorities – the United Nations Declaration on the Rights of Persons Belonging to National or Ethnic, Religious and Linguistic Minorities, the Council of Europe Framework Convention for the Protection of National Minorities, and the first international mechanism expressly created to address threats to stability resulting from minority/majority tensions, the High Commissioner on National Minorities of the Organisation for Security and Cooperation in Europe (OSCE). This was primarily in response to another seismic change to international borders, and more newly created minorities with existential fears, after the break-up of the Soviet Union and Yugoslavia.[23]

---

21 C. Chapman, 'Still Missing a Trick: Minority Rights, Indigenous Peoples' Rights and Conflict Prevention', in L. Lyra Jubilut, A. G. Melo Franco Bahia and J. L. Quadros de Magalhães (eds.), *Direito à diferença: Volume I – Aspectos teóricos e conceituais da proteção às minorias e aos grupos vulneráveis* (Saraiva, São Paulo, 2013) p. 404.

22 R. B. Bilder, 'Can Minority Treaties Work?', 20 *Israel Yearbook on the Human Rights* (1991) p. 74–75.

23 C. Chapman, *supra* note 21, p. 405.

Currently the international consensus on the question which is the main point of consideration in this chapter, may be considered to be summarised in the preamble of the UN Minorities Declaration:

> Considering that the promotion and protection of the rights of persons belonging to national or ethnic, religious and linguistic minorities contribute to the political and social stability of States in which they live.[24]

The Declaration was adopted unanimously by the General Assembly. Academic and other non-governmental studies have also reached conclusions that support this position:

> The Centre for Research on Inequality, Human Security and Ethnicity at Oxford University has undertaken detailed quantitative and qualitative research into conflict and horizontal inequalities (inequalities between ethnic, religious or linguistic communities) in 8 countries in three regions, and statistical desk research in 55 countries. The Centre analyses inequalities in access to economic opportunities, participation in political decision-making and the status accorded to cultural practices and symbols. The Centre concluded that in the top 5 per cent of countries with the greatest socioeconomic inequalities, the risk of conflict is tripled when compared with the average. The risk of conflict increases again if socio-economic inequalities are combined with inequality in access to political decision-making, and inequality in cultural status adds a further risk factor.[25]

Similarly, The Carnegie Commission on Preventing Deadly Conflict, a three-year research project involving 16 eminent scholars in the field of conflict prevention and resolution, concluded that:

> [T]ime and again in the twentieth century, attempts at suppression of ethnic, cultural or religious differences has led to bloodshed, and in

---

24 General Assembly Resolution A/RES/47/135, 18 December 1992.

25 G. McDougall, *supra* note 20, p. 7, citing F. Stewart, G. K. Brown and A. Langer, 'Major findings and conclusions on the relationship between horizontal inequalities and conflict', in F. Stewart (ed.), *Horizontal Inequalities and Conflict: Understanding Group Violence in Multi-ethnic Societies* (Palgrave Macmillan, Basingstoke, 2010).

case after case, the accommodation of diversity within appropriate constitutional forms has helped to prevent bloodshed.[26]

6 How Many of the World's Conflicts are Driven by Factors Relating to Minority/ Indigenous Identity?

As a contribution to this debate I carried out an analysis, based on desk research, of the world's most severe conflicts over the period 2007–2013 to come up with a figure of how many are driven by issues relating to minority / Indigenous identity.[27] The analysis was peer-reviewed by a panel of 5 conflict prevention/resolution experts/practitioners.

Incidences of conflict are taken from the Conflict Barometer at the Heidelberg Institute for International Conflict Research (conflicts with an intensity rating of 4 or 5) and the Uppsala Conflict Data Program (conflicts with a best estimate of 360 deaths in a year or more – equivalent to level 4 in the Heidelberg set).[28] Narrative descriptions are taken from the Conflict Barometer except where otherwise stated. I also included conflicts suggested by the peer-review panel when a convincing case was made.

The fact that conflicts are included in the table on the basis of battle deaths means that frozen conflicts (conflicts which at one point involved intense fighting but were fought to a situation of stalemate) are not likely to be included. However, a conflict is classed as a level 4 conflict in the Heidelberg set if it involves at least 18,000 refugees in any given year, which could include some frozen conflict situations.

26 D.A. Hamburg and C.R. Vance, *Preventing Deadly Conflict* (Carnegie Corporation of New York, New York, 1997) p. 29.

27 The analysis was carried out with the institutional support of Minority Rights Group International. Fawzi Barghouthi, Courteney Leinonen and Julie Louisa Andrus provided invaluable research support. The peer-review panel was composed of: Conor Foley (Consultant in Human Rights and Humanitarian Aid), Jérémie Gilbert (Professor of International and Comparative Law, University of East London), Hurst Hannum (Professor of International Law, Fletcher School of Law and Diplomacy, Tufts University), Andreu Solà Martín (Associate Professor, Open University of Catalonia and Blanquerna – Universitat Ramon Llull), Stefan Wolff (Professor of International Security, Department of Political Science and International Studies, University of Birmingham)

28 Conflict Barometer at the Heidelberg Institute for International Conflict Research: https://www.hiik.de/en/konfliktbarometer/index.php; Uppsala Conflict Data Program: http://ucdp.uu.se/?id=1.

Issues of MIPs[29] are for the purposes of the study understood to include:

- exclusion of MIPs from politics or economic life
- denial of MIPs' identity, prohibition of its expression
- MIPs are treated in a discriminatory way, or attacked violently, by another community or armed actors – the state colludes / knowingly fails to protect
- tensions between MIPs and majority, or between MIPs, over real or perceived unfairness in access to resources, historical grievances, etc.
- MIPs seek autonomy / secession (may or may not be due to systematic persecution or failure to include them in national politics)
- the state expresses (and/or acts on) a long-standing suspicion of MIPs based on prejudices / historical tensions / conflict
- MIPs are scapegoated by the state, which may lead to violence, including genocide

The conflicts were classed according to four categories (with the percentage of conflicts found in the category indicated in brackets):

- Issues of MIPs are one of the main drivers of the conflict (47%)
- MIPs' issues are a secondary or additional driver, or have emerged or receded over time as a significant driver (24%)
- MIPs' issues are not a driver of the conflict; however there are targeted attacks on MIPs by armed actors (11%)
- MIPs' issues are not a driver of the conflict; MIPs are not specifically targeted based on their identity (18%)

29 In this analysis, the terms 'minority' and 'indigenous peoples' are understood as a fluid, social construct, often with variable levels of consensus within the community in question as to the use of terms. Many communities prefer a different term e.g. people, or nation. Community members have the right to self-identification and this table in no way implies the imposition of a label on any group.

Issues of minorities and indigenous peoples (MIPS) as a driver of armed conflicts 2007–13

MIP issues are one of the main drivers of the conflict	MIP issues are a secondary or additional driver, or have emerged or receded over time as a significant driver	MIP issues are not a driver of the conflict; however there are targeted attacks on MIPs by armed actors	MIP issues are not a driver of the conflict; MIPs are not specifically targeted based on their identity
Burma / Myanmar (KNU-Karen) 1948[1] Although a ceasefire was signed at the end of 2011 with the government, fighting between Karen rebels and the government army claimed around 1000 lives in 2011.Conflict de-escalated in 2012 but ceasefire signed in 2011 broke down.	**Afghanistan** (Taliban) – 1994 Taliban had persecuted minorities under their control (e.g. Hazara, Uzbek, Tajik). Their ousting achieved through international support for Northern Alliance, essentially a Tajik-Uzbek coalition against the (Pashtun) Taliban. Over time, other issues have come to the fore, relating to sovereignty, anti-West rhetoric, and relationships with neighbours, but minority issues are still relevant.	**Colombia** (FARC, ELN, AUC) 1964 – Primarily a conflict based on political ideology. Afro-Colombian and Indigenous groups targeted disproportionately because of lack of protection by the state, poverty, and ambitions to seize their land.	**Algeria** (AQIM/MUJAO) 1989 conflict over national power and the orientation of the political system between al-Qaeda in the Islamic Maghreb (AQIM) and its splinter group Unity Movement for Jihad in West Africa (MUJAO) and the government.

Issues of minorities and indigenous peoples (MIPS) as a driver of armed conflicts 2007–13 (cont.)

MIP issues are one of the main drivers of the conflict	MIP issues are a secondary or additional driver, or have emerged or receded over time as a significant driver	MIP issues are not a driver of the conflict; however there are targeted attacks on MIPs by armed actors	MIP issues are not a driver of the conflict; MIPs are not specifically targeted based on their identity
Burma / Myanmar (SSA-S / SSA - N- Shan) **1952** (northern and southern Shan State Army vs government) over autonomy. The Shan State Army-South signed a ceasefire agreement with the government after sporadic clashes.	**Central African Republic** (APRD, CPJP, CPSK, FDPC, UFDR vs Government) **2005** – Primarily a national power conflict between rebel groups and central government, although grievances of Gula community are at base of rebellion according to HRW. Gula also suffering most at hands government forces as a result. Some rebel groups formed the Séléka coalition which seized power in 2013. The conflict has taken on a religious aspect in 2013, with the Séléka coalition, and the anti-balaka coalition that	**DR Congo** (FDLR, Nyatura vs. Mayi-Mayi Cheka, Raia Mutomboki, FDC vs. APCLS vs. Mayi-Mayi Shetani vs. M23) **1997 / 2011** A complex conflict system with various groupings, particularly Mayi-Mayi, fighting with other rebel groups including the FDLR and M23. Raia Mutomboki had been mostly dormant for the past few years but resurfaced in 2011 after continued FDLR presence in South Kivu.	**Brazil** (poilce vs armed gangs) **Unknown start date.** NB this conflict does not appear in the Uppsala or Heidelberg datasets. Although other situations of large numbers of killings by police are not listed (for example in USA, police killed 371 people in 2008, which would reach the threshold for this assessment) it was felt that the nature of the violence in Brazil, with armed gangs operating in specific urban

MIP issues are one of the main drivers of the conflict	**MIP issues are a secondary or additional driver, or have emerged or receded over time as a significant driver**	**MIP issues are not a driver of the conflict; however there are targeted attacks on MIPs by armed actors**	**MIP issues are not a driver of the conflict; MIPs are not specifically targeted based on their identity**
	was formed to combat it, being mainly associated with the Muslim and Christian communities respectively. Atrocities were targeted at unarmed Muslim and Chris tian communities because of their religious identity.	Raia Mutomboki was composed of members of the ethnic groups Tembo and Hunde. A number of massacres took place in which villages appear to have been targeted because of their ethnicity. The FDLR drew most of its membership from Hutus who fled to the DRC after being defeated by the Rwandan Patriotic Front after the Rwanda genocide.	locations and the police undertaking operations against them resulting in many human rights violations, is effectively a conflict situation. cf. Mexico situation listed below. A very significant proportion of slum dwellers in Brazil are Afro-Descendants, but evidence does not seem to have been presented to make a case that minority issues are a driver of the conflict or that they were specifically targeted. HRW reported that 1137 people were killed in Rio de Janeiro state in 2008.

Issues of minorities and indigenous peoples (MIPS) as a driver of armed conflicts 2007–13 (cont.)

MIP issues are one of the main drivers of the conflict	MIP issues are a secondary or additional driver, or have emerged or receded over time as a significant driver	MIP issues are not a driver of the conflict; however there are targeted attacks on MIPS by armed actors	MIP issues are not a driver of the conflict; MIPS are not specifically targeted based on their identity
Burma / Myanmar (KIA/ KIO - Kachin State) **1948** Autonomy and resource conflict flared up after 17 year ceasefire broke down in 2011. Deaths estimated in the thousands in 2012.	**Chad** (various rebel groups - FUC, UFDD, UFDD-F, RFC, FSR, UFCD, UDC, MDJT, NA vs. government) – **2005** essentially a political conflict, but ethnicity has played a role in affiliations. Clashes between the ethnic groups of Tama and Zarghawa erupted in eastern Chad in September and October, leaving 20 people dead. The Tama supported the FUC, while the Zarghawa were the native ethnic group of President Idris Deby.	**Egypt** (opposition groups vs government) **1954** Popular protests against Mubarak regime; then military, then Morsi govt; some sectarian violence in the aftermath of Mubarak's surrender, and then again in 2013 after the ouster of Morsi (when in particular Christians were blamed by pro-Morsi supporters for supporting his ouster). Peaked 2011.	**Burundi** (Palipehutu-FNL) **- 2005** Essentially a political conflict between a Hutu militia and Hutu-dominated govt but has its roots in the Hutu/Tutsi conflicts. One grievance of P-FNL is the prohibition on using the word "Hutu" in its name – the militia defines itself in terms of revindication of Hutu grievances.

MIP issues are one of the main drivers of the conflict	MIP issues are a secondary or additional driver, or have emerged or receded over time as a significant driver	MIP issues are not a driver of the conflict; however there are targeted attacks on MIPs by armed actors	MIP issues are not a driver of the conflict; MIPs are not specifically targeted based on their identity
Burma / Myanmar (Buddhist vs. Rohingya Muslims / Rakhine state) 2012 - Conflict between the majority Buddhist population and the minority Rohingya Muslims in Rakhine state over sub-national predominance. Violence claimed the lives of around 180 people as well as the displacement of an estimated 110,000 people in 2012. Recent years have seen increasing evidence of the involvement of the national army in violent attacks on the Rohingya.	**Côte D'Ivoire** (supporters of Ouattara, FN vs. supporters of Gbagbo) 2000 post election violence between Gbagbo and Ouattara supporters continued until August 2011 resulting in many hundreds of deaths and IDPs. Although starting largely as a political power struggle, the conflict increasingly took on both ethnic and religious dimensions as each party was identified in terms of religion and ethnic belonging of their supporters. Hate speech/crimes played a significant role in the conflict.	**India** (Naxalite) – 1997 a lot of support amongst tribal peoples of Andhra Pradesh, Maharahstra, Madhya Pradesh and Orissa but also amongst non-minority poor and landless. Indigenous peoples have suffered immensely, as they face brutal human rights violations perpetrated by the militants and are targeted by the Indian military on the assumption that they are supporting the rebels. Encounters between security forces and CPI-M militants, abductions, bomb attacks, and strikes inflicted a total of over 360 casualties in 2012.	**Mexico** (drug cartels) 2006 Conflict between various drug cartels and the government over rule of law, subnational dominance and resources in addition to inter-cartel violence.

Issues of minorities and indigenous peoples (MIPS) as a driver of armed conflicts 2007–13 (cont.)

MIP issues are one of the main drivers of the conflict	**MIP issues are a secondary or additional driver, or have emerged or receded over time as a significant driver**	**MIP issues are not a driver of the conflict; however there are targeted attacks on MIPs by armed actors**	**MIP issues are not a driver of the conflict; MIPs are not specifically targeted based on their identity**
Chad (ethnic groups). **2003** conflict between Arab Janjaweed groups, located on both sides of the Chad-Sudan border, and black African communities in the eastern part of Chad. Peaked in 2007. Regional Predominance conflict	**DR Congo** (Ex-RCD-G, FDLR, Interahamwe vs. government) **1997** – conflict beginnings in Rwandan genocide. FDLR is rebel group drawing from Rwandan and Congolese Hutus, now fighting for resources and subnational predominance in DRC. Also states that long-term aim is to topple Rwandan government.	**Libya** (opposition / popular protest vs. Govt) **2011** Conflict between anti-Gaddafi rebels and forces loyal to Gaddafi, significant civilian casualties but no ethnic group singled out. Some clan / tribal affiliations mirrored the pro-/anti-Gadaffi divide, with clashes reflecting that.	**Pakistan/Afghanistan/Somalia** (USA and other allies vs Al Qaeda and related groups based on Wahabi / Islamist ideology) International conflict (political / ideological / state control). 391 deaths in 2009 (UCDP / PRIO dataset).
DR Congo (CNDP/M23 vs. government) **2004** Conflict concerning subnational predominance and control of resources in North Kivu	**DR Congo** – (Enyele vs Boba) **2009** local ethnic conflicts over farming and fishing rights have become absorbed into the larger government/insurgency conflict.	**Peru** (Shining Path) – **1980** conflict between the left-wing rebel group Shining Path (SP) and the government over regional predominance.	**Philippines** (CPP/NPA vs govt.) **1968** Conflict over system/ideology pitting Communist Party of the Philippines (CPP) and its military wing,

MIP issues are one of the main drivers of the conflict	MIP issues are a secondary or additional driver, or have emerged or receded over time as a significant driver	MIP issues are not a driver of the conflict; however there are targeted attacks on MIPs by armed actors	MIP issues are not a driver of the conflict; MIPs are not specifically targeted based on their identity
and south Kivu, eastern DR Congo, with the National Congress for the Defence of the People (CNDP), later M23. CNDP justified their armed struggle as defending the Banyamulenge ethnic group, related to Rwandan Tutsi, against the threat presented by Hutu militias in the eastern DR Congo. Banyamulenge suffered long-term deprivation of citizenship, not accepted as Congolese. Alleged / documented role of neighbours (Uganda, Rwanda). Conflict escalated in 2012;the UN accused Rwanda of backing M23.	Drew in FARDC, MONUC. FARDC accused of human rights abuses in attempts to tackle Enyele. Conflict peaked 2010, ended in 2011.	According to Minorities at Risk Project: "Shining Path and Tupac Amaru claimed to represent Indigenous interests, which attracted some initial support from Quechua and other Indigenous groups, although these organization cannot be said to be authentically indigenous movements". Systematic abuses and violent attacks on indigenous communities by both SP and govt.	the New People's Army (NPA) against government, essentially an ideology-based conflict, although indigenous peoples have been severely affected (displacement). Peaked 2008.

Issues of minorities and indigenous peoples (*MIPS*) *as a driver of armed conflicts* 2007–13 (cont.)

MIP issues are one of the main drivers of the conflict	MIP issues are a secondary or additional driver, or have emerged or receded over time as a significant driver	MIP issues are not a driver of the conflict; however there are targeted attacks on MIPs by armed actors	MIP issues are not a driver of the conflict; MIPs are not specifically targeted based on their identity
DR Congo (Bundu dia Kongo vs govt) **2000** BdK demanded the creation of a political system and society based on indigenous cultural and social values, and the resurrection of the Kingdom of Kongo (a Bantu ethnic group). Demanded establishment of federal system while seeking to eradicate social and economic injustices. Peaked 2008.	**Iraq** (AQI, ISI, Ansar al-Islam, 1920 Revolution Brigades, Sunni militant groups vs. government, Al-Sahwa militia) **2003** - began as rebellion against multi-national forces, since 2006 the conflict has become increasingly sectarian (Sunni/Shi'a). Tensions also growing between Arab and Kurdish political movements particularly in Nineveh and Kirkuk. Smaller minorities targeted to pressure them to join one side or the other, or because perceived as allied with international forces in Iraq.	**Somalia** – **2006** (Somaliland vs government, Al-Shabaab vs. TFG, KDF, ENA) Primarily a conflict over state control, ideology and application of Islam. Minorities, for example Bantu, particularly targeted, because lack protection of large clan – members of minority clans forcibly recruited, including children, women are abducted. Conflict over system / ideology, national power, with international involvement (Kenya/ Ethiopia, AU peacekeeping mission).	**Somalia** (Somaliland vs SSC) **2009** conflict over subnational predominance in the regions of Sool and Sanaag, as well as Togdheer's Cayn Section, between the self-declared independent state of Somaliland and the local resistance group from Sool, Sanaag and Cayn (SSC). Peaked 2012.

MIP issues are one of the main drivers of the conflict	MIP issues are a secondary or additional driver, or have emerged or receded over time as a significant driver	MIP issues are not a driver of the conflict; however there are targeted attacks on MIPs by armed actors	MIP issues are not a driver of the conflict; MIPs are not specifically targeted based on their identity
Ethiopia (OLF, OLA - 1973 ONLF- 1984) Small scale clashes continued to occur between the OLF, OLA and the government in the Oromiya area and the ONLF and the government in the Ogaden area. The ONLF fought for the independence of the predominantly Muslim-inhabited Ogaden region bordering Somalia. Conflict peaked in 2009 and 2010.	**Israel/Occupied Territories** (Fatah, Palestinian Islamic Jihad, Hamas) -1948 – cannot be classed as an international conflict because of failure to establish sovereign Palestinian state; occupation of a people that puts them in position of de facto minority. Discriminatory laws and occupation of lands.		**Sudan - South Sudan (2011)**, international conflict over contested border areas in particular Abyei, including Heglig, an oil rich area.

Issues of minorities and indigenous peoples (MIPS) *as a driver of armed conflicts 2007–13* (cont.)

MIP issues are one of the main drivers of the conflict	MIP issues are a secondary or additional driver, or have emerged or receded over time as a significant driver	MIP issues are not a driver of the conflict; however there are targeted attacks on MIPs by armed actors	MIP issues are not a driver of the conflict; MIPs are not specifically targeted based on their identity
Georgia/Russia - South Ossetia 1989 grievances relating to demands for autonomy, intensified by involvement of Russian Federation, flaring to an intense but brief peak in 2008. South Ossetia strived for independence from Georgia and unification with ethnic kin in Russia's North Caucasus republic of North Ossetia.	**Kenya** (PNU/ODM) **- 1999** post-election violence was essentially political, between supporters of rival political parties. However political camps were formed largely along ethnic lines and framed by a long history of ethnic tensions. Grievances held by respective ethnic groups include exclusion from land and government jobs. Peaked 2008.		**Tajikistan (Gorno – Badakhshan)** - Tolib Ayombekov's Militia vs. Government - **2012** Conflict over subnational predominance in the Gorno-badakhshan autonomous Province. Conflict resulted in 47-200 deaths in 2012. Ayombekov also accused of smuggling and human and drug trafficking.

MIP issues are one of the main drivers of the conflict	**MIP issues are a secondary or additional driver, or have emerged or receded over time as a significant driver**	**MIP issues are not a driver of the conflict; however there are targeted attacks on MIPs by armed actors**	**MIP issues are not a driver of the conflict; MIPs are not specifically targeted based on their identity**
India (Assam separatists) **1979** The peace process with Assam Separatists ULFA - PTF (pro-talk Faction) proceeded in 2012,violence by ULFA -ATF (anti-talk Faction) continued. Related conflict: ULFA, ATTF, NDFB, NLFT, AASU, Bodos vs. Bengalis, Biharis, AABYSF **(1981)** Conflict escalated in 2012, mainly took place in the Assamese parts of the semi-autonomous Bodo Territorial Autonomous District (BTAD), where many Bodos perceived Muslims and Bengali-speakers to be illegal immigrants.	**Pakistan** (Taliban, tribes in Federally Administered Tribal Areas) – **2001** the conflict is ideological but also has ethnic elements, with Taliban tribes generally being Pashtun, and therefore connected with neighbouring tribes in Afghanistan. The conflict de-escalated in but remains violent, with more than 240 people killed in fighting with the government in 2012. The wider conflict between Islamist groups and the government claimed a total of 4000 lives, with further attacks on religious minorities by fundamentalist groups occurring.		**Yemen** (opposition groups inc. Islah and tribal federations vs government) **2011** anti-Saleh demonstrations, southern separatists, army mutiny, clan rivalry, and al-Qaeda militants. Govt cited 1500 killed between Jan and Sep 2011.

Issues of minorities and indigenous peoples (MIPS) as a driver of armed conflicts 2007–13 (cont.)

MIP issues are one of the main drivers of the conflict	MIP issues are a secondary or additional driver, or have emerged or receded over time as a significant driver	MIP issues are not a driver of the conflict; however there are targeted attacks on MIPs by armed actors	MIP issues are not a driver of the conflict; MIPs are not specifically targeted based on their identity
India (Kashmiri Insurgency) **1947** secession conflict particularly affecting the Indian-administered Jammu & Kashmir, between the government and Kashmiri and Pakistani insurgency groups. Primarily an identity-driven conflict, with issues relating to the partition of India in 1947.	**South Sudan** (Shilluk militias, Militias David Yau Yau, SSLM-Gadet, SSDM, Militias Gatluak Gai, Militias Gabriel Tang-Ginye vs GoSS) **2010** Conflict over distribution of resources and orientation of the political system in South Sudan. Conflict peaked 2011, de-escalated in 2012. Some militias formed along ethnic lines, and citing grievances based on Dinka dominance of government & resources.		**Yemen** (AQAP, Ansar al-Sharia) **1992.** Peaked 2011. conflict over national power and the orientation of the political system between al-Qaeda in the Arabian Peninsula (AQAP) and linked Islamist militants of Ansar al-Sharia, on the one hand, and the government supported by the USA, on the other.

MIP issues are one of the main drivers of the conflict	MIP issues are a secondary or additional driver, or have emerged or receded over time as a significant driver	MIP issues are not a driver of the conflict; however there are targeted attacks on MIPs by armed actors	MIP issues are not a driver of the conflict; MIPs are not specifically targeted based on their identity
Iran (PJAK - Kurds) 1979 The autonomy conflict between PKK offshoot PJAK and the Iranian government peaked in 2011 then de-escalated in 2012 but remains violent with casualties on both sides.	**South Sudan** (Forces allied to Riek Machar vs govt.) 2013: After Vice-President Riek Machar was ousted from government in June, tensions rose, resulting in all out conflict in December. Although tensions have focused on perceived / real exclusion of Nuer from political participation and resources, the conflict is also a political one between rivals for power within the SPLM. Dinka and Nuer civilians have been victims of targeted killings.		

Issues of minorities and indigenous peoples (MIPS) *as a driver of armed conflicts 2007–13* (cont.)

MIP issues are one of the main drivers of the conflict	MIP issues are a secondary or additional driver, or have emerged or receded over time as a significant driver	MIP issues are not a driver of the conflict; however there are targeted attacks on MIPS by armed actors	MIP issues are not a driver of the conflict; MIPS are not specifically targeted based on their identity
Kenya (SLDF, MF, Kenyan govt) **2002** violence between majority Soy and minority clans of the Sabaot community over contested allocation of land led to government intervention.	**Sudan** (JEM, SLM/A-AW, LJM, SLRF, SLA-Unity, SLA-Juba, SLA-BA, URF vs. government, Janjaweed, SLM/A-MM) **2003** increasingly, the battle lines are defined in terms of political groupings/militias and less in minority terms. But at the root of the conflict lie economic and political marginalisation of Darfuri tribes. Supremacist ideologies have also been used by central govt. to provide a basis for armed action.		

MIP issues are one of the main drivers of the conflict	MIP issues are a secondary or additional driver, or have emerged or receded over time as a significant driver	MIP issues are not a driver of the conflict; however there are targeted attacks on MIPs by armed actors	MIP issues are not a driver of the conflict; MIPs are not specifically targeted based on their identity
Kyrgyzstan (Kyrgyz, Uzbeks following ouster of Bakiyev) **1990** Conflict over regional predominance and resources between Uzbeks and Kyrgyz. Reached crisis point in 2010.	**Syria** - (opposition (SNC, FSA vs government) **2011** Began as conflict over national power, protest against authoritarian rule, and the orientation of the political system. By the end of 2012, 60,000 fatalities were reported, more than 500,000 refugees in neighbouring countries, and approx. 2.3 million IDPs. In 2013, with Hizbollah declaring open support for Assad, conflict took on more overt sectarian Sunni/Shi'a elements. Minority communities targeted because of real/ perceived support for Assad.		

Issues of minorities and indigenous peoples (MIPS) as a driver of armed conflicts 2007–13 (cont.)

MIP issues are one of the main drivers of the conflict	**MIP issues are a secondary or additional driver, or have emerged or receded over time as a significant driver**	**MIP issues are not a driver of the conflict; however there are targeted attacks on MIPs by armed actors**	**MIP issues are not a driver of the conflict; MIPs are not specifically targeted based on their identity**
Libya (Inter-ethnic violence - Warffallah tribe vs. Zwai vs. Tibu tribe vs. Berber ethnic groups vs. Ethnic Arab settlements vs. El-Mashasha tribe vs. al-Fawatra tribe et al.) **2012** Conflict over subnational predominance, orientation of the political system and resources following the 2011 civil war. Accusations by parties that state failed to protect them / supported other parties. **Mali** - (Tuareg rebels - ANM, MTNM, MNLA, Ansar al-Din vs. Government). **1989** Following increasing calls	**Uganda/South Sudan**/CAR/DR **Congo** (LRA vs governments) **1987** at its origin the war was closely tied to Acholi grievances. Acholis have suffered gross violations at hands of Ugandan army, also in relation to the operations undertaken against LRA. LRA declared that it began fighting in Uganda to impose a government based on 10 commandments. Increasingly appears to have no political agenda apart from own survival.		

MIP issues are one of the main drivers of the conflict	MIP issues are a secondary or additional driver, or have emerged or receded over time as a significant driver	MIP issues are not a driver of the conflict; however there are targeted attacks on MIPs by armed actors	MIP issues are not a driver of the conflict; MIPs are not specifically targeted based on their identity
for secession by Tuareg groups, there were clashes in early 2012 between National Movement for the Liberation of Azawad (MNLA) and the Islamist Tuareg group Ansar al-Din and government forces. The President was deposed in an army coup in March. In April the MNLA declared the independence of Azawad (traditional Tuareg homeland in the north). Following further government / rebel clashes, and splits between MNLA and Ansar al-Din, ECOWAS agreed to deploy peacekeepers.			

Issues of minorities and indigenous peoples (MIPS) as a driver of armed conflicts 2007–13 (cont.)

MIP issues are one of the main drivers of the conflict	MIP issues are a secondary or additional driver, or have emerged or receded over time as a significant driver	MIP issues are not a driver of the conflict; however there are targeted attacks on MIPs by armed actors	MIP issues are not a driver of the conflict; MIPs are not specifically targeted based on their identity
Nigeria - (Farmers – Pastoralists) 1960 conflict primarily concerned with arable land, exacerbated by ethnic, political, and religious issues between predominantly Christian farmers of the Berom and Tiv tribes on the one hand, and the mainly Muslim Fulani nomads on the other. Hausa and Fulanis - are both Muslim communities and perceived as strangers to Plateau state (without indigene-state rights[2]); but many Hausa for example have been residing in the			

MIP issues are one of the main drivers of the conflict	MIP issues are a secondary or additional driver, or have emerged or receded over time as a significant driver	MIP issues are not a driver of the conflict; however there are targeted attacks on MIPs by armed actors	MIP issues are not a driver of the conflict; MIPs are not specifically targeted based on their identity
State for several decades. Situation now so polarised that mixed Christian and Muslim neighbourhoods barely exist. Conflict escalated to a war in 2012 causing 600 deaths over the course of the year.[3] **Nigeria** (Christians - Muslims) **1960** Christian/ Muslim tensions, including communal *violence in Jos, and uprising* by the group Boko Haram which aims to create a "pure" Islamic state ruled by Shari'a law (USIP). Caused approximately 600 deaths in 2012. Amnesty International has said that 950 suspected Boko Haram militants died in government detention facilities in 2013. Since			

Issues of minorities and indigenous peoples (MIPS) as a driver of armed conflicts 2007–13 (cont.)

MIP issues are one of the main drivers of the conflict	**MIP issues are a secondary or additional driver, or have emerged or receded over time as a significant driver**	**MIP issues are not a driver of the conflict; however there are targeted attacks on MIPs by armed actors**	**MIP issues are not a driver of the conflict; MIPs are not specifically targeted based on their identity**
August 2011 Boko Haram has planted bombs almost weekly in public or in churches in Nigeria's northeast (USIP). **Nigeria** – (Ijaw and Itsekeris tensions in Niger Delta) **1997** in context of struggle for oil involving government and foreign companies. Minorities at Risk project: "ethnic groups of the region are often in conflict with one another over resources and government access, yet are also allied against the government and the oil companies in the Delta".			

MIP issues are one of the main drivers of the conflict	MIP issues are a secondary or additional driver, or have emerged or receded over time as a significant driver	MIP issues are not a driver of the conflict; however there are targeted attacks on MIPs by armed actors	MIP issues are not a driver of the conflict; MIPs are not specifically targeted based on their identity
Pakistan (Mohajirs, MQM vs. Pakhtuns, ANP, Balochis, PPP, Sindhis, Awami Tehreek) 1947 Conflict over subnational predominance de-escalated, caused approx. 700 deaths in targeted killings in 2012. **Pakistan** (Tehrik-e-Taliban Pakistan et al vs various religious groups) 1985 Sectarian violence Sunnis, Shi'ites and Ahmadis. 537 people were killed in 2012, in 202 sectarian attacks over the course of the year. Most of the victims were Shiites but at least four Hindus and four Ahmadis were also killed.			

Issues of minorities and indigenous peoples (MIPS) as a driver of armed conflicts 2007–13 (cont.)

MIP issues are one of the main drivers of the conflict	MIP issues are a secondary or additional driver, or have emerged or receded over time as a significant driver	MIP issues are not a driver of the conflict; however there are targeted attacks on MIPs by armed actors	MIP issues are not a driver of the conflict; MIPs are not specifically targeted based on their identity
Philippines (MILF vs Government 1977, ASG vs govt 1991, BIFM/BIFF vs Milf & govt 2011) conflict between various Bangsomoro groups - Moro Islamic Liberation Front (MILF), Bangsamoro Islamic Freedom Movement (BIFM), its military wing the Bangsamoro Islamic Freedom Fighters (BIFF), Abu Sayyaf Group (ASG) and the government concerning secession/autonomy, ideology, access to resources in the			

MIP issues are one of the main drivers of the conflict	MIP issues are a secondary or additional driver, or have emerged or receded over time as a significant driver	MIP issues are not a driver of the conflict; however there are targeted attacks on MIPs by armed actors	MIP issues are not a driver of the conflict; MIPs are not specifically targeted based on their identity
Autonomous Region in Muslim Mindanao (ARMM) and SOCCS KSARGEN region. ASG/MILF conflicts peaked 2008/2009, BIFM/BIFF is a breakaway group from the MILF that entered into conflict with MILF and the government, peaking 2012. MILF and govt signed a peace agreement 2013. **Russia** (Northern Caucasus) (Islamic militants vs. government) (Chechnya 1989, Dagestan 1999, and Ingushetia 2004). The conflict in Dagestan claimed at least 413 lives in 2011. In the Northern Caucasus approximately 600 died in 2012.			

Issues of minorities and indigenous peoples (MIPS) as a driver of armed conflicts 2007–13 (cont.)

MIP issues are one of the main drivers of the conflict	**MIP issues are a secondary or additional driver, or have emerged or receded over time as a significant driver**	**MIP issues are not a driver of the conflict; however there are targeted attacks on MIPs by armed actors**	**MIP issues are not a driver of the conflict; MIPs are not specifically targeted based on their identity**
South Sudan (Murle vs. Lou Nuer vs. Misseriya vs.Dinka Gok vs. Dinka Rek vs. Dinka Bor vs. Bari vs. Fartit) **2008** violence between neighbouring ethnic groups over access to fertile grazing land. In a series of Lou-Nuer attacks on Murle villages in 2012, 20,000 to 60,000 people were displaced and 612 killed.			
Sri Lanka (LTTE vs government) **1948.** LTTE were defeated in 2009. Tamils and Muslims in post-conflict areas continued to be at risk of discrimination			

MIP issues are one of the main drivers of the conflict	MIP issues are a secondary or additional driver, or have emerged or receded over time as a significant driver	MIP issues are not a driver of the conflict; however there are targeted attacks on MIPs by armed actors	MIP issues are not a driver of the conflict; MIPs are not specifically targeted based on their identity
and violence from the army. Autonomy/secession/ language rights/political participation. **Sudan** (SPLM/A - North vs Central government) 1955 Autonomy conflict between Sudan Revolutionary Front (SRF) and the government in the Sudanese provinces of South Kordofan and Blue Nile. After independence of the South, conflict has shifted to contested resource rich territories along the border, in particular South Kordofan, home to the Nuba ethnic groups. **Thailand** – Malay-Muslims in southern border region vs government: 1902.			

Issues of minorities and indigenous peoples (*MIPS*) *as a driver of armed conflicts 2007–13* (cont.)

MIP issues are one of the main drivers of the conflict	**MIP issues are a secondary or additional driver, or have emerged or receded over time as a significant driver**	**MIP issues are not a driver of the conflict; however there are targeted attacks on MIPs by armed actors**	**MIP issues are not a driver of the conflict; MIPs are not specifically targeted based on their identity**
Narathiwat, Pattani, Songkhla and Yala. At least 600 people were killed in 2012. Secession / ideology conflict. **Turkey** (PKK vs government) **1974** War between PKK and the government over autonomy, Kurdish language rights, political participation, civil/political rights. The PKK ceasefire ended in February 2011 **Yemen/ Saudia Arabia 2004** (Shi'a followers al-Houthi) conflict erupted as order broke down in Yemen, between al Houthi rebels			

MIP issues are one of the main drivers of the conflict	MIP issues are a secondary or additional driver, or have emerged or receded over time as a significant driver	MIP issues are not a driver of the conflict; however there are targeted attacks on MIPs by armed actors	MIP issues are not a driver of the conflict; MIPs are not specifically targeted based on their identity
and Sunni tribal forces. Throughout 2012, clashes claimed over 400 lives. Al Houthi leader accused Saudi government of assisting Yemen govt in its fight against his group.			
Total number of conflicts:			
62			
Total per column:			
29	15	7	11
Percentage of total:			
46.8%	24.2%	11.3%	17.7%

NOTES

(1) The start date of conflicts is indicated. All conflicts included in the analysis were either still ongoing by the end of 2013, or ended at some point between 2007 and 2013.

(2) In the Nigerian Federal system, within each Federal state, natives of that State ("indigenes") have greater rights regarding work and residence than Nigerians from another Federal State.

(3) Input from Andreu Solà Martín.

Thus if we merge the first two categories, we have a very significant majority of conflicts – 71% – in which minority / indigenous issues are a primary or secondary factor. In only 18% of conflicts can minority or indigenous belonging be said to be irrelevant. Conflicts are highly complex phenomena, and I do not pretend to boil them down to one simple issue. In many conflicts, there is debate around what the root causes of the conflict are, but in most cases the main issues at stake can be understood from a) who is fighting who; b) statements and demands made by belligerents; and c) strategic decisions of belligerents e.g. to seize control of a specific resource or territory. The maximum claim that I would make is that MIP issues are *one of* the principle causal factors in a conflict. In fact, this complexity of conflicts is one of the issues that clouds some observers' and decision-makers' understanding of conflicts. It is not uncommon to hear observers remark that a given conflict is not about identity, but about resources. This was the case, for example, of the conflict between North and South Sudan leading up to the 2005 Comprehensive Peace Agreement. However, it is always necessary to ask for any given conflict, a) what are people fighting over and b) who is fighting whom? In the Sudan war, it is true that the two sides were fighting (in part) over resources, particularly oil-rich territories, but the way the battle lines were drawn also needs to be considered. The North was fighting the South, and while there was significant ethnic inter-mixing, the two sides identified to a large extent in terms of ethnicity and religion. Identity factors such as the desire by Khartoum to impose Sharia law on the South, and its refusal to allow independent decision-making structures to be set up in the South, played a significant role in the conflict. Khartoum mobilised proxy militias drawing from ethnic groups and incited them against neighbouring ethnic groups using appeals to supremacist ideologies or long-held animosities. So the fact that the conflict was (in part) over resources, does not mean that it was not about identity as well. If ethnic groups are fighting each other over resources, we need to ask ourselves why this is happening. Why are these groups not peacefully collaborating and sharing the resources? It is also necessary to bear in mind that MIP issues alone are not sufficient in generating conflict; means and opportunity – money, guns, safe havens, political platforms, etc. – are also relevant.

It should be noted that MIP issues can be used (by the state, majority and/or MIPs) as the basis for appeals to use violent means to gain redress. Community leaders may misrepresent or exaggerate issues in order to sharpen tensions and build a power base, potentially leading to conflict. This is the phenomenon of so-called ethnic entrepreneurs.[30] However, it should not be assumed that

30 With regard to ethnic entrepreneurs, Stefan Wolff made the following useful remarks: "[I]n some of the literature there is a distinction between ethnic activists (people who have

a platform for conflict can be built out of nothing. As Isaiah Berlin noted, whatever exploitation or manipulation of national sentiments may have occurred, the identity issue was there to be exploited or manipulated.[31] The inclusion of a conflict in one of the above categories implies no judgment on the credibility of a particular party's appeal to MIP grievances, merely that the grievance – whether real or perceived – exists.

These statistics indicate that governmental, inter-governmental and NGO actors who work on conflict prevention, mediation and resolution, need to have a close understanding of minority and indigenous issues. However the United Nations Independent Expert on Minority Issues found that United Nations bodies and other inter-governmental organisations dealing with conflict did not have expertise on minority issues.[32] In most cases staff did not receive training on minority rights. The Independent Expert recommended that "Minority rights expertise should be strengthened and integrated comprehensively across the United Nations system".[33] These findings are in line with my experience of engagements with governmental and inter-governmental actors. The picture with regard to Indigenous Peoples is not substantively better, despite the generally greater visibility given them within the UN system.

There have been some welcome developments. A report by the UN Independent Expert on Minority Issues, on minority rights and conflict prevention (cited extensively here) was presented to the General Assembly; it shed much needed light on the issue and set out necessary actions to be taken both by inter-governmental organisations and states.[34] However there remains a need to strengthen the capacity of government and IGO officials working on conflict to engage with MIP issues. This can be done by setting up dedicated units or advisers on MIPs and conflict, drawing up guidance notes, and providing training. Such officials should have the necessary expertise and knowledge to (among other things):

---

an 'exaggerated' need to identify ethnically and exercise peer pressure on others to do so as well) and political entrepreneurs (people who 'play' the ethnic card for their own political advancement). Distinctions are often fluid between them, but as a rule of thumb, for ethnic activists, power is a means to an end (ethnic 'purity' or whatever they may seek), whereas for political entrepreneurs, ethnicity is a means to an end (gaining power, wealth, etc.)." (Interview with author, 16/9/2014).

31 I. Berlin, 'Nationalism: Past Neglect and Present Power', in H. Hardy (ed.), *Against The Current: Essays in the History of Ideas* (The Hogarth Press, London, 1979) p. 352.

32 G. McDougall, *supra* note 20, pp. 15–20

33 *Ibid.*, p. 22.

34 G. McDougall, *supra* note 20

- identify minorities and Indigenous Peoples
- know what their rights are, and the mechanisms for implementing them
- understand possible barriers to engaging with MIPS, such as geographical isolation, suspicion of outsiders, and language, and how to overcome them if necessary
- be able to identify the early warning signs of situations in which MIPS, not previously parties to or victims of a conflict, could become targeted due to the way in which the conflict is developing
- be aware of how information communicated to the public via national media, governments, and even mainstream civil society, may be negatively affected by prejudice and/or ignorance
- be aware of tools for involving MIPS in consultation processes

It is important to note that even when MIPS are not a party when a conflict starts, they can be attacked by one or other party for a number of reasons: a) they are located in strategically important or resource-rich territories; b) they will not be protected by other armed groups (including the state); c) more powerful parties will not protest attacks on them; d) if one party to the conflict has made an appeal to a specific community based on existing grievances, the community becomes an automatically suspicious potential constituency of that party.[35] Parties may attack MIPS also in an effort to cast themselves as protectors of the nation, attempting to depict MIPS as foreign or otherwise unpatriotic agents. These dynamics can be hard for outsiders to spot, thus supporting the argument for the need for specialised expertise. Unfortunately the evidence indicates that this expertise does not yet exist. In 2003, the United Nations Secretary-General, Kofi Annan, commissioned a High Level Panel on Threats, Challenges and Change to develop recommendations for the organisation in facing up to a new generation of security challenges. In its report, the panel recommended:

> The United Nations should seek to work closely with regional organizations that have taken the lead in building frameworks for prevention … regional organizations have gone farther than the United Nations in setting normative standards that can guide preventive efforts … The

35 An example is the Nepal civil war, in which the Maoist movement appealed to Dalits with a pledge to uproot the "feudal caste system" (S. Kharel, 'The Struggle for Full Citizenship for Dalits in Nepal: Approaches and Strategies of Dalit Activists', 27 *Himalaya, the Journal of the Association for Nepal and Himalayan Studies* (2007) p. 61).

> Organization of Security and Cooperation in Europe (OSCE) has developed operational norms on minority rights. The United Nations should build on the experience of regional organizations in developing frameworks for minority rights.[36]

Almost 15 years later, there is evidence that the organisation – and other actors in the conflict prevention field – would do well to heed this advice.

7 Conclusions

In this chapter, my aim has not been to give the last word on the causal link between minority rights and conflict prevention. As I have said elsewhere, "[v]iolent conflict, being by nature both endlessly complex, and hard to study firsthand, has given rise to a predictably broad range of theories attempting to explain how it happens, what makes it persist, and the measures needed to bring it to an end".[37] But at the very least, the evidence presented must give pause for thought, both for governments of conflict-affected states, and mediators, diplomats and IGO officials who deal with conflict prevention, conflict management and conflict resolution. It is essential that these actors do not give into the easy attractions of assimilationist discourses; but also that they understand who minorities and indigenous peoples are, and what their internationally recognised rights are.

The accommodation of groups within a state is in part a question of the development of fine-tuned laws, policies and implementation / monitoring mechanisms at the national level – and global and regional human rights frameworks have a role in guiding that process. But on another level, a fundamental shift in the approach to state-building is necessary. As a general principle, the tendency towards absolutist, zero-sum thinking must be avoided – for example that security concerns must always trump human rights, or the construction of a strong, unified national identity must win out over the promotion of diversity. However, one constant is that states must not create categories of citizens who have less rights. Hannah Arendt argued that, in Nazi Germany, the process of stripping an entire class of people of citizenship – and therefore rights – would inevitably result in the toppling of the edifice of human rights the world over:

36 *A More Secure World: Our Shared Responsibility: Report of the High-level Panel on Threats, Challenges and Change*, UN Doc. A/59/565 (2004), para 94.

37 C. Chapman, *supra* note 21, p. 406.

> The official SS newspaper, the *Schwarze Korps*, stated explicitly in 1938 that if the world was not yet convinced that the Jews were the scum of the earth, it soon would be when unidentifiable beggars, without nationality, without money, and without passports crossed their frontiers. And it is true that this kind of factual propaganda worked better than Goebbels' rhetoric, not only because it established the Jews as scum of the earth, but also because the incredible plight of an ever-growing group of innocent people was like a practical demonstration of the totalitarian movements' cynical claims that no such thing as inalienable human rights existed and that the affirmations of the democracies to the contrary were mere prejudice, hypocrisy, and cowardice in the face of the cruel majesty of a new world.[38]

While almost all violations of human rights are cited at some point by cynics and *Realpolitiker* as proof of the fundamental non-viability of the human rights framework, it is certainly true that human rights cannot be imagined if they are not enjoyed equally and universally – as illustrated by the very title of the United Nations' foundational human rights document, and its first article ("All human beings are born free and equal in dignity and rights").[39] This is one reason why the European Court of Human Rights could surely not have reached a different conclusion in the *Sejdić and Finci* case; and all the more so because such blatant, *de jure* expressions of discrimination are becoming rarer, with the entrenchment of the non-discrimination norm as an *erga omnes* obligation,[40] which no state dares to question openly, either on legal or moral grounds, and are ceding ground to forms of indirect discrimination, whose existence is harder to document and prove.

However, discrimination is not only perceived by minorities. If specific mechanisms are put in place to protect the identity and address forms of discrimination faced by MIPs, these need to be carefully explained to majorities. Politically and economically marginalised sections of majority communities can easily be convinced by populist politicians that the blame for their situation lies with minorities or immigrants; this can then be used to build a platform that wishes to question the human rights basis of national constitutions – a

38 H. Arendt, *The Origins of Totalitarianism* (Meridian Books, Cleveland, 1958) p. 269.

39 Universal Declaration of Human Rights, United Nations General Assembly resolution 217 A (10 December 1948).

40 *See* for example International Court of Justice, *Barcelona Traction, Light and Power Company, Limited* (*Belgium v. Spain*) (1962–1970), Second Phase, Judgment, I.C.J Reports 1970.

process that can ultimately have the destructive consequences that Arendt outlined.

Beyond these red lines, there are few absolutes. Seeing human rights and security concerns as mutually antagonistic and exclusive, as has often been the case in national-level debates around the *Sejdić and Finci* case, is an oversimplification.[41] Post-conflict political settlements should not be viewed wholly in terms of security, nor wholly in terms of human rights, and in reality this approach can work against the aim of consolidating security in the long-term. I have tried to show here that violations of human rights – in particular group rights – are often a source of instability; human rights norms should therefore be seen as an ally in nation-building. Furthermore it is wrong to see human rights obligations as absolute and inflexible. In most cases they allow for a balancing with other legitimate concerns of the state and its people. In the case of power-sharing agreements, many of which involve at least an element of exclusion on identity lines, one suggested possible solution is to enshrine a "sunset clause" (a time limit on a particular provision, after which there is a transition to another arrangement). An example of this is South Africa's interim constitution of 1993, which provided for power-sharing between the African National Congress, the National Party (traditionally the party of Afrikaner interests) and others. It was superseded in 1997 by a permanent constitution which allowed for government based on traditional majoritarian democracy. Both documents are also a good example of the nestling of political arrangements within a strong human rights framework.

Sejdić and Finci found that the Bosnian arrangement violated the complainants' rights, but did not find against power-sharing as a system. It would be difficult to say that a particular political system, in all its applications, is either friendly or inimical to human rights (fascism, apartheid and absolute autocracies would probably have to be exempted from that analysis). Power-sharing can be effective in giving minorities a voice, whereas majoritarian democracy can have the effect, if not the intention, of leaving them out in the cold. The specific system adopted will always depend on the particularities of the context.

Similarly, and especially at times of crisis, questions of individual and national identity are posed in terms of a necessity to choose which side of the fence you are on. Britain's Prime Minister, in a keynote speech to her party's annual conference, claimed "if you believe you're a citizen of the world, you're

41 V. Bojicic-Dzelilovic, 'The Politics, Practice and Paradox of 'Ethnic Security' in Bosnia-Herzegovina', 4 *Stability: International Journal of Security and Development* (2015) p. 1.

a citizen of nowhere. You don't understand what the very word 'citizenship' means".[42] May's rejection of transnational forms of belonging had special resonance – intentionally, no doubt – in the aftermath of the referendum on Britain's membership of the European Union. In reality, as a citizen of her country explained,[43] a feeling of being a global citizen does not in itself cast doubt on one's sense of belonging to one's country. Similarly, in 1972, M.N. Larma tried in vain to explain to the Bangladesh parliament that indigenous individuals of the Chittagong Hill Tracts were no less Bangladeshi, for being also Chakma, or Marma, or Khiyang. History has shown that the zero-sum identity game often leads to forced assimilation, genocide, or secession, usually after a bloody war, and no country illustrates that better than Bangladesh.

42 'Theresa May's Conference Speech in full', Daily Telegraph, 5 October 2016 (http://www.telegraph.co.uk/news/2016/10/05/theresa-mays-conference-speech-in-full/).

43 J. Eskenazi, 'It's May who misunderstands world citizenship', letter to the editor (Financial Times, 10 October 2016).

CHAPTER 10

The Post-Conflict Security Dilemma and the Incorporation of Ethno-Cultural Diversity

Padraig McAuliffe

1 Introduction: The Ambiguous Place of Ethno-Cultural Protections in Peace Agreements

Of the most vicious and/or intractable civil conflicts fought since the end of the Cold War (e.g. Rwanda, Darfur, Sri Lanka, Syria, Kosovo, Chechnya), a majority have seen ethnic, cultural, linguistic or religious differences emerge as a catalyst for conflict. Under grievance-based theories of war where groups rebel over issues of identity and exclusion from power, the failure of the state to respect the rights of distinct ethno-cultural groups (usually minorities and/or other subnational groups like indigenous communities) is seen as the critical precursor to civil conflicts. These grievances can inflame minority nationalism or transnationalism that diminishes any attachment to a single nation-state. The violence will usually originate from members of a minority community (or majority community without sufficient access to state power) resorting to violence out of a conviction that justice or security cannot otherwise be ensured in a pluralistic political environment characterised by discrimination, assimilation or exploitation. Violence may also stem from majoritarian ethno-nationalist states inflicting violence against their citizens in order to control a territory or suppress a group's identity. Many ethnic conflicts experience the deliberate provocation of violence by antagonists on both sides to solidify confrontational polarisation that is exacerbated in cycles of violence and over-reaction. The conflict may stem from a fight for autonomy from the state, a fight against the removal of autonomy by the state, or secession from the state. Even those conflicts that revolve around economic issues that do not appear strictly attributable to ethno-cultural differences may nevertheless see issues of identity embraced by conflict entrepreneurs as a means of mobilizing a constituency.[1]

1 For a good primer on the ethno-cultural roots of civil conflict, *see* L.E. Cederman, A. Wimmer and B. Min, 'Why Do Ethnic Groups Rebel? New Data and Analysis' 62 *World Politics* (2010) p. 87.

 | DOI 10.1163/9789004328785_012

Though differences in size, history and power of minority groups, to say nothing of the dissimilarities between ethnic, linguistic or religious oppression, mean that no two ethnic conflicts are the same, there is a general confidence among scholars and policy-makers that "[d]ealing effectively and efficiently with minorities and minority problems in the aftermath of ethnic conflict is crucial for durable and stable peace."[2] Minority rights, those individual rights permitting members of a given group "to enjoy their own culture, to profess and practice their own religion, or to use their own language,"[3] provide rights of protection (against discrimination or extinction), rights of empowerment (participation in national-level decision-making and/or authority to regulate the groups' own affairs or autonomy) and preservation (of the group's culture and identity).[4] Their inclusion in peace agreements is believed to grant them efficacy in addressing the ethno-cultural roots of conflict because peace agreements are seen within this literature as the bargained "blueprint" for a new human rights framework for the state and its constituent groups[5] or as an opportunity for quasi-constitutional embedding of minority protections.[6] It is assumed that a peace agreement should serve as a "first expression of a new form of relationship" between the state and marginalized groups or indigenous people, a recognition by both the state and the group of the need to respect the diversity of the state.[7] Peace agreements are believed to establish constructive solutions that harmonize concerns relating to order with those relating to minority rights.

Ethno-cultural protections can be achieved through claims by right and by what protections the group can negotiate with other groups or the state. As Eide argues, effective protection for an identifiable group requires the full suite of core human rights without discrimination, a commitment by the state to allow the group to preserve its dignity as part of a given community based on

2 T.K. Reuter, 'Including Minority Rights in Peace Agreements: A Benefit or Obstacle to Peace Processes after Ethnic Conflicts?' 19 *International Journal on Minority and Group Rights* (2012) p. 359.

3 Article 17 of the International Covenant on Civil and Political Rights.

4 T.K. Reuter, *supra* note 2, pp. 364–365.

5 J. Gilbert, 'Indigenous Peoples and Peace Agreements: Transforming Relationships or Empty Rhetoric', in G. Ore Aguilar and F. Gomez Isa (eds.), *Rethinking Transitions. Equality and Social Justice in Societies Emerging from Conflict* (Intersentia, Antwerp, 2011) p. 229.

6 C.L. Sriram, 'Making Rights Real? Minority and Gender Provisions and Power-Sharing Arrangements', 17 *International Journal of Human Rights* (2013) p. 278, drawing on C. Bell, 'Peace Agreements: Their Nature and Legal Status', 100 *American Journal of International Law* (2006) pp. 391–394.

7 J. Gilbert, *supra* note 5, pp. 208 and 209.

language, religion or ethnicity (which may or may not require special positive measures) and protection for the material basis of its culture or lifestyle.[8] Some guarantees can be rectificatory, like affirming the rights of those who once occupied land to resources from which they were removed, recognizing historical abuses (truth commissions, apologies), securing accountability (trials and reparations) and facilitating refugee returns. Others are more prospective measures to prevent a recurrence of grievance or violence, most notably the creation of political institutions that transcend ethno-cultural boundaries through democratization, rule of law reform and creation of human rights bodies or ombudsmen with guarantees of effective participation. Education systems can be reformed to resist assimilation, reject divisive ideologies and be accessible in non-majority languages, while advocacy of religious, racial or national hatred can be criminally prohibited. Groups can be empowered to implement personal laws in relation to family and culture, consultative or dialogue-based bodies can inform government policies on ethno-cultural issues, minorities can be consulted on development or poverty-reduction plans and schemes for affirmative action employed creatively.

Any number of examples could be offered of peace agreements that attempted to create an effective architecture for preserving ethno-cultural diversity in states that heretofore had not done so sufficiently. Nicaragua's Autonomy Law No. 28 helped bring armed struggle to an end by guaranteeing cultural rights like the right to religious freedom and the right of coastal communities to be educated in their own language, while extending official status to indigenous languages and providing that municipalities or town councils should be created according to communal traditions. Macedonia's Ohrid Agreement entailed greater representations of ethnic Albanians in government and society and made any language spoken by over 20% of the population (like Albanian) co-official with Macedonian on municipal level. The peace agreement between the Philippine government and the Moro National Liberation Front guaranteed autonomous administrative divisions for Muslims in the south, the establishment of an autonomous government and distinct judicial systems for Sharia law. The Indian and Assamese (state) governments signed a Memorandum of Settlement with the Bodo Liberation Tigers to establish a Bodoland Territorial Council to provide constitutional protection for autonomous government, to fulfil economic, educational and linguistic aspirations and the preservation of land rights, socio-cultural and ethnic identity of the Bodos,

8 A. Eide, 'Minority Situations: In Search of Peaceful and Constructive Solutions', 66 *Notre Dame Law Review* (1990) p. 1341.

as well as improve infrastructural development in the area concerned. Bangladesh's Chittagong Hills Tract Accord recognised the distinct ethnicity and special status of the tribes and indigenous peoples of the Tracts. It founded a Regional Council made up of the local government councils of the three districts of the Hill Tracts and guaranteed central government consultation with regional councils over all issues concerning the area.

However, as Section 3 goes on to argue, though accompanied by strong language on the need to acknowledge diversity, ethno-cultural protections are often underspecified and under-implemented in peace settlements. Furthermore, minority rights and indigenous rights are sometimes excluded completely in some agreements. For example, references to minority or indigenous rights were negligible or non-existent in the agreements made by the Sudanese government relating to the conflicts in Darfur and the south or in the Pretoria Agreement in the Democratic Republic of Congo.[9] As Section 1 illustrates, it is difficult to demonstrate that minority rights are seen as core components of peace agreements even in those pacts that address what are most obviously ethno-cultural cleavages. For most of its history, UN work on conflict prevention has had few or no minority rights specialists.[10] This neglect may flow from what Macklem identifies as the historic lack of attention paid to minority rights issues by international legal scholars,[11] which itself may flow from their perceived vagueness (the belief they offer little by way of detailed guidance on what states actually have to do to guarantee their realisation),[12] the post-World War II eclipse of minority rights by human rights and the less-advanced nature of the corpus of minority rights relative to other special regimes.[13] Notwithstanding similarities in subject area, there are few cross-overs between the work of scholars on group rights or multicultural co-existence like Kymlicka and conflict resolution specialists like those who study consociationalism and institutional design.[14] Scholars of peacemaking and peacebuilding who address

9 C.L. Sriram, *supra* note 6, p. 279.

10 C. Baldwin, C. Chapman and Z. Gray, 'Minority Rights: The Key to Conflict Prevention', Minority Rights Group International (2007), at <http://minorityrights.org/wp-content/uploads/old-site-downloads/download-174-Minority-Rights-The-Key-to-Conflict-Prevention.pdf> p. 4.

11 P. Macklem, *The Sovereignty of Human Rights* (Oxford University Press, Oxford, 2015).

12 *Ibid.*, 107.

13 G. Pentassuglia, *Minorities in International Law* (Council of Europe, London, 2002) pp. 26 and 241.

14 As argued by S.G. Simonsen, 'Addressing Ethnic Divisions in Post-Conflict Institution-Building: Lessons from Recent Cases' 36 *Security Dialogue* (2005) p. 312.

power-sharing rarely examine provisions dealing with minority groups or indigenous peoples who fall outside it.[15] While the need for including women in the specific context of peace negotiations has attracted a copious scholarly literature and dedicated Security Council Resolutions,[16] no equivalent literature or generalised political commitments have attached to minority rights at the end of civil conflict.[17] The strikingly small literature on minority and indigenous rights and peace agreements bears out the disjuncture between the apparent faith of legal scholars of ethno-cultural diversity in the necessity of minority rights to ground peace and a much more ambivalent practice by conflict principals and mediators.[18] As one study puts it, "despite the fact that a disregard for minority issues lies at the heart of these conflicts, minority rights have been marginalized in international conflict prevention. Too many conflicts that have minority rights at their centre are not being understood as such."[19]

Most peace agreements that resolve ethno-culturally-based conflicts do have ethno-cultural protections (most notably forms of power-sharing and territorial autonomy), but the success of these agreements does not depend on a fuller suite of individual or group rights guarantees that would go some way towards significantly remedying legitimacy deficits arising from state formation. While international scholars use international legal categories of equality, culture and self-determination to understand, support and structure ethno-cultural claims,[20] a distinctly different set of motivations and justifications underpin the demands made in the largely endogenous course of peace negotiations. These motivations and justifications are based primarily on achieving the group's physical security, a reality that distinctly impacts the types of protections that are emphasized. Guarantees like state support for ethno-cultural groups, or finding the means to enable a minority to engage on a sustainable basis in activities the majority takes for granted, or recognizing the need for legal pluralism, are of less importance to minorities than enjoying the wherewithal to politically or militarily resist majority encroachment. The basis for these claims is different to those found in the case-based jurisprudence on group-based rights. The intent is less to ensure that constitutional

15 C.L. Sriram, *supra* note 6, p. 276.

16 UN Security Council Resolutions 1325 and 1820

17 C.L. Sriram, *supra* note 6, p. 278.

18 The works thus cited in this particular section make up a sizeable proportion of the works dedicated specifically to the role of minority rights in general to peacemaking.

19 C. Baldwin, C. Chapman and Z. Gray, *supra* note 10, p. 2.

20 G. Pentassuglia, 'Ethnocultural Diversity and Human Rights: Legal Categories, Claims, and the Hybridity of Group Protection', 7 *Yearbook of Polar Law* (2015) p. 257.

or legislative frameworks are developed to respond to indigenous or minority claims in the long term than it is to ensure the state or army are not turned against demobilized or disarmed minorities in the short term. The rest of this chapter outlines four reasons why this is so:

(a) The regime of minority rights is essentially preventative of war, and so is less equipped to deal with the aftermath of situations where prevention has already failed and latent hostility or mistrust has metastasised into warfare.
(b) Once a minority group becomes a conflict principal, the group's antagonists and international mediators must treat the group as belligerents, as opposed to minorities or as indigenous groups, and so all sides elevate security or order over rights. Minority and indigenous groups enjoy improved ethno-cultural protections from the state, but not as rights holders from rights enforcers. Instead, they enjoy them as belligerents. However, because they are belligerents, soft guarantees of human rights may not respond to the security dilemma they face.
(c) The state in question is both post-conflict (with a state infrastructure wholly or partly destroyed) and hybrid (a form of governance where liberal and illiberal, democratic and undemocratic elements coexist), meaning that neither a government nor minorities can fully trust implementation of any agreed minority rights provisions.
(d) Those elements of peacemaking like power-sharing and autonomy that bear affinity with those governmental policies that are believed to give meaningful effect to minority rights operate in radically different ways after conflict than they might before conflict. Attempts to reduce the emphasis on ethno-cultural identity or to foster national inclusivity or representativeness give way to defensive ethno-cultural entrenchment.

Before examining these reasons in greater detail, it is necessary to define the scope of this chapter. This chapter addresses post-conflict peace agreements between a majority group(s) and a minority group(s). Generally speaking, these are negotiated peaces where neither side has achieved victory in conflict, as opposed to wars where either the government or rebel forces emerge victorious. This goes far beyond a ceasefire or cessation of violence to those agreements that approximate Christine Bell's three-part peace agreement process of pre-negotiation agreement (preliminary matters of security, inclusion and agenda), framework (fundamental provisions, interim arrangements for governance and the permanent institutions for resolving the conflict) and implementation agreements (outlining how the framework will be given effect).[21] It does not address the important issue of the exclusion of minorities with little political influence from the peace guarantees who are not belligerents, like the familiar examples of the Roma and Jews in Bosnia, or Egyptians, Gorani and Ashkaelia in Kosovo. Nor does the chapter address the occasional inclusion of minorities in peace agreements in which they are *not* among the main belligerents solely in relation to instruments affecting minorities. Other core overarching issues implicated by the theme of the chapter such as (i) the tension between the focus on individual protection in the international minority rights framework and the collective nature of minorities or (ii) the links between minority rights and internal/external self-determination are not addressed in the interest of more fully developing the chapter's core themes.

2 The Preventative Nature of Minority Rights

One explanation for why ethno-culturally-based conflicts that have minority rights at their centre are not being understood as such might lie in the nature of the rights themselves and the different ante and post bellum contexts in which they apply. Minority rights, after all, are premised on the value of a universal commitment to protect ethnic, religious, cultural and linguistic affiliations as essential characteristics of what it means to be human. However, because these affiliations sharpen distinctions between communities, there is a danger that they divide peoples within larger regional or state communities, creating in-groups and out-groups and, through autonomy, potentially creating opportunities for defined groups to opt out of a common state project. It is for this reason that two goals for minority rights are generally identified, not merely the preservation of a minority or indigenous culture (which primarily benefits that culture), but to maintain peace and security (which benefits all within the larger political community).[22] As Baldwin, Chapman and Gray note, minority rights were developed over ninety years ago "as a tool of conflict prevention" by prohibiting states founded on exclusive conceptions of national identity from repressing other identities, thereby averting the aforementioned

21 C. Bell, *Peace Agreements and Human Rights* (Oxford University Press, Oxford, 2000) pp. 20–32.

22 T.K. Reuter, for example, notes these twofold goals (*supra* note 2, p. 360).

risks of state violence against minorities or minority rebellion against majority rule.[23] This prophylactic raison d'etre was explicitly outlined in the seminal 1935 advisory opinion by the Permanent Court of International Justice in the Minority Schools in Albania case. It noted:

> The idea underlying the treaties for the protection of minorities is to secure for certain elements incorporated in a State, the population of which differs from them in race, language or religion, the *possibility of living peaceably alongside that populations and co-operating amicably with it*, while at the same time preserving the characteristics which distinguish them from the majority, and satisfying the ensuing special needs.[24]

The UN Minorities Declaration again reiterates this, stating that that the promotion and protection of the rights of persons belonging to national or ethnic, religious and linguistic minorities "contribute to the political and social stability of States in which they live".[25]

Along similar lines, Levy argues that while minority protection is valuable in and of itself, international law values minority protections because they mitigate "dangers of violence, cruelty and political humiliation [that] so often accompany ethnic pluralism and ethnic politics."[26] For Macklem and Preece, the function of international minority rights lays less in universal elements of human identity than an implicit desire to monitor the encroachments or injustice of majority communities, and hence insecurities of minorities, caused by the anomalies created by the distribution of distinct communities inside and outside certain sovereign borders.[27] This preventive nature is also apparent if we examine the justifications for establishing official bodies and frameworks to deal with minority rights, which typically envision a state where latent divisions exist but have not led to military conflict. The 1995 Framework Convention for the Protection of Minorities notes that "the protection of minorities is essential to stability, democratic security and peace" and intends cultural

23 C. Baldwin, C. Chapman and Z. Gray, *supra* note 10, p. 32. One can of course look further back in time towards group protections in the Peace of Westphalia, the discussion of Jews and partitioned Poles at the Congress of Vienna or 1856 Congress of Paris in 1856 which attended to the status of Christians and Jews in the Ottoman Empire.

24 PCIJ Series A/B, No. 64, 1935, at 17.

25 General Assembly Resolution A/RES/47/135, 18 December 1992.

26 J.T. Levy, *The Multiculturalism of Fear* (Oxford University Press, Oxford, 2000) p. 12.

27 P. Macklem, *supra* note 11, pp. 124–131 and J. Jackson Preece, 'Minority Rights in Europe: From Westphalia to Helsinki', 23 *Review of International Studies* (1997) p. 77.

diversity to constitute a source of "enrichment" as opposed to "division", emphasizing the Convention's roots as more precautionary than rectificatory. Similarly, the UN Sub-commission on the Prevention of Discrimination and Protection of Minorities speaks of "peaceful and constructive solutions to *situations* involving minorities," defining "situations" as a "widespread sense of frustration among members of minority groups, and that frustration is related to their belonging to the group", suggesting latent tensions where the powder keg of conflict has yet to be lit.[28]

As such, a minority rights framework that prohibits discrimination, operates affirmative action, fosters intercommunal understanding through the media and education or guarantees voice and participation for all is best understood as a 'how to' guide for preserving already peaceful (if far from unproblematic) pluralistic societies.[29] Recognizing minority rights serves as a means to discourage subversive action preliminary to conflict initiation and to foster mutually-acceptable political activity, thereby stopping 'evil spirals' in the early stages.[30] The early warnings generated by minority rights monitoring and systematic review of constitutional and statutory provisions concerning minorities offer a form of 'structural prevention' that mitigates the effect of inherited hierarchies and inequalities to maintain sustainable peace.[31]

However, many elements of the minority rights framework of free and open democracy with sufficient freedom of expression, movement, information and association to satisfy the needs of minorities to forestall any conflict cannot fully respond to the more immediate and acute anxieties of post-conflict ecologies in a way that other guarantees like participation rights in decision-making and autonomy can. The minority rights regime is predicated on a degree of trust on the part of minority groups and remedial good faith on the part of majority groups which cannot be assumed after conflict, even where both sides are agreed on the necessity of peace. For reasons explored in the next section, peacebuilding after ethnic conflict takes places on the basis of an implicit "assumption of intransigence", a reluctance to compromise or to abandon extreme positions based on a supposition that the nature of the antagonism is beyond immediate transformation.[32] While domestic and international

---

28 UN Sub-commission on the Prevention of Discrimination and Protection of Minorities, Special Rapporteur Asbjorn Eide, *Study on Peaceful and Constructive solutions to Situations Involving Minorities*, UN Doc. e/CN.4/Sub.2/1993/34, para. 44.

29 C. Baldwin, C. Chapman and Z. Gray, *supra* note 10, p. 27.

30 A. Eide, *supra* note 8, pp. 1338 and 1339.

31 C. Baldwin, C. Chapman and Z. Gray, *supra* note 10, p. 28.

32 S. G. Simonsen, *supra* note 14, p. 298.

negotiators will work creatively to resolve impasses and build confidence, both parties live in fear of defection by the other belligerent. Minority rebels fear defection by the government that enjoys a monopoly of violence after they disarm and/or demobilize, while governments fear defection by rebels after the latter enjoy the advantages of recuperation and possible rearmament. Realist scholars of war and peace have long argued that after a conflict which demonstrates that the once merely potential employment of mass violence is henceforth a concrete reality, disarmament "creates vulnerabilities that local disputants find intolerable."[33] It is undoubtedly important to work towards systematically including marginalized groups politically and economically while at the same time granting autonomy and affirmative action in areas essential for the preservation of identity. However, the language of rights is more likely to be embraced by minority groups in particular *before* war where social trust is brittle but intact, as opposed to *after* war where that trust has been eradicated and where social extinction or institutionalized discrimination are distinctly imaginable. As Spears notes, "decisions made in environments where security is in jeopardy often differ from decisions made in environments where survival is not in question."[34]

Before conflict, the institutionalisation of minority protections can be explained by the government's acceptance of minority rights norms (though they may do so to avert the risk of conflict), but after war, minorities are aware their ability to affect governmental decisions that concern them may be more a function of the power they demonstrate against the government than the government's remedial goodwill. Many of the essential conditions of trust, compromise and cooperation that underpin a preventive approach are not present in the very different political ecology of post-conflict states, where existential uncertainty leads to inflexibility and self-reliance. By the same token, many of the dilemmas that typically attach to minority rights protections at the preventive stage (most notably the fear that minority protections can harden ethnic differences or legitimise the use of ethnic/religious/linguistic identity politics to gain political power) diminish as concerns largely because these outcomes have already been realized through the vehicle of warfare. The obvious and understandable confidence expressed about the ability of minority rights to prevent conflict may not be applicable to the very different task of preventing the *recurrence* of conflict, for reasons explained below.

---

33 I. Spears, 'Anarchy and the Problems of Power Sharing in Africa' in S. Noel (ed.), *From Power Sharing to Democracy: Post-Conflict Institutions in Ethnically Divided Societies* (McGill-Queen's University Press, Montreal, 2005) p. 188.

34 *Ibid.*, p. 191.

3 The Security Dilemma

Civil wars that divide antagonists across ethno-cultural lines typically manifest an asymmetry of one strong party (usually the state) and a weaker party (a rebel force representing a linguistic, religious or ethnic group). The government can call upon its better trained, equipped and experienced national military to prosecute warfare against rebels who typically lack these advantages. However, modern asymmetric war allows weak rebels to pursue indirect attacks via guerrilla warfare instead of direct defence, permitting them to forestall defeat indefinitely. This is made easier where there is civilian support, where a topography of mountainous terrain and/or many borders permits rebels to endure as moving targets, where arms and explosives are plentiful and where they can secure outside military assistance. As Holl notes, the ability to wage war is dependent on two factors – resources available and the strength of the commitment to apply available resources to securing conflict goals.[35]

Even where governments are militarily much stronger in terms of resources available, rebels can compensate for lack of numbers and weaponry with an intransigent commitment to bear costs in pursuit of the conflict objectives, a belief in ideological or moral superiority of their position and use of violence that exerts disproportionate amounts of disruption.[36] Even where rebels cannot win a war, they can escalate the costs to their state adversary by increasing the costs of failure to come to a settlement. As the old military adage goes, rebels win by not losing. Attrition of will, as opposed to destruction of power, is the main goal of rebels. Most contemporary civil wars therefore become 'contests of punishment' where one belligerent tries to bend the other to its will, but generally fails to do so fully. Once this becomes apparent, much warfare becomes less about victory than about extracting a better deal in negotiation, a process that makes war "indistinguishable from bargaining".[37] The military impasses (often labelled 'mutually hurting stalemates') that characterize contemporary civil conflict compels an acceptance of the need for negotiated peace, a tendency exacerbated by the growing international normative shift

35 J. Holl, 'When War Doesn't Work: Understanding the Relationship between the Battlefield and the Negotiating Table', in R. Licklider (ed.), *Stopping the Killing: How Civil Wars End* (New York University Press, New York, 1993) p. 279.

36 I.W. Zartman, 'Dynamics and Constraints in Negotiations in International Conflicts', in I.W. Zartman (ed.), *Elusive Peace: Negotiating an End to Civil Wars* (Brookings Institution, Washington D.C, 1995) p. 3.

37 R.H. Wagner, 'The Causes of Peace' in R. Licklider (ed.), *supra* note 35, pp. 238 and 260.

towards peaceful settlement of civil war.[38] Since at least 2000, negotiated peaces have tended to outstrip battlefield victories in frequency, a trend that continues to the present day.[39]

Two assertions can confidently be made about peacemaking: (a) it is a fundamentally rationalistic process even where tempered by mistrust, and (b) negotiating stances are adopted through a veil of confusion over antagonist commitment and intentions that should gradually become clearer through discussion and mediation. Peace terms must of necessity fit the expectations of belligerents who assess what they secure at in negotiations by comparison to what they might still potentially achieve on the battlefield. Existential questions of group survival will dominate the thinking of minority groups, while fundamental questions about the nature of the state, territory or power will be key in the mind of the government. Negotiation strategies therefore are competitive, emphasizing self-interest, wealth and autonomy that advance or decline relative to those of the other conflict principals. Negotiations are rarely about objectively identifying and remedying definable failures to protect minorities, but are instead about reconciling different conceptions of national or group interest. As Talentino argues:

> If the terms are considered wrong or out of step with what local actors think they need to be secure, or what they think they might be able to achieve, they will not support the terms no matter how fair others may consider them. Effective peacemaking and peacebuilding are thus only partially connected to equity and right. Being fair is not so much the challenge; instead, the task is to address the cognitive and perceptual issues that will make groups feel both satisfied and secure.[40]

However, fostering this sense of satisfaction and security is immensely difficult, particularly for minorities. As Baker reminds us, the duration of peace agreements ultimately rests primarily on the goodwill of the disputants, and not on the legal authority of the settlement or the institutions it

38 I.W. Zartman, 'Ripeness: The Hurting Stalemate and Beyond', in P. Stern and D. Druckman (eds.) *International Conflict Resolution after the Cold War* (Washington D.C., Committee on International Conflict Resolution, 2000) pp. 225–250.

39 T. Pettersson and P. Wallensteen, 'Armed Conflicts, 1946–2014', 52 *Journal of Peace Research* (2015) p. 544

40 A.K. Talentino, 'Perceptions of Peacebuilding: The Dynamic of Imposer and Imposed Upon', 8 *International Studies Perspectives* (2007) p. 158.

created.[41] The confusion, violence and hardening identities that result from war do not conduce to rational cooperation among factions.[42] There is a crisis of credibility on the part of disputants as to whether they will uphold past and future undertakings. As noted above, the pacific bona fides of each side are untested, and all sides have legitimate fears that the other side will opportunistically exploit the peace to pursue victory. The buffer created by peacekeeping agents and third-party mediation are familiar ways of reducing this uncertainty.

However, though mediation implies that both sides are equal in standing to negotiate (even where unequal in power or military success), the weaker party generally fears the consequences of defection more than the stronger one. To the extent that rebels are the weaker party, they fear non-implementation the most as the majority of peace reforms are the responsibility of the government. Minority leaders will be aware that signing a peace treaty does not end political bargaining as parties continue to compete for advantage. Many peace settlements are at best agreement to struggle in more constitutional ways.[43] After international peacebuilders leave or the benefits of institutional guarantees like power-sharing or elections prove less beneficial than imagined, what appeared like wholehearted commitment to peace may be revealed to have been a temporary acquiescence to a more pacific politics, a strategic manoeuvre which did not entail a fundamental commitment to the terms. In particular, governments may later attempt to renegotiate terms they conceded when they were militarily weak. As their strategic situation improves in conditions of peace, they may wish to renege on the settlement or not fully implement their side of the bargain.[44]

It is well established, therefore, that the higher the intensity of the war (usually a matter of deaths and duration), the number of factions and the greater the salience of identity all tend towards the diminution of mutual confidence and lead disputants to emphasize security over other goals.[45]

---

41 P. Baker, 'Conflict Resolution Versus Democratic Governance: Divergent Paths to Peace', in C. Crocker and F.O. Hampson (eds.) with P. Aall, *Managing Global Chaos: Sources of and Responses to International Conflict* (United States Institute of Peace, Washington D.C., 1996) p. 760.

42 M. Doyle and N. Sambanis, *Making War and Building Peace: United Nations Peace Operations* (Princeton University Press, Princeton N.J, 2006) p. 28.

43 M. Doyle, *UN Peacekeeping in Cambodia: UNTAC's Civil Mandate* (Lynne Rienner, Coulder, 1995) p. 66.

44 K. DeRouen, J. Lea and P. Wallensteen, 'The Duration of Civil War Peace Agreements', 26 *Conflict Management and Peace Science* (2009) p. 369.

45 C. Zürcher, C. Manning and K. Evenson, *Costly Democracy: Peacebuilding and Democratization After War* (Stanford University Press, Stanford, 2013) p. 44.

Because peace agreements are born of mistrust (after all, an antagonist with a proven capability of engaging and matching one's forces in conflict probably retains the ability to inflict further harm), there is generally an attempt on the part of all sides to restrain power and to moderate political behaviour so as to diminish competition and extremist tendencies. Two overarching strategies have emerged to regulate security dilemmas, namely (a) enhanced political and security guarantees relating to power-sharing and autonomy (addressed below in Section 5), and (b) other political and security guarantees based on the human rights 'respect, protect, fulfil' framework, though it should of course be acknowledged that significant elements of the former find their origins or legitimacy in minority rights standards. As noted in the Introduction, there is great optimism among scholars and international policy-makers that the human rights 'respect, protect, fulfil' framework to address breaches of minority rights could play a valuable role in fostering the sense of security and inter-communal harmony that would underpin a sustainable peace. Such judgments, however, are not made in the domestic post-conflict ecology of commitment problems, competitive bargaining and existential dilemmas that characterize actual peace negotiations. Here, weakened governments and inherently vulnerable rebels elevate security-based reassurance in the short-term over long-term, highly conditional and administratively difficult aspirations for ethno-cultural protections like education reform, language equality and development consultation. This is not simply the case for minority rights, but for human rights overall. Human rights protection, be it specific regimes of civil and political rights, socio-economic rights or minority rights, are rarely fundamental to the reassurance antagonists seek to assuage their security concerns when entering a peace agreement and transition to revised modes of social ordering. An assessment of the UN peace agreement database reveals that notwithstanding the increased emphasis on human rights in peace agreements, the most common substantive issues included are security arrangements (69 per cent), rule of law (53 per cent) and military issues (47 per cent).[46] Human rights, by contrast were included in 31 per cent of agreements. A survey conducted for the World Bank and UNDP of the frequency of provisions in peace agreements demonstrates that security issues like security reform, civilian oversight and DDR are present more than twice as often as issues like minority rights and land reform.[47] The average specificity of these provisions is

46 J. Easterday, 'Peace Agreements as a Framework for Jus Post Bellum', in C. Stahn, J. Easterday and J. Iverson (eds.), *Jus Post Bellum: Mapping the Normative Foundations* (Oxford University Press, Oxford, 2014) pp. 388–9.

47 *Ibid.*

also illustrative – provisions relating to security issues, power-sharing, elections and property rights are far more specific in terms of benchmarks and timetables for implementation than minority or socio-economic rights issues.[48] As noted in the introduction, minority rights are sometimes omitted completely even when ethno-cultural issues lie at the root of the conflict.

The failure to seriously depend on, or commit to, human rights (and minority rights in particular), should come as little surprise if we consider the position of the ethnic majority government. All civil war peace processes pit power-holders (usually those who historically control political, economic and social arrangements, and benefit from them) against power-seekers (those who seek to amend the prevailing arrangements).[49] As Bell argues, to the extent that there is pressure for a human (or group) rights component, it generally comes from the weaker side's analysis of the causes of the conflict. This pressure is seen to challenge a status quo against which they are fighting.[50] Though human rights are premised on universalism, there is therefore a perception that one side to the peace stands to benefit from their inclusion, while the other (and usually the stronger of the two) stands to be the net loser. A firm commitment to minority rights on the part of the stronger party cannot be assumed, nor indeed can any commitment to addressing deeper issues of ethno-cultural equity or thoroughly reorganizing the broader political community.

4 Problems of Implementation

The inclusion of individual, minority and/or indigenous rights guarantees can be assumed to work to the benefit of ethno-cultural groups who heretofore have suffered from their absence. However, minority groups may prove reluctant to fully trust in the state's willingness or ability to guarantee them in a political environment where the possible dissatisfaction of majority public opinion and the reality that politics as usual will require further negotiation among competing interests can overtime undermine the willingness of governments to fulfil commitments undertaken. While the Introduction outlined a number of examples of ethno-cultural protections included in peace agreements, their record of implementation affords little confidence even where

48 *Ibid.*

49 J. Darby, *The Effects of Violence on Peace Processes* (US Institute of Peace Press, Washington D.C, 2001) p. 120.

50 C. Bell, 'Negotiating Human Rights' in J. Darby and R. Mac Ginty (eds.), *Contemporary Peacemaking* (Palgrave Macmillan, Basingstoke, 2008) p. 215.

governments appear willing to give genuine effect to them. Strong guarantees in peace agreements like affirming the diversity of a state or the need to eradicate discrimination are always welcome, but will appear merely hortatory if no mechanisms for implementation are provided. As Reuter's study of the fulfillment of minority rights obligations concludes:

> Findings suggest that the inclusion of minority rights in peace agreements and post-conflict constitutions is only beneficial to the peace process if adequate institutional mechanisms and sufficient local political support for the implementation of human rights and minority rights is established.[51]

Ethno-cultural guarantees like large-scale development projects, budget monitoring, affirmative action and systems to eradicate or punish discrimination require some degree of pre-existing state functionality to be made credible. However, outside of fully developed Western states like the UK (where statutory protections against religious discrimination, civil and cultural rights, decommissioning of weapons, justice and policing were guaranteed by an enormous, highly-skilled and fully accountable administrative apparatus), implementation consistently proves to be the weakest element of peace agreements. This is not necessarily a matter of will, but of ability. Outside of the OECD world, the existence of governmental institutions capable of at least minimally exercising authority, formulating and executing policies, appropriating and using revenue in effective budget plans, regulating social relationships and monopolizing violence cannot be assumed. Ethno-cultural guarantees must be secured in areas of limited statehood where these conditions do not obtain. Weak and narrow tax collection, corruption in public services and lack of human resources are typical features of post-conflict states, and rank among the main reasons why the record in implementation has proven so disappointing, and in turn why so little reliance is placed on rights guarantees even when specifically included. This is evident from a study of some of the most familiar examples of ethno-cultural protection in Bosnia, Macedonia and Kosovo. Because all three areas lacked strong central institutions, they needed international support (in Bosnia and Kosovo the international community enjoyed near-sovereign power) to stabilize and to implement the human rights provisions agreed at the end of conflict. While Bosnia has had some success in technically addressing minority rights

51 T.K. Reuter, *supra* note 2, p. 360.

concerns (albeit with unprecedented degrees of external involvement), the other two have seen state incapacity undermine ethno-cultural protections. Within seven years of the Ohrid agreement, Albanians in Macedonia suffered from extensive discrimination in political, administrative and economic areas and suffered violence and intimidation during elections.[52] Kosovo, similarly, did not enjoy the coordination and oversight competence (nor, it must be said, the political will) to give effect to legal frameworks for ethno-cultural protection of Serbs, resulting in a situation where discrimination, impunity for offences and lack of linguistic integration bedevil inter-communal relations.[53] Notwithstanding considerable UN and European support, Kosovo's minority protection laws have been criticised as "too ambitious" in light of its weak institutional and financial capabilities.[54]

Macedonia and Kosovo showed signs of limited statehood but nevertheless had reasonably functional governance, bureaucratic capability and the ability to penetrate and/or regulate society. The problems they suffered with implementation and minority trust are multiplied if we look at states further down the spectrum of declining performance to severely fragile and failed states, i.e those that cannot perform core national duties.[55] Many of these will occur in Africa where problems of state bureaucratic weakness mean structures of government may not be mature enough to effect promised structural reforms or ensure specific ministries or actors will discharge specific responsibilities. One can also look to states like Bangladesh. As Chris Chapman points out in his chapter in this volume, the aforementioned Chittagong Hills Tracts accord has been characterised by an inoperative Land Commission, non-existent elections to the Hill Councils, continued army rule in the area and denial of the existence of Indigenous Peoples in the country.[56] Because of the reluctance of the international community to meaningfully intervene or build peace, peace agreements become self-enforcing, a deeply problematic situation for

52 *Ibid.*, p. 383.

53 *Ibid.*, p. 392.

54 E. Lantschner, 'Protection of Minority Communities in Kosovo: Legally Ahead of European Standards – Practically Still a Long Way to Go' 33 *Review of Central and East European Law* (2008) p. 488.

55 On the spectrum of limited statehood, see T. Risse, 'Governance in Areas of Limited Statehood' in T. Risse (ed), *Governance Without a State: Policies and Politics in Areas of Limited Statehood* (Columbia University Press, New York, 2013) p. 1.

56 C. Chapman, 'Ethno-Cultural Diversity and Conflict – What Contribution Can Group Rights Make?', in G. Pentassuglia (ed.), *Ethno-Cultural Diversity and Human Rights* (Martinus Nijhoff Publishers, Leiden, 2018).

minorities in states where governments have difficulty consolidating their rule. In Aroussi and Vandeginste's survey of peace agreements in over 20 sub-Saharan African states concluded between 1989 and 2011, they observed a steady trend whereby human rights were being formally included in peace agreements as substantive issues in the form of cross-cutting themes when dealing with other matters, guarantees in designated sections as self-standing or autonomous entitlements in themselves, or in frameworks for future bills of rights or constitutional provisions.[57] While these agreements contain commitments to ratify human rights conventions, to fight discrimination and inequality and to a raft of substantive civil and political rights, none of the settlement they analysed made these commitments core element of the implementation, monitoring or evaluation of the agreement.[58] It is increasingly apparent that human rights institutions 'can end up almost hastily tacked on to an agreement without the institutional detail which would make them effective ... This can produce institutions with serious gaps which leave them largely rhetorical and symbolic, rather than capable of effecting real change'.[59] It is for this reason that the formal enumeration of rights provisions in peace agreements "correlates only weakly, if at all" with the quality of human rights protections citizens enjoy in their aftermath.[60]

These failures may owe something to a lack of political will inasmuch as there remain competing visions of state-minority relations, but they also reflect the hybrid nature of post-conflict, semi-liberal states that are typically made up of pluricentric power structures mixing the sort of functioning state familiar in the West with residual deep-rooted, traditional forms of government and social organization. The state is characterised by superficial democracy, has low capacity to secure social minima beyond security, and is mediated by non-state institutions that employ their own methods of resolving social problems within the rebuilt state.[61] Instead of establishing a liberal and democratic society (with or without defined group accommodations), international intervention invariably leads to a hybrid condition in which liberal and

---

57 S. Aroussi and S. Vandeginste, 'When Interests Meet Norms: The Relevance of Human Rights for Power-sharing', 17 *International Journal of Human Rights* (2013) p. 185.

58 *Ibid.*

59 C. Bell, *supra* note 21, p. 231.

60 T. Putnam, 'Human Rights and Sustainable Peace' in S.J. Stedman and D. Rothchild (eds.), *Ending Civil Wars: The Implementation of Peace Agreements* (Lynne Rienner, Boulder, 2002) p. 238.

61 B. Bliesemann de Guevara, 'The State in Times of Statebuilding', 10 *Civil Wars* (2008) p. 349.

illiberal, democratic and undemocratic elements coexist.[62] There is a lack of the type of civil society than can monitor and censure state non-performance of duties or connect all ethno-cultural groups. The hybrid condition of liberal and illiberal, democratic and undemocratic means that state actors must again co-operate with parastatal and non-state actors to achieve functionality, but this cannot be guaranteed. As Cheng notes, there is a distinction between the open theatre of negotiations over the formal political order and the interactions of informal actors and networks. Clans, families, religions, secret societies, to say nothing of individuals, may have little control over state-level cease-fire or political design, but form comprehensive ecosystems that can undermine provisions needed to secure harmony between minority and majority groups.[63] This has had ruinous effects even in post-conflict areas of limited statehood outside sub-Saharan Africa. In Nicaragua, the government could not compel the co-operation of mestizos with autonomy schemes for Atlantic Coast communities who dominated political positions within those schemes, which compounded state failure to adequately secure budgets for autonomous organs.[64] Guatemala's 1998 agreement on Identity and Rights of Indigenous Peoples provided for the creation of legal offices for the defence of Mayan rights and a commission on reform and participation for indigenous peoples, but implementation was conditional on constitutional reform which was defeated after elites rallied to defeat it and the government failed to adequately inform the communities concerned.[65] In examining the experience of peace agreements involving indigenous groups, Gilbert notes a "history of forgotten promises," a recurring problem of non-implementation where "several promises are made in the text of the peace agreement,[but] the concrete implementation of these promises is often severely lacking."[66]

62 R. Belloni, 'Hybrid Peace Governance: Its Emergence and Significance', 18 *Global Governance* (2012) pp. 21, 27.

63 C. Cheng, 'Private and Public Interests: Informal Actors, Informal Influence, and Economic Order after War' in M. Berdal and D. Zaum (eds.), *Political Economy of Statebuilding: Power after Peace* (Routledge, Abingdon, 2013) pp. 65–70.

64 *See generally* S. Brunnegger, 'From Conflict to Autonomy in Nicaragua: Lessons Learnt', Minority Rights Group International (2007), at http://minorityrights.org/wp-content/uploads/old-site-downloads/download-105-From-Conflict-to-Autonomy-in-Nicaragua-Lessons-Learnt.pdf.

65 W. Stanley and D. Holiday, 'Broad Participation, Diffuse Responsibility: Peace Implementation in Guatemala' in S.J. Stedman, D. Rothchild and E. Cousens (eds.), *Ending Civil Wars: The Implementation of Peace Agreements* (Lynne Rienner, Boulder, 2002) p. 421.

66 J. Gilbert, *supra* note 5, p. 220.

By contrast, those few states that emerged from conflict in under-developed regions that nevertheless enjoyed a post-colonial legacy of relative but genuine "stateness" like South Africa and post-independence Zimbabwe found that a functioning bureaucracy would allow commitments to be centrally implemented in a credible manner, reducing the vulnerabilities post-conflict conditions of anarchy gave rise to.[67] While there is still a possibility that choices of factional leaders can overcome post-conflict fears of non-implementation and that confidence can be built where governments succeed in some forms of implementation, minority leaders will be aware that they bear most of the risk of non-implementation of peace. Gilbert is speaking for indigenous peoples but could just as easily be speaking of any minority when he argues these parties are "particularly vulnerable to the non-implementation of the agreement" because by giving up their weapons they have "very little room for leverage" to ever force government responsiveness again.[68] Structural realist perspectives suggest that in conditions of weakened or non-existent central authority, "actors feel tremendous uncertainty and this focuses them to the actions to defend their security."[69] They therefore put much more emphasis on those elements of agreements that permit them to guarantee their own security as self-reliantly as possible, even at the expense of a more holistic governmental approach that would prioritize removing all or most elements of ethno-cultural discrimination. As De Waal puts it:

> In a weakly institutionalized country in which patrimony rules, any attempts to address supposed root causes such as injustice, lack of liberal democracy and unequal development may not help—or may even hinder—the achievement of more modest but realizable goals based on elite bargains ... the elite bargain is the first and most essential component.[70]

These elite bargains revolve around power-sharing, which has consistently proven a much more attractive means than other minority or indigenous rights guarantees alone or in combination to consolidate security.

---

67 I. Spears, *supra* note 32, p. 189, citing J. Ginifer, Managing Arms in Peace Processes: Rhodesia/Zimbabwe (UNIDIR, New York 1995) p. 55

68 J. Gilbert, *supra* note 5, p. 221.

69 I. Spears, *supra* note 33, p. 191.

70 A. De Waal, 'Mission Without End? Peacekeeping in the African Political Marketplace', 85 *International Affairs* (2009) pp. 112–113.

5 Power-Sharing and Autonomy

As noted above, peace agreements typically provide that the weaker of the parties must disarm. This makes them vulnerable if we take into account the (re)centralization of power and the means of violence in the hands of the government with the cessation of hostilities. Armed ethno-cultural groups will predictably refuse to demobilize or disarm if any agreement implies reinforcing the power of the incumbent government as this might ultimately allow them to evade obligations assumed in the prior accord. They therefore seek degrees of political, military and territorial power that either reduce the danger of one side reneging or provides them with some security in the event that this occurs. Out of all of the examples of individual and collective minority rights provisions outlined in peace agreements, therefore, the effective protection of ethno-cultural diversity in both non-conflicted and post-conflict states most requires an elaboration of the means by which minority groups are both included in the decision-making process of the state (inclusion) and given a distinct zone within which the group can define, protect and develop self-governing capacities (autonomy). Most contemporary peace agreements provide both national inclusion through political power-sharing and autonomy through territorial power-sharing.[71]

As a result, external observers of peace agreements tend to view the constitutional and territorial arrangement of peace agreements as forms of what Bell calls "hybrid self-determination" comprising a procedural right to be heard through direct negotiations with the state and a substantive right to effective and fair participation in public decision-making.[72] These forms of self-determination will usually be secured through periodic elections. However, in deeply divided societies, elections alone cannot induce permanent minorities to agree or implement a peace settlement as they find it difficult to accept the potentially prejudicial effects that come with majoritarian democracy or the uncertainty that comes with proportional representation.[73] As a result, fair participation is secured by the disaggregation of power through devices such as consociationalism, territorial subdivision or autonomy, and robust

---

71 Most negotiated settlements contain at least two forms of power sharing – territorial, political, economic and military – and less than a third contain only one mechanism (M. Cammett and E. Malesky, 'Power Sharing in Postconflict Societies Implications for Peace and Governance', 56 *Journal of Conflict Resolution* (2012) p. 992).

72 C. Bell, *On the Law of Peace: Peace Agreements and the Lex Pacificatoria* (Oxford University Press, Oxford, 2008) p. 219.

73 C. Zürcher, C. Manning and K. Evenson, *supra* note 45, pp. 3–4.

human rights and minority rights protections.[74] The limitations, and hence marginality, of minority rights protections in providing sufficient security for minorities in post-conflict states have already been addressed. By contrast, there is much stronger evidence that political and territorial power-sharing assuage suspicions that the security, territory or other interests of antagonists could be harmed once arms are relinquished. In particular, the inclusion of minorities in federal or regional governments has been consistently shown to pacify ethnically diverse societies.[75] These concepts are, of course intertwined – a federalist solution within a unitary state is one of the most common sources of territorial autonomy, while power-sharing in the form of grand national coalitions is often associated with a high degree of cultural autonomy for one or all groups to run their own internal affairs.

Bell argues that hybrid self-determination can be understood in two quite different ways. In one sense it can be understood as a genuine attempt to forge new creative solutions that circumvent the inherited strictures of the Westphalian state as manifest in the hitherto unchanging relationship between a diverse people, a unitary territory and the hegemonic sovereignty of the nation-state. This, she argues, is an "optimistic" approach that views hybrid self-determination as having an emancipatory dimension.[76] On this view, self-determination is not merely a means of off-setting the pathologies that flow from earlier majoritarian domination but rather a positive means of creatively re-articulating the relationship of this group with the larger national political community. Hybrid self-determination suggests "a complex disaggregation of concepts of statehood, territory, peoples, and nationalities, so that these can be reconstituted in a broad variety of permutations to enable the accommodation of complex, overlapping and mutating group identities and competing conceptions of the state," negotiated on an ongoing basis in the course of an evolving and implicitly improving relationship between erstwhile belligerents.[77]

The more positive explanations for political and territorial power-sharing suggest that these mechanisms firstly accustom antagonists gradually into moderation and compromise, while secondly gratifying some pre-war aspirations of combatants through the opportunities produced within

74 C. Bell, *supra* note 72, p. 219.

75 G. Schneider and N. Wiesehomeier, 'Rules That Matter: Political Institutions and the Diversity – Conflict Nexus', 45 *Journal of Peace Research* (2008) p. 183.

76 C. Bell, *supra* note 72, p. 231.

77 *Ibid.*

inclusive governance structures. In the short term, it is assumed that autonomy and self-governance regimes "can provide the institutional structures that offer sufficient space to non-dominant groups to experience genuine self-governance, while simultaneously making dominant groups less insecure about the future existence of the overall state."[78] The longer-term hope for hybrid self-determination is that inclusion is coupled with a transformation of the political economy of social arrangements that redresses the "overlap" between identity and socio-economic disadvantage.[79] It is assumed that as guarantees become institutionalized and trusted, power-sharing can create incentives to decentralize further, fully embrace minority cultures and promote the redistribution or retention of resources to or by ethno-cultural groups to a much greater degree. Some argue that the conscientious observation of ethno-cultural autonomy, guaranteed representation at national level and provision of state benefits can convert formerly separatist movements into willing parts of the state.[80] The spirit of the "optimistic" view of hybrid self-determination is captured by Nicaragua's autonomy law:

> [T]he process of Autonomy enriches the national culture, recognizes and strengthens ethnic identity; it respects the specificities of the cultures of the communities of the Atlantic Coast; it redeems the history of the same; it recognizes property rights to communal land and repudiates any type of discrimination; it recognizes religious freedom and without deepening differences it recognizes distinct identities as coming together to build national unity.[81]

It can be surmised that this view of hybrid self-determination appeals to the rebellious minority group that realizes it will never succeed in secession, but seeks the greatest freedom to secure identity and autonomy.

---

78 M. Weller and S. Wolff, 'Recent Trends in Autonomy and State Construction', in M. Weller and S. Wolff (eds.), *Autonomy, Self-Governance and Conflict Resolution: Innovative Approaches to Institutional Design in Divided Societies* (Routledge, London, 2005) p. 236.

79 T. Sisk, *Statebuilding* (Polity Press, Cambridge, 2013) pp. 35–36.

80 Argued for example by M. Chadda, 'Minority Rights and Conflict Prevention: Case Study of Conflicts in Indian Jammu and Kashmir, Punjab and Nagaland', Minority Rights Group International (2006), at <http://minorityrights.org/wp-content/uploads/old-site-downloads/download-82-Minority-Rights-and-Conflict-Prevention-Case-Study-of-Conflicts-in-Indian-Jammu-and-Kashmir-Punjab-and-Nagaland.pdf> p. 5.

81 Ley 28 Estatuto de la Autonomía de las Regiones de la Costa Atlántica de Nicaragua – Law no. 28, Autonomy Statute of the Regions of the Atlantic Coast of Nicaragua, Section v.

The second, more "pessimistic" view of hybrid self-determination is that of a temporary device adopted primarily to stabilize statehood of a fairly traditional form.[82] It can be surmised that this is the view of hybrid self-determination that most appeals to a state that realizes it must concede some power to minorities it cannot fully subordinate but who will try as far as possible to replicate elements of the pre-conflict dispensation. These more negative explanations for power-sharing foreground the ability of power-sharing to mitigate the greatest fears of disputants that the other side will defect or resile from the agreement, but are ambivalent about the prospects for more substantive ethno-cultural rapprochement.

For the reasons outlined in the two previous sections, it is clear that most peace agreements represent the working out of a distribution of dissatisfactory aspects until a mutually agreeable position is reached.[83] Those who negotiate power-sharing and autonomy must balance the imperative to reassure minorities that the state cannot renege on the powers awarded to them in the agreement with the obligation to ensure these powers are not so unlimited that the weaker party can use them to obtain ever more prerogatives.[84] This essential compromise is something the international community generally accepts as it too reflects the "security approach" of the belligerents, with concerns for stability trumping the types of normative concerns that might guide more meaningful forms of autonomy on the one hand, and factional control over given areas by armed groups prevailing over concerns to maintain the state's undiminished internal sovereignty on the other.[85] It is likely, therefore, that in most cases of ethno-cultural conflict the model of hybrid self-determination ultimately agreed upon will reflect an exchange of preferences falling somewhere between the optimistic view of a constructive re-articulation of relationships between minority and majority that empowers states to build a responsive state and the pessimistic view of it as the minimum re-organisation of the state consistent with pacification. The widespread enthusiasm on the part of international mediators, scholars and advocates for hybrid self-determination,

82 C. Bell, *supra* note 72, p. 231.

83 On this, *see* for example S. Puri, *Fighting and Negotiating with Armed Groups: The Difficulty of Securing Strategic Outcomes* (*Adelphi Book 459*) (International Institute for Strategic Studies, London, 2016).

84 P. Roeder, 'Power Dividing as an Alternative to Ethnic Power Sharing', in D. Rothchild and P. Roeder (eds.), *Sustainable Peace: Power and Democracy after Civil Wars* (Cornell University Press, Ithaca, 2005) pp. 58–9.

85 G. Pentassuglia, 'Do Human Rights Have Anything to Say About Group Autonomy?', in G. Pentassuglia (ed.), *supra* note 56.

needs to be tempered by an acknowledgment of how political inclusion and autonomy are negotiated and implemented.

5.1 *Autonomy*

In non-international armed conflicts fought by groups seeking independence or autonomy from the state for their region, territorial power-sharing that grants autonomy to a particular ethno-cultural group distinct from the state majority is a standard response to guarantee those regions greater control over their own political, economic and cultural affairs at a sub-national level. It is designed to minimize the potential for conflict by reducing opportunities and motivations for friction with a state characterized by the dominance of another group, most notably by limiting its authority. The most common examples of territorial power-sharing after those conflicts where rebels from a given region have fought for secession or autonomy from the state are ethnofederalism (where territorial governance units are explicitly designated as ethno-cultural homelands but include other minorities) and regional autonomy (the legal grant of specific responsibilities or powers to a regional authority). Territorial power-sharing is considered, along with military power-sharing, more reassuring than other forms because it allows ethno-cultural groups to check the central government's coercive force and provides a defensible geographic area they can control.[86] Indeed, the government's loss of control of a territory is considered so high a cost that it serves as a strong signal of conciliatory intent.[87] Post-conflict states have also employed ethnocorporatism (jurisdictions that extend to members of a community but not all citizens within the territory) and non-territorial federalism (where distinct responsibilities and powers are devolved to a community in areas like traditional law, education, language or religion). The primary aim of all of these decentralizations of power is to impose institutional limitations on unbridled central authority by giving an ethno-cultural group rule over itself in matters that are the group's exclusive concern.[88] It can include control over taxation, rights to natural resources, enhanced status for local leaders and self-governance over cultural and social issues.

---

86 M. Hoddie and C. Hartzell, 'Power Sharing in Peace Settlements: Initiating the Transition from Civil War', in D. Rothchild and P. Roeder (eds.), *supra* note 84, p. 102.

87 A. Jarstad and D. Nilsson, 'From Words to Deeds: The Implementation of Power-sharing Pacts in Peace Accords' 25 *Conflict Management and Peace Science* (2008) p. 207.

88 D. Lake and D. Rothchild, 'Containing Fear: The Origins and Management of Ethnic Conflict', 21 *International Security* (1996) p. 87.

However, autonomy within a certain territorial area or in relation to certain matters cannot rectify all conflicts between groups and the state. For example, Nicaragua's aforementioned autonomy law did not resolve disputes between communities on the Atlantic coast with the state over land and resource exploitation.[89] One of the paradoxes of autonomy is that it attempts to increase pluralism, but will often depend on pre-existing traditions of pluralism that did not suffice to mitigate tensions and prevent disputes before the conflict.[90] After an intense conflict, there is no "culture of accommodation" to sustain the power-sharing bargain given the pre-existing lack of a civic/pluralistic culture within which autonomy regimes can operate.[91] Autonomy seldom satisfies the preferences of either side. On the one hand, states fear a "slippery slope" towards disintegration of territory.[92] On the other hand, far from preparing a minority population for more integrated social and political practices, territorial power-sharing "instead tends to deepen the expectation of autonomy among separatist populations and those who fought for it."[93] This tension over autonomy makes it less likely in the longer term that root causes of minority dissatisfaction can be redressed to mutual satisfaction as it has to a greater or lesser extent in non-conflict areas like the Aland Islands, Puerto Rico, the various Lapp or Catalonia territories a sufficiently robust democratic/civic culture has matured that can both establish and limit group autonomy over the longer term within a multilayered structure.[94] It cannot be assumed that autonomy laws are passed with a genuine intention on the part of the national government to yield real power. There is an obvious risk that the powers of local authorities can be curtailed by controlling their financing. As Sriram notes:

> [A]utonomous territories may not be sustainable without serious resource commitments from the central government or the international

89 C. Baldwin, C. Chapman and Z. Gray, *supra* note 10, p. 8.

90 Y. Ghai, 'Territorial Options', in J. Darby and R. Mac Ginty (eds.), *supra* note 50, p. 242.

91 D. Rothchild and P. Roeder, 'Power Sharing as an Impediment to Peace and Democracy', in D. Rothchild and P. Roeder (eds.), *supra* note 84, p. 29.

92 T. Sisk, 'Power Sharing After Civil Wars: Matching Problems to Solutions' J. Darby and R. Mac Ginty (eds.), *supra* note 50, p. 201.

93 C.T. Call, *Why Peace Fails: The Causes and Prevention of Civil War Recurrence* (Georgetown University Press, Washington D.D, 2012) p. 122

94 *See*, for example, H. Hannum, *Autonomy, Sovereignty, and Self-Determination: The Accommodation of Conflicting Rights* (University of Pennsylvania Press, Philadelphia, 1990) and M. Suksi, *Sub-state Governance Through Territorial Autonomy: A Comparative Study in Constitutional Law of Powers, Procedures and Institutions* (Springer Science & Business Media, Heidelberg, 2011).

> community. Obviously, central governments, which are likely to be dominated by a group that is ethnically, linguistically, or religiously distinct from the majority of the autonomous region, may not be committed to financing that autonomy.[95]

In particular, the more geographically isolated some minority regions are from the rest of the country, the more likely governments are to maintain an attitude of neglect and disinterest towards them.[96] As Mehler observes, it remains very much an open question whether decentralization can in anyway reduce structural disparities (particularly those in terms of public goods and services) between groups in conflict.[97] It is far from clear that political power-sharing at national level can resolve these disparities or other disputes over issues of common interest.

5.2 *Political Power-Sharing*

Post-conflict political power-sharing is understood by most scholars as the participation of an ethno-cultural group in a joint executive coalition government with the possibility of mutual veto over some or all decision-making. It is considered essential in addressing existential questions of the use of the state's resources and coercive power against or on behalf of minority groups. As Wolff argues, "it is likely, and in fact probable, that without power-sharing arrangements non-majority communities will find themselves permanently disenfranchised, socially and economically excluded, or culturally discriminated against."[98] It also gives those communities that would never be victorious in central government elections a "concrete stake" in national governance[99] and weakens prevailing concepts of government as founded on exclusive concepts of nationhood or the implicit/explicit exclusion of ethnic, religious or linguistic groups.

---

95 C. L. Sriram, *supra* note 6, p. 188. A similar point is made in A. Jarstad and D. Nilsson, *supra* note 87, p. 207.

96 C. Baldwin, C. Chapman and Z. Gray, *supra* note 10, p. 12.

97 A. Mehler, 'Not Always in the People's Interest: Power-Sharing Arrangements in African Peace Agreements', German Institute of Global and Area Studies (2008), at <https://www.giga-hamburg.de/en/system/files/publications/wp83_mehler.pdf> p. 14 (visited on 19 December 2016).

98 S. Wolff, 'Building Democratic States After Conflict: Institutional Design Revisited', 12 *International Studies Review* (2010) p. 134.

99 N. Bermeo, 'What the Democratization Literature Says – Or Doesn't Say – About Postwar Democratization' 9 *Global Governance* (2003) p. 166.

The 'optimistic' assumption is that broad-based and inclusive political institutions that give ethno-cultural groups access to decision-making creates incentives for co-operation and joint problem-solving that in turn lays the ground in the long-run for democratization,[100] notwithstanding concurrent critiques from liberal positions that autonomy and power-sharing arrangements can contradict democratic and normative ideals of non-discrimination.[101] This hope flows from an essentially Lijphartian conception of consociationalism derived from the Western European experience as government by elite cooperation and consensus that gradually works to build inclusive, democratic government resolved to eliminate or mitigate causes of intercommunal tension.[102] However, post-conflict power-sharing tends not to resemble liberal consociationalism on bases that developed organically in Europe (and in some cases after colonialism) because peace is negotiated at the point in time when group identities are most politically salient and divisive.[103] There is something of a consensus in the peacebuilding literature that in post-conflict states power-sharing works in radically different ways to essentially democratic, problem-solving Lijphartian paradigm.[104]As Jarstad notes, the research on political power-sharing can be divided into two distinct spheres – a "democracy" strand that focusses on using the policy to achieve stable democracy with all the human rights and consensus-building this entails, and a "conflict management" strand that focusses mainly on its role in achieving

100 *See e.g.* P. Norris, *Driving Democracy: Do Power-Sharing Institutions Work* (Cambridge University Press, Cambridge, 2008) and B. Reilly, 'Does the Choice of Electoral System Promote Democracy? The Gap Between Theory and Practice', in D. Rothchild and P. Roeder (eds.), *supra* note 84, p. 159

101 On normative counter-ideals see H. Steiner, 'Ideals and Counter-ideals in the Struggle over Autonomy Regimes for Minorities', 66 *Notre Dame Law Review* (1991) pp. 1551–1555. Perhaps the most notable expression of this concern is found in European Court of Human Rights, Grand Chamber, *Case of Sejdić and Finci v. Bosnia and Herzegovina*, Applications nos. 27996/06 and 34836/06, Judgment, Strasbourg, 22 December 2009 which found the Roma and Jewish applicants' ineligibility to stand for election to parliament violates Article 14 of the European Court of Human Rights (ban of discrimination in the field of Convention rights) taken in conjunction with Article 3 of Protocol No. 1 (free elections).

102 *See* A. Lijphart, 'Consociational Democracy', 21 *World Politics* (1969) p. 207 and subsequent refinements of the work.

103 A. McCulloch, 'Consociational Settlements in Deeply Divided Societies: The Liberal-Corporate Distinction', 21 *Democratization* (2014) p. 501.

104 C. Hartzell and M. Hoddie, 'The Art of the Possible: Power Sharing and Post – Civil War Democracy', 67 *World Politics* (2015) p. 37

stable post-conflict peace.[105] The conflict management approach is essentially defensive, as opposed to constructive, more about overcoming commitment problems and mitigating security fears than fundamentally re-imagining the holistic range of majority-minority relations.[106] It tends to apply in situations where a more pluralistic, rights respecting culture (and the institutions necessary to support it) is underdeveloped. As Schneckener points out, most of the conditions that historically underpin power-sharing deals in the liberal West like extensive political participation, relative parity in relation to group size, absence of sizeable socio-economic inequalities, underlying allegiance to the broader state and/or pluralist representation of ethnicities by more than one party may not exist elsewhere.[107] As such, power-sharing outside this context, and particularly in post-conflict states, is essentially a matter of "fear reduction", more about curtailing the risk that disputed claims can escalate from protests, demonstrations or even terrorism into renewed warfare than actually addressing those claims or laying the foundation for democratic governance.[108] However, in so doing, power-sharing embeds the divisions of the civil war on a permanent basis that may become conflictual once more if the emerging post-conflict institutions of governance are unprepared to manage their unexpected consequences.[109] Because they are based on elite consensus, the parties to power-sharing seldom need or seek to build bridges across the different groups within society or to foster co-operation across ethnic lines.[110] Scholars of power-sharing point out a "second-generation problem" where the need for the majority group to behave in a conciliatory and accommodative manner towards minorities decreases over time, calling into question the majority's continuing commitment to a fuller expression of ethno-cultural diversity.[111]

105 A. Jarstad, 'Power Sharing: Former Enemies in Joint Government' in A. Jarstad, and T. Sisk, (eds.), *From War to Democracy: Dilemmas of Peacebuilding* (Cambridge University Press 2008) p. 108.

106 *See* H.M. Binningsbø, 'Power Sharing, Peace and Democracy: Any Obvious Relationships?', 16 *International Area Studies Review* (2013) p. 102

107 U. Schneckener, 'Making Power-sharing Work: Lessons from Successes and Failures in Ethnic Conflict Regulation,' 39 *Journal of Peace Research* (2002) pp. 211–217.

108 M. Mattes and B. Savun, 'Fostering Peace after Civil War: Commitment Problems and Agreement Design', 53 *International Studies Quarterly* (2009) p. 737.

109 C.L. Sriram, *Peace as Governance: Power-sharing, Armed Groups, and Contemporary Peace Negotiations* (Palgrave Macmillan, Basingstoke, 2008) p. 1.

110 T. Sisk and C. Stefes, 'Power Sharing as an Interim Step in Peace Building: Lessons from South Africa', in D. Rothchild and P. Roeder (eds.), *supra* note 84, p. 297.

111 D. Rothchild and P. Roeder, *supra* note 91, p. 38.

Furthermore, it is something of a commonplace that inclusive power-sharing government is less apt to result in cooperation that it is in "institutional deadlock and ineffective government" that that fosters a politics of "delusion" and "procrastination."[112] The fundamental rationale of power-sharing for conflict-management is that if all antagonists are brought within the political fold, they are more likely to trust it and cultivate an interest in its stability and effectiveness.[113] This can operate to the detriment of a conflict-eradication approach to ethno-cultural divisions. Many African wars in particular appear to be fought less by the leaders of non-majority communities to fundamentally address deep ethnic or social grievances than they are to reintegrate themselves into a system of power rotation/bargaining from which they have been excluded.[114] As Bryden notes, power-sharing at the centre tends to operate to the exclusion of re-organising those elements of government that crucially relate to the divisions that led to conflict:

> Transitional, power-sharing governments are often reluctant to address these issues since they would often require a dilution of central control over systems of patronage and representation. As a result, transitional governments too often fail to reshape government in ways that mitigate the root causes of crisis.[115]

6 Conclusion

This article has attempted to explain a paradox that puzzles many minority rights advocates and scholars – why, if the salience of ethno-cultural issues increases in the course of making war and negotiating peace, does any

112 M. Basedau, 'Managing Ethnic Conflict: The Menu of Institutional Engineering', German Institute of Global and Area Studies, (2011) at <https://www.giga-hamburg.de/en/system/files/publications/wp171_basedau.pdf> p. 18 (visited on 19 December 2016), citing N. Cheeseman and B.M Tendi. 'Power-sharing in Comparative Perspective: The Dynamics of 'Unity Government' in Kenya and Zimbabwe' 48 *Journal of Modern African Studies* (2010) p. 203.

113 M. Cammett and E. Malesky, *supra* note 71, p. 1016.

114 P. Englebert and D. Tull, 'Postconflict Reconstruction in Africa: Flawed Ideas About Failed States', 32 *International Security* (2008) p. 122.

115 M. Bryden, 'Disarming Somalia: Lessons in Stabilization from a Collapsed State', unpublished paper for project on 'Conflict, Security and Development', King's College London, March 2009, cited in M. Berdal, *Building Peace After War* (Routledge, Abingdon, 2009) p. 128.

corresponding commitment to minority rights fail to extend commensurately? It is submitted that the rights-based discursive frameworks of jurisprudence and scholarship that explore the many ways in which claims for ethno-cultural protection can be justified are not irrelevant to post-conflict states, but are of secondary importance because they do not speak directly to the existential concerns over group survival. The faith that rights-based frameworks, power-sharing and autonomy guarantees can guarantee ethno-cultural protection follows from a view of peace agreements as progressive, problem-solving institutions concerned with the purposive achievement of normative goals. However, this vision of the normatively-infused just peace that reconciles minority with majority interests is but one way of understanding peace. The other, more prevalent way of framing peace is a conflict management imperative which sees the obligation to end conflict as the sole, fundamental objective of peace.

For reasons examined in the previous sections, this tension between conflict management in the short-term and more long-term rights guarantees indispensable for a 'just' sustainable peace is more often than not resolved in favour of the former. Peace agreements are only ever concluded between belligerents with strong contrasting views as to whether and how ethno-cultural diversity can or should be respected. Peace agreements revolve around give-and-take bargains struck by majority and minority communities instead of shared holistic, rational political visions. While it is true that many peace agreements contain generic language on inclusion and minority rights, the particular context of post-conflict states has a strong effect on the types of ethno-cultural protections that are emphasized and those that are peripheral. Autonomy and power-sharing are the most commonly emphasized, but the degree of mistrust that exists between former antagonists means that they are rarely oriented towards incorporating and reconciling distinct identities to build national unity, ethno-cultural balance and co-operation. Again, both policies respond more to acute security concerns arising from the conflict than the original root causes of it. The main objective of autonomy schemes and political power-sharing is to contain conflict within the constitutive rules they are based on and to avoid escalations of ethno-cultural claims that jeopardize them.[116] This is often a recipe for political sclerosis at the national level and enduring the endurance of mistrustful relations between autonomous regions and the state.

116 P. Roeder, 'Power Dividing as an Alternative to Ethnic Power Sharing', in D. Rothchild and P. Roeder (eds.), *supra* note 84, p. 54.

As noted in the Introduction, those who argue that minority rights are essential in post-conflict situations do so on the basis that they can sustainably protect communities from discrimination, assimilation and encroachment by the majority community. It is premised on a vision of the state derived from non-conflict situations as hegemonic at its strongest and overweening even at its weakest, a state where the potential for conflict is latent but as yet unrealised. This vision of the state as the potential abuser or assimilator of minorities remains appropriate in the aftermath of the types of stalemated conflict that compel contemporary peace agreements, but this is only half the story. The other half of the story is that of minorities with a proven capacity to defend itself, to disrupt the state and to underline its legitimacy internationally. This vision of the state as itself vulnerable (to violence and disruption, if not defeat) means that group rights approaches as manifested in the form of traditional minority rights to remedy discrimination or to acknowledge the need of groups for recognition are always balanced by a discourse of security. Similarly, the more advanced guarantees like political and territorial power-sharing are characterised less by the need for representation and voice for one community as the pre-conflict discourse around such assurances suggests than they are by a sense of *mutual* security on the part of the minority that the state's coercive apparatus of army and police might be turned against it, but also on the part of a majority who fears the other side will use the period of peace to re-arm. Advanced political or territorial group protections are essentially forms of 'fear reduction', more about curtailing the risk that disputed claims can escalate from protests, demonstrations or even terrorism into renewed warfare than laying the foundation for a culture of rights. Because the parties' existential concerns over security dominate such agreements, more normative, yet no less real, concerns, are sidelined. It may suffice to bring an ethnic conflict to an end in the short- to medium-term. However, where security in and of itself becomes the primary normative goal, it may reflect a counter-productive political and legal myopia over the longer term as resentments fester, needed solutions for structural problems are put on the long finger and as communities self-sort on the basis of the cleavages established in post-war governance. The one obvious escape from the myopia is the intervention of the international community and/or reliance on international law to perform a transformative role that eschews 'normal' (conservative) statehood for 'post-sovereign' or reconfigured orders where group guarantees trump the chauvinism or permanent victimhood of ethno-nationalism. It is possible to point to internationally-brokered peace settlements, most notably from Versailles 1919 and Dayton 1995, which firmly, if imperfectly, established internationally-recognized standards of minority treatment as the basis for future co-existence in post-conflict states. However, it is worth pointing out that these are examples where the international community (or alliances within it) became active participants in, and active guarantors of, the settlement. Observers hope that peace negotiations where the international community is involved can escape an exclusively domestic security logic to become susceptible to international norms and values. It is expected that mediators can exercise 'directive' influence, fashioning the substance of the agreement through judicious employment of deadlines and ultimatums or offering material inducements to introduce minority rights concerns into the negotiation agenda.[117] However, the international community in contemporary conflicts is welcomed by domestic antagonists for its impartiality and not the leverage it may enjoy to control the process. Consequently, third party actors invited to participate are rarely those 'mediators with muscle' we see in examples like Dayton that can dictate more long-term, pluralistic and human rights-based solutions to the roots of conflict. Peacebuilders and minority rights advocates may find arguments in favour of ethno-cultural protections normatively attractive and press for their inclusion in peace agreements, but the primary concern of conflict principals ultimately remains with strategies that best meet their interests and security needs. The political and legal challenge that remains is to blend holistic rights-based frameworks with security-based conflict management approaches, and to systematically infuse conflict-management approaches with a sensitivity to broader minority rights concerns. A better appreciation of the logics of security and containment at play in contemporary peace negotiations will lend credibility to the normative arguments of international mediators, NGOs and domestic reform constituencies.

117 S. Aroussi and S. Vandeginste, *supra* note 57, p. 192.

General Index